THREADS OF THINKING

Young children learning
and the role of early education

Cathy Nutbrown

P·C·P
Paul Chapman
Publishing Ltd

Paul Chapman Publishing Ltd
144 Liverpool Road
London
N1 1LA

British Library Cataloguing in Publication Data

Nutbrown, Cathy
    Threads of Thinking: Young Children
    Learning and the Role of Early Education
    I. Title
    370.15

    ISBN 1-85396-217-1

Typeset by Dorwyn Ltd, Rowlands Castle, Hants
Printed and bound by Athenaeum Press Ltd, Gateshead, Tyne & Wear.

B C D E F G H   9 8 7 6 5 4

For

Bethany Martha Trevorrow

with love
October 1993

ACKNOWLEDGEMENTS

Over my years as a teacher of young children, and during my work with parents, teachers and other early childhood educators, I have met and worked, in different ways, with many different people. It is dialogue and the sharing of thoughts and ideas which shapes everyone's thinking. I would like to thank all those with whom I have worked, children, parents and educators, who have given me things to think about, questions to ponder and suggestions and ideas to develop. I am grateful to Chris Athey for her professional support, her comments on the manuscript and for sharing her own work which stimulated my work and challenged my thinking. Tricia David, Mary Jane Drummond, Ann Hedley and Kath Hirst willingly shared in the process of writing this book, giving generously of their time to comment on the developing manuscript. Their roles were critical to my thinking but the responsibility for the final version rests with me. Marianne Lagrange of Paul Chapman Publishing has offered me immediate and effective professional advice whenever I sought it. I have been fortunate to have someone who has always been there for me, and so I express my love and thanks to Andrew Nutbrown for all his practical help, understanding and encouragement.

CONTENTS

INTRODUCTION

This book is about young children and their educators working together. It is about the promotion of high-quality thinking and action of children aged 3–5 years. Some thoughts about children aged from birth to 3 years, and 5–8 years, are also included as part of the discussion of continuity in teaching and learning.

Throughout the book I have included examples of children's talk, action, representation and thinking drawn from observations made over a ten-year period to illustrate some aspects of their schemas, to demonstrate their capacity as learners and to suggest ways of developing practice in the education of young children. This kind of data could have been used and analysed in many different ways. The interpretations given in the book are my way of making sense of the complexity of children's behaviour as they grow and learn. In any book of this kind there is room for debate and the many observations have been included for readers to consider my conclusions.

Most of the observations in this book were made in nursery education settings, others draw on children 'in action' at home. It is important that the terms used to describe the adults who work in different contexts with young children are clear. The Rumbold Report (DES, 1990a) tried to overcome this difficulty by using the term 'educator' to apply to everyone who engaged with young children in some way, arguing that all adults, parents, childminders, playgroup workers, teachers, nursery nurses, nannies and so on had a part to play in helping young children to learn. Whilst this attempts to embrace the multidisciplinary nature of work with young children, and the diversity of settings in which they might learn, it makes for a lack of clarity of roles and responsibilities and clouds issues about provision offered and the training, status and qualifications of the people who work with young children. There can also be a dangerous assumption that anyone and everyone can work effectively with young children. If we call everyone involved with young

children an 'educator', discussion which separates out roles and responsibilities of parents and other educators can become confused, and the
specialised nature of the work of different kinds of educators can become blurred or misunderstood. Throughout this book I have tried to
overcome this problem in several ways: using specific professional titles
to describe adults where they have arisen from certain observations;
referring to parents as parents, but acknowledging their important and
distinct role in children's learning and development; and referring to
educators in a range of group settings as 'professional educators'. I use
the term professional educator to mean adults who have some relevant
training and qualifications and understand something of how children
learn, and who are active in their thinking and interaction with young
children in group settings. In many cases I have referred specifically to
teachers because it was those professionals who were involved in the
observations described.

This book is intended to provide evidence of children's thinking
about, and learning from, their world. It draws, where appropriate, on
theories to illuminate the examples of children's language, action and
representation. In particular the work of Athey (1990) is used to explore
ways of understanding children's learning.

This book is an attempt to think more deeply about children's action
and a voyage of discovery into the riches of children's minds. Here I give
my ways of thinking about and working with young children. I invite
readers to consider my thoughts and, returning to the children they
know best, to make their own observations, develop their own thinking
about children's thinking and their own role in the dynamic process of
supporting, challenging and extending children's thinking and learning.

Cathy Nutbrown
September 1993

Part I
Young children learning

Our knowledge of young children's cognitive development has been extended by the early work of Piaget, Vygotsky, Isaacs and other 'Great Educators' who, in different ways, set out to illustrate the characteristics of children's thinking. Chapter 1 gives some examples of children trying to make sense of, and reason why things happen. Chapter 2 considers some of Athey's work and deals with some questions which educators often raise about schemas and young children's learning.

1
THINKING ABOUT YOUNG CHILDREN LEARNING

Children are complete and whole persons. They are not divided into parts which need to be educated, parts which need to be cared for and parts which need to be healthy. Ensuring their health, care and education requires a holistic approach. Children need to grow up in a caring, educational and healthy environment. Their quality of life must embody these things.

Young children cannot be taught effectively if planned learning is divided into man-made compartments called subjects. Children will explore science, learn about maths and develop language skills through activities and experiences which are planned to encompass these and many more elements of thinking and learning.

It is best to illustrate these points with some examples of children learning through realistic and immediate experiences. In the following examples all the children are using and exploring water. I recall one headteacher's comment: 'If they have nothing else, they must play with water. I could teach the whole curriculum through the theme of water.' These observations show how the immediate and engaging experience of playing with water can provide learning opportunities in a play setting. Three observations follow, Zoe (aged 4), Ashaq (age 6) and Karmen and John (age 8 and 7).

Zoe age 4

Zoe was playing in the water trough at the nursery. She was experimenting with a jug and water wheel, spending a considerable time filling the jug, pouring the water over the wheel and watching it turn. She poured water at different speeds, and from different heights. Her teacher watched and eventually asked: 'Can you tell me what is happening?' Zoe

looked at her and began her explanation: 'The wheel doesn't like to get
wet, so it runs fast to get away from the water. When all the water is
gone, it stays still again!' Zoe knew that the water made the wheel turn
but ascribed attributes of thought and feeling to the wheel. Early experiences of the scientific principles of force, gravity and power are present
in this example, as well as the beginnings of reasoned thought. Zoe was
beginning to grapple with ideas of speed and of cause, function and
effect.

Ashaq age 6

Ashaq was watching his mother using a jet spray at the garage to wash
her car. He observed intently for some time and then asked if he could
have a turn. After concentrating the jet of water on one muddy wheel
and watching the dirt wash away he said: 'If I put it nearer the dirt goes
away faster. That's because the water hits it harder if it doesn't spray so
far. If I spray a long way away then not all the dirt goes.'

This 6-year-old told his teacher about the car washing. She used jets,
sprays and the advantage of a hot summer day to work with him to
develop further this understanding and to extend his interest. Water
flowed from the hose pipe in the yard outside the classroom as did
questions of 'How?', 'Why?' and 'What if?' Ashaq made reasoned answers to all the questions the teacher raised. He also asked questions of
his own. The principles of syphoning were mastered and the appropriate
terminology was introduced by the teacher. A small group of children
worked purposefully to create and solve their own water-oriented
problems.

Learning does not begin and end in school. The visit to the garage
with his mother uncovered some thinking which Ashaq, with the help of
his teacher, was able to extend further in the classroom.

Karmen and John age 8 and 7

Karmen and John were at home in their garden bathing dolls and washing all their clothes. The dolls and clothes were covered in an ever-
increasing amount of soap suds. The children had rather overestimated
the quantity of washing powder they needed, reasoning that the dolls
were extremely dirty and so must need a lot of soap to get them clean.
John decided to change the water and wash everything again, this time
not putting in any more soap. The following conversation gives an inter-

esting (and amusing) insight into the children's reasoning and understanding:

Karmen: Make the water cooler this time, it disperses the bubbles.

John: How?

Karmen: Not sure, but it does, mum does that with the jumpers in the sink. It sort of pops them.

John: Is it that cold water is too cold for them and it makes them pop?

Karmen: Maybe, it's thinner and gets through the membranes.

John: Brains! Do bubbles have brains?

Karmen: No! Membranes! It's like an invisible sort of film, like a sort of skin thing – to keep the air trapped, they have them on *Tomorrow's World* on telly sometimes.

John: How does the air get in there?

Karmen: Well, it's the soap. Get the cold water now.

John: How cold?

Karmen: Cold! Don't put any warm in, though you could put a bit, tepid water, 'hand hot' my mum calls it I think.

John: Does that mean as hot as my hand?

Karmen: It means you can put your hand in and it doesn't make it red hot or freezing cold so it hurts your fingers.

John: I bet we could do it quicker than changing all this water.

Karmen: How?

John: Stick them all under the tap 'til all the bubbles run off then squeeze them!

Karmen: Or! We could use the shower thing in the bathroom and give them a shower. That would work.

John: I saw that on telly.

Karmen: What, doing the washing?

John: No, spraying the oil.

Karmen: What?

John: If you spray oil it breaks up, pollutes the environment and the sea, oil does.

Karmen: Like if you get soap on your hair and use the shower to rinse it off. We'll do the dolls first, their hair is all bubbles.

John: The particles bombard the oil and hit it to break it up. Dad said.

Karmen: Does oil have membranes?

John: Don't know. Give me that jacket. Oil's not as heavy as water though. It floats on top. I saw that on telly too!

Karmen: We've got brains!

John: If it works we have. But I bet it does. My mum puts me in the shower on holiday!

Karmen and John were transferring elements of their knowledge, gleaned from different sources, including their parents and the

television, and using what they knew to try to solve their present difficulty. They were exploring, discovering, checking out each others meanings, predicting results, forming hypotheses and drawing conclusions.
They played co-operatively and with intensity of purpose.

As children get older and more experienced, if adults have spent time
with them, extending their interests and explaining things about the
world, stimulating their actions and thoughts into new areas, and talking
with them, children will use different language and terminology to explain their reasoning. It is their language which gives us a good clue to
their stage of development and their understanding. If children are obli-
ging enough to tell us what they are thinking, their parents, teachers and
other educators are in a better position to help them to develop further.

If we reflect on the use of language in the three examples of children
using water we see different thoughts and understandings. Four-year-old
Zoe explained: 'It runs away from the water.' Six-year-old Ashaq observed: 'If I put it nearer the dirt goes away faster.' Seven-year-old John
said: 'The particles bombard the oil and hit it to break it up.' Eight-year-
old Karmen said: 'Membranes, it's like an invisible sort of film like a sort
of skin thing, to keep the air trapped.' If children have played in their
earlier years with the stuff of the world (water, sand, mud and clay), they
are in a better position to develop further concepts through these medium. Children with few encounters with these natural materials will
need time to explore their properties and attributes before they can
progress to other elements of learning.

The restrictions which are placed on children and the consequences of
this in terms of their subsequent development were considered by Tinbergen (1976), who discussed the ways in which young children learn
through play in their natural environments. Tinbergen suggested that
society has inhibited children's freedom to play and, just as young animals find their own way of learning, young children could do the same if
they were in an appropriate environment.

Worries about children's safety and urban living now inhibit the freedom of our own children – they are not free to explore their world.
Concerns for children's well-being include fear of illness from polluted
rivers and beaches and abduction and abuse. Adults who wish to support
children's learning must now bring the stuff of the world into safe,
defined, but falsely created boundaries. Instead of the vastness of the
seashore, children play with small quantities of sand and water in
troughs designed for the purpose, and they often wear aprons to keep
their clothing clean and dry when part of the learning comes from get-

ting sandy and wet. Instead of making mud pies in the outdoors, children use clay, in a confined space. The role of the adult in protecting the opportunities for learning and enabling children's own ways of thinking and exploring is crucial. To learn truly, children need the freedom to play, and educators need to create opportunities which provide this freedom to learn in a protected environment which, as far as possible, removes the inhibiting restriction which arises from fear for children's safety.

John Brierley made an important contribution to our understanding of children's brain growth and development. He provides useful insights for all who have responsibility for and concerns for young children. Brierley firmly asserts that the years from 0 to 5 are crucial for brain development and that the first ten years are the years during which the brain reaches 95% of its adult weight. He writes:

> During these years of swift brain growth a child's eyes, ears and touch sense in particular are absorbing experiences of all kinds through imitation and exploration. It is obvious that the quality of experience is vital for sound development. In addition to sensory experience, talk is as vital to human life as pure air.
>
> (Brierley, 1987, p. 28)

Brierley continues to discuss 21 principles for teaching and learning based upon knowledge of brain development. He makes it clear that the more children learn, the more their brains will have the capacity to learn. The following two principles help to focus on implications for young children's learning:

> All forms of play appear to be essential for the intellectual, imaginative and emotional development of the child and may well be necessary steps to a further stage of development.
>
> The brain thrives on variety and stimulation. Monotony of surroundings, toys that only do one thing, a classroom display kept up for too long, are soon disregarded by the brain.
>
> (*Ibid.*, p. 111)

It was variety and stimulation and the important experiences of talking with adults which prompted the questioning and thinking from the children in the following two examples. Young thinkers construct some wonderful and apparently bizarre reasons for why things happen, drawing on their present knowledge to create explanations which are logical to them at that time (Paley, 1981). The following examples illustrate children's skills as thinkers as they struggle to explain and reason things which puzzle them about their world.

A five-year-old boy asked his parents 'Why are there trees?' A satis-factory answer took his parents into many reasons and a long discussion which justified the existence of trees: shady places to sit on a hot day; for making wooden furniture; equatorial rain forests; conservation; food and habitats for wildlife; and finally 'somewhere for Robin Hood to hide'. This last reason followed a visit to Sherwood Forest and the Major Oak. One part of the answer led to another question or a further reason and so dialogue between parents and child continued with an interested and lively 5-year-old applying his mind and pursuing this line of thought, continuing to think, assimilate and understand, acquiring more informa-tion along the way which extended and further stimulated his thinking. The questioning stopped when, for the moment, he was satisfied with the explanation which had been generated.

A 4-year-old girl asked her father, 'Why does the sea go in and out?' Her father gave the most honest explanation he could, mentioning the moon and the spinning of the earth and the need for the sea to come into the harbours of other parts of the world. She thought that the sea came into the harbour of the small town where she lived to let the boats float, and that it went out to stop children swimming in the sea all day so that their skin did not get wrinkled! She thought that this going in and coming out of the sea was all 'a waste of time' and that the sea should stay in the harbour all the time so that the boats could always float and the children could swim whenever they wanted to. Her search for reason and justification led her to create an explanation and some logical rea-soning from what she presently knew.

Piaget's insights into children's thought and language contribute to our understanding of young children's minds. Piaget gave some fascinat-ing lists of *'why'* questions which were asked by children, providing illustration of children's thinking and their search for reason. The chil-dren about whom Piaget wrote asked questions of *causality* and ques-tions of *justification*. Those who spend time with young children will find a familiar tone in questions like 'Why does the sea go in and out?' and 'Why are there trees?' Young children ask questions which Piaget would categorise as 'Whys of logical justification' when they look for logical and sensible reasons for the things they see and are told. Whilst Piaget thought young children 'ego-centric', this term need not be considered in a selfish sense, nor should children's egocentricity be thought of as a deficit. Young children work hard to make sense of the things they encounter and use all that they know to try to understand. To reply to a child's why question with an answer such as 'because it is' or even 'because I say so!' will not suffice because such responses are neither logical nor satisfactory in terms of their thinking, and do not do justice to children's capacity to think through what they encounter as they try to make sense of what they find.

Children's questions, puzzles, problems, solutions and fascinations have formed the substance of this chapter. They have demonstrated active and creative ways in which children learn, how they think about the world and make sense of their experiences of it. It is in the context of children as capable and serious learners and thinkers that this book is written.

2
QUESTIONS ABOUT SCHEMAS

This chapter is about teachers and other professional educators thinking. When early childhood educators first learn about schemas they often need time to reflect on what this new information means to them. People I have met on numerous courses and conferences which focus on schemas and young children's learning experience a number of emotions: anxiety, concern, excitement, fear and puzzlement to name but a few. On one occasion I was talking about schemas with a group of nursery nurse students in their second year of their initial training course, when one student said 'I think you're making all this up!' So for some, the initial reaction may be disbelief.

These different reactions and emotions reflect the challenge which new-found information can offer us. Thinking about newly encountered theories may challenge established practices and threaten the values which have been held, and even cherished, for some years. Teachers of children under 5 think deeply about the learning and development of the young children with whom they work and, having pondered, they often ask many questions.

This chapter considers some of the questions which I have heard teachers and other early childhood educators ask about schemas, and offers some personal reflections in response. The following questions are typical examples of those which arise when professional educators begin to think about the implications of theory which suggest that children's thinking can be developed by following their intrinsic forms of thought, their schemas.

In the absence of a large bank of research data to draw upon, the responses to some questions are in the form of personal interpretations which may highlight areas for further research. Where possible, relevant theory and research evidence are used.[1] Such a chapter represents something of a risk. To say 'I think' is to expose what is at the heart of one's actions in working with young children and their parents. Here I am sharing my present thinking and my understanding, not because it is definitive but because I believe that it is important that those who are interested in children's learning and development share their thinking and their questions in the hope that a clearer understanding will be reached through professional and pedagogical dialogue.

I hope that this chapter will help to put together a few pieces of the jigsaw puzzle of our understanding of children's thinking. It is written with the intention of making a contribution to the discussion rather than a conclusive statement.

What are schemas?

We are now more knowledgeable about the learning patterns of babies and how they might think and learn. Goldschmied (1989) demonstrates how babies, given safe, stimulating and supportive opportunities, will use their senses to learn about objects they encounter. In so doing they enter into a world of discovery, puzzlement, social encounter and communication. Anyone who watches a young baby will see that some early patterns of behaviour (or schemas) are already evident. As babies suck and grasp they rehearse the early schematic behaviours which foster their earliest learning. Early patterns of behaviour seen in babies become more complex and more numerous, eventually becoming grouped together so that babies and young children do not perform single isolated behaviours but co-ordinate their actions. Toddlers work hard, collecting a pile of objects in the lap of their carer, walking to and fro, backwards and forwards, bringing one object at a time. They are working on a pattern of behaviour which has a consistent thread running through it. Their patterns of action and behaviour at this point are related to the consistent back-and-forth movement. The early schemas of babies form the basis of the patterns of behaviour which children show between the ages of 2 and 5 years, and these in turn become established foundations for learning.

Athey (1990) maintains that children will notice elements from their surroundings, depending upon their interest at the time, and that they have their own intrinsic motivation which must be facilitated by materials and support from adults. She focused on how 2–5-year-old children also work on particular patterns of behaviour, referring to each of these patterns as a schema and defining a schema as: 'a pattern of repeatable behaviour into which experiences are assimilated and that are gradually co-ordinated' (*ibid.*, p. 37). A number of patterns of behaviour were identified and named by Athey according to their characteristics. For example the 'vertical schema' is so called because it relates to up-and-down movements. Athey discusses children's learning and development in terms of:

- dynamic vertical
- dynamic back and forth/side to side
- dynamic circular
- going over and under
- going round a boundary
- enveloping and containing space
- going through a boundary.

The actions and marks related to these descriptions of movement can be identified in young children's drawing and markmaking, but Athey illustrates how such patterns can be represented in children's play, their thinking and their language. Athey argues that patterns pervade children's actions and speech as well as their markmaking. Detailed description and discussion on ways in which different patterns of learning can be represented through action, speech and markmaking are given by Athey, who further illustrates in theoretical and practical terms how *forms of thought* (schemas) once identified can be nourished with worthwhile *content*.

If a child is focusing on a particular schema related to roundness we could say that the child is working on a circular schema. The *form* is 'roundness' and the *content* can be anything which extends this form: wheels, rotating machinery, rolling a ball, the spinning of the planets!

Similarly a child interested on 'up and down ness' could be working on a vertical schema. The *form* is 'up and down'; related *content* can include using ladders, using the climbing frame, watching parascending or skydiving, riding in a lift or on an escalator. In the same way, if a child is interested in enclosing and enveloping schemas, the *form* is 'inside-ness', and related *content* may include wrapping presents, hatching chick eggs, *en croute* cookery, mining and burrowing.

Why do some children get obsessed with one particular activity, repeating it over and over again?

For example: Liam was observed on many occasions putting cups, saucers, plates and other home-corner crockery in the home-corner sink. As soon as he had put all he could find in the sink he walked away and left them. This child might have been interested in spaces which contain and his own ability to put things inside things. He was perhaps seeking out experiences which enabled him to work on different aspects of enclosing and containing. Nursery staff need to make further observations of Liam and, if the pattern is consistent, provide other ways of extending the 'enclosing' schema. Extension activities need to embrace challenging curriculum content so that his thinking is extended and challenged. Children who are apparently repeating actions which seem aimless should be observed carefully by staff who can note precisely what children are doing. Staff can try to decide from their observations how valuable children's activities are. New experiences and interventions need to be based on detailed observations underpinned by the educator's knowledge of each child as an individual learner.

What happens to a schema once a child has established it?

Schemas, or repeatable patterns of behaviour, speech, representation and thought can extend learning as they become fitted into children's patterns of thought. Early schemas seem to provide the basis for later learning. Athey (1990) describes how early 'back and forth' schemas can be observed in young children 'toddling and dumping'. Later 'back and forth' actions can be supported and extended with, for example, stories of 'going and coming' (see Chapter 7) or through experiences involving map-reading and map-making. Much more research is needed, but early schemas can connect together to provide the basis for later related experiences which can be assimilated into more complex concepts.

For example: 16-month-old Declan walks back and forth between a pile of toys and his father. Each time he delivers one toy from the pile into his father's lap. Eventually there are no toys left in the original pile and they are all heaped on the father's lap. Declan was experiencing several things. He was moving between two points: A, the toys, and B, his father. This early backwards and forwards action could lay the foundations for concepts of 'here' and 'there', beginning and ending, starting and finishing, as children move physically and later think about moving between, for example: 'my house' and 'my friend's house', 'my house' and 'my playgroup'. Declan was perhaps also making a social and emotional connection between himself and his father. Declan was giving, his father was receiving. Many who work with young children with schemas in mind see connections between children's 'academic' learning and their social and emotional development. Children can be seen not only making cognitive connections but also making relationships between themselves and others. An 18-month-old girl was waiting in the departure lounge of an airport with her parents. She had her own bag of toys beside her and there were two other carrier bags which contained duty-free purchases, perfume, chocolates and whisky. The little girl began moving between her mother and father, first giving a toy to her mother then retrieving it and walking to her father to offer it to him. The parents played the game, smiling and saying 'thank you' each time they were given a toy, and waving 'bye-bye' each time she left them. The game was then extended to include another passenger, waiting on a seat near the family. This person was offered the toy and followed the 'rules' of the game as they had been demonstrated. The little girl then began delivering a number of toys to the stranger, leaving them on the seat beside her. When she had emptied her own bag of toys, she then began to offer the stranger the contents of the parents' duty-free purchases, smiling at the stranger each time she offered something and looking back at her parents too. This game ended when mother and father stepped in to prevent their perfume and whisky being donated to a complete stranger! This little girl, like Declan, was moving backwards and forwards, testing the power of her own actions, and making a new relationship, a new connection between herself and someone else who, up to now, she had not met. This she could do in the safety of her parents' gaze, to whom she looked from time to time for reassurance and approval.

It is interesting to think about the future of the 'going and coming' patterns of toddlers. Seven-year-old Craig was able to represent his knowledge of space and place and of going and coming by drawing a map of the area around his school (Figure 2.1). It shows the position of the school and the streets which surround it. Some roads are labelled, arrows show the direction to approach the roundabout and buildings are named. Craig explained: 'I know where you go around here because this is where I go with my brother on my bike. To get to my house you go down this road and then turn and go across there.' This 7-year-old's map represents knowledge, connection of ideas and understanding derived from experiences. In terms of pattern, it builds upon early experiences of toddling backwards and forwards, from A to B, and shows again how important the early behaviours of young children are in their learning.

What do you do when you think you have identified a child's schema?

This is a fundamental question. It is not sufficient simply to identify a child's interest: early education needs to challenge children's thinking

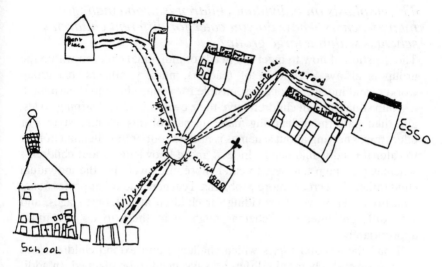

Figure 2.1 Craig's map

and extend their learning. When a child appears to be paying attention to a particular pattern, he or she needs to be provided with a range of interesting and stimulating experiences which extend thinking along that particular path. For example: Heather's teacher had noticed that she seemed interested in circular patterns and movement. She planned several 'extension' activities which might 'nourish' Heather's schema:

- A small group of children (including Heather) visited a tyre fitters to watch car tyres being changed.
- Gyroscopes were introduced, adults demonstrated how to use them and children experimented with them.
- Heather's mother took her to the visiting fairground where Heather delighted in several rides down the helter-skelter and on the carousel.

Extensions to children's schemas need to provide opportunities for further learning, for children to talk and for more nourishment for children's fertile minds. Simple extensions for a child's circular schema might include: playing ring games or singing songs (Mort and Morris, 1991) and making collections of circular or round objects. More challenging extensions might draw upon real life happenings, as in Heather's case, which widen children's experiences of the world and so deepen their knowledge and appreciation of it.

The emphasis on individual children is problematic for many teachers – how do you cater for different children's schemas within a large group?

The question of how to meet the needs of individual children within the group is always a concern of teachers, nursery officers, playgroup workers and indeed anyone responsible for young children's learning in a group situation. All children have their own individual learning styles, and their patterns of learning make up part of this learning style. For educators, knowing about schemas is not the root of the dilemma of how to cater for individual needs. Indeed, more knowledge about children's schemas may help teachers to cater more effectively for the individual child rather than create more problems. Teachers and other professional educators seek ways of providing for children at different stages, and with different interests. Schemas might help them to do this more appropriately.

Broad themes and topics which challenge and extend children, and nourish several schemas in different ways, need to be planned. In addition one-off experiences, small-focus exhibitions and planned opportunities which aim to extend one particular schema for a small number of children, or for an individual, can be incorporated into the curriculum. Working, hands-on exhibitions which match children's schematic interests will attract children who find such things most meaningful to them. Such exhibitions can focus on such themes as packages, wheels, grids and coverings, and are most valuable when they are filled with objects which children can examine, draw and talk about.

When educators have offered a topic to all children, it does not follow that all children have learned the same things from it. All teachers have responsibility for the education of individual children who are grouped together for organisational as well as educational reasons. The match between what educators teach and what children learn is a key issue which involves observation, planning, teaching, assessment, record-keeping and reflection. These processes are further discussed in Chapter 10.

Professional educators who have become interested in children's schematic development will know that children will pursue their schemas anyway, whether adults like it or not! Rather than being an additional burden, and something else to worry about, knowledge of schemas can be a useful tool for teachers who work alone, in early entry classes, for example. Such knowledge can help with observation, planning, interaction with children, intervention in their work and assessment of their learning. Teachers and nursery nurses working together in nursery schools and classes and other professional educators in day nurseries, playgroups and crèches can, together, provide a quality of experience which challenges young children, enables 'fine-tuning' of thinking and action, and ensures equality of access and curriculum opportunity.

When children play in groups do they choose to play with children who are working on the same schema?

It may be that some children play well together in a sustained and involved way because they 'match' in terms of thought and action. For example, 'house' and 'den' play may well attract children who are interested in ideas of 'inside' and 'outside'. However, many children play co-operatively in groups together and perhaps children also play with children whose schematic interests are different but not conflicting.

In a nursery class a group of three children (aged between 3:9 and 4:6), two girls and a boy, were using large hollow bricks to make a 'castle'. The two girls set about the foundations, laying down a square of bricks, one brick high. Both girls worked together, one inside and one outside. At the same time the boy built up the walls, putting more bricks on top of the foundation layer which the girls set out. The girls paid attention to making the doorway and the windows, whilst the boy concerned himself with the height of the walls. Two important ideas were being pursued here. The girls were apparently interested in enclosing and enveloping, and in 'getting in' and 'seeing out'. The boy appeared to be more interested in building towering walls, and the concept of height. As they worked, the three children were engaged in different tasks related to the same project. They discussed questions of 'how big', 'how high', 'how many people can fit in', 'where could the door go', 'how to make the door open and close', 'would there be a letter box'. (They decided there would be no need for a letter box, because in old castles they did not get many letters and if they did someone delivered it on a horse and would knock on the door and ride in!) The three children co-operated, negotiated and worked together purposefully. They worked independently of the teacher who, wisely, allowed this valuable interactive and co-operative exchange to continue uninterrupted, and observed from a distance.

The question of whether schemas can influence children's choice of their partners in play is one which needs further research. Those who work with young children are in a position to research this for themselves, drawing out instances of co-operative schematic play from their observations of children and making careful analysis of these data.

Catherine Arnold (1990) worked with parents and colleagues to investigate her notion that children who play together have similar schemas. Nine children were observed during her project, which concluded that the project children all seemed to display repeated patterns of behaviour which were generalisable and that 'On the whole, children tended to play with other children, who were interested in doing similar things' (*ibid.*, p. 31).

Arnold's study indicates the difficulties of carrying out such research, even on a small scale, and the importance of trying to overcome the difficulties of professional educators doing their own research. Some children need more than co-ordinated schemas to help them to play together co-operatively, and to be able to negotiate plans and tasks with other children. They need professional educators who are much involved with children's play to encourage co-operation, individual potential and the positive development of children's interests in a climate of mutual discovery, learning and support. This is emphasised in the work of the Froebel Blockplay Project, where Bruce concludes 'Rich blockplay does not just occur. It develops when the adult acts as a powerful catalyst working hard to enable it' (Bruce, 1992, p. 26). The crucial role of adults working with children is discussed in Chapter 10.

Can a knowledge of schemas help me to change the behaviour of a 3-year-old in the nursery who is persistently throwing objects?

Clearly adults need to intervene when children behave in ways which are disruptive, dangerous or damaging. Obvious questions to ask include: What triggers the behaviour? What happens before? What reaction does it attract? What are the consequences? Educators need to observe and attempt to intervene before unacceptable behaviour occurs. Identifying children's schematic interest, and providing appropriate activities to match, may help. Many professional educators use what they know about schemas to divert children from disruptive activities and to focus them on more worthwhile endeavours.

Children who throw in inappropriate contexts may respond to more challenging opportunities for throwing. They may throw to attract attention, to try to gain entry to a group or for other reasons! Finding out 'why' is one issue, tackling the behaviour may well be another. Often the first reaction to a child's throwing is to try to stop him or her. One possibility is to identify the throwing as a way of linking into something which might be important to the child and channel his or her skills and energy more positively. This was the case with Simeon. He was 3 years and 3 months old when he began nursery. His young mother was anxious about his temper tantrums and his bouts of throwing whatever he could find.

Nursery staff observed Simeon carefully and tried to engage his interest in experiences which involved throwing before situations arose which prompted a throwing tantrum. Challenged to find worthwhile curriculum opportunities which involved throwing, the nursery staff became very creative and inventive. Obvious activities such as throwing and catching balls, quoits and bean bags had their place in Simeon's daily experiences but catching was a skill which Simeon was still learning and throwing was something he had perfected to a fine art! Nursery staff were keen that activities which Simeon encountered in nursery were worthwhile learning opportunities for him. He and other children became involved in making targets to throw wet sponges at – the mark left by the sponge was used to identify the score. Sometimes targets had numbers on, other times colours or shapes. Energy and interest were channelled into an activity which absorbed a group of children in a range of learning opportunities and experiences: taking turns; writing 'scores' on large charts; aiming; co-ordinating body movements; talking; moving; co-operating as a group and sometimes in 'teams'; interacting with peers and adults; and making up new 'rules' for a game. Other throwing activities included: using small balls attached to elastic which returned to the thrower; experimenting with yoyos; and flight-testing paper aeroplanes.

Early years educators with some knowledge of schemas are in a good position to tackle situations where children's behaviour presents something of a challenge. If children's behaviour becomes a difficulty in terms of its meaning or its management (or both), making detailed observations needs to be part of any course of action. Clearly young children cannot always be allowed to do exactly as they choose in school or at home. They need clear boundaries. Adults need to explain that certain habits are not acceptable, when they are not in their interests or in the interests of others. Detailed observation of a child who is at first glance creating disorder may provide further information to shed light on what is really happening. The child may be reordering, acting according to a particular schematic concern.

Children cannot be allowed, in the pursuit of their schemas, to misuse equipment or impede the work of other children. This kind of problem often arises if children are unstimulated and unmotivated by what is available for them to do. Early childhood education must offer a multiplicity of challenging activities and experiences which children can engage in and which foster a number of schemas. Worthwhile curriculum content is that which is broad and balanced and relevant to children's developmental needs. A curriculum needs to be relevant to children and pertinent to individual needs and interests. Such opportunities will lead to motivated children who are absorbed in valuable learning processes.

It seems that everything children do could be called a schema. How useful are schemas really?

When professional educators give labels to children's schemas they are using a kind of professional shorthand, identifying consistent patterns of action. What a 'schema' is called is really only a way of labelling children's consistent patterns of action. The various categories of schemas are useful as an observational tool. They provide another way of looking at children, by giving a focus to observational details which might otherwise become a list of disconnected events without much indication of learning or possible action to follow. Simply labelling a child's activities in terms of different schemas will be only the first part of the process; the next important step is to use detailed observations of children to decide how best to extend their learning. It is the detail of these observations which are important. Compare the two observations below which report the same event:

Observation version 1 Carole was playing in the home corner. She set up the ironing board and did some ironing. Then she washed the cups and saucers and tidied up. She wrote a shopping list and dressed up, took a bag to the 'shop' in the nursery garden.

Observation version 2 Carole was playing *in the home corner*. She pulled the ironing board *across* the entrance and did some ironing. She put the 'ironed' clothes *in* the wicker *basket*. She collected the *cups* and *saucers* and placed them *in* the *bowl in* the *sink*. She 'washed' them and then put them *in* the *cupboard*. She made some circular marks on a piece of paper, folded it and put it *in an envelope*. She put the envelope *in her pocket*. She put the *purse in her shopping bag* and fastened it shut. Carole *wrapped* a shawl *around* her shoulders and went out into the nursery garden where a tent had been set up as a shop. She went *inside*.

The detail in version 2 gives more information about the *form* of Carole's thinking than does version 1, which notes that she was involved in aspects of domestic play. Version 2 provides more insights into the schematic nature of Carole's play. She was exploring insideness with a continuity of thinking and consistency of action throughout all she did.

Though little has been written about schemas in the sense it is used in this book, some LEAs such as Cleveland (Nicholls, 1986) and Sheffield (Sheffield LEA, 1988; 1989; Nutbrown and Swift, 1993) have produced booklets that contain observations of children which illustrate certain schemas. In considering the work of LEAs as well as that of the Froebel Early Education Project (Athey, 1990), it appears that, given schemas as the focus, parents and professional educators are able to observe the fine detail of children's actions and to note the key elements of children's talk that illuminates their thinking and can provide the foundations on which learning can be built. According to Athey (1981, pp. 361–2): 'Systematic behaviour is curiously under researched in children from two to five years. Behaviours of this stage are often described as idiosyncratic, but schemas of action, when recognised, serve to unite a wide range of apparently different instances of children's activities.'

How can we use our knowledge of schemas to develop links between home and nursery settings?

When parents, teachers and other early childhood educators work in partnership, sharing their observations on the children they live and work with, the possibility of continuity in learning and development is increased. Underpinning knowledge of children's development and supporting theories can sometimes shed light on otherwise incomprehensible behaviour. Teachers who have shared their interest in schemas and talked with parents about the ways in which they use this theory to support children's development have often found that parents become more interested in this way of looking at and making sense of children's actions, their talk and their markmaking. Chapter 9 discusses different ways of working with parents so that ideas about schemas can be shared. The following example shows what can happen when teachers share their professional knowledge with parents who then use what they have learned further to help and understand their children's development.

Three-year-old Lulu was absorbed by and interested in circular shapes and motion. She toured the nursery looking for circular shapes, identifying circular objects – bowls, wheels, knobs, turning tap handles. The teacher told Lulu's mother about Lulu's interest, how staff were encouraging her to identify circular shapes and how this would support aspects of her mathematical development. The next morning Lulu and her mother arrived with a carrier bag filled with Lulu's 'circles'. Lulu had collected them together at her house on the previous evening – enlisting the help of her mother and baby brother!

Links between home and nursery, school or playgroup, can be reinforced as parents and professional educators draw on each other's observations of children playing in the home and in their groups settings, finding ways of extending children's ideas. Lulu and her mother went with a small group of children and a nursery nurse to visit a working water wheel which developed the concept of roundness and introduced the dynamics of movement and cause-and-effect relationships.

How long do schemas last?

Without longitudinal research to draw upon it is not possible to answer this question categorically. However, if teachers use observations to inform their daily work with children, the lack of an answer to this question is not necessarily problematic. A child will explore a schema for as long as he or she is absorbed by it. His or her pattern of thought needs to be supported by challenging content which will embellish learning and experience. Whilst it seems possible to observe particular and predominant schemas in young children, it appears that schemas connect and combine in older children as they tackle more sophisticated and complex tasks and experiences.

What do you do if a child seems 'stuck' on one schema?

Professional educators become sensitised to the times when children appear to be locked into apparently 'aimless repetition' as well as times when children are repeating actions as a valuable part of their learning process. When children get 'stuck', they are often stuck in terms of schematic 'content'. Ways need to be found to extend the content, while still matching the *form* of a child's thinking. That is to say, the form can be nourished whilst the child is diverted from repetitive *content*: Asif appeared to be interested in a vertical schema. He repeatedly (and loudly) built and demolished brick towers for his super-heroes to climb and jump from. Positive learning from this activity had been apparently exhausted. It is at this point that teachers need to intervene. If a child seems stuck on a schema, going over and over the same experiences and actions, careful planning and thought needs to be given to providing further learning opportunities. Planned interventions which are also in tune with the child's schemas and which offer the child the opportunity to learn and develop further need to be introduced. This is how nursery staff developed the curriculum for Asif.

The nursery nurse arranged for Asif, with a small group of children and their parents, to visit a local shopping mall and to ride in the glass lift and up and down on the escalator. Play experiences in the nursery reflected this when the children, on return, used the climbing frame to represent the lift and the escalator. Asif's drawings also represented 'the stairs you stand still on' and 'the box that shut you in and lift you up'. Super-heroes were not excluded from this added dimension. The children's play soon included people 'stuck' in the lift who needed to be rescued (enter Batman!). Later extensions to this theme included lifting objects with a pulley system using a rope over a branch of a tree. This introduced the children (through hard physical effort and much thought) to problems of power and weight, strength and fastenings, thus fostering ideas related to early scientific discovery.

Can you interrupt a schema?

When professional educators ask this question they are concerned about disrupting the finely balanced process of children's thought. Those who have tried to divert children's attention to activities which do not match their current developmental needs will know that children will not be interrupted in their thinking unless it suits them. Parents who have tried to dissuade babies from throwing toys from their prams or high chairs know how difficult it is to divert children from the activity which interests them.

Educators who observe, interact with and intervene in children's play, know that sometimes their interventions are well tuned and well timed whilst on other occasions they are not. Teaching young children is not an exact science; we can only use the knowledge and skills at our disposal to do the best we can and it seems that schemas can provide a better chance of teaching 'in tune' with children's cognitive concerns.

Is there an order in which children tend to go through schemas?

More research, with detailed studies of individual children, is needed to answer this question with confidence. It may help to think of some kind of continuum of schematic development where schemas become increasingly co-ordinated. Work on the development of children's early markmaking can help us to speculate about the possible existence of a sequential order of schemas. We can see a clear pattern in the area of children's markmaking development in the work of Rhoda Kellog (Plaskow, 1967), who identifies a sequence of markmaking development in young children. In her sequence, dots, dabs and straight lines precede enclosures and connected marks.

Given that children working on particular patterns of thought represent their schemas through making marks and talking as well as through their actions, it may follow that 'vertical' and 'back and forth' schemas emerge before 'enclosing and enveloping' schemas. It is probably not as simple as this, though, as children work on the same schematic theme at different stages in their development and incorporate and co-ordinate a number of schemas as they develop.

It may be helpful to think of the notion of 'schemas revisited', where children build up their knowledge through their absorption in particular schemas, move on to explore other schemas and, later, with more maturity of action, language and thought, return to explore a schema further. Only detailed longitudinal studies of children at home and in their group settings will provide further insights into the cumulative nature of schemas.

Reporting on the Froebel Blockplay Project, Gura (1992, p. 65) writes: 'Children often return to forms already mastered, to try out a novel or more complex variant, such as the stacking of vertical enclosures. Sometimes, when it looks as if a particular form has dropped out of the child's repertoire, it reappears in combination with the latest discovery'.

Do all children eventually include all schemas in what they do?

Again, more research into the development of individual children is needed. What is important is that observations of children at any point in time lead to the planning of appropriate experiences for them which match their form of thinking. Certainly in terms of graphic representation, through writing and drawing, they eventually work on numerous schematic forms. It may, therefore, be reasonable to suppose that this is so for action, and speech as well.

Whilst young children can sometimes be observed paying attention to a particular schema, older children's learning involves co-ordination of schemas. Co-ordination and connection mark important progression in learning at all stages. Combinations and co-ordinations of schemas develop into higher-order concepts.

Does all, or most of a child's, activity at a particular time fit into a single schema?

In answer to this question I will refer to the children in my own study when I observed 40 children aged 3–5 years in one nursery class over an academic year. Several of the children exhibited behaviour which could be related to a number of schemas. Other children tended to work on a 'dominant' schema for a while, selecting activities and experiences which fitted into their current schema, but co-ordination and connection of schemas is part of human development. The chapters in Part II will provide further details and examples to support theories in relation to this question.

Is work outside a child's schema counter-productive or fruitless?

No! If the curriculum is based on worthwhile content which draws on real-life experiences, engages children in talking, listening, experimenting, solving problems and thinking, it is not fruitless. The point here is that the 'match' needs to be found between what is being learned and what is being taught. This 'match' may be enhanced if curriculum material is in tune with children's schematic concerns, identified through observation.

Everything could be attributed to schemas – what about other theories and philosophies?

There are of course many ways of thinking about things, and different theories may be useful at different times. For example, whilst 4-year-old Kerrie played in the sand she said, 'Bury up the baby – cover her all up'. The teacher interested in her schema may see this as behaviour relating to an enclosing schema, whilst in a different context, a psychologist or playtherapist may attribute this behaviour to resentment of her new baby sister. It might be both. Athey (1990) gives a similar example of Lois (3:5) who drew her younger brother Jock in his cot, covered her whole drawing with a blanket (a square of sticky paper) and said, 'I've covered him up with a blanket'. She then said, 'And I'll put the cot in the cupboard [pause] and I'll put the cupboard in a cave'. Athey (*ibid.*, p. 152) remarks that this example could suggest 'sibling rivalry', 'if interpreted within a Freudian framework. However this explanation could not be applied to the dozens of similar examples that were observed around this time, including the wrapped pancake, the darkened house and the "covered over" worm.'

Those who live and work with young children use a whole range of perspectives in order to make judgements about the meanings of the things they say and do; those who include schemas as part of their thinking will do the same. Schematic theory should be used as a flexible and useful tool for teaching and learning. It should work for educators, educators should not be slaves to theories.

Adults working with young children use their knowledge of children as individual human beings, and their understanding of theories about child development to make sense of the things children do and say. Using schematic theory in the teaching of young children is a way of using positive theory which identifies and builds on children's strengths and interests and capabilities rather than focusing on the things which they as yet cannot achieve.

Where does all this fit with Piaget?

Relatively little is known about the intellectual development of young children. Despite the work of renowned psychologists such as Piaget and Vygotsky, theories about the thinking of children aged 2–5 years is still relatively meagre. Some theorists, like Piaget, tend to denote stages of development and patterns of behaviour which can be expected from children at particular times. Piaget's studies of cognitive structure contribute much to our understanding of children's development, but his work on children aged 2–5 years tends to focus more on things children cannot yet do rather than their present capabilities. Donaldson (1983) replicated some of Piaget's tests and showed children to be more able that Piaget asserted. Much more work is needed on how children think about their world.

Piaget gave us a focus for young children's thinking, but there was still a need for further insight into the development of thinking of children aged 2–6. While Piaget's studies began to fill the gap in our understanding of children's development there remained a lack of knowledge about how young children thought about their world. Much of what was said about children still concentrated on what they could not do rather than what they could do. That is a 'deficit' rather than a 'constructive' theory.

Paiget stimulated thinking about patterns of development and of the connections between thought and language in young children. He asked questions about children's ability to communicate, and the extent to which children of the same age could think by themselves. Piaget also pondered on children's understanding, considering how much young children of the same age understood each other. He concluded that genuine understanding between children occurred around the age of 7 or 8 years. Recent work challenges this, for example, Goldschmied's work (1989) points to early understanding and communication in babies of between 6 and 9 months. Examples throughout this book also show ways and situations in which children understand each other in different ways from an early age.

I feel that the idea of schemas is interesting but how can we share these things with parents? What will their reaction be?

Some teachers feel that they want to know more about theories of child development and learning before they discuss them with parents. Others feel it is important to share new knowledge with parents even though it is still new and incomplete for them. How professional educators feel depends upon the relationships they have with parents, their own depth of knowledge and their confidence in sharing their professionalism. It seems important that parents have the opportunity to find out about this way of thinking about children's learning and development, and ways of sharing this knowledge are needed. Chapter 9 discusses more fully aspects of working with parents.

This chapter has given some indication of the depth of thinking which teachers engage in when they begin to think about the development of the children with whom they work in terms of schematic theory. It shows that the quest to understand our children's minds continues and that teachers and other professional educators have a professional interest in understanding children's thinking. The questions upon which this chapter is based came from teachers who spent time developing their own knowledge and thinking. The children they work with are rich indeed for they are taught by people who ask 'why' as well as 'how', 'what' and 'when'. Nothing can stop children from thinking and our young children need to be equipped and challenged to think as well as to know. Teachers and other professional educators need theory for they cannot teach effectively without professional knowledge on thinking and knowing. They need to think about their work. Knowing about schemas enables them to extend their thinking and develop their practice. Teachers in the field of early childhood who concern themselves with new knowledge and how to apply that knowledge to their practice are well placed to help the next generation of children to grow up as thinkers too, extending children's thinking with worthwhile curriculum content.

Notes

1. For a detailed consideration of aspects of educational theory in relation to this topic, see Athey (1990).

Part II
Children's patterns of
behaviour and learning

3

CONSISTENCY, CONTINUITY AND PROGRESSION IN YOUNG CHILDREN'S LEARNING

The notion of consistency in the behaviour and minds of children under 5 years of age might raise an eyebrow or two, particularly when adults consider very young children to be inconsistent, spasmodic and idiosyncratic in their approach to life and learning. Pattern and consistency, however, are important features in young children's development.

The identification of children's schemas (their patterns of learning) can help their teachers, parents or other educators to provide learning experiences that are matched to and in tune with their pattern of interest, and therefore provide a consistency of learning opportunity.

Effective educational provision for young children needs to be consistent. Consistency can be considered in terms of three 'constants':

- adults and their behaviour
- routines and information
- experiences and materials.

Adults and their behaviour

That children under 3 need their own 'key worker' who is with them for the majority of the time that they are in group care is a concept presently under debate (Rouse, 1990). At certain times children under 5 need the consistency of a particular adult. This special 'someone' the child often chooses him or herself after an initial attachment is formed during a settling-in period, or it may be a worker who is allocated to a particular group of children. This kind of consistency is important. Parents know whom they first need to talk with, should they want to share something about their child or discuss a concern. Children also know who to turn to if they need help or want to share an excitement.

Teachers, nursery nurses and other educators and carers in group settings need to be consistent in their approaches with children and with their parents. They need to provide one of the constants in children's lives. Children need to be able to predict how adults might react to certain situations so that they can sometimes take some risks. They may risk asking questions, trying out something new or tackling a new problem. Children are more likely to 'risk' new things if they have a sense of adult support.

Routines and information

The second 'constant' leads on from that of adults and how they behave. Children need to 'know where they are' to be able to operate with confidence and effectiveness in their nursery or group. If things change, they need their 'constant' of adult support to help them to cope with and learn from the new, sometimes puzzling, frightening and challenging experiences. Children need to know what will happen and when. They need to have clear explanations if things change and time to adjust to these changes. Information which they can understand is important in helping children to adapt to new situations and to make the most of their daily experiences.

Experiences and materials

The third 'constant' of early education centres on the actual provision that is made for children on a day-to-day basis. Those things which children see when they enter the nursery in the morning, the experiences that unfold and in which they engage need to have an element of constancy so that children can get on with the business of learning and are not encumbered with such worries as where to find things, who to ask or what to do. Children need to know that some things will remain the same each day, for example: that the woodworking bench and necessary materials and tools will always be there for them to use; that there will always be some paint; those favourite books, or a story read today, will be there again to enjoy tomorrow. They need to know that something they begin today will be there for them to complete or add to tomorrow so that they can develop their own continuity of thought and action.

These three 'constants' help to create a consistency of curriculum which enables young children to be *active* learners:

- Tackling new things because they feel safe in doing so and because they know that adults will help them.
- Planning what they will do when they arrive – for example deciding 'When I get to nursery this afternoon I'm going to paint some wood and fix it together'.
- Revisiting familiar materials to build on previous experiences.

Knowing that adults, space, time and materials will be 'constant', the same today as yesterday, helps young children to assume more responsibility for what they do and to follow their own consistent threads of thinking and doing without unnecessary hinderance.

The notion of consistency leads us to think about issues of *continuity* and *progression*, which are also necessary elements for effective learning. The National Curriculum, introduced by the Education Reform Act 1988, aimed to ensure continuity and progression in learning and achievement for children aged 5–16 years and defined how children's learning should progress. The following excerpt from the Report of the Parliamentary Select Committee on Educational Provision for the Under Fives asserts the view of early education as part of an ongoing, continuous process between home, and statutory schooling:

> . . . early education should be seen not as something separate and apart, but rather as the first step on the path into a relevant, coherent and integrated curriculum . . . 'education is a seamless robe . . . the pre-school experience of three year olds and four year olds is part of a continuum'. At the same time, nursery education does not, and never can, replace the home, but is an extension of it.
> (House of Commons, Education, Science and Arts Committee, 1988, para. 2.5)

This view has since been further endorsed by subsequent government documents (Her Majesty's Inspectorate (DES, 1989a); Rumbold Committee (DES, 1990a)):

> The best work with under fives has always taken account of the need for continuity with the teaching and learning which takes place in the next stage of their education. The new legislation (ERA 1988) adds considerable importance to ensuring that full account is taken of the need to promote curricular continuity and progression.
> (DES, 1989a, para. 73)

> The wide range of developmental stages and needs of very young children puts a great responsibility on educators to provide a curriculum which can take into account the similarities and differences within any group of under fives and also provide continuity with what went before and progression to what will follow.
> (DES, 1990a, para. 63)

Issues of continuity and progression linking previous, present and future experiences, and their significance for the curriculum for children under 5, need careful consideration. There needs to be clear understanding of what is meant by 'continuity' and 'progression', and of the ways in which early education might achieve continuity and progression for young children's learning and development. Let us consider, briefly, some of the issues.

First, are we considering continuity of *thought* as well as *action*? That is, are we paying attention to and providing for continuities of children's ideas and interests as well as continuity of the things they *do*? Are we considering continuity of *process* as well as *content*? Is there an over-emphasis on the products of early educational experiences? To address these questions it is helpful to think about different facets of continuity and progression.

Teacher-imposed (or teacher-controlled) continuity

In practice, this view of continuity requires (or supposes) that children can focus on a thematic content over some weeks. Whilst an initial idea for the theme might be derived from a child's idea or experience, it is usually nursery teachers, leading a team, who plan and extend further content of the theme. The cross-curricular nature of the thematic approach to teaching young children is intended to contribute to the all-round learning opportunities and to a 'broad, balanced, relevant and differentiated' curriculum (DES, 1989a). Thematic approaches to curriculum planning and organisation can be a way of ensuring curriculum balance and breadth, and a way of integrating elements of learning rather than falsely compartmentalising them into subjects. However, experience suggests that continuity in terms of a theme lasting a number of weeks is typically imposed by nursery staff, offered to the children, and is content based. For example, a theme on 'Journeys and journeying' can focus on elements of this topic that touch on all the nine areas of learning and experience advocated by HMI (DES, 1989a) and the Rumbold Committee (DES, 1990a) to provide a broad and balanced curriculum: 'The aesthetic and creative, the human and social, the linguistic and literary, the mathematical, the moral, the physical, the scientific, the spiritual and the technological' (DES, 1989a, para. 20).

Such a topic could include early mapwork, related stories told and read, considerations of forms of transport and ways of getting to different places, how different modes of travel work, forms of energy, historic journeys and so on. Early years educators will be familiar with this method of constructing a broad and balanced curriculum. Such planning embraces a holistic view of the curriculum, sets learning in real and realistic contexts and does not compartmentalise particular sets of ideas, rather integrating them into a sensible and coherent whole. This type of planning also draws upon children's interests and can be a way of making learning opportunities dynamic and worth while. But this is only the *offered* curriculum and teachers and other educators who claim to offer high-quality educational provision need to find out the extent to which each child has *received* and learned from that which is offered.

The type of continuity across the curriculum achieved through thematic work can be a useful planning tool. However, *teacher-constructed continuity* is not necessarily the kind of continuity that fulfils children's need for continuity in their learning and thinking. Observations of children thoroughly absorbed in their work as part of the curriculum offered to them are needed to find out how much the children have gained and learned from it. Watching children, and listening to children, provide ways of doing this. Mary Jane Drummond (1993, p. 59) writes: 'Our attempts as teachers to get inside children's heads, and understand their understandings, are enriched to the extent that children themselves are prepared to give us, through their talk, access to their thinking.'

Continuity constructed by children

Children's schemas provide opportunities for continuity in learning. Children's persistent threads of action and thought seem to be a fundamental elements which link children's thought and action with process and content. This kind of continuity is that which children create in the process of exploring, thinking and learning. Viewed in this way, schemas can be considered the core of children's developing minds.

Some of the continuity constructed by individual children may be identified as a thread of thinking, or schema which 'connects' different areas of content. Without accurate identification, without observation and reflection on the part of professional educators, these threads remain invisible and children's chosen activities appear to lack continuity either of content or of thought. When children's individual patterns of action and thought have not been observed and identified it might be said that they are *inconsistent*, that they lack *concentration* and are unable to choose for themselves. Young children are often described as 'flitting'. However, when professionally informed educators look closely at what children are doing in each apparently unconnected activity they sometimes find and understand links which remain invisible to those

who are uninformed and lack an underpinning knowledge of the theories of children's learning. For example: a 3-year-old spends his time
moving from one activity to another. First he digs in the sand; he
moves on to make a cup from some clay; then he goes outside to 'hide'
under the branches of a willow tree; next he paints – two ovals on a
large sheet of paper and puts a dab in the centre of each. 'Mices in
cages', he says. Viewed from the point of view of *discontinuities of
action*, he moves in about six minutes between four different activities
– sand, clay, willow tree, paint. Considered in terms of *continuity of
thought* he creates: *a hole* (in the sand), and *a container* (in the clay), he
hides in an *enveloping space* (under the willow tree), and he represents
two mice *enclosed* in cages (using paint). Reflected upon in this way,
the links or *continuities* in his behaviour become apparent and can be
described as part of his enveloping/enclosing schema, his predominant
intellectual concern.

When children's actions are observed with schemas, rather than
simply content in mind, it becomes possible to interpret children's approaches to learning differently. It is through schemas, and the fitting of
content to different schematic threads, that children's own construction
of reality and subsequent continuity can be identified. Looking at learning in this way can be a little like unlocking a door, shining a light on
previously darkened areas, seeing anew.

Four-year-old Vicky irritated her parents when she persistently removed tea towels from the kitchen to wrap her teddies in and put them
to bed. When participating in a discussion about children's schema held
at Vicky's nursery, her mother realised that it was not just the teddies
who were being used in this wrapping-up behaviour. Vicky always carried a bag with her when she went out. In the bag there was often a
smaller bag and then several other bags and purses filled with small toys,
coins, a hanky, notepaper, indeed whatever would fit. Vicky's mum had
always accepted this behaviour as Vicky 'being a little girl' and wanting
to be like her mum. Vicky probably was modelling her mother to some
extent, but what underpinned this and other related examples of similar
behaviour was the schematic thread of consistency in her behaviour; this
child was thinking in a concentrated and systematic way about insideness. When Vicky's previously irritating behaviour was interpreted in
this new way, a way that suggested that she was exploring an area of
learning, an important kind of thinking, Vicky's mother decided that she
would make small 'teddy-bear sheets' out of an old sheet and enable
Vicky to continue her wrapping behaviour whilst keeping track of her
tea towels.

Progression in thought

The gradual evolution of schemas, and the extension of early forms of children's thought, can eventually lead to connections between schemas and therefore to the formation of new ideas. One example of progression in thought can be seen in a child's gradual development in drawing the figure of a person. Initial representations may be simple vertical lines later followed by oval representations. Later some marks may appear inside or outside the oval that represent parts of the face; finally the oval core becomes attached to vertical and horizontal lines, and the whole represents a body with arms and legs.

Over a period of two or three years the drawing of a human figure develops in this way. An area for further research lies in the possible links between children's representations and their emotional development. Children first represent themselves and their own viewpoint, their egocentric view of life, and later become more aware of themselves in the world. The development of core and radial drawings may also link with the time when children begin to make social and emotional connections, with their peers and others. Other figures appear in their drawings, seemingly at the time when children become aware of themselves and others, their brother, sister, mum, grandad, their dog, cat or goldfish.

So how does the early content of children's persistent puzzling and thought lead to progress or development?

The content of young children's thought arising from an enveloping/ enclosing schema might relate to the idea of hiding or covering up or 'being inside'. When these fundamental ideas develop, children will begin to understand ideas related to capacity or surface area. Later still children start using symbols to represent capacity, in the same way as adults understand that the petrol indication light on the dashboard of a car represents how much fuel is in the tank, or the dipstick that indicates the level of oil in the reservoir. Children who understand about 'inside' and 'outside' and about increasing and decreasing size will find the story of *The Secret in the Matchbox* (Willis, 1991), where a young boy keeps a tiny dragon in a matchbox, but when the box is opened the dragon grows and grows, both understandable and amusing.

Quality in the early-childhood education curriculum

Continuity is an essential element of a quality early years curriculum. The curriculum content that is offered to children must match the content of their thinking and capabilities. Some continuity and progression of learning can be achieved by building on children's capabilities. Bruce (1987, p. 25) reminds us that 'what children can do (rather than what they cannot do) is the starting point in the child's education'.

Teachers and other early childhood professionals need provide for continuity in ways which are linked to children's ideas and children's interests. The progression of skills, and the introduction of new materials and content, should support progression of children's thoughts and ideas. All these elements are needed, but where skills and content dominate the curriculum it is at the expense of other important elements. There is a risk that some quality and balance can be lost and growth of independent and creative thinkers is limited where skills dominate. Continuity and progression in children's learning can only be achieved if the children as people and as a learners are respected as central to and active in the learning process. Learning opportunities must be meaningful and motivating to children.

Ways of making learning meaningful have been central to the work of many respected educators who laid the foundations of early childhood education as it is known today. Reflecting on the work of Froebel, Montessori and Steiner, Bruce (1987, p. 26) writes: 'Through careful observation, based on knowledge of the stages of child development, the adult can work with the child rather than against what is natural. In this way, children are more likely to be prepared to struggle and persevere when difficulties in learning are inevitably encountered.'

The Russian psychologist Vygotsky made a significant contribution to theory on children's thinking. He saw learning as a profoundly social process which needed dialogue and mediation. He identified the clear and crucial role for adults in developing young children's thinking. Early childhood educators today have this awesome task for they can make a profound difference to young children's quality of thought.

According to Vygotsky every piece of learning had a history, a base on which it was built, beginning before formal education and based in real-life experiences. This kind of learning occurs when children spend time with adults, working on real situations such as baking, filling the washing machine, gardening. Vygotsky regarded the match between a child's learning and his or her developmental level as all important. He suggested that children had two developmental levels, their actual developmental level, what they could actually do independently, and a higher level, that which they may next be able to do. Vygotsky identified the interchange between these two levels as the 'zone of proximal development', the difference between what children can do alone and what they can do with help, support and guidance. He argues: 'what a child can do with assistance today she will be able to do by herself tomorrow' (Vygotsky, 1978, p. 87). This notion emphasises the important role of the adult in fostering progression in children's thinking: helping children to move forward in, and develop their ideas through, positive and interactive learning encounters between children and adults.

One of the clearest ways to understand progression in children's learning is to look at individual children over a period of time, observing their schematic interests, seeing how these relate to the development of their behaviour, their speech and their thinking. The next chapter consists of case studies of three children: Gary, Jeanette and Stuart, who are pursuing three different schemas.

4
SCHEMAS AS CONSISTENT PATTERNS OF BEHAVIOUR – STUDIES OF THREE CHILDREN

Introduction

In this chapter the activities and learning experiences of three children, Gary, Jeanette and Stuart, are presented and discussed. Three short case studies use observations of the children's daily work, play and development in their nursery environment and illuminate different elements of continuity and progression in their thinking. By focusing on individual children we can begin to identify ways in which theory about patterns of development and schemas might be useful in practice.

Observations of them were made over three terms whilst the children attended a nursery class. All three children show consistencies in their actions that can be analysed to find consistent patterns of thought, as well as continuity and progression in their learning.

In looking at Gary, Jeanette and Stuart we can consider three of the schemas identified by Athey (1990): dynamic vertical, containing/ enveloping and dynamic circular. We can see how children meet and use opportunities for further learning through the exploration of their schemas. In these examples there is visible consistency of *forms* of thought (the schemas) and a variety of related *content* of thought (curriculum and life experiences) (Athey, 1990).

Whilst a dominant schema is discussed for each child, this does not mean that the children did not work on other schemas. In each case all observations of children were analysed and the schema occurring most often in observations is discussed here in detail to illustrate the learning arising for each child. It was the dominant schema, once identified, that enabled staff to plan learning opportunities that matched the child's concern and interest. Observations are presented and discussed in terms of each child's subsequent learning.

This chapter illustrates consistent patterns that seem to run through the whole of children's behaviour: their actions, their language, their drawings and their thinking. In discussing the schemas of Gary, Jeanette and Stuart, we will see how speech, graphic communication and actions seem to fit together to form a cohesive pattern.

Examples given here draw on original data from my study of 40 children. The temptation to draw comparisons between these and observations from other publications has been resisted. What is needed is a 'bank' of information that will help professional educators to discuss and identify schemas and extend children's learning from a schematic base. This is similar to the call by Stenhouse (1975) for multiple cases that can be drawn upon in the search for commonalities. Different authors have taken different approaches in the search for schemas, but many will recognise the patterns of action, speech, representation and thought illuminated by Athey (1990).

Gary: Dynamic vertical schema

Gary attended the nursery full time for a term before he transferred to the infant school. He had recently moved into the area and had previously attended another nursery in the same local authority. He lived with his mother and younger, 2-year-old brother, in a two-bedroom terraced council house that was just a few minutes walk away from the nursery.

Gary's markmaking, his movement, the things he constructed and his use of language seemed connected in his dynamic vertical schema. The following observations show a thread of thinking and doing which seemed to run throughout the work he engaged in.

Gary (4:7) frequently used the climbing frame in the nursery garden. He climbed to the top, using various routes and usually descended by way of the slide. Gary also used his body to extend and explore height when jumping, bouncing and climbing tree logs, often launching himself into the air with the cry and gestures of the current television super-hero! The experience of climbing higher and dropping down is important for the development of ideas related to increasing and decreasing height and for children to gain a sense of control of their bodies. If children experience such dimensions with their bodies they are better equipped to understand them in the abstract and to represent height and different levels in their drawings and through talk. If children have a

Figure 4.1 'That's a ladder . . .'

variety and richness of experiences they are better equipped to create abstractions from their experiences.

Gary (4:7) painted a series of pictures that included ladders. Figure 4.1 represents 'That's a ladder, that's a man who's gonna climb up it, and that's the sun'. Whilst Gary's drawings were clear and apparently uncomplicated he was able to produce a set of marks that enabled him to portray most things. He could draw straight lines, dots, arcs and circles. He could connect these marks, he could place marks inside other marks and add marks to the outside of others. His use of the grid to represent 'a ladder' matches his interest in climbing up and down. He described the ladders in his drawings as 'useful, 'cos it helps you to go up'. Positioning also seemed important in Gary's drawings. There was always something at the bottom of the ladder, for example the ground, himself, another person or a car, and the sun or a bird was often featured at the top of the ladder.

Playing with the doll's house (4:8) Gary walked some small figures up the stairs saying, 'They need to go up the stairs. They sleep at the top'. Later his play involved people working on the roof of the doll's house. 'They're working up high. They climb up the ladder to fix the slates.'

Understanding and appreciation of gender issues and equal opportunities mean that nursery staff encourage children to use the whole range of equipment and experiences. In this example Gary demonstrated his interest and competence whilst using the doll's house to create a story that fitted his schematic concerns. Constraints of gender stereotype that reduce children's access to various learning opportunities were not apparent here. The doll's house provided the opportunity to play in a creative and representative way with his earlier real-life experience of seeing the roofers repair damaged roof tiles.

A conversation with Gary's mother revealed that he had been 'helping' some workers who arrived during the school holidays to replace roof tiles. She commented that he would not be distracted from watching them, seemingly fascinated that they were walking on the roof. At the time he commented: 'They're up a lot, aren't they mum?'

Gary's mother recalled her amusement with the way Gary expressed his observation that the men were up high, and told him that the men were 'up high'. It is noteworthy that Gary then used the word *high* when he was playing with the doll's house. Children are more likely to assimilate language used by adults when what they say matches children's interests. Words that are out of context or not in harmony with children's current schematic concerns and interests are less likely to be meaningful for children.

Continuing to pursue his interest in vertical movement, Gary (4:8) used the small ladder in the nursery garden and placed it against the wall. He asked if he could 'paint the wall'. This was not encouraged in its entirety (the prospect of Gary and 38 other children with brushes and gallons of paint needs no explanation). Instead the teacher found a way to satisfy this request. She gave him a large bucket of water and a large brush and suggested that he pretended to paint the wall. Gary was happy with this and began to 'paint' the outside wall. Other children joined him, and he explained the technique: 'I have to climb up four steps first, you do up high first, then you come down lower to do the bottom bits. I saw them do it outside my house.' Gary paid attention to the brickwork he was 'painting' with water. He counted the bricks he had painted and commented that he had 'half the water left' in his bucket. He was able to combine ideas of space and number, achieving some continuity of thought and connection between different ideas.

There had been decorators working on the estate recently, redecorating the outsides of some houses. Again this experience matched Gary's current interest and he represented it in his play. Nursery staff supported and extended Gary's interests, providing the materials he needed in response to his requests, and following their own observations of Gary. Such methods of working served to enhance Gary's learning opportunities.

Figure 4.2 'I did a car . . .'

Gary (4:9) drew a vehicle (Figure 4.2) and said, 'I did a car and it was going really fast and it's got one wheel that's pumped down so it stopped'. He pointed to the smaller wheel in the drawing to indicate which wheel he was referring to. It seems that Gary had found a way to represent his schema through drawing on the experience of riding in his uncle's car when it had a puncture. The opportunity to see the deflated tyre, the jacked-up car and the process involved in making the car mobile again provided 'food for thought' for Gary and matched his current schema.

When talking about this drawing with Gary, his teacher told him that when a tyre was 'pumped down' it was called 'deflated'. She explained that the tyre in Gary's picture was deflated because it had a hole in it which was called a 'puncture'. Gary liked these words and soon introduced a game where he pretended that all the bikes in the nursery garden were in need of repair because they all had punctures.

The ladders in Gary's drawings and his understanding of 'upness' and 'downness' seemed to be a development of his vertical schema. Later drawings often included a grid or cross of some kind. He filled in spaces using vertical and horizontal lines and made a series of drawings that included numerous crosses. This combination of vertical and horizontal marks and movements seems to herald the arrival of more complex thinking for Gary.

Gary (4:10) was looking at pictures of spiders' webs in a book, then he saw a photograph of a child drawing around his hand. Gary spent some time staring hard at the palms of his hands and tracing the lines on them with his finger. Later he drew around his hand and filled the outline with a grid pattern (Figure 4.3). After drawing this he said: 'It's spiders' webs all over my hand. I saw them in a book'. Gary had seen the match between the crossed lines in a spiders' web and the crossed lines that

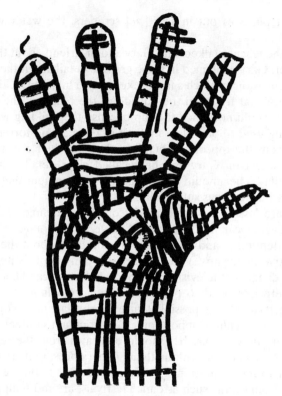

Figure 4.3 'It's spiders' webs all over my hand'

naturally occur on the skin of the palm. This illustrates the potential source and richness of stimulating material in books when combined with the child's own patterns of thinking, markmaking and language.

Gary refined his lines and grid patterns to the point where he could draw sophisticated representations of a palm of his hand. Gentle (1985, p. 40) observed that a child's markmaking evolves according to a 'repertoire of marks, schemata and observations already made'.

Gary (4:10) utilised much of the nursery equipment and appeared to extend his schema spontaneously. He subsequently represented his experiences. On one occasion he used a number of large foam cubes to build a tower, saying: 'This is the tall fire tower that goes up higher than you can get.' Then with his friend they played a game of fighting the fire with hoses and used wooden boxes as the crane to reach the top of the tower. Eventually (after a helpful push) with dramatic sound-effects the tower crashed to the floor. Again Gary explained: 'They built it too high.

You can't put fires out in scry [*sic*] scrapers, the water won't go up there.'

When the teacher talked with Gary and his friend about their burning skyscraper, Gary explained in some graphic detail about the film he had seen on television in which a fire broke out in a high tower. He described the elevator that travelled the outside of the building; the raised plat-forms that would not reach the top because the building was too high; ropes being used to provide a method of escape; and torrents of water pouring from the top of the building. The film had clearly had some profound effect on Gary and he recalled clear details for use in his dramatic play. The amount of vertically related content that this 4-year-old had assimilated was substantial.

There are lessons to be learned from this example. Television, as many will agree, can have a powerful influence on young children. They can pay attention to and retain elements of detail about the images (be they positive or negative) which they see. This book is not about the virtues or dangers of television for children, but we can heed a message. Whilst there is a need to protect children from images that may be disturbing, it can also be possible to use appropriate media opportunities to enhance curriculum opportunities. Curriculum content (to be dis-cussed more fully in Part III) should be drawn from the real world. It should provide children with firsthand experiences, visits to local places to see, for example, machinery, animals, the fire station, and to enjoy and learn from events such as dance festivals, art and sculpture exhibi-tions. All these things can be important elements of a worthwhile curric-ulum and such experiences need frequently to be built into the curriculum for children under 5. This may be familiar to many early childhood educators, but for so many, the familiarity lies in the content of visits rather than the forms of thought that they might inform, nourish and extend.

Gary's interest in firefighting was apparently fuelled because it matched the form of his thinking, his schema. Powerful images captured his imagination: falling debris, cascading water, elevators moving up and down the building, people abseiling on ropes from a great height. Whilst in this example the drama cannot be ignored, it is useful to focus in on the structures of thinking which made Gary represent this scenario in his play. Those working with young children need to consider forms of thinking when they plan visits as part of a topic or theme. A visit to the fire station can nourish a number of schemas and ideas and serve a number of interests, especially when the *forms of thought* (or schemas) are identified and where the *content* is worth while and informative.

Children interested in ladders may be focusing on the structure rather than the content 'ladder'. So the job of the teacher is not necessarily to focus on *ladders* but to work with the child to explore the question, 'What other things can be used to increase height and nourish a vertical schema?'

Jeanette: Containing and enveloping schemas

Jeanette began attending nursery when she was 3 years and 9 months old. She needed about four weeks to settle happily, during which time her mum and grandma spent quite a lot of time in the nursery with her each morning. Jeanette lived in a semi-detached council house on the estate in which the nursery was situated. She lived with her mum and dad, two older brothers (12 and 14 years) and younger sister who was 6 months old. Jeanette spent much time with her grandma when her mum was working at her part-time job in the local chipshop.

Jeanette made full use of the nursery environment and seemed very imaginative in her play. Observations of Jeanette in the nursery suggested that containing and enveloping actions underpinned her play, though there were observations that suggested other schematic concerns. This would be expected where children are engaged in a range of experiences and making use of whatever they come across as they develop their thinking, knowledge and understanding about the world. Much of Jeanette's language reflected the underpinning structures of her thinking and helped staff to identify her interests.

Brown (1973) wrote that speech representations which relate to enclosing and enveloping begin at about 2 years old. Piaget and Inhelder (1956) described three types of enclosure: one-, two- and three-dimensional. Jeanette put herself inside enclosures many, many times. She sorted through the dressing-up clothes and then enclosed herself behind the trolley on which they hung. She used the hanging clothes as curtains. She seemed intent upon hiding or being covered up. 'This is my house, come in', she said, indicating that she had used the dressing-up trolley and clothes to make a house and this was the content of her schema.

This type of play continued when Jeanette climbed inside a climbing frame that formed an enclosed and defined space. Again her language matched her actions: 'This is my little house, I'm in bed.' There were two references to enclosures in this remark, *house* and *bed*. In this sentence, having described her actions, Jeanette added content to her schema: 'I'm in bed.' What she *said* and what she *did* corresponded, showing co-ordination between her speech and her actions.

Several observations of Jeanette playing in the home corner include a reference to her blocking off the entrance with furniture: an ironing board, a chair and a piece of fabric fastened between cupboard units. Indeed, she used whatever she could find to bridge the open gap so that she was completely enclosed within the house. Often, when doing this she would say something like, 'I'm inside now', or 'The door is closed now'. It appeared that there was a need to be entirely enclosed, so sealing the entrance was an important part of her play.

Through these observations, staff were able to identify the patterns of thinking which seemed to link Jeanette's actions and language. The role of early education is not simply to recognise children's patterns of behaviour and learning and to understand their actions. Teachers can find ways of extending children's thinking and learning, basing their decisions on children's needs as ascertained by careful and detailed observations and their knowledge of child development, child psychology and continuity and progression of learning strands. Teachers of young children develop ways of matching the curriculum they plan, and their own knowledge of potential curriculum content, to the current interests and concerns of the children with whom they work. Such teachers are inventive, ingenious and imaginative in their work and involve themselves and intervene in children's play, when appropriate, to extend and challenge their thinking and their doing.

Jeanette's teacher used the opportunity of a sudden and heavy snowfall to do this. A group of children, including Jeanette (4:1), was playing outside in the snow. The teacher watched as Jeanette and other children played with the buckets and spades, digging, moulding, throwing and sliding on the snow. She wondered if she could, or should, channel Jeanette's enjoyment of the snow and help her to work with other children and engage in further experiences of 'insideness'. The teacher suggested that they might try to build a house of snow. The children moulded the snow, talked about it, rolled it into small balls and added more snow to make the balls larger. Jeanette jumped into mounds of snow, pretending to hide and a spontaneous and joyful game of 'snow hide-and-seek' followed. Children piled snow into a heap to make a wall, then Jeanette, knowing that her house was made of bricks, organised a number of children to make some bricks out of snow. This was a rather ambitious undertaking, but two passing parents were happy to stop and join in! A retired gentleman who lived opposite the school came to offer his garden spade and the nursery nurse donated her car snow-shovel to the effort. The addition of these tools made construction work easier. The teacher prompted talk about the size and weight of the bricks, and how wide the wall should be. Jeanette was most concerned about how big the 'inside' would be so that everyone could fit in.

Jeanette's interest here seemed, through this dynamic and co-operative experience, to have moved from simply *being inside* to thinking about the purpose of space, the importance of size and fitness for purpose. She was concerned that there should be a roof '*to keep the people dry*'. When offered a blanket (used as a tent in the summer) she said that it would 'still let the rain through to the inside' and chose instead to use plastic sheeting supported by a plank of wood. She explained the reasoning for her choice: 'My dad put that on the window when it broke and the rain won't to through this stuff.'

The house building complete, the children shared some warming soup that had been prepared indoors by another group of children with the nursery nurse. Jeanette remarked that children needed to 'go in and out because they can't all fit in together'. She also offered that some of the children who made the soup should be allowed to sit inside the house. 'They helped us to get warm inside our tummies so they can play in the house too.'

This experience was a balanced episode of sharing and co-operating, involving children, staff, parents and neighbours. There were opportunities to learn about working together and communicating effectively, about physical effort and the need for good tools and warm, waterproof clothing. Children talked about many mathematically rooted aspects: how big, how many, too heavy, too small, just right, will it fit. They discussed angles, corners, shape and position. They talked about, as they experienced, the properties of the snow, whiteness, coldness, its melting, the noises on the streets and in the garden, how it might change if the sun shone or if it got even colder. All these early scientific notions were included in the chatter of this busy and tenacious group. The teacher made the most of opportunities to maximise individual children's interests and to help them to develop and appreciate different things: working with others, considering size, sharing the digging tools, estimating and measuring spaces.

Clearly the children involved in this rich outdoor experience had meaningful opportunities to talk and learn. Their work was stimulated and extended by a teacher who was tuned into children's interests and skilled at motivating children to work purposefully and co-operatively. These children were learning about working together as well as gaining worthwhile cognitive experience. They were sharing their ideas, their plans and their pleasures as they played with peers and adults to make the snow house. The spontaneous experience of building the snow house fitted well with the planned event of making soup. The teacher and nursery nurse dovetailed these two activities with skill and gave the children the opportunity to share together and with parents in the outcomes of their morning's work.

Markmaking can also provide a clear indication of what children are paying attention to. Jeanette rehearsed the movements and actions of containing and enveloping by making clear marks on paper that matched her motor-level actions. From a range of geometric designs printed on paper, Jeanette selected a page printed with divided, concentric circles. Using a way crayon she covered the whole area with one colour. Explaining her work she said, 'I've covered up all the pattern – it's hidden'.

The notion of being inside and the enclosure marks Jeanette was able to make were combined in a verbal account which Jeanette gave to describe one of her drawings: 'It's rain, and that's the umbrella, those are the metal things and that's the material that covers over and that's the spider. It's inside the sink, that's the sink.' In this example Jeanette was recalling the objects that she knew were coverings or containers and her vocabulary reflected this interest. Gardner (1980, p. 26) observes that preschool children generate 'fixed patterns' or 'schemas' for familiar objects in their world. These include a circle radiating lines that typifies the sun. Jeanette used this core and radial (Athey, 1990) to represent *spider* and *umbrella*. Gardner (1980) suggests that these basic schemas, having been established, can be assimilated into more organised and complex representations of their experiences. Jeanette applied the objects within her experience of containing and enveloping to make an illustration that incorporated objects that are covered, coverings or contained and containing.

She drew three examples which she described as 'Me *covered up*'; snowman, snow *all around*'; 'a car *covered in* snow'. She represented these things within her experience and in doing so picked out of those experiences the elements which matched her current schematic interests. The words she used to describe her drawings were linked to covering and enveloping ideas.

Other drawings seemed to represent her containing/enveloping schema. She made a series of marks on the same day that were all types of enclosure or coverings and she named each differently, ascribing content to each:

- a tree, 'a big big tree'
- a snail

- a head
- a sock
- a snake.

Gardner (1980, p. 11) suggested that children often make their drawings in sets of three, four or five, which explore one particular schema.

Jeanette also used paint to cover paper, puting layer upon layer of paint on a page. Those who have worked with young children will be familiar with those paintings that are so covered in paint that they have become a *soggy hole*. On several occasions Jeanette placed another piece of paper over the top of her painting, often remarking 'I've covered it up'. On one occasion she covered her painting with more paper and pulled it apart to reveal a print of her original on the top paper. She remarked, 'I've made two, one for you and one for Mrs P. I'll put them together again'. In this example we can see Jeanette's understanding and application of one-to-one correspondence and her attitude of giving her paintings to others as presents.

Jeanette sometimes made her wet paintings into little presents, folding them into tiny 'parcels' which she took pleasure in presenting to interested adults. This scenario will also be familiar to many who know young children. It is another excuse to enclose and a way children find to offer something special to familiar adults with whom they spend their time.

Jeanette dipped toy cars in paint, then she moved the cars along the paper making first an arc, then a straight line. She placed three cars inside the enclosure she had created and said, 'Three cars in the car park' (Figure 4.4). The mathematical work which Jeanette spontaneously undertook included: organising space, using numbers, thinking about size, shape, proportion and early tessellation. Action, graphic and speech representations were combined in this example.

As the examples of Jeanette's learning and development show, she seemed to keep up a 'running commentary' of her work, often using language linked to the ideas of containing and enveloping. In further work, Jeanette made some marks and covered them with another piece of card then secured them well with a large amount of a sticky tape. When she was apparently satisfied that sufficient tape had been used she held up the card and said, 'there, all covered up'. The smile on her face indicated her pleasure and satisfaction at a job well done. She had learned about the materials she had used to fasten her card. She had persevered for some time to develop a technique that enabled her eventually, and with skill, to cut the tape without ending up with a sticky ball

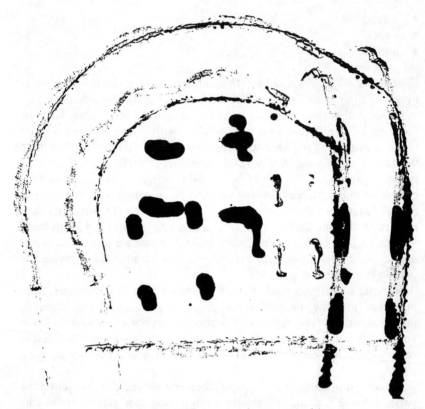

Figure 4.4 'Three cars in a car park'

of useless tape and the belief that the material had a mind and will of its own!

Jeanette's interest in covering things extended to three-dimensional works. She wrapped cardboard tubes in paper and said they were 'crackers for a party'. The *form* of thought was enclosure; the *content* in this instance was party crackers. Jeanette filled paper bags with a variety of contents. She gave one to each adult working in the nursery telling them, 'It's for you'. In doing this Jeanette was making and giving presents. The learning underpinning this leads to ideas of degrees of fullness and emptiness, and to one-to-one correspondence. Jeanette made sure that there was one bag filled for each adult. Later she filled a plastic container with small objects and stuck the lid on. 'I helped Ben to make this present for his mum. I showed him how,' she said. In fact, Ben had been allowed to watch Jeanette as she worked on the 'present' with industrious attention. He was not permitted to do anything else to it!

Further presents were made for a pretend party happening in the home corner, using books and small toys collected from around the nursery and enclosed in sheets of paper. The desire and the act of making and giving presents were as important a part of this little girl's affective development as was her learning related to areas of mathematical experience. Jeanette took pleasure in making something for and giving it to others.

Nursery teachers know that foundations of mathematical ideas of surface area, size and capacity can be laid in the process of early play with natural materials including water, sand and clay. These materials are used in nurseries on a regular basis. Such provision of natural materials with a range of complementary equipment gives children an open-ended resource with which to explore, discover, invent and create.

Water

Having filled a jug with sponges and water, this initial action of containing led to some experiences of functional dependency (Athey, 1990, p. 70). Jeanette tried to make some plastic bottles stand up. They were empty and unstable, so fell over. She puzzled for a while and after repeated attempts to make them stand up said: 'Oh! I know why they won't stand up, 'cos they've no water in them, water makes them stand up.'

Jeanette had created her own 'logical structure' and was able to reason and express orally (Piaget, 1972). Jeanette reasoned that the bottles standing upright were functionally dependent upon being filled with water. Piaget considered the experience of objects to be a basic factor in the development of cognitive structures. He suggested that physical experience consists of acting upon and drawing knowledge from the results of these actions: knowledge being drawn not from the objects but from the actions that effected the objects (Stendler, Lavatelli and Stendler, 1972).

Sand

Jeanette filled a small bowl with pebbles and wet sand. She said, 'It's your dinner'. She continued to bury the 'dinner' in the sand: 'It has to go in the oven to cook, then you can get it out and eat it.' This example happened a few days after the nursery had held a barbecue party in the garden. Parents and other guests attended and potatoes wrapped in foil were placed in the barbecue fire to cook. Jeanette may have been drawing on this experience when she buried the dinner she had made in the sand to cook. Real-life experiences of cooking in different ways, and different kinds of food, are a good source of curriculum content to nourish children's schemas.

Clay

Jeanette filled containers with clay. She said, 'Shampoo and talc. It's a shop'. On another occasion she wrapped pieces of clay in some pieces of brown paper and put them in a small box, closing the lid. 'I'm cooking the tea', she said, 'it's a surprise tea tonight!' The underpinning form of thought (containing and enveloping) which is continually represented in Jeanette's learning and thinking is represented is different ways as she plays with the clay.

If we reflect on the *content* of Jeanette's play and actions over time we can see a child who is apparently flitting from one experience to another: house play, drawing, water, sand, clay, making crackers for an imaginary party, giving presents, playing at cooking. However, if we focus on the underlying *form* of her thinking that is present in these actions it is evident that, far from flitting, she is systematically fitting relevant experiences together which match her schematic interest. She is selecting from materials, activities and opportunities available to her, a set of experiences bound by an almost invisible thread of thinking. Athey discussed the notion of flitting and fitting:

> . . . focusing on content at the expense of form can lead to the conclusion that young children flit from one theme to another and that they are unsystematic or even idiosyncratic . . . One of the uncharted areas of early cognitive functioning is children's own search for commonalities. While it is true that children often name a drawing as one thing and then change it to another, it is also true that, more often than not, there is a common form underlying differences in content.
>
> (Athey, 1990, p. 83)

Jeanette had put herself inside spaces, covered spaces and places, filled spaces. This illustrates at a basic motor level the containing and enveloping schemas through which she was learning about mathematical ideas of size, position, capacity, shape, quantity and space. Through these early motor experiences she had a basis for developing these ideas further when she met or created for herself similar and challenging situations. The work Jeanette did was self-motivated and it appeared to involve her in significant steps in her learning. Curriculum processes must enable children to interact in this way, facilitating their developmental knowledge and supporting their actions and discoveries.

Jeanette's explorations were systematic and fitted together as a cohesive, well planned and relevant whole. This shows the need to reconsider the notions that 4-year-olds have short concentration spans and have only a limited ability to make choices for themselves. Jeanette was able to select from a wide range of experiences, to extend her thinking and to work in depth with adults who challenged, extended and supported her learning. She also illustrates how graphic representations, actions, language and thought can be combined in common purpose of learning and making sense of the world.

The opportunities Jeanette had in the nursery to explore her interests depended upon the structure of the nursery and the roles of her teacher and other nursery staff. These are further considered in Chapters 8 and 10.

Stuart: Dynamic circular schema

Stuart began nursery when he was just 3 years old. He lived in a mid-terraced council house 10 minutes' walk away from the nursery. He lived with his mum, gran and 2-month-old baby sister.

Stuart's interest in circular objects and movement fell into four categories identified by Athey (1990, p. 69): graphic representation (using marks or models); action representations (movement); speech representations; and functional dependency relationships: 'In early education *functional dependency relationships* are manifest when children observe the effects of action on objects or material. For example . . . melting wax is *functionally dependent* on heat' (*ibid.*, p. 70). It is sometimes helpful to understand this idea by thinking about simple cause-and-effect relationships. This would mean that the above example could be expressed as heat (the cause) makes wax melt (the effect). In the interests of accuracy and of consistency the words *functional dependency* will be used throughout.

Observations of Stuart working at different levels on a dynamic circular schema show that he often used two kinds of representation together. Here, observations of Stuart will be discussed in terms of their representations and will look at these categories of representations in groups of two: speech and graphic; action and speech. Stuart, like many 3-year-olds, often did more than one thing at once; therefore it is not surprising that different forms of representation occurred simultaneously. He usually made a running commentary about what he was doing so was rarely seen playing silently, either when he was alone or with others. Stuart appeared to give a running commentary on his thinking and his actions. This was a great help in interpreting his actions because he was obligingly descriptive about what he was doing!

Speech and graphic representations of a circular schema

Some of Stuart's (3:2) early markmaking showed a predominance of circular motion. Many looked similar to the examples in Figure 4.5 which he called *tractor wheels*. Other similar representations were named *Father Christmas*, *wheels-car* and *snake*. These examples begin to illustrate early and uncomplicated representations, both through speech and graphic means, of the dynamic circular schema.

Sceptics will suggest that children make circular marks because the paper might suggest that shape. To test out this challenge, a range of different sizes and shapes of paper were made available. When Stuart decided to paint, he made circular marks on all the sheets he used, calling each one *snake*. Those in doubt are invited to try this for themselves. Some children will follow the boundary suggested by the paper (another schema), but children are likely to pursue their schematic

Figure 4.5 'Tractor wheels'

concerns and will be influenced by the shape of paper provided only if it matches their schematic concerns at the time.

From a range of printing tools of different shapes and patterns, Stuart (3:3) chose some round shapes. He made several round marks with them and then, using a paintbrush, made large sweeping curves that encompassed the page. He simply said, 'Going round'. Later circular mark-making was labelled *mummy, daddy, Davey, Stuart, bike*.

Stuart was at the stage of using language to label things. Isolated words, then, were typical of his stage of language development. It is interesting that he is able to use the words he needs to represent his schema through speech. The words *going round* could well have been used by an adult working with him, describing his actions as he painted and words which Stuart chose to repeat. If adults use appropriate descriptive language when working with children, language of *form* as well as appropriate *content* descriptions, children are more likely to obtain meaning from it.

Action and speech representations of a circular schema

Action and speech representations were combined when Stuart turned the handle of a hand-operated sewing machine (without a needle fitted!) and said, 'Going round'. He wound up a clock (a rare artifact in this digital world), saying 'round and round'. He puts cars on a sloping ramp of a toy garage and said, 'Look, round here, look wheels going round'. He used a cylindrical rotating puzzle and said, 'It goes round, look!'

It appears that Stuart was interested in the power of his own actions. He was absorbed with discovering what he could make things do. There was also an extending role here for the adults who worked with him. When he was using the hand-operated sewing machine the teacher spoke about it with him:

Stuart: It goes round and round.
Teacher: Yes, it turns, it rotates.
Stuart: Then I stop it, I let it go.

This short dialogue shows how Stuart knew that he had control over the machine. He had worked out for himself how it operated and what he needed to do to make the parts move. The dominant interest in this example was the *functional dependency relationship*. The movement of the wheel handle and the vertical action of the other part of the machine were functionally dependent upon Stuart operating the machine by turning the handle.

Adults play a crucial role in extending and developing children's learning through schemas. This was evident on another occasion when Stuart (3:3) spent ten minutes spinning a rotating model with a figure of a person on one end and a weighted sphere on the other for balance:

Stuart: Look, Look! Spinning, going round.
Teacher: It's rotating (*making a circular gesture with her hand*).
Stuart: 'Tating, round and round, look, look! Spinning, 'tating, spinning.

He was very excited by this and made circular hand gestures similar to those made by the teacher. The teacher showed that she valued Stuart's interest. Whilst extending his vocabulary with other words to describe the movement of the model, and adding a hand gesture (another action representation) to accompany the word she matched her response to Stuarts' interest. Tait and Roberts (1974) discuss the technique of 'reflecting back'. In this case that technique was extended to introduce a new word as well as validate the words of the child. The meaning was maintained whilst the vocabulary extended.

On other occasions Stuart's actions were used by the teacher in 'reflecting back' and providing a speech representation of his actions as a kind of accompanying dialogue. Going up the ramp outside, Stuart stopped and turned a full circle, he looked at the teacher who said: 'You went up and you turned right around. 'Stuart replied, 'Right around'.

It seems that a key to the development of ideas and understanding can be a child's schema. A Land Rover was driven into the nursery garden. Stuart saw it and was immediately compelled to get a closer look. He was not as tall as the large wheels on the vehicle and so was on the appropriate level to examine them in detail. He commented with excitement, 'Look, big wheels look!'

Through an interest in things that rotated, his observational skills were heightened and he also paid attention, not surprisingly, to their size.

Functional dependency relationships

Stuart was talking with the teacher about round objects. The teacher was drawing his attention to different things in the environment, circular and otherwise:

Teacher: This fence has pieces of wood going up and down, this truck has wheels which go round and round.
Stuart: Like that (*making a circular gesture with his hand*).

Teacher: Yes! Like that.
Stuart: Round and round and round.
Teacher: They rotate as they move along the ground.
Stuart: Rotate, go along, I like them.

This conversation illustrates how adults can introduce further extensions to schemas. Stuart was clearly interested in *going round*. The teacher introduced the notion that going round was connected with going along. This could lead to future work with older children regarding circumference and land-measuring techniques. Curriculum issues will be discussed in Part III.

Functional dependency relationships can be reinforced in different ways; many simple songs and musical experiences can help to support such understanding. While Stuart turned the handle of the sewing machine the teacher sang (to the tune of here we go round the mulberry bush:

Sewing machine goes round and round,
Round and round, round and round,
Sewing machine goes round and round,
While Stuart turns the handle.

By observing happenings in the nursery environment Stuart was able to identify functional dependency relationships. He watched a joiner drilling a hole in a door in the nursery. Later he made a 'drill' using construction materials and 'worked' at the door. He explained: 'Goes round and round and round, goes zzz and makes that hole, look!'

He also represented this graphically, using vertical lines then a circular mark and said: 'That's a man up on chair, doing it in.' As he said *doing it in*, he gestured as if holding the drill and drilling the hole. Stuart showed interest in a similar tool to the one used by the joiner. The brace and bit was introduced to the woodwork tools to extend children's experiences of rotation and the consequent hole making. He spent some time after watching the real-life experience representing and repeating it using the woodwork equipment.

Nurseries, wherever possible, must provide a range of equipment which children can operate with developing confidence, skill and competence. Working with household equipment and tools that perform a real function provided endless opportunities to extend thinking and understanding.

What can we learn from Gary, Jeanette and Stuart?
The brief case studies of Gary, Jeanette and Stuart show how these children with different needs and at different stages of physical, cognitive and affective development were thinking and learning.

The snapshots into the experiences of these children show how concrete and realistic experiences can nourish the exploration of ideas, fantastic and factual. We have seen the important role of factual experience for Gary: the punctured tyre and the spider's web. The co-operative and tenacious venture of building the snow house illustrates how interests can be extended and developed in the outdoor environment, building on spontaneous happenings and knowledge of children's interests. Stuart's exchanges with his teacher reinforce the importance of nourishing children's language with relevant adult talk.

For these three children, working sometimes independently and sometimes in harmony with a skilled and supportive adult, we can see the potential for learning which 'fits' what children are interested in. This chapter has highlighted the natural learning processes which can occur from an open-ended and vibrant curriculum where children work in a carefully planned and 'well stocked' environment and where trained and skilled and interested adults understand some of the theories about how children learn. Later chapters will develop these issues.

Part III
Schemas and the development of knowledge and understanding

The next three chapters will examine and discuss children's early exploration of ideas which are the roots of mathematical and scientific development, children's patterns of literacy learning and the use of stories in extending children's knowledge and thought.

Throughout these three chapters run two themes: 'match' between children's *forms* of thought and curriculum *content* which enriches their learning; and the importance of reflection and evaluation of children's learning in these 'matched' encounters.

5
CHILDREN'S DEVELOPING UNDERSTANDING OF MATHEMATICAL AND SCIENTIFIC IDEAS

If we accept the likelihood that young children can and do learn as they follow particular patterns of behaviour and interest, the next step is to consider how such patterns, or schemas, might be the foundation of their growing knowledge and understanding. This chapter presents the findings of my own research carried out in a nursery class in the mid-1980s, and suggests how children's pursuit of particular schemas can lead to the exploration of certain ideas and understandings. Observations of 40 children aged between 3 and 5 years were made during one academic year. The observations were reflected upon and analysed in terms of the ideas that the children seemed to be exploring. Many of the ideas had mathematical or scientific foundations.

A great variety of ideas were being investigated, and these were evident when the observations of children's actions were closely studied. The wealth of ideas that children explored during the observation period included: capacity, tessellation, spatial order, size, shape, height, angles, perimeter, circumference, numbers, sorting, time, matching, quantity, position, estimation, transformation, addition, length, equivalence, distance, symmetry, properties of natural materials, cause, effect and functional relationships, centrifugal force, rotation, colour, magnetism, gravity, trajectory, natural science, change and speed.

Three major schemas emerged in the analysis of these observations: dynamic vertical, dynamic circular and enveloping/containing. Detailed inspection of these anecdotal observations showed that it was possible to make two generalisations:

- In each schema there emerged an idea that appeared to dominate.

- Some ideas were identified as arising from children's pursuit of all three schemas.

Thinking over these first generalisations I generated three main questions as I tried to explain my observations. I wondered if it was possible to make some statements about *all* children's learning and not just the children I was observing. This chapter considers three questions which arose from my observations and draws on those observations of the children in the study to draw some conclusions.

Question 1: Do some ideas dominate in the pursuit of particular schemas?

When observations of the children were analysed in detail the three schemas revealed distinctive and, in a sense, obvious sets of ideas:

- The dynamic vertical schema was evident where some children were involved in activities and ideas concerned with height.
- Dynamic circular schema was evident where some children were exploring aspects of rotation and roundness.
- Containing/enveloping schemas were evident where instances of capacity were observed.

These three simple ideas are discussed next with examples of children's activity by way of illustration.

Dynamic vertical schema and ideas related to height

Emmie gained some experience of changes in height when using the slide and steps repeatedly. She said: 'I went up there and up there.' Her language matched her actions and included the idea of an increase in height.

Linda connected a number of bricks, one on top of the other. She said: 'It's a sword, I need a bit more to make it better.' Linda knew that she could increase the height of her construction by connecting more bricks and thereby improve it.

Lucy indicated that a ladder was a useful aid for increasing height when she said: 'That ladder is to go up.' Russell wanted to see out of the window so he put one brick on top of another and stood on them saying, 'I can see now I'm up here'. He had used his awareness and skills to make a step construction that would increase his height. This example reinforces the importance of motor actions and the relevance of *doing* as opposed to being told or explained to. Piaget (1953) emphasised that practical experiences were needed in order that understanding could occur in a linguistic form.

William pretended to go up some stairs, lifting his feet as if mounting an imaginary staircase. He said, 'Up the stairs, up the stairs', then he turned and pretended to go down the stairs saying, 'Down the stairs, down the stairs'.

Later in the same month William tried to climb on to the top of some 2-foot cubes which were piled up on a trestle platform. It was too high for him to manage and he could not reach the top. He fetched a stool and then a large brick to enable him to climb on to the top of the pile. He said: 'There are two steps, one big one and one little one.'

William had built up a map of understanding about size and increase in height that meant that he could eventually solve his problem. The development of thinking and problem-solving strategies should be fostered by open-ended and limitless experiences which involve children in creating and seeking solutions to their problems. The responsibility of the educator is to provide the opportunity; the children will solve the problem.

HMI (DES, 1989b) identified four main areas in which children need to develop scientific skills:

1. making and recording observations
2. identifying patterns
3. developing hypotheses
4. investigating and experimenting.

They state:

> For the youngest children many scientific interests begin with exploratory play. In nursery and infant classes children frequently demonstrate an ability to explain their observations and test their ideas as they take part in early scientific activities . . . Work with sand and water . . . and activities involving constructional materials such as wooden bricks and toys with moving parts, invariably involve children in investigations that lead them to explain scientific phenomena and sequences of events as far as their understanding allows.
>
> (*Ibid.*, para. 57)

The dynamic circular schema and the development of ideas about rotation

Francis showed some interest in rotation. She seemed intrigued by objects that rolled, and by the rotation of an old record-player turntable.

She chose two model elephants, one larger than the other, and placed them on the turntable. Francis set the turntable in motion and said, 'The baby elephant is chasing the daddy', then she laughed and said, 'The daddy is chasing the baby too!' As Francis described her observation she conceptualised the notion of rotation and circular action. Chapman and Foot (1976) consider that humour in infancy is characterised mainly by the way children are amused by things they understand. Humour, they say, is related to cognition. Francis had some sense of the 'circleness' of a circle, never really ending or beginning, and her understanding led to her amusement.

Francis's teacher felt that her interest was clear and developed the activity to support her schematic interests and extend her learning. On one occasion this involved Francis and two other children helping to make pumpkin soup. The equipment used for this included a can opener, pepper and salt mills, and an electric liquidiser.

Francis found the liquidiser fascinating, observing that: 'Its spinning faster and faster and making the big bits little.' Using language related to rotation she described the process she saw and included a comment on two important basic concepts, change and size. She investigated the salt and pepper mills, and was delighted to discover how they worked. The mills provided more experience of rotation and of cause, effect and functional relationships. Frances carefully turned the handle of the can opener noting that: 'If you turn this handle the tin turns too, and if you keep turning the lid comes right off.'

Through her interest in rotation Francis was grasping the principles of cause and effect, learning about what made things happen; what is more, she was able to talk about these things. She included in her talk the vocabulary of rotation, matching her words to the things she saw and making some precise comments. As well as using the kitchen tools competently and with understanding of how they worked, Francis remembered to stir the soup frequently, watching the circular pattern the stirring made. The task of making soup for a party was a real job and suitable mechanical tools were provided to extend the learning opportunities involved.

Francis (with the support of the teacher) was totally involved for the whole of the hour it took to make the soup. The two other children quickly lost interest and left the activity but Francis remained involved and actively interested until the soup was ready to eat. This incident highlights the need for more adults to be available to give intensive one-to-one attention to children's learning opportunities, through their finely tuned interactions with individual children.

Why did Francis stay with the soup for so long? Might prolonged concentration be linked to a match between a child's schema and what the child is currently doing? Suggestions that young children can only concentrate for short periods and have a low level of persistence have been disputed for some time. Young children, time and time again, prove themselves capable of serious persistence when the task in hand matches their interests.

Other children in the same nursery were interested in rotation:

- David spent fifteen minutes turning the blades on a small toy helicopter.
- Gary turned the handle on an unconnected tap and later found a rotary spinning toy and asked how it worked. He spent time spinning it and exploring the action it made.
- Guy demonstrated his interest in rotation when he painted pictures of a washing machine. He said: 'They're clothes going round and round and getting clean.'

His experience of technology in the real world enabled him to add to and represent his understanding of rotation in a creative medium and through appropriate language.

John was interested in how things worked. He was sorting through a collection of metal objects and found a screw. He took it to the teacher and said, 'Here's a screw'. The teacher asked what it was for and John replied, 'A screw driver', making a circular gesture with his hand as if using a screwdriver. John was combining his knowledge of what goes with what (one-to-one correspondence) and function (the screwdriver makes the screw go into the wood), linked through his interest in finding things that rotated. John found a brass tap, he turned the nut at one end until it came off, then he turned the handle. Through these actions John gained more feedback and information about rotation and its effect on objects.

Guy found three wooden circles and said, 'Oh! More rounds!' In so doing he showed that he could identify the shape and classify them as part of a set. He used the language of addition *more* to indicate his discovery. Matthews (1984) discussed the development of mathematical concepts in the nursery and considered the use of mathematical terms such as *more*, *not enough*, *bigger* and *fit* in spontaneous experiences to be the best method of facilitating mathematical development. Guy later found a small wheel and said, 'There's another wheel here, I've got these, that's one and that's another one'. He was adding to his collection of circular items and reinforcing his own ideas of addition and using a range of mathematical terms.

Containing and enveloping schemas and the development of knowledge of capacity

Writing about the beginnings of measurement, Dowling (1988, p. 46) states:

> For young children to learn how to measure accurately they need a range of experiences in making judgements about amounts . . . This happens through children handling materials and conversing with one another, suggesting who has more or less milk or who has collected bigger stones. Children need to judge how much paper or material they require to cover a surface, and the teacher may join in at this stage to ask if the amount is too large or too little.

I made many observations of children exploring ideas related to capacity and volume by using a variety of materials to contain objects or to envelop spaces by covering or surrounding. Natural materials, construction tools, the home corner and imaginative play were all used by the children to develop their ideas related to containing and capacity.

Adam used sand and water to fill or cover objects and containers. Francis filled bottles with water and poured from small bottles into larger ones. In doing so she provided for herself an experience of capacity in relation to the size of an object.

Kelly wrapped sand, string and dry spaghetti in a paper parcel. She had made her own container and used what was at hand to create her experience of volume.

In the home corner, Lulu sorted plates, saucers and cups into a drawer. Here she was not only fitting objects into a space and gaining experience of capacity, she was also sorting and classifying. She later placed small plastic shapes in a container, a simple action that added to her experience of containers and containing; as such her actions contributed to her idea of volume.

Guy found an open-mouthed toy monster that he began to fill with pieces of Lego. He was using the things he found readily available in his unique way to continue his interest. Athey (1986) considers that children will use whatever they can find to extend their schemas. This preposition raises questions about appropriate provision, resources and curriculum content that will be discussed in the final chapters of the book.

Question 2: What other ideas do children explore whilst pursuing particular schemas?

Reflection on the observations of the 40 children in my study suggested that, as well as exploring the ideas already discussed, other ideas were encountered by children as they pursued particular schemas.

Particular experiences arising from children's pursuit of dynamic vertical and straight-line schemas

As some children explored ideas related to height, they also encountered problems and situations leading to awareness of length, equivalence, distance and symmetry, and these were only identified in observations that indicated children's interest in dynamic vertical and straight-line schemas.

Adam constructed a line by fitting construction pieces end to end and placing them between the tables on the nursery floor. In this activity, Adam gained experience of length and space. He saw that he could increase length by adding more elements and in the visual impression of his construction he saw the length of his work in comparison to the length of the floor.

Gerry walked to the top of the yard and rode down on a truck. This gave him the experience of the equivalence of distance and comparison of speed, since walking up took him longer than riding down, even though the distance travelled each time was the same. This basic motor-level experience provided potential for understanding. Gerry performed a similar action when he crawled from one end of a constructed platform to the other and then ran back along the outside. This too gave him experience of equivalence of distance and difference in speed. These kinds of experiences provide opportunities for young children to build their own foundations for mathematical and scientific understanding. The validity and relevance of these kinds of experiences need to be emphasised and recognised in terms of their potential for learning. As Dowling (1988, p. 45) puts it, 'The nursery can thus provide a seedbed for mathematical thinking. A range of potentially helpful activity can be explored, but as with other aspects of development the cue must come mainly from the child. These cues need to be observed, then taken up and developed by the teacher.'

David and Saul used the climbing frame, walking up the slide, turning and running down, then later using the steps to ascend and descending by way of the slide. These children were experiencing asymmetry of movement as well as developing their growing bodies.

Particular experiences arising from the dynamic circular schema

As well as exploring ideas of rotation, activities leading to experiences in the areas of transformation and change were also identified in observations indicating a dynamic circular schema.

Colin chose cups, dishes, a jug and plates in the home corner and turned each one upside down on the table. These objects were then transformed to give a different configuration. Colin gained visual feedback of what he had done and the change he had created by turning each object through 180°.

The observation of Francis making the pumpkin soup earlier in this chapter gives another example of children's use of mathematical language. She was describing the effect of the liquidiser on the food inside it when she said: 'It's spinning faster and faster and making the big bits little.' This shows her clear understanding of the term *faster* and of the effect of increasing speed on the changing size of the food inside.

Particular experience arising from containing/enveloping schemas

Ideas of capacity arising from children's exploration of containing and enveloping schemas have already been discussed. A great variety of experiences can support the further development of ideas which are evident through children's exploration of containing/enveloping schemas. These include corners and angles, position, estimation, space and place.

Francis used the term *corner* when she played with the doll's house, as she put various pieces of furniture into the corner spaces of the rooms. Her actions indicated that she understood her use of the term.

Lucy sat in a corner and then placed a doll's bath in a corner of the doll's house.

Both children were experiencing 'cornerness' through interaction with and manipulation of their environments. Such physical experiences put them in a position to understand more abstract ideas of corners and angles later.

Seb buried a toy in the sand. 'It's on this side', he said when giving another child a clue about where to find it. Seb knew that there was another side and therefore had the basis of some understanding of position and perspective.

In the observations of these children the beginnings of ideas about perimeter and area seemed to be linked closely with children's work in markmaking and representation. Lulu and Lucy both enclosed spaces with paint by painting around the edges of the paper they used. Linda did a similar thing using ribbon to edge a piece of card. Mathematics is never far away from young children's actions. Fontana (1984) considered mathematics to be present: in the selection of materials for collage, in the home corner, stories and in music. Mathematical ideas are not only present in children's choices and selections of materials but also in the way in which they use the materials they are offered. The ways in which children use materials often dictate their learning potential.

The skill of estimation was demonstrated clearly by Francis when she was trying to build a house using some large bricks. Part way through the construction she looked at her building and at the remaining bricks. 'There's no more bricks to build a house, there's not enough.' She had not counted the bricks but could see that the remaining materials were insufficient to complete the task. Early play is vital to future mathematical development (Hodgkin, 1985) and the importance of blockplay in the development of children's mathematical and scientific ideas has been highlighted by the Froebel Blockplay Project (Gura, 1992).

Guy used a puzzle that entailed fitting cylinders into holes. He counted 'One, two, three, four' then he placed a cylinder in each hole. He used what he knew about numbers, the language of number and one-to-one correspondence to complete the task he set himself. Susan was wrapping a parcel. She understood ideas of size, classification and numbers. This was apparent when she said: 'I'll put a big one and two small ones in this parcel.'

Saul used his matching skills at a complex level of thinking when he looked at some construction plans and asked another child to 'make a house like that one'. The language 'like that' is indicative of children's developing mathematical appreciation of comparison, similarity and difference. HMI assert the importance of teaching children in ways that encourage them to talk mathematically: 'Their [children's] ability to use mathematical language discriminatingly and accurately is increased through well planned practical activities and play experiences designed to help them understand aspects of number, weight, size, capacity, time and measurement' (DES, 1989, para. 39).

Lucy worked on her containing/enveloping schemas through imaginative play and construction. She built a house with large wooden bricks. There was no opening. She said, 'There's no doorway', but this did not seem to concern her. She began to put a variety of objects into the house and seemingly enjoyed being inside the house herself. Then she commented, 'Only one more can come in, there's not much space'.

She was using the language of containing and of mathematics, and through what she did and what she said, showed her knowledge of number, quantity, size, position, space and estimation. Later, in her play, Lucy put a doll into a bath and clothes into a washing machine.

The teacher provided boxes to improvise as the bath and the washing machine as Lucy requested them. Lucy dressed the doll, using her finely developed manipulative skills for this kind of enveloping. Lucy decided that the clothes were still wet and needed to be put in 'the tumbler' to dry. She asked the teacher for sticky tape, 'Because I want the clothes to stay in', she explained, again using language related to containing.

In this observation Lucy was intent on enclosing a variety of objects in a number of different ways and for different purposes. She used the teacher as a provider of resources to develop and extend her play.

Lucy used a variety of materials to build houses for make-believe and miniature people. On one occasion she attached a garage to her house and put a truck inside it. 'They're all inside that truck in the garage', she said. Later she put the people inside the house: 'People are in the rooms, that's where they live, that ladder is to get up, when they're up they can get in there and go to bed.' Here she was combining ideas of *going up* with ideas of *going in* and using appropriate language to describe her thinking.

Russell enclosed himself in a space under some steps where it was quite dark. He kept moving out of the space and going back inside again saying: 'It's dark in here, but it's daytime out here!' He seemed excited by his experience of darkness and light that resulted from changing his own position.

Question 3: Are some similar ideas developed as children explore different schemas?

Observations of the 40 children in the study showed that some mathematical and scientific ideas arose from all three schemas: dynamic vertical, dynamic circular and containing/enveloping. These ideas include: capacity; tessellation; spatial order; surface area; shape; sorting; cause, effect and functional relationships; and colour.

Children's ideas of and experiences of capacity have already been discussed. The discussion in this section will focus on aspects of children's thinking and understanding in three of the areas listed above: tessellation, cause, effect and functional relationships; and surface area. These have been chosen because they relate to aspects of learning not normally associated with the development of children aged 3 and 4 years. The areas that will be given less attention in this discussion are sorting, size, colour and shape. These are ideas already fully established as fundamental in the early years curriculum (Fontana, 1984).

Tessellation and spatial order

Examples of children's exploration and understanding of tessellation and positioning show clearly the capability of young children to focus on complex mathematical ideas.

Guy chose a wooden puzzle and fitted shaped bricks together to fill the outline. Some days later he fitted squares of wood together on a large sheet of paper. A week later he arranged four footballs together on a square and kicked one which had the effect of moving all four. He exclaimed: 'They go all over!' It is possible that Guy was aware of the ways in which two-dimensional shapes fitted together and was experimenting with the tessellation of three-dimensional shapes. He was interested in watching a bricklayer who was working in the nursery garden. This provided the opportunity to see the tessellation in action as bricks of the same shape and size were fitted together in different ways to form a pillar.

Leo piled three-dimensional cubes on top of one another; these seemed to correspond to the brick wall alongside. He later built up the cubes, three high and two deep, a progression from his earlier attempt. Lulu used paint and paper marked with a grid pattern to produce an example of tessellation; she printed with various shapes to make a design where the different shapes fitted together. William filled a gap in the parcel he was wrapping, fastening it by sticking another piece of paper over the hole, thereby filling the space. Some weeks later he fitted two cubes into a box to make a 'speed bike'. This was part of his exploration and use of positioning three-dimensional shapes.

The children in these examples used what was generally available to develop individual experiences for themselves. They manoeuvred and organised shapes and space. Piaget and Inhelder (1956) found that children's early concepts of space were topological which later give way to Euclidean concepts. Ideas of space can be difficult for educators to understand and discuss, but some understanding is important if children's understanding of space is to be fully nurtured. Helpful definitions and examples of types of space are given by Dickson et al. (1993). They describe topological properties as 'global properties which are independent of size or shape' (p. 13) and Euclidean properties as 'those relating to size, distance and direction and hence leading to the measurement of lengths, angles, areas and so on' (p. 14).

Considering the examples above, where children explore space in a flexible way, the usefulness of jigsaws that are provided for children to fit shapes together in a set fashion, and colouring books that require children to fill in fixed spaces of colour, need to be questioned. Such activities do not support and nourish the ideas of flexible space where children pay attention to activities which allow them to manipulate space and develop their own ideas of measurement and size.

Surface area

Sally seemed to be interested in a dynamic vertical schema. She used paint, moving the brush up and down on the page producing patches of colour until she had covered the whole page with red paint. This example illustrates how young children create their own firsthand experience – here of the concept of covering a flat space. Saul, whilst interested in a circular schema, made a similar painting using circular actions and marks.

Many examples of surface area arose when children covered themselves, or each other. Fiona put an adult into bed in the home corner and covered her up. Imaginative play provided the opportunity for Fiona to work on mathematical ideas. She needed to use two sheets to cover the teacher because one sheet was not long enough to cover her, even though one sheet was usually all that was needed to cover up other children.

Gwen found a piece of wrapping paper. She looked at a small farm building, intending to wrap it in the paper. 'Not big enough', she said and went to look for a bigger sheet of paper. She did not find anything suitable, so chose a smaller item to wrap! Gwen was able to estimate size and had an idea of relative size. She concluded her activity by singing 'Happy birthday' and placing her actions in the context of a make-believe situation.

Cause, effect and functional relationships

This study of 40 nursery children found that children had an interest in the outcomes of their own actions. Many were fascinated with how things worked and what they could make things do. The following examples illustrate how children investigate and deduce the function of an object and then articulate it through language.

Gail was turning the handle of a vice on the woodwork bench. She said: 'Look, when I turn it [the handle] that comes out and I can get the wood in.' She had ascertained the function of the vice by manipulation and observation. Four weeks later Gail was playing with water. She took a container to the sink to fill it with water. The water kept coming out of the container and Gail eventually discarded it after many unsuccessful attempts to fill it. She remarked, 'It's got little holes in so the water will always go on the floor'. She had clearly understood the effect of holes on the ability of the container to hold water and that this was not a 'one-off' occurrence, but that a container with holes in would never hold water.

Ann was using the toy garage and petrol pump. She turned the handle and said: 'When I turn this, that bit over there moves and when the car is on it it turns around.' She was able to express quite clearly the cause (turning the handle) and the effect (movement of a small platform), and the function (turning a car around).

Lulu saw a cylindrical tin roll off the table. She said, 'This is silly, it fell down there because it is round'. She had the basis of a hypothesis that round things roll, because she had understood the action of the rolling tin.

When we listen to children's talk, as they manipulate their words and meanings, we have many opportunities to see that children have established an understanding of cause, effect and functional relationships. It is difficult to establish whether children have understood cause-and-effect relationships if they do not talk about their thinking. Part of the responsibility of teachers and other educators is to ensure that children hear a wide range of talk and terminology and can therefore generate the words they need to be able to talk about their own findings and communicate their important and developing ideas through language. It is important that the needs of bilingual children are addressed in this context, and that they have opportunities to develop their ideas through their home language, working with bilingual staff.

Carol put the water pump into the water and seemed fascinated by the up-and-down action she was making. She said nothing, so it cannot be confirmed that she understood the relationship between her actions and the pumping of the water. The teacher had watched her and moved alongside her, describing what Carol was doing. 'You're moving the pump handle up and down and it fills with water and the water is coming out of the top.' The teacher described what was happening in a way which Carol could understand and use herself should she choose to. This would have been an opportunity for the teacher to introduce the language of cause and effect, saying things like 'it's doing that because' or 'that's why . . .'

This section, based on the detailed analysis of a large set of observations of 40 children aged 3–5 years, has considered three questions about schemas and the development of children's mathematical and scientific ideas. What is clear from the observations given here is that these children have acquired a wealth of knowledge and understanding that enables them to develop a *command* over a range of mathematical and scientific ideas:

> It is the basic themes that lie at the heart of Science and Mathematics and the basic themes that give form to life and literature are as simple as they are powerful. To be in command of these basic ideas, to use them effectively, requires a continual deepening of one's understanding of them that comes from learning to use them in progressively more complex forms. It is only when such basic ideas are put in formalized terms as equations or elaborated verbal concepts that they are out of reach of the young child, if he has not first understood them intuitively and had a chance to try them out on his own. The early teaching of Science, Mathematics, Social Studies and literature should be designed to teach these subjects with scrupulous intellectual honesty, but with an emphasis upon the intuitive grasp of ideas and upon the use of these basic ideas.
>
> (Bruner, 1977, p. 12)

The learning of the children described in this chapter has been 'intellectually honest', derived as it is from an extensive range of activities most of which are rooted in their play. Various areas of experience provided in the nursery facilitated the development of children's minds according to their individual capabilities.

This chapter has examined ways in which children can develop understanding of mathematical and scientific ideas through firsthand experiences and a furtherance of their schemas. It has indicated how action, thinking and language are inextricably linked in the process of developing ideas and understanding. The children whose learning has been discussed here showed themselves capable of considerable exploration and discovery. They were active in the learning process, which was facilitated according to their individual learning patterns. Extensive opportunities were provided by well informed professionals who understood the ways in which children learn. Some issues raised in this chapter have implications for curriculum provision and the role of the teacher; these concerns will be discussed in Chapters 8 and 10.

6
PATTERNS OF LITERACY

Razia and four other children who began school the term before their fifth birthdays were playing in the 'office' that was set up just outside the reception class. The office was equipped with two typewriters, one manual, one electric, a computer set up with a word-processing package and a concept keyboard, several telephones, a working intercom between the classroom and the office, note pads, order books, pens, catalogues, envelopes, 'in' and 'out' trays, and other office paraphernalia. The children had been to the school office to see the equipment there in use and they had also, in small groups, visited the large offices of a local business.

Picture Razia, aged 4 years and 8 months. She was sitting at the typewriter, typing a page of notes from her note pad. She was having some difficulty 'reading' from the writing on her pad. 'If this was on tape it would be much easier – I can't read her writing!' This was probably a reference to something a secretary told her when she went to the local office, about how difficult it sometimes was to read people's handwriting and how it was often easier if they dictated their letters on to tape using a dictaphone.

Another child told her that there was a telephone call for her and passed her the telephone. Razia tucked it between her chin and right shoulder and continued to type whilst she spoke to the caller! Then she took a pen in her left hand and scribbled a note on her pad. 'Yes, yes OK I'll tell her. Thank you for calling.' Razia replaced the telephone and finished writing the message. In her play this little girl reflected some of what she had learned about how some people work, how they communicate, the words they use, the postures they assume and that office life can be very busy.

This example shows that literacy learning in school can have a real purpose and context. Razia, a developing writer and reader, already knew how useful these skills were and wanted to use what she knew about reading and writing in her play. Her playing had purpose, it was grounded in real-life experiences, but what would her teacher do to challenge and extend Razia's literacy even further?

The teacher wanted to spend some time writing with Razia. She had let her spend most of the morning in the office play area and wanted to give her some individual time. Razia, however, was engrossed, her language was flowing, something the teacher wanted to encourage in this young bilingual child. The teacher drew on what she saw, and what she knew about children's development and learning to help her decide her next step. She needed to make certain that her intervention did not become interference in Razia's thinking and learning processes. The teacher approached Razia with some 'typing'. 'Razia, could you type a letter for me please? I want to write to the office to say "Thank you" for letting us visit. If you type it, everyone could sign it and then it can be posted – we'll need an envelope too.' Razia glowed with pride at the prospect of the task. She set to work immediately and typed the letter, which had been drafted by the teacher, following through the task by getting children to sign their names at the bottom of the letter, in the conventional style. She selected a brown envelope and typed 'OFIS' on the front. The teacher wrote a 'covering letter' to accompany the letter, in case the office staff were not conversant in emergent typing!

Razia and her teacher were engaged in a dynamic teaching and learning process, grown out of real situations and leading to purposeful outcomes. Razia gained more experience of focusing on writing and identifying individual letters, she made a good attempt at reading the teacher's letter and had a clear understanding of what she was typing. She identified individual letters and some whole words and was able to find the letters she needed on the typewriter keyboard. Children can be motivated when creative and flexible teachers provide them with real purposes, real tasks and real audiences, and are prepared to adapt their learning objectives for children when necessary.

What did Razia learn by being asked to type the letter? She learned that she and her contribution to the task were valued by the teacher. She learned a little more about communicating with others, conventions of saying 'Thank you' to their hosts, and she learned that her letter was worth writing and worth sending. She sensed real purpose and real achievement. She used capital and lower case letters as appropriate. She checked her typed version against the teacher's draft. These are some of the building blocks of early literacy.

How is Razia's teacher supporting and extending her development? How does she decide on her role? The framework set out in Figure 6.1 is

MODEL

PROVIDE

OBSERVE

INTERACT

INTERVENE

EVALUATE

Figure 6.1 Framework for encouraging emergent literacy

a useful way to define the role of the teacher in encouraging children's emergent writing.

Give children rich and varied *models* of literacy, in a variety of settings, shops, offices, homes, schools, printers, leisure centres. Let them see people using their literacy skills and tools to communicate with others. As Wray suggests, children need to see literacy happening: 'A literate environment is a fairly meaningless concept without people who are using that environment, people who, through a variety of ways in which they use print, demonstrate when it is used, how it is used, where it is used and what it is' (Wray, Bloom and Hall, 1989, p. 66).

Children need dynamic opportunities to write in context. Readers and writers can flourish when a variety of models of literacy are presented to children and when the literacy environment is richly *provided* for. Teachers and other early childhood educators must first consider what children know about literacy and what kinds of models of literacy they are familiar with. They must provide opportunities for children to write and to read, and the equipment and materials they need to do this: quality books (as discussed in the next chapter), writing tools, examples of print and the written word in a variety of scripts and fonts.

Those who work with young children must employ their skills of *observation*, watching what children do and say, assessing what children know and deciding where they might need help. Observation helps educators to decide what to do next in terms of supporting, developing and extending children's development as writers and readers. As well as observing what children do and say in terms of literacy, *interaction* with children as they read and write is all-important. Observation and interaction can help to determine the nature of *intervention* on the part of the educator. To make certain that positive intervention does not become futile interference in a child's learning process, it must be preceded with sensitive observation and interaction with the child. All of this takes a high level of skill, knowledge about young children and how they react and act in different circumstances. This framework for the educator requires knowledge about literacy and a sense of progression in literacy acquisition. The practical framework of *model, provide, observe, interact, intervene* is not complete without the educator's *evaluation*. There must be a time for reflection upon what happened, and an assessment, however brief, of the strategies used and the resulting outcomes. Questions need to be asked: What did Razia learn? Was the teacher's strategy a successful one? What will the teacher do next?

Much has been written about the development of children as writers. The National Writing Project (1989) provides clear and accessible accounts of children's early development of writing systems. There are also several studies which document in fine detail the early writing development of individual children (Payton, 1984; Bissex, 1980; Schickedanz, 1990). A booklet *Writing for All* (Oldham LEA, 1992) stresses that children with special educational needs are entitled to be taught to write in the same way as pupils in mainstream schooling, and suggests that there are three main elements to becoming a writer: composer (creating meaning); communicator (conveying meaning); and secretary (markmaking). It is when all three elements are supported and developed effectively through interactive teaching and learning processes that children emerge as competent and confident writers.

Thinking about children's schemas and their writing development, there appear to be two questions about *form* and *content* which are worth pondering:

- Should writing *form* and the *content* of writing be given separate and different value and attention?
- Are there links between the *form* and *content* of young children's writing and other underpinning threads of children's thought and action?

Form and content in young children's early writing

If the voices of children are to be valued, the content of their writing, the essence of its meaning and its subject-matter must always be important.

What children choose to write about, why they write, whom they write for, are important elements in the making of a writer. The content of children's writing will be influenced by the experiences they have and what they find meaningful. Children's writing often reflects events which they feel are important to them, real and imagined happenings, the plots from favourite or influential stories they have read or heard told to them.

In parallel with children's development as authors, developing meaningful content is their development of what can be described as 'secretarial skills'. The understanding they show in their early markmaking of what a writing system is about: signs, symbols, conventions. These early writing attempts are useful evidence of learning about the form that writing takes and the structure of a writing system. Young, developing bilingual and multilingual children are often developing symbols and strategies to understand and use several scripts which have different signs and different conventions.

The *form* the structure and markmaking of the written code, and *content*, the essence, subject-matter and meaning of writing, are both important factors in the making of a writer. Form and content need to be developed in parallel. Well formed, legible marks which have nothing to communicate are of little use. The writer must have something to say. Neither form nor content should be sacrificed in the interests of the other.

Should writing form and the content of writing be given separate and different value and attention? In the early developmental stages of children's writing, is there an emphasis on getting the form of writing correct at the expense of listening to the messages children have to convey through writing? There is an emphasis on correctness of form contained within the requirements of the National Curriculum where, by the age of 7, children should have considerable control over handwriting form. Though there is also a requirement that children should write in an interesting way, there is a danger that things which are more easily assessed, such as the correct position of capital letters and full stops, are given greater value than children's ability to convey meaning in their composition. This is well argued by Armstrong (1990, p. 15), who expresses the belief that meaning is central to children's writing, and states: 'One of the most important tasks in interpreting children's work is to describe its patterns of intention: the interests, motifs, orientations, forms of meditation that govern a child's thought and seek expression in her practice.' This puts the case that attention should be paid to the content of children's writing if their 'voice' and the meaning of their writing and thinking is to be valued.

Links between writing form and content and other areas of children's thought and action

Are there links between the form and content of young children's writing and other underpinning threads of children's thought and action? Sophie (7.5) was writing about a train ride. The content of her writing included several references to *connections*, a tunnel, gates at the station, stepping-stones across a river. There was an apparent link with her self-motivated interest in joined-up writing and the connection of letters (and words). Her teacher explained that the class had not tackled joined-up writing, but that Sophie seemed intent on joining not only letters within words but also the words together. This interest in connection also linked with her interests in art and dance, which included content related to joining and connecting.

Angie (4.2) drew a picture which appeared to the teacher to be a solid block of colour. Her description of the picture included several references to coverings, and Angie illuminated the thinking it represented as she labelled parts of her drawing:

That's the house.
That's the little girl covered in paint.
That's the rain dropping down.
This is snow. The snow will be covered up with rain.
That's rain dropping down on to it and covers over the snow.

Angie's composition included several references to covering, suggesting a link between her thinking and her representations in drawing and speech.

Writing as representation

Another aspect of writing development needs to be considered, that is the notion of writing as a means of representation.

Writing representing writing

As they begin to pay attention to the act of writing, young children seem to write 'for the sake of it'. They move their pen quickly across the page, as they have seen their mother do when she writes a quick letter, seated at the kitchen table. They produce a series of linear squiggles which represents the look of writing and, in the act of doing this, they get the feel of being a writer. Adults who watch young children at this stage of their writing development will notice that children assume the posture

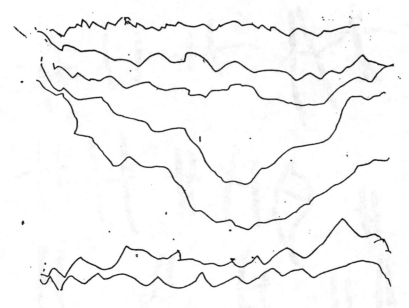

Figure 6.2　'I'm writing'

of a writer, they 'write' with intensity, their faces show concentration and they 'write' with a certainty of focus and purpose. The child who writes in this way will probably produce something similar to that in Figure 6.2. Adam (3:2), who wrote this, looked up at his mother and said 'I'm writing'. He was representing the act of writing.

The child who knows a little more about marks which make up writing may write something similar to the example in Figure 6.3. When Joanne (4:4) wrote this she said, 'This is writing'. She used what she knew about writing and writing conventions to produce a page of symbols which look like writing. There is no message as such, it simply *is* writing.

Some children know the power of the written word and can produce writing which has influential content before they have developed sufficient skills to make their own marks convey the message in a way which resembles convention. Shaun (4:3) was not fond of writing and preferred to be outdoors engaging in more vigorous and energetic activity. On one occasion he wanted to go down to the school office to photocopy some of his drawings. It was a Monday and inconvenient for the school clerk who was involved in the usual start-of-the-week administration. Children from the nursery were in the habit of going to the school office. They always took with them a note from the teacher to show that they

Figure 6.3 'This is writing'

were on 'official business'. Shaun pestered to go to the office, his photocopies were essential and he could not wait. He tried to persuade each member of staff to let him go. Finally the teacher said: 'Shaun, you haven't got a note to say you can go. I can't let you go this morning, especially without a note, and it's so busy in the office this morning.' Undaunted, Shaun wrote his own note, in his own way (Figure 6.4). He returned with it to the teacher: 'That says "boys can go down to the office" ', he said, confidently presenting the note to his teacher, 'So can I go now? The teacher endorsed the note with a translation for the clerk

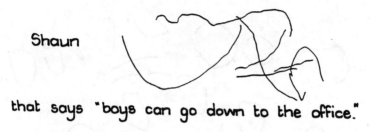

Figure 6.4 'That says "boys can go down to the office"'

and agreed that he could go later in the morning when the clerk was less busy. Shaun was satisfied. His knowledge about writing, its power and his tenacity had won the day.

Representing something with writing

For young children, the understanding that they can make a mark or series of marks which means *them* is an important discovery. At this point the child's autograph appears on every picture and painting, regardless of whether an adult has already written it for them.

Lori (3:9) produced a piece of writing which at first glance seems to be an attempt to represent the letter *c* (Figure 6.5). Lori volunteered the real purpose of this writing. 'It's the bit of Lori I can't get.' It seems that Lori was practising hard, at her own motivation, to represent the oval which made the *o* in Lori. She knew it should join up but couldn't quite manage to get her hand to do what she knew she wanted it to. Some adults who remember learning to write recall the frustration of trying to get the *o* to join up neatly without crossing over.

Stuart was 3 years old when he began nursery. His speech was limited and he tended to point and label when he wanted to draw attention to something. Writing was apparently new to him. He was acutely aware of his world, noticing minute details in pictures and in the nursery both indoors and outdoors. He was constantly on the move, exploring and discovering. Stuart's own markmaking was at an early stage, but he understood that writing had meaning and could be used to represent things. After seeing a notice about story books on the quiet-room door Stuart wrote something himself (Figure 6.6). This, he said, was 'Writing a door'.

As well as representing parts of their names and objects, children can use their writing to represent stories which are full of action. James

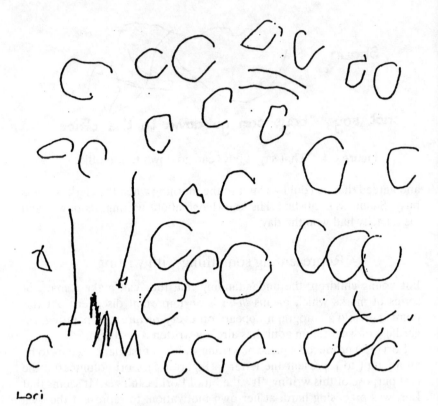

Figure 6.5   'It's the bit of "Lori" I can't get'

(3:11) drew his picture (Figure 6.7) before he dictated the following story to his teacher who wrote it on the computer.

James's picture
This is the story about the picture . . . This is something important, it's going to get the lights. This is a dog waiting for the spaceship. This is the line that the spaceship is going on. It goes all up and down all the way across. This is a helicopter, they are flying round. This bit is Father Christmas, his house is in space. This is an aeroplane, he's flying to the dog and to the helicopter. This is Airwolf, he's going to get something important, that other aeroplane.

James composed this description of his picture where the words, like the illustration, are full of movement and action. There is attention to space and place and to going and coming. It clearly illustrates the intertwining of form and content in young children's writing development.

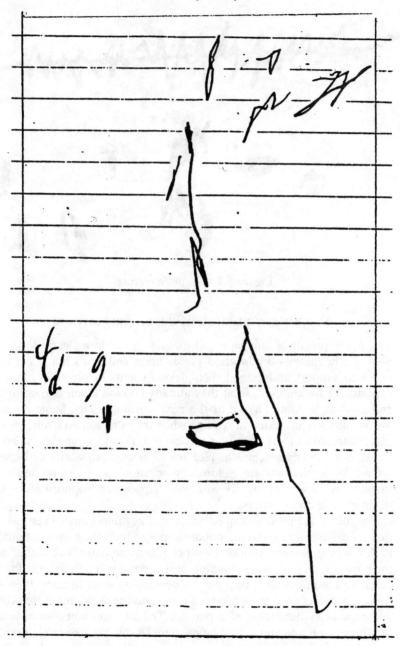

Figure 6.6 'Writing a door'

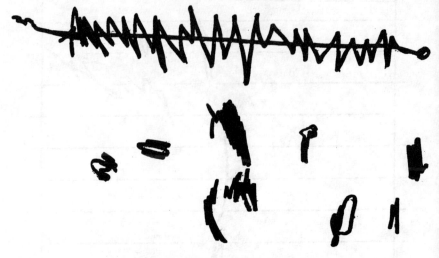

Figure 6.7 'James's picture'

Supporting children as developing writers

The development of language and literacy in children's early years is vital. Early childhood education builds upon children's home experiences to support and extend their development. In planning literacy experiences for children, what they already know is taken into account and used as building blocks, or the next starting points. Some 3- and 4-year-olds are interested in reading when they first attend a nursery or playgroup, and others have yet to develop an understanding of how books work and experience the pleasure of listening to stories and sharing books. Similarly some children know a lot about writing and see themselves as writers; others will need support and opportunities to begin to develop as writers.

The role of the professional educator is of key importance in ensuring that all children are given the opportunities to fulfil their own potential in developing literacy. Working with children and parents according to their own stages of understanding and according to their individual needs and interests must be a part of developing early literacy. Professional educators need to be aware of value and use their important skills and be able to share these with parents. The all-important communication between home and school helps to make this big step in children's lives go more smoothly and helps teachers to know more about the children. This is useful when planning and providing for each child.

Because literacy is so important, no time should be lost in developing and extending children's interests and skills in literacy. Talking with parents and finding out what experiences of literacy a child has had in their earliest years at home will help in planning and extending children's opportunities in their first group setting, be it playgroup, nursery or school.

Reading and writing are skills for living, providing the user with a means of access to information and an effective means of communication with others. The power of literacy should never be underestimated. Children need to begin to acquire the invaluable skills, knowledge and understanding about literacy from an early age. It is a partnership between all involved with the child which will maximise opportunity for children's early literacy development.

How can parents support children's literacy development?

There has been increased involvement of parents in children's education generally in recent years and in reading in particular. There is a diversity of ways in which parents are now involved and some agreement on the need to work with parents (Griffiths and Edmonds, 1986; Lujan, Stolworthy and Wooden, 1986; Winter and Rouse, 1990; Hannon, Weinberger and Nutbrown, 1991).

Some parents have involved themselves in their child's literacy development well before the child begins school, demonstrating that, given information about how young children might begin to understand elements of literacy and with appropriate support, parents can play a key role in promoting their children's literacy development. Parents on a course focusing on young children's learning and development were asked to talk about the things they did which helped to focus children's attention on literacy and to develop their learning. These are some of the things they said they did with their children:

- Pointing out signs when on the bus and signs in shop windows.
- Writing invitations to a party.
- Looking at the labels on tins, naming the soup, spaghetti, other packages.
- Playing the part of a character in the book after reading it together.
- Looking at books, describing pictures, saying which is a favourite and why.
- Putting an alphabet poster on their bedroom wall, looking at letters and saying them.
- Making words from alphabet spaghetti at tea time!
- Choosing books together in the library.

Parents on the same course talked about their ideas and experiences in helping to support their children's literacy development. They recalled doing different things at home with their young children:

> She likes writing her own cheques, sending them for bills!
> We read catalogues, she helps to fill in the form for the order!
> I'm always reading adverts on TV, and names that go up at the end of *Neighbours*.

Perhaps one of the most significant comments came from the parent who said: 'I suppose I do help her to learn but it's all sort of, natural. I don't think, "this is helping her to learn", I just do it. It's part of life isn't it – reading and writing!'

The Sheffield Early Literacy Development Project (Hannon, Weinberger and Nutbrown, 1991) identified three ways in which parents supported the literacy development of their children under 5 years of age: being a 'model'; providing opportunities (time, space, experiences, materials); and giving recognition to children's efforts in writing and reading behaviour.

Parents who are aware of and have some knowledge about early literacy development are in a better position to enhance further the things they often do naturally. They can then enjoy, value and support their young children's literacy development.

How can nurseries, schools and other group care settings support children as developing writers?

Earlier in this chapter the framework for developing emergent literacy was discussed (Figure 6.1). Teachers, nursery nurses, playgroup and crèche workers who want to offer children opportunities to develop their literacy can use that framework of *model, provide, observe, interact, intervene* and *evaluate*, to develop their strategies for working with young developing writers and readers.

Children's early markmaking needs to be encouraged and developed, for these early marks and the beginnings of writing included in this chapter form the basis of writing in the conventional form as we know it. To write all the letters in the English alphabet children need to be able to represent straight and diagonal lines, circles and arcs, to connect marks together and to place marks inside and outside enclosing marks. Much of the early writing done by young children includes this repertoire. After that point it is a matter of understanding about writing, gradual development of a writing system, gaining control and repetition as well as experimentation. Young children have the capability to de-

velop all the marks they need to write and, with the support of professional educators following a framework similar to that given in Figure
6.1, they can develop as competent writers. Simultaneously, they need
opportunities to forge the words they need and to have something to
say. Content and form must be nourished in parallel and given equal
value. Children's writing must be nurtured, with opportunities to prac-
tise signs and symbols; good models to understand conventions and
purposes, and knowledgeable educators who are well placed to time and
tune their interventions to children's current learning needs.

There is a wealth of published material to draw on in order to provide
a richness of learning opportunities. Barnsley LEA (1990) have produced a booklet which suggests ways of developing literacy in a variety
of play situations. The Sheffield Early Years Literacy Association (1990)
gives teachers' accounts of developing literacy through activities such as
using environmental print, storytelling and book making. The important
place of story books in children's learning to read has been discussed by
Waterland (1985) and Bennett (1991) who acknowledge that children
become readers in the true sense of the word when their reading material is wide ranging and includes picture and story books. Chapter 7
considers the place of stories in children's learning, not just as material
for learning to read but as nourishment for their minds.

7
STORIES: NOURISHING CHILDREN'S THINKING

Stories are a vital means of extending children's thinking and fostering their knowledge and attitudes. In this chapter the importance of story books in early education is stressed and the potential of stories in fostering children's development and learning is illustrated with examples. A number of stories are used to illustrate their important role in developing children's thinking.

Two aspects of stories will be considered:

1. *Quality in children's literature*, because it is important to ensure that literature available to children is the best which can be offered.
2. *Stories as teachers*, because there is a wealth of information and stimulus in stories which teach children much more than literacy or learning to read.

The chapter concludes with a list of 'Stories as nourishment for thinking' which gives details of stories which can be used to support the ideas developed throughout this chapter.

Quality in children's literature

It is difficult to talk about 'quality books' for children without taking some time to define, however inadequately, what might be meant by this term. One possible interpretation of the term 'quality' could be that books should be neither racist or sexist, should be well illustrated, and well written. Directly the problem of defining quality is compounded. Who decides what is 'well illustrated'? Who decides what is 'good writing' for children? To some extent, these are matters of personal opinion. Some books which children would consider to be 'good' may well represent bad taste for their parents or teachers! Because of this dilemma of quality, the choices teachers make when they choose books for their classrooms, and when they read stories to the children, are of crucial importance. There is more choice in children's literature now than ever before. Teachers need to ensure breadth of choice and a range of quality books in their classrooms so that children are not restricted to a narrow view of literature and ideas. Those educators who work with children under 5 in a wide variety of settings, playgroups, parent and toddler groups, crèches, nursery schools and classes, private nurseries, libraries, children's play co-operatives, all need to ensure that they provide a wide range of literature for children to share, learn from and enjoy. To do otherwise would be to deny children opportunities in their early encounters with the written word.

Quality in children's books is more than promoting equal opportunities and positive images of ethnic minorities, and male and female. Quality is much more than skilful and compelling illustrations. It is more than poetic and memorable turns of phrase and a story line which absorbs young readers. Children's books need to include all of these things and more. Children need books which nourish their minds and their emotions, because quality is about feelings as well as thought and knowledge. Many books can help to support children's emotional development, reflecting and affirming their feelings by challenging their thinking and presenting characters with different emotions including fear, sadness, excitement, love and care.

Victor Watson (1992, p. 1) challenges readers to define what we mean by children's literature, arguing that the very idea of a category of literature called 'children's' is an 'uncertain concept'. It is important that educators reflect on what they mean by a 'good book' and children also need the freedom and the opportunities to decide what makes a 'good book' for them. For children to begin to develop their own views of quality in the literature they read, they need to experience the most wonderful, the most magical, and the most entrancing literature available. Books can illuminate for children parts of life which are difficult, sad, lonely, exciting, strange, challenging, scary. Books can show the importance of being fair, and can stimulate thinking about equality of opportunity. Quality literature can be shared between children and their parents at home and between children and professional educators in group settings such as nurseries, playgroups and schools. Used in these ways books become not just an instrument for learning about words and happenings but part of a loving and warm family or group experience.

Children will be able to develop discerning qualities and the ability to decide what they feel is 'a good book' if they have the opportunity to share stories, to hold on to books, and to lose themselves in the pages of a mystery, a fantasy, a thriller, which is just for them.

The National Curriculum Programmes of Study for English (DES, 1990, p. 29, para. 3) states that:

> Reading should include picture books, nursery rhymes, poems, folk tales, myths, legends and other literature which takes account of pupil's linguistic competences and backgrounds. Both boys and girls should experience a wide range of children's literature . . . Pupils should encounter an environment in which they are surrounded by books and other reading material presented in an attractive and inviting way.

Teachers have the responsibility to ensure that literature used by children in school, books which they read for themselves and those which are read to them, is wide ranging, of high quality and helps to make readers flourish.

The books which children encounter in classrooms and nurseries, playgroups and at home, the books which adults share with children at special times, must be books which light in children that flame of the love of literature which will burn and burn throughout the whole of their lives. Books of quality can spark that passion in children. Adults responsible for children's learning need to find ways to make this possible Sharing books in the early years of childhood is not just about learning to read, it is an experience which is enhanced through the quality of relationships between adults and children. The wide range of literature for children supports the development of children's language development, helps them to listen attentively, to talk about things which interest them and are meaningful to them and write their own versions of the familiar and favourite stories they read and hear.

What are books of quality?

It is all very well to talk of 'quality books', but it is not so easy to define what 'quality' consists of. Quality can be very much a question of personal taste. It could even be said that quality, a bit like beauty, is in the eye of the beholder. Reading a book, or sharing a story, is often a personal encounter – a book which one child loves and enjoys over and over again will be firmly rejected by another. Those who work with young children do not simply need a list of 'good books' to use with children. They need to be able to decide why they select certain books for children to explore, why they read particular stories, why they tend to shun others. For example, *Where the Wild Things Are* (Sendak, 1967) is a humorous and exciting fantasy for some children whilst others find it a terrifying horror story they wish to avoid. Such books are still important for all children to experience, because children bring their own experiences, ideas, thoughts and feelings to the books they read, and books bring ideas, experiences, information and emotions to the children who read them. When children's own experiences connect in some way to those contained within a story a meaningful literacy experience can take place. This match between what children find important and the story material they are offered at that time makes the crucial difference between hearing a story and really listening with absorbed intent.

There are some elements of quality which are fundamental to 'good practice'. Margaret Meek (1988) writes of the 'intertextuality' and the 'multiconsciousness' of books which contain much more than words. There may be two or more stories, different layers of text, illustration, timing, one story being conveyed through the text and another, or an embellishment of this story, continuing in the illustrations. Early years workers need to develop their own criteria for choosing books for children which maximise opportunities for children to develop their language, literacy and understanding of the world. The following criteria are used by Madeleine Lindley[1] when choosing books for the developing reader and are based on work done during Manchester's Early Literacy Project (1984–8):

Appeal
- Does the book look inviting?
- Consider size, colour, illustration, title.

Readability
- Does the book's form/structure make reading easy?
- Do illustrations complement the text?
- Is the story line predictable, making sense to children and thus encouraging reading for meaning?
- Does the language flow naturally, not sounding stilted or contrived? How close is it to children's own speech patterns (important at early stages)?
- Is the print helpful and appropriate for reading level? Look at size of type, position on page, amount on page, line endings.
- Consider the length of the book.

Content
- Is the content worth reading?
- Does the story hold the reader's characterisation or plot?

- Does it extend the child's imagination and emotional range *or* relate to the children's own lives, experiences and feelings?
- Do you enjoy it yourself? (But remember that tastes vary.)
- Does non-fiction present interesting information in an accessible manner, appropriate to the age of the reader but without trivialising the subject?

Development
- Will this book help the child to develop into a more skilled reader?
- Does it enrich the child's vocabulary and develop an understanding of different language uses (e.g. literary language)?
- Does it enable use of variety of reading strategies depending on purpose?
- Does it raise questions and encourage reflection?
- Does it stimulate a creative or imaginative response?

Equal opportunities
- Is the writer conscious of equal opportunities and attempting to avoid bias?
- Consider the implicit message of the book as well as the detail.
- Are there positive views of minority-group people and reference to their cultural traditions, where appropriate?
- Are female characters given equal importance and status as males?
- Are stereotypes avoided and are images of ethnic origin, religion, class or disability fairly and positively shown?

Books can convey powerful images and messages to young children, therefore the books they are offered need to be chosen carefully. Bearing in mind these thoughts, the following books have been examined to see what they offer children in terms of a literacy experience and in terms of widening their experiences, knowledge, ideas and thoughts.

The Tooth Ball (Pearce, 1987) tells the story of Timmy, a young boy who is sad, shy and without friends. His wobbly tooth falls out. He wraps it first in some gold foil which comes from his grandmother's birthday chocolates. Gradually further layers are added, silver foil, a leaf, Christmas paper, writing paper, brown paper, computer paper. The ball gets bigger as layers of wrapping are added, but it also gets lighter. As the tale progresses, Timmy meets another boy who helps him to put more layers of wrapping on the 'tooth ball', an old sock, kitchen paper, newspaper, wallpaper, a duster, cotton wool, a tea towel, an old woolly hat, a table cloth, a pillow case, a sack, and finally: 'It got bigger and bigger – and lighter and lighter, too, in a most surprising way. They had to wrap it in garden-netting so that Timmy could wind his fingers in it firmly, to stop the toothball from bouncing away'. The two boys took the tooth ball to the park and met several children who became new friends.

This a book about relationships, burning heartfelt desire for friends and a grandmother's love. It is a fantasy with a happy ending but has another ingredient as well. It also contains within it a strong notion of 'covering' described in great detail. This story can stimulate further learning experiences and act as a starting point for work on coverings and wrappings as well as discussions about friends and loneliness. After telling this story to her class of 5-year-olds, a teacher introduced some work on wrapping and packaging. Using different types of wrapping material, including paper, fabrics, plastics, children began to create their own multilayered balls. Children learned that each time a layer goes on, the size of their ball increased, but also recorded that the weight increased too. Children recorded the type and size of the layering material, and the increasing weight of their layered balls. Working in small groups they needed to discuss, experiment, hypothesise and try out different ideas. Later they tested their products for durability, seeing how long they would stay intact when used outdoors for throwing, rolling and bouncing. The absorbing and worthwhile activities which arose from this story experience contained several links to subject areas in the National Curriculum including English, mathematics, science, design and technology.

A Book of Boxes (Mason, 1989) is more than a book. It demonstrates a perfection in the craft of colour and imagination, concealing surprises in the boxes contained on each page. It is a book full of wonderment, and surprise. A nursery nurse was sharing this book with two 4-year-olds. It was their first encounter with *A Book of Boxes* and together they explored each page, talking about experiences of which the boxes and their contents reminded them. The two children were keen to see 'What's inside this one?' as each page was turned. Later that day one of the children brought a box to the nursery nurse. She offered it to her and said, with a broad smile, 'What's inside this one?' The adult knelt down to open the box. Inside she found six books. The little girl laughed and said 'It's a box of bookses!' She had used her experience of the story and understanding that things the wrong way around might be funny; she made her own joke in reversing both the title and the object she had created. Both the book and the child's subsequent 'box of bookses' were content related to 'insideness'.

A Dark, Dark Tale (Brown, 1983) is an example of the power of illustration and the economy of words. The enchantment of repetition

and the expectation in this book is known and enjoyed by everyone who
turns the pages:

> Once upon a time there was a dark, dark moor.
> On the moor there was a dark, dark wood.
> In the wood there was a dark, dark house.
> At the front of the house there was a dark, dark door.
> Behind the door there was a dark, dark hall.
> In the hall there were some dark, dark stairs.
> Up the stairs there was a dark, dark passage.
> Across the passage was a dark, dark curtain.
> Behind the curtain was a dark, dark room.
> In the room was a dark, dark cupboard.
> In the cupboard was a dark, dark box.
> And in the box there was . . . A MOUSE!

After hearing this story many, many times both at home and at nursery,
Annie (3:7) wrote her own version of the book. She used four sheets of
paper fixed together with staples. On each page she drew an oval. She
brought the book to her teacher who wrote Annie's words on each page:

Front cover	'Dark Book' 'by Annie'
Page 1	'Dark house'
Page 2	'Dark mouse'
Page 3	'Dark cat'
Back cover	'finished!'

This example of a young child's book making shows how children who
are absorbed by certain stories and ideas can extend these ideas further
when there is match between their ideas and new ones. Resources and
information needs to be offered to them and adults need to be 'tuned in'
to extend and support children's efforts and interests.

These books (and many hundreds more) all have their own distinct
qualities. They each offer something particularly special to younger and
older readers. They are 'multilayered' (Waterland, 1992). Children must
see, handle, own and experience reading books like these. They must
talk about them and hear stories read by their teachers, their childminders, their friends, their parents. They should have the experience of
sharing stories and books with people who share the passion of story and
of literature. Books and stories have a prime place in the quality early
childhood curriculum, providing experiences for children which will last
a lifetime.

As well as the written story, the tradition of storytelling contains
compelling and memorable themes and motifs which sustain both younger and older listeners. Traditional stories told by storytellers arose from
real-life experiences and listeners can often find links with their own

lives. Listeners bring their own experiences to the story just as the storyteller brings experiences of the story to them.

The 'Story of the Tailor'[2] tells of a tailor who acquired a large length of cloth of a quality he had never worked with before. The tailor proudly made a fine long overcoat which he wore until it was all worn through Unable to bring himself to throw the cloth away he remade the overcoat into a jacket ('for there was still some good cloth in the overcoat'). Over time the jacket wore out and so the tailor made a waistcoat out of the good cloth which was not so worn and still had some quality left in it. The waistcoat in its time was made into a cap, the cap into a tie. Finally, when the large piece of cloth had been made into garments reducing in size each time, the tailor realised that his tie of fine cloth was truely worn out. But there was one tiny piece of the tie which was not so worn and the tailor made the smallest thing he could, a button 'the finest he ever had'.

Alongside the compelling style of the storyteller (lost here in the 'potted' version) are two main themes: the first of decreasing size, and the second of the pride and pleasure of the craftsman. The first is a theme which can link with certain mathematical notions of decreasing size, and the second bears a message about feelings of pride and pleasure in creating and owning something beautiful, and never really wanting to part with it. Such themes recur in many stories and link with children's schematic interests in 'something inside something inside something'. Storytelling is an important part of many cultures and a way of passing on the history of a people. The storytelling tradition is important to Native Americans who, in parts of Utah, Arizona, Colorado and New Mexico, produce the 'storytellers'. These are clay models of storytelling dolls, figures with mouths open (telling a story) and many children sitting on their knees, at their feet, leaning over their shoulders. Traditional tales of the tribe are passed on in this way to the youngest children and stories of traditions and history are told and retold through generations.[3] Often these traditional tales are full of pattern, repetition and information which are intended to equip the listener with guidance for life.

Picture books and pop-up books

There are many books where the most attractive features are often the illustrations and the pop-up or movable features. There seem to be a number of stories which interest children where illustration is strongly schematic and the text may tell a different story. For example, other books attract children because of their compelling mastery of paper technology, as in *The Wheels on the Bus* (Zelinsky, 1990) and *The Magic Window* (Nister, 1981). These can be sources of dynamic exchanges between children and adults who share their books. Adults need to develop finely tuned skills of observation so that they can be alert to the things which children find important in the books they read.

Picture books and books which contain examples of skilful paper engineering provide examples and stimulus for children to design and create their own books with illustrations and with flaps which lift, as in books like *Where's Spot?* (Hill, 1980) and surprises in pockets such as the letters in *The Jolly Postman* (Ahlberg and Ahlberg, 1986) and the variety of unexpected delight in *A Book of Boxes* (Mason, 1989). Six-year-old Josie created her own version of *The Jolly Postman*. She made her book by stapling sheets of paper together and then stuck an envelop on each facing page. Over a week she wrote various letters to the characters in her book, illustrated the pages and made up rhymes to link the letters together as the pages were turned.

Stories as teachers

The examples given earlier in this chapter show that some stories can help children to learn. Parents, teachers and other early childhood educators often seek out a book which they hope will help a child through difficult or challenging times in their lives. *I'll Always Love You* (Wilhelm, 1985) is the story of a small boy and his dog, whom he loves very much. Finally the day comes when the old dog does and the sadness felt by the little boy is shared by all who read this story. *Ben's Baby* (Foreman, 1989) tells the story of a little boy whose mother is expecting a second child and the events in his life during this time of change. Books convey many images and messages about feelings, about the environment, about social etiquette. Many books written for children portray powerful messages through graphic as well as textual images. For example, in *Rosie's Walk* (Hutchins, 1969) the main characters are Rosie, the hen and the fox. There are 32 words of text in which there is no mention of the fox, but without the fox in the illustrations, *Rosie's Walk* would have been a quite different story. Margaret Meek (1988) discusses the important interplay between text and illustration and describes a child's reading of this book and the messages conveyed through word and picture.

Earlier chapters have discussed both form and content of children's thinking. Here stories are considered as a source of rich nourishment for children's developing and lively minds. The themes which run through many stories can nourish children's patterns of learning. Many stories seem to have in common a number of different themes, which form a kind of 'structure' or 'sub-theme' which lies beneath the content of the story. Watson (1992) finds that ideas of 'space and place' are important in children's stories (p. 11). He draws attention to the substructures in *Tom's Midnight Garden* (Pearce, 1958), which is: '. . . full of openings – doors, windows, gaps in hedges' (p. 23).

This next section considers stories which contain such underlying structures. The themes such as 'insideness', 'up and down', 'rotation and roundness' and 'journeys' will be discussed and illustrated with examples of stories and children's responses.

Insideness in stories

All young children, at different times in their lives, seem to be interested in ideas and experiences of being inside or putting things inside. Being inside, hiding, wrapping things, hiding objects are all part of this apparently compulsive behaviour of young children which could collectively be called ideas of 'insideness'. Many stories nourish the theme of insideness in a number of different ways. Whilst the 'form' of thinking – 'insideness' – is common in all of the following stories, there is a wide variety of content. These stories can stimulate and extend children's ideas and knowledge.

Inside – inside – inside
The development of mathematical concepts of decreasing size can be fostered with stories which tell of an object or objects inside other objects which are themselves inside something else. This idea is the literary equivalent of the Russian Doll which opens to reveal a smaller doll, which also opens to reveal another doll and so on until finally a wee small doll is found inside the penultimate tiny doll. Stories like Ruth Brown's *A Dark, Dark Tale* (see earlier), and *Funny Bones* (Ahlberg and Ahlberg, 1982) and Vyanne Samuels's *Boxed In* fit into this category.

This pattern of thinking is part of the same interest which prompts older children at the point where they become aware of a larger world and their place in it, to augment their home address by adding, for example: 'London, England, Great Britain, Europe, The World, The Solar System, The Milky Way, The Universe, Infinity'.

One enclosure – many things inside

Other ideas of insideness which attract children to ideas of 'fitting in' are the ideas of a single enclosure, for example, a house, a bag, a box, which contains an increasing number of things. This is like the carpet bag carried by Mary Poppins, out of which come all manner of objects, large and small, which in reality are far too large to fit inside the bag. Similarly, *A Witch got on at Paddington Station* (Sheldon and Smith, 1991) tells of a happy witch who gets on a crowded bus on a rainy day. In a tussle with the grumpy conductor her bag breaks and, to the delight of the passengers, out pour its fantastic contents, filling the bus:

> There was a blue moon. There were pink stars.
> There was one fountain. There were two toucans.
> There were three parrots. There were four kittens.
> There were five garden gnomes.

One Snowy Night (Butterworth, 1991) tells the story of a park keeper who is snug and warm in his house on a cold, snowy, winter night. One by one the animals living in the park arrive and ask to be let in to stay the night away from the winter elements. Percy eventually ends up with a squirrel, two rabbits, a fox, a badger, a hedgehog and some mice in his bed. Eventually the animals find other places to snuggle inside: a dressing-gown pocket, a coat pocket, a drawer, a woolly hat and some slippers.

Three-year-old Shelley, having been told this story at home, represented the story in two ways. First she hid her toy mouse in her father's slipper. When the mouse was discovered she said, 'He was hiding because it was snowy'. Secondly, she drew a rectangle with several ovals inside it and one outside it. She said: 'It's the house and the animals inside but the mole is outside.' She had selected from the story some parts which had meaning for her, and later represented them, first through action, and second through drawing. Her language also matched her representations when she used words like *hiding* and *inside*.

Four-year-old Alistair was retelling his favourite story, *Dinner Time* (Pienkowski, 1980) in which various animals swallow another in turn: a fly, frog, a vulture, gorilla, tiger, crocodile and a shark. Alistair mimicked the voices of each animal as he repeated the words in the story, 'I'm going to eat you for my dinner'. Later, playing with a set of zoo animals Alistair re-enacted the story. 'Speaking' for each animal in turn he selected a set of animals ranging from a tiny rabbit to a large elephant. He told the teacher: 'They have to eat the one smaller than them because otherwise it won't fit inside.'

Stories which include repetition of an idea or a phrase help children to place some 'order' on their thoughts and on their world. Repetitive patterns help children to predict what might come next and to incorporate their thoughts into their own story making.

Traditional stories based on the theme of insideness include the song of the old woman who swallowed a fly, illustrated in *Fancy That!* (Pienkowski, 1986), 'The House that Jack Built', 'Peter and the Wolf' and 'The Old Woman who Lived in a Shoe'.

Types of enclosure
Stories like *My Presents* (Campbell, 1988), *Dear Zoo* (Campbell, 1984), *The Jolly Postman* (Ahlberg and Ahlberg, 1986) and traditional tales such as 'The Three Little Pigs' also contain themes about different types of enclosure. Many stories include ideas of 'gobbling up', for example: 'Little Red Riding Hood', 'The Three Billy Goats Gruff', and Aesop's fable of 'The Wolf and his Shadow'. Others tell of deep enclosing forests as in 'The Sleeping Beauty'. Similarly the Bible story of 'Jonah and the Whale' tells of Jonah who is swallowed by a large whale and spends three days and nights inside the whale and is eventually spat out on to land. Another Old Testament story of Joseph, made popular through the musical show *Joseph and his Technicolor Dreamcoat* contains several enclosures. Marcia Williams retells this tale in *Joseph and his Magnificent Coat of Many Colours* (Williams, 1990) where Joseph experiences many types of enclosure: his magnificent coat, a deep pit and a prison cell.

One enclosure – many uses
Stories which show many uses of one kind of enclosure often introduce the ideas of the passing of time. *Jack's Basket* (Catley, 1989) is written in rhyme and tells of different uses for Jack's baby basket; his bed for the first few months, a wool basket, a pretend car or boat, a picnic basket, a laundry basket, something to gather apples in from the tree in the garden and, finally, battered and worn, it becomes a home for mice in the garden shed. *Fur* (Mark and Voake, 1986) tells of a cat making nests ready to give birth to her kittens; she uses a hat, a basket in a cupboard and a skirt, but finally the hat is filled with fur and the kittens have arrived. Familiar with this story, 4½-year-old Maya made 'a hat' from clay. She explained to her mother, 'I did this hat, and tomorrow there will be kittens but they haven't been born from the mummy cat yet'. Children who have some understanding of time realise that some time needs to pass before things happen. Maya knew that there was some waiting involved when a cat has kittens.

Coverings

Ideas of 'coverings' include many possible images: several covers on top of one another, making coverings, disguise and dressing up. Some stories in this category link closely to the content of several stories already mentioned. Many stories have several interrelated ideas which can be drawn out according to children's interests and imagination, and the present curriculum content.

The Hans Anderson tale 'The Emperor's New Clothes' is a story which appeals to children who understand about clothing and covering (Anderson, 1992). Children who can imagine the scene may find humour in the story of so many people being too silly to say the Emperor was not wearing fine clothes. A modern story, *Mr Nick's Knitting* (Wild and Huxley, 1990) includes the making of a blanket from knitted squares. This story describes the feelings of real friendship and the wish to give something particularly unique to a person who is a special friend.

Children can be attracted to dressing up and pretending to be a different character. Stories which feature children or animals dressing up or changing their appearance can be used to nourish and extend children's ideas of coverings, and of being wrapped inside. Two animal stories suggest that it might be possible to become disguised by taking on a different covering. *Elmer* (McKee, 1989) tells of a multicoloured elephant who covers himself with grey mud so that he is acceptable to the rest of the herd. It is a story about being different and about the need to be accepted by one's peers. It shows how effective disguise can be. Accidental disguise, as featured in *Harry the Dirty Dog* (Zion and Bloy Graham, 1960), can also show how people react to a familiar friend when they look different from their normal selves.

Children find the idea of disguise quite intriguing. After telling both *Elmer* and *Harry the Dirty Dog* to a group of 4-year-olds, their teacher noted how a small group continued the theme of coverings from the stories into their play that afternoon. The children draped themselves with fabric lengths from the dressing-up trolley and approached other children, attempted to disguise their voices and asked children to guess who they were. The teacher extended this idea by suggesting that they make some masks. The necessary materials were assembled and the interested children made masks of different characters. Most of these were representations of favourite television super-heroes, but the teacher swallowed her prejudices and allowed this in the interests of promoting co-operative work between a group of young children, who were being creative, learning about making connections, fastenings, enjoying the whole idea of surprising and puzzling their friends and parents when they wore their masks.

Up and down

There is a rich abundance of stories which include aspects of vertical movement. The following examples of stories and children's response to them show the variety of ideas which can be introduced through this theme.

Some traditional stories are filled with concepts of increasing height and of problem-solving related to height. Jack climbs the beanstalk to explore and encounter the Giant and eventual wealth and happiness. Rapunzel lets down her long hair for her suitor to use as a ladder.

Illustrators represent variations in height in many different ways. Shirley Hughes' *Up and Up* (1991) is a picture book which tells in detailed illustrations the story of a little girl, so enthralled with the flight of a bird that she tries to fly. First she makes some wings and launches herself (into an abrupt landing) from the top of a step ladder; then she inflates some ballons and, holding tight to the strings, she lifts off, only to fall to ground again when the balloons burst. An enormous chocolate egg is delivered to her house, and after eating the contents she seems able to fly; the story proceeds from here with her flight (and the pursuit of many).

This story allows children to tell their own version of events. They can speculate on why she wanted to fly, which other ways might she have tried: can chocolate really make you fly? Or they may, as the following example shows, begin to tell their own story. This transcript contains the story which one little girl had to tell, starting from her interest in a particular illustration in the book, and building on her ideas about life and her own experiences. The adult tries throughout to reflect the child's own language and ideas back to her without asking new questions or imposing her own 'adult' agenda:

Child: She's going up, right up to the roof.
Teacher: She's up on top of the roof, she's getting higher.
Child: I think she might be in Heaven soon.
Teacher: You think she might be in Heaven?
Child: Well she's nearly high enough to be in Heaven, that's why the people are chasing her.
Teacher: The people are chasing her because they think she's getting as high as heaven?
Child: Yes, as high as heaven, they don't want her to go as high as that!

Teacher:	They don't want her to go as high as heaven?
Child:	If you go as high as Heaven you get stuck and can't get down. You can get up there but you can't get back. My rabbit did that. Aeroplanes go high but not as high as Heaven, so they're OK. I went to my holiday in an aeroplane, but it wasn't in Heaven, I went for a long time though.

The picture book *Up and Up* was the trigger for this little girl to tell her own story. Both the book and the reflective language (Tait and Roberts, 1974) of the teacher enabled the child to tell the story she had formed within her. It illustrates the way she has, in her young mind, begun to understand about death and parting. She has taken the explanation that her rabbit has 'gone to heaven' and attached to it her own meaning. To her, going to heaven is not about death, but it is about parting because that loved rabbit is now stuck in a place and unable to get back to her. The teacher enabled the story not by asking why or how or by adding in ideas of her own, but by creating a space in which the child could tell her story.

There are many stories which include the idea of increasing size, woven into the text along with other concepts. *Titch* (Hutchins, 1972) conveys the feelings and experiences of many children who are always the little one of the family. Eventually, after always seemingly playing a less significant role to everyone else in the story, Titch planted a tiny seed which '. . . grew and grew and grew'.

Alfie Gets in First (Hughes, 1982) is another story of a little child who needs to solve the problem of his lack of height. *Jolly Snow* (Hissey, 1992) includes ideas of height and problem-solving. It tells of some toy animals who want it to snow so that they can play in it. They try several ways of making pretend snow indoors and using a sheet they create a toboggan run:

> 'Now if we had a slope', said Rabbit, 'we could whizz down it on the sledge.' . . . Bramwell Brown disappeared into the bedroom and came back pulling a large white sheet. He gave a corner to Jolly. 'Now', said Bramwell, 'when the others climb on, lift up your end and they should slide all the way down.'

The animals try this but have rather a dubious landing:

> 'I think we need a softer landing,' said Rabbit, fluffing up his flattened fur and helping Little Bear to his feet. He piled up a heap of cushions against the wall and then all three toys bravely climbed back onto the sheet. 'Ready, steady, go!' they called to Jolly. Up went the sheet. Down went the toys – straight into the heap of cushions . . .

This short extract serves to illustrate ways in which ideas of height, and problem-solving in relation to height, can be introduced or expanded in children's literature. Jane Hissey captures the fun and the thinking which goes on in order to solve the problems of pretend snow, and hard landings!

In *The Teddy Bear Robber* (Beck, 1989) Tom pursues the giant who steals his teddy: '. . . he slipped down a massive arm, swung on a big iron key and slithered down a mighty leg . . . They came to the Giant's castle. Tom clambered up the steep steps after the Giant . . . higher, and higher, and higher, and higher . . . until they came to a giant door . . .' The use of the words 'higher and higher, and higher and higher' vividly describe the scene and the interweaving of language and illustration illuminates for young readers and listeners the climb which Tom is undertaking.

Other stories which include an element of 'up and down' and of increasing or decreasing height contain plots which require certain knowledge really to be appreciated. Children who understand the prickliness of a hedgehog can appreciate the notion of being catapulted high into the air after sitting on a hedgehog's sharp spines. Such is the fate of *Willoughby Wallaby* (Alborough, 1986). Similarly children need to understand the concept of displacement to appreciate the story of 'The Fox and the Grapes' (Aesop).

Rotation and roundness

Many traditional rhymes and jingles include ideas of roundness and rotation, for example: 'Here We Go Round the Mulberry Bush', 'Sally Go Round the Sun', 'Round and Round the Garden', which adults can share with children and which can be sung, changed and acted out. Stories too can nurture the ideas of movement and action linked to this concept. *Cupboard Bear* (Alborough, 1989) includes the idea of rolling and rotation as Bear dreams of a huge ice-cream ball.

Books with moving parts can also be useful for developing children's interest and ideas about rotation. *The Wheels on the Bus* (Zelinsky, 1990) is a feast of movement and colour based on the rhyme and finger song. It includes wheels (and text!) which rotate. Some pseudo-Victorian pop-up books contain rotating parts whereby the picture scene changes to match the text.

Journeys

The idea of journeys and journeying in children's stories seems to begin with ideas which include children and different connecting points between them, for example, their house and their friend's house. Stories which depict journeying, whether around the house, in a local area or across continents, have a relevance for children who are interested in trajectories, that is ideas of movement from point A to point B and so on. The journeys and journeying theme will nourish elements of back-and-forth schema, giving children ideas in fantasy and reality of going and coming. There is a wealth of material in children's literature which supports this theme.

In *On the Way Home* (Murphy, 1982), Claire meets various friends who ask how she hurt her knee. This gives her the opportunity to tell a number of quite fantastic stories. Eventually when she gets home she tells her mum what really happened. The characters Claire introduces to the story through her own interwoven stories make a simple journey home into quite an adventure. *Hold Tight, Bear* (Maris, 1990) describes the walk of some toys into the forest where they have a picnic: 'Over the hills, across the stream, to a meadow near the woods . . . Bear walks under the tall trees, through the cool quiet woods . . .' The passages which describe the journey introduce children to the language of mapping and mapwork. The story also includes the notions of direction, position and of space and place. Similar ideas are contained in *The Ball* (Lloyd and Rees, 1991), which not only describes the path of the moving red ball but also depicts this with illustrations showing the bouncing movement, indicating where the ball has been as well as where it presently is. Some journeying stories have become classics. *Where the Wild Things Are* (Sendak, 1967) and *The Snowman* (Briggs, 1980) reveal imaginary journeys. Are they dreams or are they fantasy? The reader must decide. Both stories tell of boys who set off on fantastic journeys. Maurice Sendak (1967) uses language which describes journeying through time and place to take Max to his adventure with the wild things. Max travels in a private boat:

> . . . he sailed off through night and day
> and in and out of weeks
> and almost over a year
> to where the wild things are.

Oi! Get Off Our Train (Burningham, 1991) tells of another bedtime journey where a little boy and his pyjama-case dog travel on their train through fog, heat, wind, marshland, rain, forest and snow rescuing endangered species as they go. *We're Going on a Bear Hunt* (Rosen and Oxenbury, 1989) tells of a journey and the return home.

Some young children who are interested in places and journeying create their own maps and diagrams of spaces and places which they know. Kirstie was absorbed with ideas of space and place and, in particular, with the idea of getting from one place to another. She used wooden bricks to create her own built environment, labelling various blocks, 'my house', 'auntie June's house', 'nursery', 'Adam's house'. She used small people to represent different characters and moved them from one place to another. Her talk took the form of a running commentary to her thinking and the action:

Kirstie doll: I'm going to Auntie June's house.

Mummy doll: (*Protests*) You can't go on your own.

Kirstie doll: Yes I can – I won't talk to the wolf.

Mummy doll: Oh all right – but don't pick flowers in the forest. (*Kirstie walks the doll around her brick world to Adam's house*)

Kirstie doll: Knock knock – is Adam coming with me? (*Adam doll is brought into the game and Kirstie with Adam in one hand and the doll representing herself in the other continues her tale as she moves both dolls around the brick village she has created*)

Kirstie doll: Shall we go to Auntie June's?

Adam doll: Oh all right.

Kirstie doll: We're there now – knock knock (*nothing happens*)

Adam doll: She's not in.

Kirstie doll: Well we can't go in the woods – 'cos the wolf might get us. (*Kirstie walks the dolls around again, humming to herself. She takes them in and out of brick enclosures, through tiny gaps in the bricks and eventually back to her house*)

Kirstie later drew what she called 'my house'. It consisted of four angular enclosures and connecting dotted lines. Pointing to appropriate parts of her drawing Kirstie told her teacher, 'My house, auntie June's house,' 'Adam's house', 'nursery', then tracing her finger along the dotted line she said: 'That's the way we go to nursery. We get Adam first, then go through there and along there and down there, past the phone box and to nursery in there.' Kirstie's map which showed the way to nursery was created from her knowledge of her local environment, her life experiences and her understanding and experience of stories. Her journey may not have been quite as fantastic as those of Max, or the boy who flew with the Snowman, but it was enriched with the language of mapping which is also present in many of the stories she had heard.

Stories and the National Curriculum

The stories discussed so far demonstrate their tremendous potential for stimulating learning. As well as nourishing more 'traditional' areas of learning as defined in terms of subjects such as mathematics, science, history, geography and others identified in the National Curriculum, stories can nurture other important elements in children's learning and development. For example, *The Stop Watch* (Lloyd and Dale, 1986) is a story which focuses on timing events; it could be valuable for concepts of time and timing. It is also about competition and the relationship between a brother and sister. Similarly, stories such as *Oi! Get Off Our Train* (Burningham, 1991) can be used to highlight and reinforce effects of environmental damage with human and emotional content as well.

Children's ways of learning have not changed because of the National Curriculum. The successful understanding of curriculum content depends upon classroom practice, on teachers' interactions with children and on stimulating and challenging resources and experiences. Stories are a rich source of curriculum content. Often a balanced topic can be planned around a single, well chosen story.

The practice of planning curriculum around stories has been developed by several sources in recent years. The result is publications which promote science, design and technology (Creary *et al.*, 1991; Williams, 1991; Design Council, 1992; Nutbrown and Hirst, 1993); history, (Cox and Hughes, 1990); geography (Lindley[4]); and cross-curricular themes and issues, (Development Education Centre, 1991; Emblen and Schmitz, 1991; Hardwick and Moore, 1991).

Those who work with children under the age of statutory schooling have a curriculum freedom which allows them, whether they work in nursery schools and classes or other forms of provision such as playgroups and crèches, to draw on the richness of the world to provide nourishment for the minds of young children. Teachers working with children in the early stages of Key Stage 1 can take those ideas from the programmes of study which suggest meaningful curriculum content for children, and add to and enrich them according to the various interests and concerns of the children. Curriculum freedom means that children under 5 can have the 'natural curriculum' which their young minds yearn for, rather than a diluted version of a National Curriculum which is written for older children.

This 'natural curriculum' must contain the wealth of stories: myths, legends, traditional stories from many different cultures, stories from children's own, local histories and localities, and Greek myths, Aesop's fables, Bible stories and the Anansi stories. Stories, told, read, retold and re-enacted, become the hidden teachers of young children and open the doors of their minds to the wider world.

Stories as nourishment for thinking

In the following pages stories are presented under broad themes which can be related to the different concepts, topics and schemas which have been discussed in this chapter and throughout this book. Such themes can provide profitable curriculum content and stimulate children's interests and imaginations. This illustrates the wide range of content to be drawn from stories to nourish specific threads of children's thinking.

The stories are presented here under the themes already discussed in this chapter: insideness, coverings, up and down, rotation and roundness, and journeys and journeying. These lists are by no means comprehensive and are included to exemplify the range and depth of material which stories can offer.

Insideness

Inside – inside – inside
Ahlberg, J. and Ahlberg, A. (1980) *Funny Bones*, Collins Picture Lions, London.
Brown, R. (1983) *A Dark, Dark Tale*, Scholastic Publications, London.
Pienkowski, J. (1980) *Dinner Time*, Gallery Five, London.
Pienkowski, J. (1986) *Fancy That!*, Orchard Books, London.
Samuels, V. (1991) *Boxed In*, Red Fox, London.

Traditional tale: 'Peter and the Wolf'.

One enclosure – increasing amount inside
Allan, P. (1988) *Who Sank the Boat?*, Picture Puffin, Harmondsworth.
Burningham, J. (1978) *Mr Gumpy's Outing*, Puffin Books, Harmondsworth.
Burninghan, J. (1980) *The Shopping Basket*, Jonathan Cape, London.
Butterworth, N. (1991) *One Snowy Night*, Picture Lions, London.
Sheldon, D. and Smith, W. (1991) *A Witch Got on at Paddington Station*, Red Fox, London.
Williams, M. (1988) *Noah's Ark*, Walker Books, London.

Traditional tale: 'The Old Woman Who Lived in a Shoe'.

Types of enclosures
Ahlberg, J. and Ahlberg, A. (1986) *The Jolly Postman or Other People's Letters*, Heinemann, London.
Campbell, R. (1984) *Dear Zoo*, Puffin, Harmondsworth.
Campbell, R. (1988) *My Presents*, Campbell Blackie Books, London.
Hill, E. (1980) *Where's Spot?*, Heinemann, London.
Mark, J. and Voake, C. (1986) *Fur*, Walker Books, London.
Mason, L. (1989) *Books of Boxes*, Orchard Books, London.
Roffey, M. (1982) *Home Sweet Home*, Piper, London.
Sieveking, A. and Lincoln, F. (1989) *What's Inside?*, Frances Lincoln, London.

Aesop's fable: 'The Fox and the Grapes', in Clarke, M. and Voake, C. (1990) *The Best of Aesop's Fables*, Walker Books, London.
Traditional tale: 'The Three Little Pigs'.

One enclosure, different uses
Catley, A. (1987) *Jack's Basket*, Beaver Books, London.
Prater, J. (1987) The Gift, Puffin, Harmondsworth.

Coverings
Anderson, H. C. (1992) 'The Emperor's New Clothes', in Ash, N. and Higton, B. (1992) *Fairy Tales from Hans Anderson – A Classic Illustrated Edition*, Pavilion Books, London.
McKee, D. (1989) *Elmer*, Andersen Press, London.
Pearce, P. (1987) *The Tooth Ball*, Picture Puffins, Harmondsworth.
Wild, M. and Huxley, D. (1988) *Mr Nick's Knitting*, Picture Knight, London.
Zion, G. and Bloy Graham, M. (1960) *Harry the Dirty Dog*, The Bodley Head, London.

Up and down
Alborough, J. (1986) *Willoughby Wallaby*, Walker Books, London.
Dale, P. (1991) *The Elephant Tree*, Walker Books, London.
Edwards, H. and Niland, D. (1982) *There's a Hippopotamus on our Roof Eating Cake!*, Hodder & Stoughton, London.
Hissey, J. (1992) *Jolly Snow*, Random Century, London.
Hughes, S. (1991) *Up and Up*, Red Fox, London.
Hutchins, P. (1972) *Titch*, The Bodley Head, London.
Inkpen, M. (1991) *The Blue Balloon*, Picture Knight, London.

Aesop's fable: 'The Fox and the Grapes', in Clarke, M. and Voake, C. (1990) *The Best of Aesop's Fables*, Walker Books, London.
Traditional tales: 'Jack and the Beanstalk' and 'Rapunzel'.

Rotation and roundness
Alborough, J. (1989) *Cupboard Bear*, Walker Books, London.

Books with rotating parts
Nister, E. (1981) *Magic Window*, Harper Collins, Glasgow.
Zelinsky, P. (1990) *The Wheels on the Bus*, Orchard Books, London.

Journeys and journeying
Bayley, N. and Mayne, W. (1981) *The Patchwork Cat*, Jonathan Cape, London.
Beck, I. (1989) *The Teddy Bear Robber*, Doubleday, Toronto.
Briggs, R. (1980) *The Snowman*, Puffin, Harmondsworth.
Burningham, J. (1963) *Borka – The Adventures of a Goose with no Feathers*, Jonathan Cape, London.
Burningham, J. (1991) *Oi! Get Off Our Train*, Red Fox, London.

Cartwright, R. and Kinmonth, P. (1979) *Mr Potter's Pigeon*, Hutchinson Junior Books, London.

Dale, P. (1991) *The Elephant Tree*, Walker Books, London.

Fair, S. (1989) *Barney's Beanstalk*, Macdonald, London.

Flack, M. and Weise, K. (1991) *The Story about Ping*, Random Century, London.

Hughes, S. (1991) *Up and Up*, Red Fox, London.

Hutchins, P. (1969) *Rosie's Walk*, The Bodley Head, London.

Lloyd, D. and Rees, M. (1991) *The Ball*, Walker Books, London.

Lear, E. and Cooper, H. (1991) *The Owl and the Pussycat*, Hamish Hamilton, London.

Maris, R. (1990) *Hold Tight Bear!*, Walker Books, London.

Murphy, J. (1982) *On the Way Home*, Pan Macmillan Children's Books, London.

Prater, J. (1987) *The Gift*, Puffin, Harmondsworth.

Pearce, P. (1987) *The Tooth Ball*, Picture Puffins, Harmondsworth.

Rosen, M. and Oxenbury, H. (1989) *We're Going on a Bear Hunt*, Walker Books, London.

Sendak, M. (1967) *Where the Wild Things Are*, The Bodley Head, London.

Shapur, F. (1991) *The Rainbow Balloon*, Simon & Schuster, London.

Wild, M. and Huxley, D. (1988) *Mr Nick's Knitting*, Picture Knight, London.

Zion, G. and Bloy Graham, M. (1960) *Harry the Dirty Dog*, The Bodley Head, London.

Aesop's fable: 'The Hare and the Tortoise', in Clarke, M. and Voake, C. (1990) *The Best of Aesop's Fables*, Walker Books, London.

Notes

1.   I am grateful to Madeleine Lindley, of Madeleine Lindley Ltd, for permission to reproduce her criteria for choosing books for children, and for the invaluable help she and her team have given in identifying and obtaining many of the books referred to in this chapter.

2.   The story of the tailor was told by Pat Ryan at the Sheffield Early Years Literacy Association Conference, June 1991.

3.   More information on this topic can be found in Bahti, M. (1988) *Pueblo Stories and Storytellers*, Treasure Chest Publications, Tucson, Ariz.

4.   *Geography through Story – Keystage 1* lists stories which relate to particular attainment targets for geography in Key Stage 1. This is the outcome of work by Pat Hughes which has been developed by Madeleine Lindley. From Madeleine Lindley Ltd, 79 Acorn Centre, Barry Street, Oldham.

Part IV
Implications for early childhood education

8
A CURRICULUM FOR THINKING CHILDREN

This chapter will consider the kind of curriculum that is needed to foster the development of children's thought, knowledge, skills and understandings as illustrated throughout this book. The debate about the 'gifts' of nature and the 'effects' of nurture have rumbled on through the decades. Those responsible for the education of young children must believe that nurturing young minds can have a positive effect on their learning and development. To ascribe to a theory that asserts that potential intelligence understanding and achievement are decided in the womb, rather than developed from the cradle, leads nowhere and guarantees that early education will be ineffective. Nourishment for the mind, the emotions and the body must be matched to children's needs, their present needs, and must include educators' high expectations of the children with whom they work.

The work of Athey (1990) suggests that early intervention, an education that involves parents, professionals and a clear pedagogy, can enhance children's intellectual development. It would be reasonable to suppose that increased knowing, ability and understanding will lead to higher self-esteem, increased emotional security and a fuller all-round development for children. These issues are fundamental to the way in which young children are taught and how a curriculum to foster their learning might be constructed.

The examples of children's learning and thinking in this book suggest two questions that need to be addressed if curriculum developments in nurseries and other group settings are to provide ways for children to develop as thinkers:

- How can professional educators ensure breadth, balance and relevance in the curriculum they offer?

- How can a curriculum for young children nourish children's *forms* of thought with worthwhile and interesting *content*?

These two questions raise many different issues and they will be considered in turn.

How can educators ensure breadth, balance and relevance in the curriculum they offer?

There is some agreement that curriculum for children under 5 exists in its own right. Curtis (1986, pp. 2–3) writes that there is a recognisable and distinctive curriculum for under 5s that is distinct from that curriculum for children of statutory school age: '. . . there is a recognisable curriculum for children under statutory school age based on skills and competencies to be developed in a flexible and child-centred environment, and . . . there is ample material with which to challenge and extend children without offering them a "watered-down" reception class programme.'

The Preschool Playgroups Association (1991, p. 2) have also endorsed the idea of a curriculum for playgroups catering for children aged 2–5 years:

> Every group has a curriculum, though it might not be a written one and may never have been consciously studied or decided upon. A curriculum is simply a course of learning, formal or informal. The curriculum of a playgroup is what the children learn during their time in the group.

There is also a suggestion that there is a developing curriculum for babies and toddlers. As the demand for more group care of the youngest children grows so does the debate about what kind of quality it should offer: 'Day care must not just be a safe, clean parking place with good food, fresh air and kind bustling adults. Babies and toddlers must learn to express and exchange emotions, to communicate, and to learn about people, objects, and experiences' (Rouse, 1990, p. 7).

Government documents have also endorsed the idea of a specialist curriculum for children under 5. The Education Reform Act 1988 instigated a curriculum for children aged 5–16 designed and defined in terms of subjects and assessed in terms of attainment targets with levels of attainment for each key stage. This curriculum has been the subject of controversy, debate and revision since its inception and changes continue. During the early implementation stages of the National Curriculum, the Rumbold Committee (DES, 1990a), reporting on the quality of educational experience of 3- and 4-year-olds in all settings, considered a curriculum 'framework' based on broad areas of experience and learning opportunities, which together made up a balanced and broad curriculum, was the best way to proceed for young children under 5 years of age. HMI (DES, 1989b) had already set forward this view so far as nursery schools and classes were concerned, so there was some agreement about its appropriateness.

It is important that educators focus not just on areas of experience but also on ways of extending and linking different strands of knowledge and understanding and experience. Such teaching can give young children opportunities for learning and development that are rich and full and create an experience of early education that is satisfying in holistic terms. A balanced, broad, relevant and differentiated curriculum is much more than rhetoric. It is a sound philosophy of curriculum entitlement for all children.

Subjects are one way of categorising elements of knowledge into convenient groupings so that teaching and assessment can be managed and curriculum discussed, but this is not the only way and the compartmentalisation of learning in terms of subjects can be less than helpful in terms of understanding and challenging young children's thinking. In reality, young children do not think in subjects. Neither do adults. Human beings think in terms of situations, puzzles, problems to be solved, questions to be answered; it is the same for adults and children alike. When children are thinking, talking and applying their existing knowledge the children attend to the task in hand. They do not analyse their knowledge in terms of subjects, as the following example shows.

A group of children (aged 4:8–4:11) in a reception class were using the sand and making up a story. Their story began when one child declared that all the animals had died and needed to be buried. A mass burial of tigers, monkeys, giraffes, elephants, whales, seals, penguins and tigers followed. Next the children dug up their animals and decided they would start again. They made the sand slightly damp, taking care not to add too much water. The children patted the sand to make it flat and then arranged some twigs in a circle to make a forest. Inside the twigs was the forest. The circle represented the 'edge' of the forest. Shells were made into a patterned arrangement to represent 'the sea at the edge of the forest'. The group agreed that some of the animals lived 'inside the forest' whilst others lived 'under the sea'. The animals were located in their respective habitats. One child began sprinkling sand over the twigs and said, 'it's snowing, the forest is all covered with snow because it hasn't got a roof on. The animals are covered in snow. They'll die if they freeze to death'. Again, many of the animals died. It was the small animals who suffered this fate for they were 'too small to survive the cold winter'. They were given respectful burials, with due ceremony, in graves of suitably measured sizes, in the centre of the forest. Small memorial notices were written and stuck in the ground to mark the graves.

Educators who watch and interact with children who are employing all that they know in purposeful play can learn things about those children which focusing on subject knowledge alone would never reveal. These children were working with a sensitive co-operation to be admired. Their story evolved as they were stimulated by the materials provided by the teacher, the stories they had heard, their ideas about dying and burial and their knowledge of the conventions of marking graves and of the survival of the fittest.

Dilemmas about curriculum, what it means, what it should be called and what it should consist of will continue. It seems timely to reflect at this point on the words of Christian Schiller (1979, p. 93):

> Curriculum is not an attractive word. Whether heard through the ear as a sound, or seen through the eye as a shape on a page, it leaves an impression of something sharp and harsh. It is, of course, a Roman word, unaltered and unassimilated by our native tongue; and this fact no doubt reveals a certain tardiness in finding a native word which says, quite simply and with feeling, 'What we do in school'. Perhaps also it reflects a certain reluctance to think in general terms of all those activities with which children find themselves engaged by our choice as teachers.
>
> And this is not surprising. Curriculum has for long conventionally been used as a collective noun to denote a collection of subjects. But in the field of primary education we are becoming increasingly clear that for young children 'subjects' have little significance.

The Early Years Curriculum Group (1992, p. 19) advocate breadth of curriculum and illustrates the diversity of learning which is possible through firsthand experience and activity:

> In the early years the child's knowledge is not separated into subject groupings. When children are cooking, for instance, they may be learning about science, maths, health education, and how to collaborate and share while extending their vocabulary and language skills. Young children learn about 'subjects' through a wide variety of play activities. Play takes many forms, both indoors and outdoors; the skilled observer recognises the significance of these activities and promotes children's understanding and learning. Real objects and materials enable children to explore and extend what they already know and can do. Through a wide range of

materials they will be covering many subject areas of the curriculum.

As well as endorsing a curriculum for under 5s made up of areas of experience, the Rumbold Committee and HMI state the importance of the process of learning – that is to say, how children learn is as important as the content of their learning, what they learn.

The 'Great Educators', Froebel, Montessori, Pestalozzi, the Mac-Millans and Isaacs left a legacy to early childhood educators which provide an underpinning of *process* of learning. That is the important place of play in young children's learning. There are many interpretations of play. Bruce (1991) examines the views and influences of researchers and theorists including Piaget, Freud, Erickson, Winnicott, Burner and Vygotsky. She concludes that there are difficulties in defining play.

Play has a prominent place in young children's learning and development. Evidence to this is available to all who watch young children as they play alone and with others. Play is not the only means by which children learn. They learn by watching and imitating others, baking at home, going shopping with their parents, going for a walk, helping in the garden, preparing and participating in family celebrations and events.

Breadth and balance in the curriculum are not just about content but about processes of learning. There must be space, time and value for children to play, talk, imitate, reflect and question and reason as they develop their understanding of things they meet with. Saul (3:9) added some water to dry sand to make it wet. He then began digging in the sand and, with a puzzled look on his face, said: 'There's water in this sand but I can't find it!'

There must also be opportunities for children to experience the new and the challenging as 'apprentices' to adults who can help to extend their thinking and doing. Children can be fascinated by watching craftspeople at work and will benefit from opportunities to see them working at their craft: for example, by visiting craft centres where people can be seen making candles, jewellery, knitting, painting, and by inviting people to demonstrate their skills in the nursery such as a carpenter working at the woodwork bench to make a small stool, or a lace maker, sitting at a low table and working at a piece of lace whilst children watch.

Having considered aspects of breadth and balance, where does this leave the question of relevance to the child? It is here that the Plowden Report, proves useful: 'At the heart of the educational process lies the child. No advances in policy, no acquisition of new equipment have their desired effect unless they are in harmony with the nature of the child, unless they are fundamentally acceptable to him' (DES, 1967, para. 9). This assertion of the important place of the child at the centre is a key to curriculum relevance. Any broadly based and balanced curriculum must have children as learners at the centre, if it is to be relevant to them. This means giving children opportunities to make sense of their experiences, information, opportunities and challenges which they encounter through their lives and through the curriculum.

Children must have opportunities to represent what they see, do and think. They need to represent through action, markmaking, models, writing and through talk. Children must have open-ended materials such as bricks, paint, sand, water and clay that enable them to represent their real experiences, their ideas and their imaginings. Russell used pipes in the water tray to create his representation of a washing machine. He explained: 'This is the washing machine and you put the water in here [funnel] and it's dirty, and you make it go through here [tubing] and you blow and it comes out here, and it's clean!' The co-ordinated schemas of containing and going through a boundary are illustrated in Russell's representation of the washing machine and the changing state of the water and the clothes.

For children to engage in experimentation, exploration, problem-solving and active thought they need to be able to work with inventive and creative educators. To make the most of a meaningful curriculum, children must have space and time as well as materials. They must have time to talk and to be listened to. They must have the support and challenge of educators who actively seek a match between what is taught and what is learned.

Brierley (1987) writes of the need for variety and stimulation. It is through such variety and stimulation that it becomes possible to provide for individuals within a group. Worthwhile experiences, both within the planned learning environment and in the wider community are never narrow. There are always numerous ways in which experiences and events can develop. Basing the teaching of the youngest children on real experiences and on avenues of learning which arise from children's play is more likely to ensure curriculum relevance as well as breadth and balance of learning opportunities.

How can a curriculum for young children nourish children's forms of thought with worthwhile and interesting content?

A great deal of learning can take place around the simple but fundamental theme of 'what kinds of things can be found or put inside different containers?' This can include trying out simple *en croute* cookery, food wrapped in pastry, stuffed vine leaves, stuffed peppers, samosas; it can include consideration of animals that live in shells, holes, caves or tunnels.

The curriculum is often planned and presented to children by way of a theme or topic. This can help to ensure that a wide range of experiences are linked to provide a range of experiences which have a curricular balance. If educators think about children's schemas as they plan different themes it is possible to facilitate learning through play and build on children's specific and individual needs and experiences. Consideration of schemas and children's particular 'threads' of thought can be a way of linking theory about how children learn with day-to-day practice. A closer link can be achieved between the offered curriculum and that which the learner takes up and develops. Curriculum 'match' can be made possible when curriculum material is planned as extensions of what children are already paying attention to, and have demonstrated interest in through their actions, speech and graphic representations.

Children under 5 can assimilate and enjoy a wide range of experiences that extend themes of 'inside', 'surrounding' and 'outside'. Such themes lend themselves to the development of ideas of measurement, mapping, cooking, exploring the environment and making sounds, to name but a few possible avenues for development. Children's schemas, which illuminate their patterns of behaviour and thought, can open the door to a wealth of learning opportunities. Educators who watch children closely are in a position to identify what children are currently paying attention to, and consequently to match curriculum content to children's overriding interests.

Children's schemas seem to make children alert to certain events and properties of objects in their environment. When professionals are able to identify children's interests in this way they are better placed to select appropriate curricular provision because their work is more clearly informed by and related to theory. Children's schemas seem to be part of their motivation for learning, their insatiable drive to move, represent, discuss, question, find out. Children seem to make clear choices in their play, taking from their environment the elements that make sense to them and match their schemas at the time.

Planning and organising the curriculum should take account of the need to nourish individual children's schematic concerns, and to provide a wide-ranging curriculum that fosters broad areas of experience and opportunity. The nursery where many of the observations in this book were made was organised as a series of 'workshop' areas, with equipment available in specific areas for the children to work with. Equipment included: painting and drawing materials; water; sand; woodwork; clay; materials for three-dimensional modellings and construction; imaginative, miniature figures and models; equipment for fantasy play (hairdressing, dressing up, shop and hospital play); music; books; bricks; home-corner play; and a range of equipment and vehicles for use outdoors. These types of materials formed the core of curriculum experiences and most were available daily in a space organised along the lines of Figure 8.1. A wide variety of materials and equipment can be provided for children to use, backed by the notion of 'a place for everything and everything in its place', at the start and end of each session. Equipment for each medium can be sited in each workshop area. A child who chooses to play with water can select from a range of equipment what he or she wants to use in the water. The equipment on offer can nourish a range of schemas, for example: jugs and bottles for filling and containing; tubes and funnels for 'going through'; pumps for 'up and down'; and water wheels for 'going round'. The equipment children choose and how they use it provides an indication of children's schemas and their learning focus. Adult observation is always a vital element of the curriculum in order to ascertain the needs of children and facilitate the further extension of schemas and learning through increasing the equipment or experience. Educators need to work flexibly in different areas and with individual children as well as small groups to build on children's interests.

Staff might plan in terms of the tools of the task, but children decide on the real nature of their work. A variety of available equipment for use with water can enable flexibility for individual learners whilst a number of children play side by side with water. For example, one child pursuing a dynamic vertical schema might choose to experiment with dropping various objects and materials from a height into the water. Another child interested in ideas related to containing or enclosing might fill a number of containers with water. The first child can think about ideas related to gravity, flotation and immersion whilst the second can explore events that prompt thinking related to ideas of capacity, size, shape and quantity. Both children are at work at their own level of development and interest and both have to deal with the properties of water. Adult intervention can be matched to each child's activity, as appropriate. Such developments can help early childhood educators to interpret children's behaviour at a schematic level and lead to more effective teaching and learning than that which arises through adults' plans for introducing a whole group of children to a particular idea because it seems a good thing to do. A curriculum which supports and

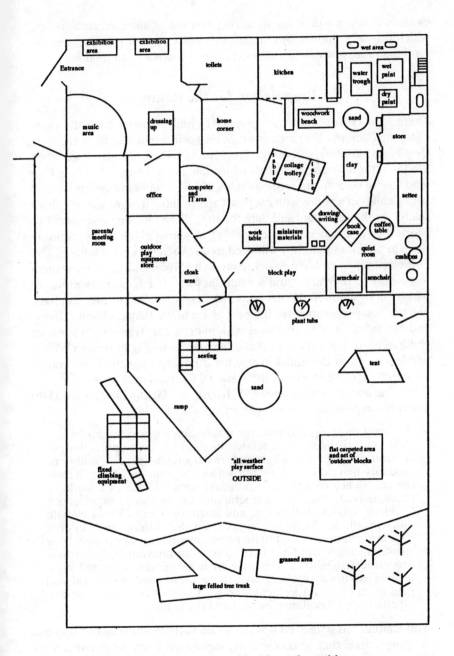

Figure 8.1 Organisation of inside and outside space

extends children's thinking by taking account of their schemas is one which provides human and material resources which provoke and extend the process which facilitates children's learning and thinking.

Preparation for the future

There is much concern about preparing children under 5 for the ever-changing National Curriculum which they will encounter from the time they begin statutory schooling. 'Preparation' is a dangerous word when used to refer to young children's education and learning. There can be a tendency to take up the precious years of early childhood, and to occupy young children's minds with exercises and training designed to 'get them ready' for the next step, and then the next. Well meaning educators can waste the time and insult the intellect of young children by requiring them to do things that they will need to do 'when they go to school'. The best way to help children to get ready to be 5-year-olds is to allow them to be 3 when they are 3 and 4 when they are 4. The early experiences which young children thrive on are the best nourishment they can have and the best preparation for the next phase of life they encounter. Being and behaving as a learner and a thinker is the type of preparation children need. The experiences and the understanding of young children which have been described in this book underpin much of the knowledge to be acquired through the National Curriculum.

Writing about children aged 0–3, Rouse and Griffin (1992, pp. 155–6) assert this type of wholeness in learning:

> We need the vision to plan for whole human beings who have a clear and realistic personal identity whatever combination of cultural or religious background, racial origins, gender, ability or disability that may be. Children who know who they are will have the confidence to love and learn and communicate in a world of mathematical, scientific, aesthetic and technological experiences. Children who can collaborate and learn together in harmony with other people are likely to respect and value differences. Children who are able to have intimate responsive relationships with their significant adult will have better access to relevant early learning experiences. Children who play in inspirational, safe and challenging environments will take these values into adulthood and pass them on to future generations. An ethos of respect for and dignity in childhood may be set from the cradle.

This chapter has suggested ways in which early learning can continue to be progressive, that is: *accelerating, advancing, continuing, continuous, developing, escalating, growing, increasing, intensifying, ongoing (Collins*

Thesaurus, 1987). Progress in early childhood education depends on the acceptance that fundamental to the process of education is the child. A learner- and person-centred early childhood curriculum gives children's minds the respect they deserve. This is the most effective preparation for whatever challenges they may next meet and an essential philosophy for any curriculum for thinking children.

9
WORKING WITH PARENTS

Five-year-old Sarah was playing in the garden of her house. It was a bright sunny day and she was bathing her doll. She skilfully carried jugs of warm water from the kitchen and poured them into the baby bath, taking care not to overfill the jug and checking after each jugful to see if there was enough water in the bath. She checked the temperature of the water with her arm and told her friend, 'You do that to check that they don't scald their skin, babies skin is so soft if the temperature is too hot they could burn'.

Sarah undressed her doll and went into the kitchen to put the clothes in the sink. 'I'll wash them later when the baby is asleep. They don't go in the machine, it makes the knitting go a funny shape', she explained. Returning to the garden she carefully put the doll into the bath, gently splashing the water over its body. She soaped its head, taking care not to get soap in its eyes. 'It stings if soap gets in and then he'll cry.' Sarah babbled and cooed to the baby doll in a sing-song sort of voice and then spoke to it. 'We'll decide what you want to wear today when you're dry.' Lifting the baby doll out of the water she laid it gently on a towel set out ready. She wrapped the towel around the doll and cradled it in her arms while she sang part of a lullaby. Then, holding the doll in one arm and resting on her hip, she began sorting through a basket of doll's clothes with the other hand. 'The green one today I think. It's sunny but it is a bit windy and this is nice and woolly and thick and warm.' She dressed the doll, chatting about the weather, about going to the shops in the pram and added, 'and then when you're asleep Mummy will wash your clothes and have a cup of coffee and watch *Playdays*'.

What did Sarah know? What can be learned from watching a child playing in this way? She knew about capacity, degrees of fullness and emptiness. She knew about temperature, the terminology related to this and the consequences of water being too hot in the baby bath. She knew about the need to keep warm by wearing woollen clothing. She knew that bathing a baby took time, that it was important, and could be a loving and pleasurable exchange, a special time which involves talking, touching and cuddling. She knew that caring and loving were experiences to give time to and to enjoy. This display of competent and human interaction is an example of a whole and worthwhile learning experience. Whom did she learn these things from? How did she know what to do? In this scenario, a little girl was using her knowledge acquired through helping her mother to care for her new baby brother. Her actions, her language and her disposition reflected the loving and sensitive encounters she had witnessed between her mother and the baby.

Recognising parents' roles as educators

Attitudes

To make the most of opportunities for children to learn and develop there needs to be a recognition of parents' roles in children's learning on the parts of educators in group settings. This includes teachers, nursery nurses, playgroup and crèche workers. These professional educators will inevitably hold certain attitudes towards parents. The following comments were made in a multidisciplinary group of people who were discussing their perception of the role of parents:

> Many parents can help with planning in an informal sense. Not necessarily at a planning meeting but in terms of helping staff identifying their children's needs and their expectations as parents and trying to find ways of satisfying them.
>
> (Nursery teacher)
>
> Professionals forget that parents know their children first.
>
> (Day nursery officer)

These words illustrate some of the ways in which professional educators are thinking about parents as their children's primary educators.

People who work with young children can, with a positive attitude, enhance opportunities they offer children. Parents and professional educators both have important and distinctive roles. There is a need to develop an attitude where these roles are recognised and respected to the benefit of the children. As Athey (1990, p. 66) puts it:

> Parents and professionals can help children separately or they can work together to the great benefit of the children. Parents can give practical help in classrooms (as many already do), but perhaps the greatest benefit to teachers in working with parents is the spur towards making their own pedagogy more conscious and explicit.

An attitude towards parents whereby teachers and other educators are prepared to think about and articulate their own philosophy and practice and to discuss it with parents and the wider community is of benefit to all.

Developing relationships

Our feelings about working with parents need to be examined. For some the idea of partnership with parents is an integral and essential part of their work. For others it is a threatening prospect. It is important that everyone who works with young children takes time to examine, for themselves, their own personal feelings about their involvement with the parents of the children with whom they work.

Some professional educators feel that they want to share their understanding and professional knowledge with parents, about how children learn. They also want parents to feel that anything they want to say will be positively welcomed. Relationships that enable parents and professional educators to share in a child's learning and thinking can enhance children's learning. Reporting on the Froebel Early Childhood Project, Athey (1990, p. 66) made an important comment about participation:

> One of the most important outcomes of the project was that all the adults watched and listened with ever-increasing interest to what the children were saying and doing. Nothing gets under a parent's skin more quickly and more permanently than the illumination of his or her own child's behaviour. The effect of participation can be profound.

The development of effective relationships between parents and nurseries, schools, playgroups and crèches need effort and commitment. A survey of parents and teachers in Maryland, USA (Junior Achievement, 1991) stated that barriers to co-operation existed within parent and teacher groups and that parents and teachers blamed each other for the lack of parental involvement.

Parents' views of themselves as their children's educators

In my study, I asked parents of the children I was observing what part they felt they played in helping their children to learn. There were three main types of reaction:

- Parents who did not recognise the things they did as helping their children to learn.

- Parents who felt that they helped 'informally' at home.
- Parents who felt they did a lot to help their children to learn but felt that the benefits of nursery education enhanced what they could do.

Parents who did not recognise the things they did as helping their children to learn commented:

> He plays at nursery. He doesn't play at home. He's too naughty, he doesn't learn anything from me. But he learns at nursery so that's OK.

> I don't think it is for me to help him learn at home, I think that's what nurseries are for. If he wants to play with his toys he can but I don't believe that home should be all about education too. They have to learn in nursery and when they go to school.

> I make sure she's got toys and things to keep her amused, but I don't think it's up to me to start trying to get her to learn colours and numbers and things like some people do.

Parents who felt that they helped 'informally' at home commented:

> I do things like singing nursery rhymes when she goes to bed.

> I don't 'teach' her as such but I do talk to her about the things she's interested in and answer her questions.

> I let him help me to make tea, he loves mixing things for cakes, and he helps with doing the washing and tidying up.

> We haven't got a garden and the twins love to climb so I take them to the play area at the bottom of the road most days. They run and climb and play hide-and-seek. They love it.

Parents who felt they did a lot to help their children to learn but that the benefits of nursery education enhanced what they could do commented:

> There are more things to do here than at home. I have jigsaws and drawing and things, but here they've got water and sand and those kinds of things to learn about too.

> I read to her at home and we look at the pictures more, I do more with books now, picking up ideas from you.

> I like going on outings with the nursery. Then when we get home we can talk about it and look at the things she collected. Then usually we bring them for you to look at with her again the next day to put on the table for the others to see too.

Parents who are informed in some way about the ways in which children learn, think about and represent their thoughts through talk, drawing and action are in a better position to support the continuity and progression of their children's learning and development between home and nursery, school or other group setting. Parents who understand what their children do, and see that it has some value to their learning and cognitive development, will be in a better position to discuss these things with teachers and other educators. Some parents are well informed and ensure that they obtain the information they need. However, it is the responsibility of professional educators to make sure that all parents have access to and opportunities to discuss information that is relevant to their children. Those responsible for educational provision for young children should recognise the need to allocate time and resources to work with parents. If equality of opportunity is to mean anything in practice, parents of all children should have opportunities to read, discuss and reflect with their children's educators upon current research. If this happens, parents may be less inclined to value the 'perfect' painting before the dynamic representation of something the child has seen, but which needs interpretation and is perhaps less aesthetically pleasing. Research suggests that many parents value this kind of involvement and information (Smith, 1980; Bennett, 1990). With this in mind the next section discusses the need to and ways in which information can be exchanged with parents.

Exchanging information with parents

The Froebel Early Education Project (Athey, 1990) was important for a number of reasons. Perhaps most significant were involvement of parents, involvement of professional educators and the identification of effective ways of discussing children's patterns of learning with parents (sharing pedagogy). This linking of three important elements, parents, professionals and pedagogy, is discussed by Athey (*ibid.*, p. 207): 'The professionals identified schemas but, once identified, parents were able to give examples . . . Professionals have useful knowledge but it is not always shared with parents.'

Another important finding of the Froebel project highlighted the importance of early experiences. This included visits to buildings, parks, gardens, events and watching people dancing, riding, demonstrating their skills and crafts. Parents and children often shared these experiences and Athey reports that as the project progressed, parents talked more with their children, pointed things out and attended with interest to what was happening and what their children were paying attention to.

The importance of the Froebel project in identifying and nourishing children's schemas, parents and professionals engaging in pedagogical dialogue and children having their parents actively involved in their learning was also evidenced in the IQ scores of the project children. The twenty project children were drawn from an educational priority area and formed a multi-ethnic group. The children were given a battery of tests at the start of the project. A comparison group of twenty children who attended the Froebel Institute kindergarten was also tested. The children in the comparison group were from families where parents had professional working lives. Athey (*ibid.*, p. 54) comments on the two groups of children:

> Although the children came from opposite ends of the social scale in terms of wealth, educational qualifications of parents, housing conditions, parental employment, and so on, they were to be given similar opportunities in the two school situations. The project and kindergarten teachers were both trained at the Froebel Institute and they had a similar pedagogical approach.

Initial test results showed the mean IQ of kindergartgen children as 124 and the project children as 90. Athey reports that project children made significant gains in IQ by the end of the project, reducing the IQ differences between the project group and the comparison group. These gains were sustained when children were tested after their first two years in primary school. Athey suggests that gains in IQ were probably due to the three main aspects of the programme, parents, professionals and a clearly articulated pedagogical approach.

If Athey's work is to be of value to professional educators and the children with whom they work, ways need to be found for incorporating Athey's 'three *ps*', parents, professionals and pedagogy, into practice.

Group meetings

Many nurseries and schools hold meetings for parents to explain what happens in the establishment, the philosophy and ethos of the school, to introduce parents to facilities available such as the toy library, book library, and so on. Some nursery schools have held successful 'workshop' evenings for parents where activities are set out for parents to try and where staff can explain the educational purposes behind the provision they make for the children. Early childhood educators are now working hard to share their knowledge with parents, to explain why they do what they do. Such meetings for parents have a valuable place in developing a partnership and enhancing understanding.

There have been some exciting developments in the area of sharing ideas about schemas with parents. Usually discussion about schemas begins with a teacher or nursery nurse mentioning something to one parent and then the interest grows. In my experience of working with parents I have been privileged to work with staff responsible for nursery schools and classes and reception classes, and to talk with small groups of parents about children's schemas and their children's patterns of development.

Group meetings can begin by viewing slides of children doing familiar activities: using the climbing frame, hiding in a tent, operating the water wheel, filling containers with sand, filling the washing machine, lining up vehicles in a 'traffic jam'. Parents, of course, immediately recognise these things as familiar, and sometimes talk about other similar activities which children do at home: hiding under the bed clothes, making dens behind the sofa, investigating locks and keys, fascination with holes. From this kind of discussion, the familiar and immediately recognisable, the idea of pattern and of schemas can be introduced. Commonly, parents reflect on the patterning behaviour of their own children and make comments similar to those made by this group of parents:

> So that's why she likes to wrap the knives and forks up in a serviette!
>
> Now I realise that he's not doing it to spite me but he just needs to collect things in little bags!
>
> Perhaps that's the reason that his pockets are always filled with stones!
>
> I thought she was being naughty when she kept tying legs of chairs together, now I think perhaps she's doing a 'connecting' schema!

These remarks are typical of the things parents say once they have an insight into their children's patterns of thinking. Educators need to move on from there and explain to parents how they use this knowledge of schemas to plan and provide for learning. The value of experience can also be discussed with parents, presenting the idea of 'food for thought' by giving children different shared experiences. Children whose parents take them to different and interesting places at weekends are better placed to extend their ideas than children who only ever spend their time in the house or in the back garden. But all parents should have the opportunity to know about ways to support their children's ideas and extend their experiences. Parents who cannot afford expensive outings can still involve their children in a range of experiences by using the local shop, the nearby playground, local allotments, a garage, talking about roadworks or happenings at a nearby building site. Schools, nurseries and other provision which provides quality of educational experience should incorporate such experiences into their provision, and can involve parents in such planned happenings.

Notices, leaflets, booklets

As well as planned times for shared dialogue to talk with parents it is also helpful to have some written information. Notices as part of an exhibition of children's work can, alongside children's drawings and photographs of them in action, give parents and other visitors insights into the value of what is happening. This is most useful when the drawings do not resemble what children say about them and when parents sometimes see an apparent 'chaos' of children playing and working when they arrive to take children home. Information presented in this way can help to communicate the idea that though learning looks (and is) messy, there is valuable and important work going on.

The following examples illustrate ways in which the main points of an exhibition of children's work can be explained. The first notice appeared in the centre of pinboard which displayed photographs of children mixing paint and painting large sheets of paper. Some photographs showed two children building up 'patchwork' paintings in a wonderful array of colours. These paintings were finally covered in a layer of thick brown paint that obscured the pattern and colour completely. One child then folded her painting into a small square. The two paintings, one folded, were displayed with the photographs and the notice to parents read:

> These children have been interested in shapes that they can fit together. They fitted together patches of colour and then covered them with one colour. They are 'enclosing' space, and shape and putting different things inside things. They are learning about space, size, colour and pattern. We thought you would like to see the photographs as well as the final products to see the work that went into it!

Another example of this kind of information sharing was on an exhibition of children's drawings and paintings. The work consisted of children's representations of vertical actions and objects. There was a drawing of a ladder against a wall and the child's comment, 'I helped to fix the broken window'. Another painting showed an aeroplane and something dropping out of the bottom. The child had explained, 'We went to the air show. The lady jumped out and landed on the field, she was OK but there was an ambulance there in case'. The notice on this display read:

> Some of the children are interested in things which go up and down. They have painted pictures and made drawings which show 'up and down' things. They have learned a lot from watching things they have seen and can draw them and talk about them. Some people call the work children do about 'up and down' part of

a Vertical Schema, this means that children's ideas seem to fit with a pattern of things that move vertically. Nursery staff will tell you more if you are interested.

Several parents found this interesting and asked for more information. They also had other examples of vertical schema to share: 'Paul keeps dropping things out of his bedroom window. I go crazy when he does it, but perhaps it's his schema. I'm not going to let him do it but I'm glad he's not just being naughty.' This parent made an important point. It is one thing to understand and recognise children's schemas and tune in to their patterns of development, but it does not mean that children must be allowed to do things which are dangerous, socially unacceptable or, perhaps, inconvenient at the time. The teacher and parents talked about ways to encourage Paul's fascination with dropping things from a height which satisfied him and that were not a danger to himself, household contents or passers-by!

One parent remarked on the importance of taking children to see different things:

> I usually take her out to keep her occupied and because it's nice to go out together. I don't know why, because it's so obvious, but I never thought of it actually giving her things to think about and things to learn about. I'll notice what she does more now when we go to different places.

It is useful to have literature available in the form of brief leaflets or short booklets for parents who want to read about schemas and children's patterns of learning. Staff at the Pen Green Centre for Under Fives and their Families wrote a short 'Schema Booklet' for parents that talks about the staff's observations of children's schemas, explains what schemas are and gives examples of different schemas and the characteristic things which children interested in a particular schema might do. The booklet ends by offering to loan interested parents more booklets about schemas and the suggestion that the best ways for parents to find out more is to observe their own children.

1–1 dialogue

As well as sharing information in group meetings and in a written form there needs to be time when parents and their children's professional educators can talk together. This is often easier said than done in the busy atmosphere of classroom or other group setting. Those responsible for staffing must be continually reminded that working effectively with young children means working effectively with their parents and that this takes time. There is no substitute for talking about children with parents on an individual basis. This needs to be an ongoing occurrence, where parents can share what has happened at home, educators can share occurrences in the group and together understandings and interpretations can be made.

Athey's project involved time in talking with parents on an individual basis. Often the activities described earlier, meetings, notices, booklets, can be supported by 1–1 dialogue.

Assessment

More and more parents are becoming involved in recording children's development. Examples of children's play and learning at home can add to these records and contribute to assessment procedures discussed in Chapter 10.

Principles of partnership

As centralisation of control over the education of our children increases, the establishment of principles upon which the education of young children is based becomes more important. It is necessary for educators to decide where they stand, and why they do what they do and believe what they believe about young children's learning. Other writers have discussed their principles of early childhood education (Brierley, 1987; Bruce, 1987). There has also been discussion of the principles that should underpin the assessment of children's learning and development (Drummond, Rouse and Pugh, 1992; Drummond and Nutbrown, 1992) and quality of provision (Nutbrown, 1992).

If professional educators are to move forward their work in partnership with parents, they must decide the principles upon which these partnerships are based. This chapter concludes with six principles of partnership which educators can consider as they decide what partnership with parents means for them and their own principles which underpin the work they do with young children and their families.

Six principles of partnership

- parents are the primary carers and educators of their children
- consistency, continuity and progression
- equality of opportunity
- working in the interests of children

- respect
- the 'loving use of power'.

Clarity of meaning is important in the establishment of principles. Each principle needs to be carefully and clearly articulated so that everyone is clear about the meaning and implications of the principles they share.

Principle 1: Parents are the primary carers and educators of their children

Everyone who works with young children, whether in schools or other settings, should acknowledge the primary role of parents as carers and educators of their children. Parents have clear responsibilities for their children's living and learning experiences. There needs to be two-way dialogue, consultation, information and partnership. Parents *are* the first and primary educators of their children, and they entrust their children's minds to nurseries, playgroups and schools for small but crucial moments of their lives. Between the ages of 5 and 16 children attend school for about 15,000 hours, that is about 625 days, less than two years.

Principle 2: Consistency, continuity and progression

The kinds of involvement which educators have with parents should have some consistency. Do parents know whom they can talk to? Are there key people who will always make themselves available to parents? Are there people who have responsibility for developing work with and partnership with parents? Is there consistency of expectations between the school, nursery or group and with parents? Is there a consistent and understood philosophy of partnership with parents?

If initiatives to involve parents are set up, there needs to be consideration of how such developments might be sustained. What kinds of continuity of involvement might there be? What is it realistic to do? How might different projects be sustained over time?

What might be done to ensure some kind of progression and development of parental involvement and partnerships between the home and the group? Does involvement and partnership always remain at the level of valuable Tuesday morning classroom-reading workshop? Does it remain at the level of fundraising for the group? Does it remain at the level of the weekly rota shift at the playgroup? Or does partnership develop from these kinds of things into a climate where parents work with professional educators in many different ways, co-operating, debating, sharing concerns and excitements together in a two-way process?

Principle 3: Equality of opportunity

Is the important role of *all* parents acknowledged? Do *all* parents believe that the workers who spend time with their children want them as parents to be involved? Are black parents, single parents, parents living in extreme poverty, disabled parents, parents who often complain and ask questions, parents of children with special needs, are they all involved in the life and developments within the groups setting as far as they wish to be? Or do educators in group settings select in some way the parents who they feel will be the 'best' fitted for the roles they have defined for them?

Principle 4: Working in the interests of children

Are partnerships with parents developing in the interests of children? Is their learning and development, their self-esteen and their thinking being enhanced because there is a spirit of co-operation between workers and parents? Are the children of mutual concern? Sometimes this may mean that workers and parents need to talk about things which make them feel angry, challenged, vulnerable, accountable and uncomfortable. Sometimes parents and workers must discuss events, incidents and practices which they would perhaps rather leave well alone and they may need to say things which they feel they would be more comfortable leaving unsaid. Parents need to be able to ask why certain practices are adopted and workers must be able to articulate their reasons for doing things.

Principle 5: Respect

Crucially, do workers and parents have a respect for each other? Do they understand and respect their respective roles and skills? Do they value the parts they both play in the lives of young children? Educators in group settings, teachers, nursery nurses, playgroup workers, crèche workers, must respect themselves. They must respect the parents of the children they work with, respecting them in their vital role as an essential and unique person in the lives of their children. Respect for each other is a necessary part of a fertile and lasting partnership. Respect is bound up in each person's feelings about the work they do and the people they meet as a part of their work.

Principle 6: The 'loving use of power'

Educators and parents are very powerful people in the lives of young children. Drummond (1993) discusses teachers' strong feelings about the idea of themselves as 'powerful' people. She noted that the teachers she worked with saw 'power' as overwhelmingly negative and argues that this denial of their own power is disconcerting. Drummond (*ibid.*, p. 173) writes: 'We do have the power to educate, for a better world, the children in our schools; to deny this power is, by extension, to deny our real responsibilities to children.'

It is important that the powerful people in children's lives, parents and professional educators, admit their power and make 'loving use' of it (Smail, 1984). This is their responsibility, though they may often feel 'powerless', to acknowledge that in the eyes of young children they are sometimes 'all powerful'. They can crush some children with a frown or make them feel on top of the world with a smile. The 'loving use of power' is an essential principle of partnership.

If the six principles of partnership discussed here are to be enacted, and if parents' wishes for high-quality education for their youngest children are to be achieved, there is a need for educators who are trained and qualified and whose qualifications have the same credibility and rigour as those who work with older children. In 1993 the Secretary of State for Education proposed changes to the training of teachers who work with young children that included lower entry qualifications and shorter courses. The implication here was that working with young children was a less complex job and therefore less training was needed. This proposal prompted protests from parents, teacher training establishments and teachers. Ironically such a proposal came at a time when there was also the beginnings of discussion about degree qualifications for those working with under 3s.

Some parents were discussing the importance of highly trained and qualified staff. One parent remarked to her daughter's nursery teacher: 'You've got her mind to see to. I need to know that you know what you're doing. I wouldn't let just anyone operate on her brain unless I knew they knew what they were doing. I don't want just anyone with a little bit of information teaching her either.' Work with parents needs to be based on firmly established principles of partnership. If parents and professional educators treat each other with mutual respect, if they acknowledge that they each have different, separate and important skills, if they share the things that are important about children's learning, they can support children's learning and extend their thinking in a fundamental way. Athey's work has demonstrated effective learning where parents and professionals talk together and observe the children and where professionals are prepared to articulate their thinking and share their expertise. It has been argued previously (Nutbrown, Hannon and Weinberger, 1991) that teachers need training opportunities to develop their work with parents in order to promote children's early literacy development. Very few opportunities exist either in the initial training of teachers or through later inservice for teachers to develop their skills, confidence and thinking in the area of work with parents. Any work on parental involvement which did take place in the initial training of teachers has effectively been eroded to make more time to fulfil legislative requirements in teacher education. Whilst the Education Reform Act 1988 was aimed at placing parents in the 'driving seat' of education, what has happened is that parents have become excluded from the curriculum as they have instead been recruited on governing bodies, and fundraising or finance committees.

The National Children's Bureau produced a training resource pack, *Working with Parents* (De'Ath and Pugh, 1986) aimed at helping all who work with young children to explore their feelings, develop their skills and examine implications of working with parents. More training opportunities are needed for early childhood educators to develop their skills in the area of sharing pedagogy with parents.

There is a clear role for parents in their young children's learning and development. There is also a clear role for well trained and qualified educators. The importance of both was considered by Susan Isaacs (1948, p. 72): 'The nursery school teacher no less than the mother must have love and sympathy, natural insight and the patience to learn; but children need more than this in their struggles with the many problems we have glimpsed. They need true scientific understanding as well as mother-wit and mother-love.'

10
THE ROLES AND RESPONSIBILITIES OF EDUCATORS

The purpose of education, what it is and how it is carried out, will continue to provide fuel for discussion and writing. John Holt suggests that the education system is driven by three metaphors of which some educators are aware and others are not. Holt argues that these metaphors largely influence what teachers do. This is his description of the first metaphor which presents education as an assembly line in a bottling or canning factory:

> Down the conveyor belts come rows of empty containers of sundry shapes and sizes. Beside the belts is an array of pouring and squirting devices, controlled by employees of the factory. As the containers go by, these workers squirt various amounts of different substances – reading, spelling, math, history, science – into the containers.
>
> Upstairs, management decides when the containers should be put on the belt, how long they should be left on, what kinds of materials should be poured or squirted into them and at what times, and what should be done about containers whose openings (like pop bottles) seem to be smaller than the others, or seem to have no openings at all.
>
> When I discuss this metaphor with teachers, many laugh and seem to find it absurd. But we need only to read the latest rash of school-improvement proposals to see how dominant this metaphor is. In effect, those official reports all say, we must have so many years of English, so many years of math, so many years of foreign language, so many years of science. In other words, we must squirt English into these containers for four years, math for two or three, and so on. The assumption is that whatever is squirted at the container will go into the container and, once in, will stay in.
>
> (Holt, 1991, p. 148–9)

Pouring in quantities of subject knowledge is not the role of any effective educator. The implication that the learner is a passive and non-participating being in the process is both a misleading notion and an insult to children's capabilities. Children are active learners who need to learn with and through interaction with knowledgeable educators. For children to learn with the support of professional educators rather than inspite of the interferences of adults, educators must be tuned into children's thinking, open to their ideas, and responsive to their ever-active minds. The roles of teachers and other early childhood educators who aspire to such quality in learning processes is complex and demanding. It is difficult to analyse this role without making it seem oversimplified. Inevitably the consideration of the work of educators results in some kind of list. The list which follows is intended as a way of highlighting some of the important skills of those who work effectively to promote the learning of young children. Throughout the discussion of these roles the educator will be referred to as the 'teacher'. This is because the ten roles and responsibilities identified here are clearly those which nursery teachers would identify as part of their work and a recognition of the fact that nursery teachers are the most highly trained and qualified educators who work with young children. Nursery teachers have had a longer time to learn about and reflect on their practice, to understand theory and practice in the education of young children and to develop effective ways of working with young children. This is not to say that other educators with training, experience, expertise and commitment may not also work towards this kind of quality of involvement with young children.

Whilst the different roles given below will be discussed separately it must be remembered that, in the reality of the nursery, many teachers find themselves doing and thinking more than one thing at a time, as the different needs of different children are identified and provided for throughout each session.

Roles and responsibilities of a nursery teacher

For effective learning to take place, teachers need to do the following (adapted from Nutbrown, 1994):

- *Plan* the curriculum and their own role in it thoroughly and appropriately, according to the needs of the children.
- *Organise* the learning environment to give children the time, space, equipment, materials and activities they need to promote their learning.
- *Observe* regularly and frequently to build up a clear picture of individual children, the value of activities and group dynamics.

- *Interact* with children, extending learning opportunities, challenging children to think, to question, to discover, to evaluate. Interaction with other members of the team, other teachers and nursery nurses to discuss planning, observation and other parts of the work.
- *Monitor* all aspects of their role: children; activities; curriculum planning; classroom organisation; parental partnership; current and developing needs.
- *Assess* children's learning, their developmental needs, their need for support, their achievements, their understanding.
- *Record* observations and assessments of children's learning, progress, needs, development, interests.
- *Communicate* with the nursery staff team, parents, children, other educators, other professionals.
- *Act* upon the knowledge and experiences gained in the above processes.
- *Reflect* on all aspects of their work.

The above roles and responsibilities of teachers and other educators who want to work with children to develop their profound capabilities as learners to the full need further thought and examination. Each of these will be considered in turn.

Planning

Teachers need clear but flexible curriculum plans which reflect the agreed and understood pedagogy of the school and nursery team. They also need to develop a clear sense of their own role in the curriculum, which should be thoroughly and appropriately considered according to the learning needs of each child. Planning the curriculum for under 5s means ensuring that the environment is organised for learning to take place in a way which enables children to use what they encounter in interaction with each other and with informed adults. It also means planning challenging curriculum content, using interesting themes and topics which can attract the attention and thought of some children. Topics can run alongside the individual interests and investigations of children. This does not mean that all children *do* 'The topic', rather it means that there exists, alongside a range of workshop opportunities, a mini-theme which provides a focus for thinking and talking. It is through planned themes such as journeys, insides or homes, to name but a few, that teachers can ensure that a range of content is introduced to nourish a number of schemas, and that the different areas of experience discussed in Chapter 8 are also introduced to the curriculum.

As well as planning content, teachers need to discuss and plan their own role and that of the team. They must consider which children they will spend time with, how and when they will introduce new ideas and content, their ways of interacting with children. Some plans can be quite clear, for example after working with Joanne on filling and emptying different containers in the water tray, the teacher decided to develop the work on a larger scale the next day. She planned to provide buckets and other large containers and a hose pipe connected to an outside tap for Joanne to continue her experiences and problem-solving in this medium. The outside, large-scale experience helped Joanne to extend her knowledge and thinking around these concepts. This kind of planning is more immediate than the pre-planned topics or themes and means that teachers need to be flexible in their thinking and able to draw on resources as needed.

Teachers also need a way of deciding how to proceed when planning for individual children. Stenhouse (1975) discusses the development of 'principles of procedure' as a way of supporting and enabling curriculum. Teachers might use the following principles of procedure to plan their own roles in the curriculum as it unfolds during their work:

1. *Select content*, developing from and drawing on:

- learning through play
- learning based on experiences
- children's schemas
- provision of a learning environment which encourages children's holistic development.

2. *Develop strategies for teaching*, including:

- observing, facilitating, communicating, comforting, assessing
- extending interests of individual children
- validating children's action, efforts and ideas
- providing experiences, equipment and materials as resources for learning.

3. *Identify strengths and areas of development where children need further support or experience*. Obtain a 'picture' of learning activities and needs by:

- observing children
- discussing with other staff

- discussing with parents
- keeping notes to identify developmental progress
- looking at children's work
- listening to what children say.

Organisation

To give children the time, space, equipment, materials and activities they need to promote their learning, the learning environment needs to be organised. A way of doing this to provide variety and flexibility has been suggested in Chapter 8. A number of things need to be organised.

Time

What are the routines of the session? Are there lengthy periods of time when children and adults can work together without the interruptions of other timetabled experiences, such as a live television programme or the need to go to assembly? Uninterrupted and focused time is a necessary ingredient for learning.

Space

Children need space to move, both themselves and objects, as they learn about arranging space and develop their play and ideas. Figure 8.1 shows one way in which space can be organised to include a range of workshop areas where children and adults can work with the equipment they need to develop the task they have in hand.

Equipment and materials

Goldschmied's (1989; 1991) work on infants and toddler play emphasises the importance of providing very young children with objects that they can use all their senses to explore and learn about. Goldschmied stresses the place of objects made from natural materials, rather than plastic toys, in children's early discovery. Good organisation should mean that necessary equipment and materials are stored accessibly and things children and adults need are close to hand. If children are to pursue different problems and ideas, and if adults are to be able to suggest new possibilities and offer additional challenges, there needs to be a wide range of equipment and materials. If workshop areas are created for 3–5-year-olds to use, the following list of equipment and materials can be included in an environment which is organised for learning, one which maximises opportunities and challenges.

Workshop areas	Equipment and materials
Woodwork	Wood: different types, sizes and shapes. Tools: 2 large claw hammers, 2 small hammers, 1 vice, 1 saw, 2 screwdrivers, 1 brace and bit, 1 pair of pliers, nails and screws of different sizes.
Water	Sponges, filters, U-bend, balls with and without holes, straws, short lengths of tubing in different widths, watering can, graded clear funnels, jugs, beakers and cups, long lengths of piping, water pumps, stones, corks, boats, small model animals and people.
Painting	Brushes: household, fine, thin, medium, thick, stencil, toothbrushes, nail brushes. Glue spreaders, sponges, cotton bobbins, cotton buds, string, corks, paint rollers, paint pads, pipe cleaners, wheels, 3D shapes. Paper: selection of paper and card in different thicknesses, various shapes, sizes, textures and colours.
Sand	Sand drill, sand wheel, scoops, large, medium and small sieves, colander, buckets, spades, containers in various sizes, small vehicles, animals and figures.
Clay	Pastry cutters, rolling pins, clay-modelling tools, spoons, knives, forks, scrapers, pipe cleaners, sticks, twigs, straws.
Markmaking	Paper: plain, lined, squared, coloured, shaped, card. Erasers, pencil sharpeners, hole punch, rulers, scissors. Variety of pencils, felt-tip pens, wax crayons, pencil crayons, ball-point pens, chalk, charcoal.
Fastening and modelling	A wide variety waste materials, natural and made such as: sequins, seeds, shiny paper, lace, gravel, cottons, fabric pieces, confetti, wool. Card and paper for 2D and boxes for 3D work. Fastenings: stapler, hole punch and threads, paper clips, split pins, sticky tape, glue.

Music and sound	A wide range of musical instruments and other objects for making different sounds and rhythms.
	Tape recorder and player and variety of blank tapes for making recordings and musical and sound tapes for children to listen to.
Building	A variety of hollow and solid 3D wooden blocks.
	Range of commercial construction kits.
	Space for creative and sustained use.
Books	A wide range of good-quality anti-discriminatory books.
	Picture, story and factual books.
	Story tapes and tapes for recording own stories.

Observation

Regular and frequent observation is necessary if teachers are to build up a clear picture of individual children, the value of activities and group dynamics. Drummond and Nutbrown (1992, p. 93) discuss issues related to the observing and assessing of young children. They ask the why, what, how and who questions of observation and assessment. They suggest that educators will observe and try to understand everything that children do: 'Watching children at their work of interacting with their environment will tell educators some of what they need to know about children's needs and development.'

Throughout this book, observations of children working on their learning have been included to illustrate their capabilities as thinkers and the importance of identifying children's schemas as a way of supporting their learning more precisely. Those who work with young children must see their skills of observation not just to identify end products of learning but to identify children's pathways of learning as well. Close and systematic observation can identify the threads of children's thinking, their patterns of development and interest. More complete pictures of children's knowing are only obtained when educators are concerned for children as a whole.

Observation such as this needs to be planned for and can be carried out more successfully when the adults who work with young children are prepared to watch with open eyes and listen with open ears. Educators must think about what they see and hear children doing and saying.

They must create meaning from their observations and be prepared to use what they learn from these processes in their interactions with children. They must trust children to show them what they are learning and they must trust themselves that time spent in observing children is not an easy option but an essential ingredient to effective teaching and learning partnerships.

Interaction

To extend learning opportunities, to challenge children to think, to question, to discover and to evaluate their learning, teachers must work interactively in partnership with children. Adults must be involved with children if they are to understand and make sense of children's processes of learning and doing as well as be able to assess the end products of their work. It is one thing to look at a model a child has made and make some judgement about what has been learned. It is quite another to be involved with a child as she makes her model, building and rebuilding, appraising and adjusting, planning, selecting materials, making decisions, as the child encounters and solves problems throughout the process. Interaction with children illuminates their thinking in a way which the appraisal of the finished product of the process never can.

Teachers also need to be part of children's activities so that they can provide feedback on what is happening (Athey, 1990; Gura *et al.*, 1992). For children to learn effectively their teachers must 'feed back' to them in order that they can be a 'feed forward' in learning. The process of feeding back to feed forward is an essential function of interaction between teachers and children.

Teachers need knowledge. They need to have a grasp of the concepts and processes which arise from different areas of learning and experience. They must be able to extend children's ideas in different areas of experience and engage children in ways of finding out more which foster continuity and progression in their learning. The Froebel Blockplay Project emphasised the importance of teacher knowledge: 'We have learnt how important it is for adults to have a good grasp of the mathematics involved, otherwise many opportunities for helping children to move forward in their thinking are lost' (Gura *et al.*, 1992, p. 91).

The importance of interaction rather than interference was discussed in Chapter 8. Teachers need to use their knowledge of how children learn, their observations of children, their respect for children as capable learners, to help them to 'tune' their interactions to children's actions. It is not a case of teachers playing the tune but of children and their educators composing the music and dancing to it responsively and together.

Monitoring

Teachers should maintain a clear view of all aspects of their work. They need to monitor their work with children, the kinds of activities and experiences they provide; their ways of helping children to use their opportunities for learning; their classroom organisation; their curriculum planning; their links with parents; the work of other members of the team; and the development of partnerships. Current and developing needs both of individual children, the group, themselves and colleagues also need to be monitored in some way. Nursery teachers are also managers, they manage situations related to children's learning and they also manage the team of nursery staff. Monitoring the needs and effectiveness of nursery staff is another task which contributes to the creating of effective learning opportunities for children. This does not mean more burdensome paperwork, it rather means teachers maintaining an overview of the situation as a whole, and keeping a clear perspective on what they do. This is part of the professionalism of teachers who, more and more, are being called to account for their time and their actions. Having a clear view of different aspects of their complex role puts teachers in a position to identify what is needed next, either for their own development or to support particular aspects of their work. Self-monitoring and self-appraisal is quite different from being assessed by an outsider or a colleague. This notion of self-monitoring is aligned to Stenhouse's (1975, p. 143) idea of the teacher as a researcher. Stenhouse suggested, 'It is not enough that teachers work should be studied: they need to study it themselves'.

Assessment

Part of a teacher's role is to assess children's learning, their developmental needs, their need for support, their achievements and their understanding. Through their work with children teachers make judgements about children's ideas and how they might be developed. Teachers make judgements about what children know, their motivation, their abilities and their thinking. Such judgements are based upon what they see children do and hear children say and the work they produce. This kind of assessment begins with careful observation. Observation can help teachers to identify children's schemas and nourish them with worthwhile curriculum content.

Assessment should be an ongoing and dynamic process which illuminates children's thinking and their capabilities. To make effective and reliable assessments teachers need to be open to what children are saying and doing, receptive to their ideas and respectful of their learning agendas. Teachers will always have some things which they want to know about all children, but they will find out most about children as individual learners if they develop a way of looking at children with open eyes rather than eyes which are blinkered because only certain aspects of children's abilities are of interest. This point was made by Christian Schiller (1979, p. 3) who wrote:

> To assess attainment it must be observed in the round. Such observation is not easy. The observer has not only to use keenly his eyes and ears, but to know where to direct them; he has not only to see and hear the shape of an event but to perceive its quality.

Recording

Observations and assessments of children's learning, progress, needs, development and interests should be recorded. Formats for written records of children's achievements have proliferated in recent years. Many suggest that learning and progress is recorded in terms of areas of experience or indeed in terms of National Curriculum subjects. This can have the effect of fragmenting a learning experience or an observation of children playing into several unconnected parts. For example children playing in a shop may well be involved in sorting and weighing goods (mathematics), they may be writing lists and cheques (literacy), they may be giving directions of where to deliver a package of groceries (geography) and through it all they are speaking and listening (oracy). Whilst it can be acknowledged that play is a vehicle for learning, play is also the intrinsic part of children's activity. To discard any reference to a play sequence as a whole and to pick out elements which occurred as part of the process is to devalue children's main activity in favour of the things with adults have decided are more important. It is important that records of children's learning should also include observations of them playing, alone and with others. In so doing assessment is recorded, as Schiller puts it, 'in the round' and the context and motivation for learning is not lost.

NAME *Danila, Age Four*

OBSERVATION	ANALYSIS OF LEARNING	ACTION	DATE & INITIALS
Following a visit to some flats, D made a construction of cardboard boxes, piling one on top of another using a chair to reach.	Motor and symbolic representation of vertical schema. Work on 'higher' and 'lower'. Introducing vocabulary using appropriate material.	Move into counting boxes. Stabilising structure. More experience of vertical e.g. lifts and escalators.	CN 6.9.91
D. on the climbing frame. Sliding down the slide. She said 'Going down' 'Going up'. Rolling cars and dolls down the slope.	Experimenting with forces and gravity.	More experiences of slopes and rolling experiences. Timing how long it takes to go down.	CN 14.9.91
D. drew a picture. Lots of //// lines. 'This is water falling out of the sky, 'It comes down and goes in the puddles,' D. said.	Understanding early scientific notions of rain and the environment.	Maybe provide different kinds of pouring tools. Showerhead, watering can to encourage observation. Feed in appropriate language.	CN 17.9.91
D's mum reported that D. is going to the top of the stairs and watching a ball bounce to the bottom. She's concerned.	Experiencing gravity and forces again.	Need to provide acceptable safe experiences for observing, bouncing and dropping objects.	CN 25.9.91

Figure 10.1   Observation record sheet

Ways of recording children's learning have been explored by the National Children's Bureau in a set of training materials *Making Assessment Work* (Drummond, Rouse and Pugh, 1992). The example in Figure 10.1 has been completed for a 4-year-old who seems to have a predominant interest in a vertical schema.

This format[1] shows one way of making observations and assessments of children's learning and progress. It begins with observations of a child which illuminates the child's needs and interests. The child's key worker notes the observation, thoughts about the learning which resulted and, importantly, what is to happen next, that is the *action* the educator will take. Dates of the recording and initials of the worker are useful for checking and reflecting at a later date. Sheets such as these can also be contributed to by parents. Some parents are happy to offer observations and discuss the resulting learning and consequent actions with teachers who spend time in such dialogues. Records such as these can become part of a child's accumulating record. Clear records of what children can do need to be developed in a form which children's future teachers can use effectively and build on as children's learning develops. Using schemas as a focus for observations ensures that children's *actions* as well as their learning are recorded. This means that 'what happened' can be noted, learning identified and further curriculum opportunities and experiences can be planned to match children's actions and their understanding.

Communication

Teachers must be good communicators. They must listen well to children, and in their work with young children they must be able to communicate their knowledge as well as their interest in order to extend children's activities and their subsequent learning. Teachers must listen well to children's parents, and to colleagues and other workers with whom they have professional contact. They must also be able to say what they think, and justify their work. They must be able to explain their meaning. Teachers in the 1990s are being required to justify their work in a language which everyone understands. Traditionally, those who have worked with young children have used words such as 'opportunity', 'facilitate' and 'exploration' to describe their work. These words have been hijacked and called into question, along with the practices of early education they describe. The true meaning of the language of early education has been distorted and, simultaneously, a notion has been introduced that 'progressive' education, something which one would suppose everyone would want, is now some kind of trendy and ineffective mischief. Good teaching must be described with words like play, exploration, challenge and opportunity. What must happen now is that teachers must say exactly what they mean when they use such words. They must explain what being a facilitator, an enabler, a supporter of learning really entails. They must do this to counteract misinterpretation and misrepresentation of the terminology which best describes their complex work and the work of children. Again Schiller's

(1979, pp. 63–4) words are apposite:

> If we think of learning as part of growth, and if we are concerned with the quality of growth and fulfilment of growth, we must define our purpose in terms which relate to these ideas and use words which relate to our thoughts. Our thoughts are always imprisoned within the words we use to express them, and we cannot solve a problem if we use the wrong language. We have need to use the language not of building and mechanics but of biology – roots, nourishment, growth – since we are concerned not with machines but with living, growing beings. If we think in terms of how children grow roots, into what they grow roots, and how these roots can best be nourished, we must use words which express such ideas.

Teachers must reclaim and use with pride the language of early education and do all in their power to ensure that their audiences understand this language as well. Teachers also need to be conversant with the new terms which are being introduced and imposed in education so that, as well as continuing to use their own language of educating to communicate together, they are able to understand and be understood by others who do not fully understand or appreciate the terminology of early childhood education. There must be more debate about the meaning of terms such as 'child centred', and teachers must also be able to use the language which others outside the profession use to make themselves understood in the wider context.

Action

The roles discussed so far carry with them the responsibility of action. Teachers must be prepared to do something about what they see, and hear. They must act upon the information they gain from their work with children, their dialogues with parents and their own experiences. Taking action is a fundamental part of teachers' work as they build on children's capabilities, obtain the resources they need, read about current research and developing practice, make changes to support developments.

Reflection

As well as ensuring that they act appropriately upon what they see and hear, teachers must take some time to reflect. They must reflect on all aspects of their work including what children, parents and colleagues say. They must reflect on what they have done and their working methods. This reflection leads to an evaluation of their work, a critical but realistic appraisal of the process and outcomes of teaching. Teachers ask themselves questions such as 'Why did I do that?' 'What made me say that?' 'How shall I solve this?' 'Who can I ask about that?'

Children need teachers who engage in professional and sensitive reflection, who think about their work and who respond to new ideas and new experiences drawn from research, attending conferences and seminars. Children need teachers who develop themselves as a part of their responsibility as a teacher.

This chapter has discussed aspects of the complex role of teachers of young children. If children's minds are to be nourished and their amazing ability to think and learn is to be acknowledged and respected, educators working with children under 5 in whatever setting must fulfil these different and demanding roles.

Children's minds are valuable and precious. Young children must receive the respect and recognition they deserve as capable thinkers and learners. Part of this respect should be demonstrated by ensuring that the adults who work with young children are well trained, well qualified, experienced to manage the diversity of the task and respected members of a professional group who receive due reward and recognition for their work.

In this chapter I have discussed roles and responsibilities of educators with particular reference to teachers in nursery schools and classes. Many children under 5 attend other settings which are staffed with educators who do not have graduate status or the benefit of lengthy professional training. Children in these settings are entitled to a high level of quality experience, they are entitled to work with adults who are able to recognise and fulfil the important roles and responsibilities of educators. To aspire to this kind of quality in a diversity of provision for children, nursery schools and classes, day nurseries, playgroups, crèches and other group settings, there must be training opportunities for all workers to explore and discuss in depth the competencies and potential of all young children. There must be more networking of provision for people working with young children in different settings to meet together and discuss their observations of children's learning. Well educated educators is a right of young children which should be realised as we approach the millennium.

Note

1. This format was first published in *Making Assessment Work* (Drummond, Rouse and Pugh, 1992) and is reproduced here with permission.

REFERENCES

Ahlberg, J. and Ahlberg, A. (1982) *Funny Bones*, Picture Lions, London.

Ahlberg, J. and Ahlberg, A. (1986) *The Jolly Postman or Other People's Letters*, Heinemann, London.

Alborough, J. (1986) *Willoughby Wallaby*, Walker Books, London.

Alborough, J. (1989) *Cupboard Bear*, Walker Books, London.

Allen, P. (1989) *Who Sank the Boat?*, Picture Puffin, Harmondsworth.

Anderson, H. C. (1992) 'The Emperor's New Clothes', in Ash, N. and Higton, B. (eds.) *Fairy Tales from Hans Anderson – A Classic Illustrated Edition*, Pavilion Books, London.

Armstrong, M. (1990) 'Another way of looking', *Forum*, Vol. 33, no. 1, pp. 12–16.

Arnold, C. (1990) 'Children who play together have similar schemas.' Unpublished project report submitted as part of the Certificate in Post-Qualifying Studies validated by the National Nursery Examining Board.

Athey, C. (1981) 'Parental involvement in nursery education', *Early Child Development and Care*, Vol. 7, no. 4, pp. 353–67.

Athey, C. (1986) Unpublished course material for INSET, Sheffield LEA 26–28 February.

Athey, C. (1990) *Extending Thought in Young Children: A Parent-Teacher Partnership*, Paul Chapman Publishing, London.

Barnsley LEA (1990) *Developing Literacy Through Structured Play*, Barnsley LEA, Barnsley.

Bayley, N. and Mayne, W. (1981) *The Patchwork Cat*, Jonathan Cape, London.

Beck, I. (1989) *The Teddy Bear Robber*, Doubleday, Toronto.

Bennett, D. (1990) *Happily to School, Topic Issue 3*, spring, 1990.

Bennett, J. (1991) *Learning to Read with Picture Books*, The Thimble Press, London.

Bissex, G. L. (1980) *GYNS AT WRK – a Child Learns to Write and Read*, Harvard University Press, Cambridge, Mass.

Brierley, J. (1987) *Give me a Child until he is Seven: Brain Studies and Early Childhood Education*, Falmer Press, London.

Briggs, R. (1980) *The Snowman*, Puffin, Harmondsworth.

Brown, R. (1973) *A First Language*, Allen & Unwin, London.

Brown, R. (1983) *A Dark, Dark Tale*, Scholastic Publications, London.

Bruce, T. (1987) *Early Childhood Education*, Hodder & Stoughton, London.

Bruce, T. (1991) *Time to Play in Early Childhood Education*, Hodder & Stoughton, London.

Bruce, T. (1992) 'Children, adults and blockplay', in Gura, P. (ed.) *Exploring Learning – Young Children and Blockplay*, Paul Chapman Publishing, London.

Bruner, J. (1977) *The Process of Education*, Harvard University Press, Cambridge, Mass.

Burningham, J. (1963) *Borka – the Adventures of a Goose with no Feathers*, Jonathan Cape, London.

Burningham, J. (1978) *Mr Gumpy's Outing*, Puffin, Harmondsworth.

Burningham, J. (1980) *The Shopping Basket*, Jonathan Cape, London.

Burningham, J. (1991) *Oi! Get Off Our Train*, Red Fox, London.

Butterworth, N. (1991) *One Snowy Night*, Picture Lions, London.

Campbell, R. (1984) *Dear Zoo*, Puffin, Harmondsworth.

Campbell, R. (1988) *My Presents*, Campbell Blackie Books, London.

Cartwright, R. and Kinmouth, P. (1979) *Mr Potter's Pigeon*, Hutchinson Junior Books, London.

Catley, A. (1989) *Jack's Basket*, Beaver Books, London.

Chapman, A. J. and Foot, H. C. (eds.) (1976) *It's a Funny Thing Humour*, Pergamon Press, Oxford.

Clarke, M. and Voake, C. (1990) *The Best of Aesop's Fables*, Walker Books, London.

Cox, K. and Hughes, P. (1990) *Early Years History: An Approach Through Story*, Liverpool Institute of Higher Education, Liverpool.

Creary, C., Storr, T., Tait, M. and Claxton, P. (1991) *Science from Stories*, Northamptonshire Science Resources, Northamptonshire County Council, Northampton.

Curtis, A. (1986) *A Curriculum for the Pre-School Child: Learning to Learn*, NFER-Nelson, Windsor.

Dale, P. (1991) *The Elephant Tree*, Walker Books, London.

De'Ath, E. and Pugh, G. (1986) *Working with Parents: A Training Resource Pack*, National Children's Bureau, London.

Department of Education and Science (1967) *Children and their Primary Schools: A Report of the Central Advisory Council for Education (England)*, Volume 1, HMSO, London.

Department of Education and Science (1989a) *Aspects of Primary Education: The Education of Children Under Five*, HMSO, London.

Department of Education and Science (1989b) *Aspects of Primary Education: The Teaching and Learning of Science*, London, HMSO.

Department of Education and Science (1990a) *Starting with Quality: The Report of the Committee of Inquiry into the Quality of Educational Experience Offered to Three- and Four-Year-Olds*, HMSO, London.

Department of Education and Science (1990b) *English in the National Curriculum*, no. 2, HMSO, London.

Design Council (1992) *The Wolf Proof House – Using Stories as Contexts for Design and Technology*, Design Council, London.

Development Education Centre (1991) *Start with a Story – Supporting Young Children's Exploration of Issues*, Development Education Centre, Birmingham.

Dickson, L., Brown, M., and Gibson, O. (1993) *Children Learning Mathematics – a Teacher's Guide to Recent Research*, Cassell, London.

Donaldson, M. (1983) *Children's Minds*, Fontana/Collins, Glasgow.

Dowling, M. (1988) *Education 3 to 5: A Teacher's Handbook*, Paul Chapman Publishing, London.

Drummond, M. J. (1993) *Assessing Children's Learning*, David Fulton Publishers, London.

Drummond, M. J. and Nutbrown, C. (1992) 'Observing and assessing young children', in Pugh, G. (ed.) *Contemporary Issues in the Early Years: Working Collaboratively for Children*, Paul Chapman Publishing/National Children's Bureau, London.

Drummond, M. J., Rouse, D. and Pugh, G. (1992) *Making Assessment Work: Values and Principles in Assessing Young Children's Learning*, NES Arnold/National Children's Bureau, available from Early Childhood Unit, National Children's Bureau, 8 Wakley Street, London, EC1V 7QE.

Early Years Curriculum Group (1992) *First Things First: Educating Young Children – A Guide for Parents and Governors*, Early Years Curriculum Group, Madeleine Lindley Ltd., 79 The Acorn Centre, Oldham OL1 3NE.

Edwards, H. and Niland, D. (1982) *There's a Hippopotamus on our Roof Eating Cake*, Hodder & Stoughton, London.

Emblen, V. and Schmitz, H. (1991) *Learning Through Story*, Scholastic Publications, Leamington Spa.

Fair, S. (1989) *Barney's Beanstalk*, Macdonald, London.

Flack, M. and Weise, K. (1991) *The Story about Ping*, Random Century, London.

Fontana, D. (1984) *The Education of the Young Child* (second edition), Blackwell, London.

Foreman, M. (1989) *Ben's Baby*, Beaver Books, London.

Gardner, H. (1980) *Artful Scribbles – The Significance of Children's Drawings*, Jill Norman, London.

Gentle, K. (1985) *Children and Art Teaching*, Croom Helm, Beckenham.

Goldschmied, E. (1989) 'Playing and learning in the first year of life', in Williams, V. (ed.) *Babies in Daycare: An Examination of the Issues*, Daycare Trust, London.

Goldschmied, E. (1991) 'What to do with the under twos, heuristic play – infants learning', in Rouse, D. (ed.) (1990) *Babies and Toddlers: Carers and Educators – Quality for the Under Threes*, National Children's Bureau, London.

Griffiths, A. and Edmonds, M. (1986) *Report on the Calderdale Pre-School Parent Book Project*, Schools' Psychological Service, Calderdale Education Department, Halifax.

Gura, P. (ed.) (1992) *Exploring Learning – Young Children and Block-play*, Paul Chapman Publishing, London.
Hannon, P., Weinberger, J. and Nutbrown, C. (1991) 'A study of work with parents to promote early literacy development', *Research Papers in Education*, Vol. 6, no. 2, pp. 77–97.
Hardwick, L. and Moore, B. (1991) *Topics with Targets*, Harmor Books, Bicester.
Hill, E. (1980) *Where's Spot?*, Heinemann, London.
Hissey, J. (1992) *Jolly Snow*, Random Century, London.
Hodgkin, R. A. (1985) *Playing and Exploring, Education through the Discovery of Order*, Methuen, London.
Holt, J. (1991) *Learning All the Time*, Education Now Publishing Co-operative, Ticknall, Derbyshire, Lighthouse Books, Liss, Hants.
House of Commons (1988) *Educational Provision for the Under Fives*, Education, Science and Arts Committee (first report), HMSO, London.
Hughes, S. (1982) *Alfie Gets in First*, Picture Lions, London.
Hughes, S. (1991) *Up and Up*, Red Fox, London.
Hutchins, P. (1969) *Rosie's Walk*, The Bodley Head, London.
Hutchins, P. (1972) *Titch*, The Bodley Head, London.
Inkpen, M. (1991) *The Blue Balloon*, Picture Knight, London.
Isaacs, S. (1948) *Childhood and After*, Routledge & Kegan Paul, London.
Junior Achievement (1991) *Quality Education Begins with Parents*, Junior Achievement of Central Arizona, Phoenix, Ariz.
Lear, E. and Cooper, H. (1991) *The Owl and the Pussycat*, Hamish Hamilton, London.
Lloyd, D. and Dale, P. (1986) *The Stop Watch*, Walker Books, London.
Lloyd, D. and Rees, M. (1991) *The Ball*, Walker Books, London.
Lujan, M. E., Stolworthy, D. L. and Wooden, S. L. (1986) *A Parent Training Early Intervention Programme in Preschool Literacy*, ERIC (Educational Resources Information Centre), descriptive report, ED 270 988.
Maris, R. (1990) *Hold Tight, Bear!*, Walker Books, London.
Mark, J. and Voake, C. (1986) *Fur*, Walker Books, London.
Mason, L. (1989) *A Book of Boxes*, Orchard Books, London.
Matthews, G. (1984) 'Learning and teaching mathematical skills', in Fontana, D. (ed.) (1984) *The Education of the Young Child* (second edition), Blackwell, London.
McKee, D. (1989) *Elmer*, Andersen Press, London.
Meek, M. (1988) *How Texts Teach what Readers Learn*, The Thimble Press, Stroud.
Mort, L. and Morris, J. (1991) *Starting with Rhyme*, Scholastic Publications, Leamington Spa.
Murphy, J. (1982) *On the Way Home*, Pan Macmillan Children's Books, London.
National Writing Project (1989) *Becoming a Writer*, Nelson, Walton-on-Thames.

Nicholls, R. (ed.) with Sedgewick, J., Duncan, J., Curwin, L. and McDougall, B. (1986) *Rumpus Schema Extra: Teachers in Education*, Cleveland LEA, Cleveland.

Nister, E. (1981) *The Magic Window*, Harper Collins, Glasgow.

Nutbrown, C. (1992) 'Principles of quality: using the Children Act to promote quality provision for young children', in David, T. (ed.) *The Children Act 1989: The First Six Months*, OMEP briefing paper, available from OMEP UK Publications, 'Midgecke', 753 Bury Rd., Rochdale, Lancs, OL11 4BB.

Nutbrown, C. (1994) 'Young children in educational establishments', in David, T. (ed.) *Working Together for Young Children*, Routledge, London.

Nutbrown, C., Hannon, P. and Weinberger, J. (1991) 'Training teachers to work with parents to promote early literacy development', *International Journal of Early Childhood*, Vol. 23, no. 2, pp. 1–10.

Nutbrown, C. and Hirst, K. (eds.) (1993) *Using Stories to Stimulate Scientific and Technological Learning and Development with Children under Five*, City of Sheffield LEA, available from Early Childhood Education Centre, Stand House School, Queen Mary Road, Sheffield S2 1HX.

Nutbrown, C. and Swift, G. (eds.) (1993) *The Learning and Development of 3–5 Year Olds, Schema Observations* (second edition) City of Sheffield Education Department, available from Early Childhood Education Centre, Stand House School, Queen Mary Road, Sheffield S2 1HX.

Oldham LEA (1992) *Writing for All*, Oldham LEA, Oldham.

Paley, V. G. (1981) *Wally's Stories: Conversations in the Kindergarten*, Harvard University Press, Cambridge, Mass.

Payton, S. (1984) *Developing an Awareness of Print: A Young Child's First Steps Towards Literacy*, *Educational Review*, no. 2, Birmingham University.

Pearce, P. (1958) *Tom's Midnight Garden*, Oxford University Press.

Pearce, P. (1987) *The Tooth Ball*, Picture Puffins, Harmondsworth.

Pen Green Centre for Under Fives and their Families (no date) *A Schema Booklet for Parents*, Pen Green Centre, Corby.

Piaget, J. (1953) *The Origin of Intelligence in the Child*, Routledge & Kegan Paul, London.

Piaget, J. (1972) 'Development and learning', in Stendler-Lavatelli, C. and Stendler, F. (eds.) *Readings in Child Behavior and Development* (third edition), Harcourt Brace Janovich, New York.

Piaget, J. and Inhelder, B. (1956) *The Child's Conception of Space*, Routledge & Kegan Paul, London.

Pienkowski, J. (1980) *Dinner Time*, Gallery Five, London.

Pienkowski, J. (1986) *Fancy That!*, Orchard Books, London.

Plaskow, D. (ed.) (1967) *The Crucial Years*, Society for Education through Art, London.

Prater, J. (1987) *The Gift*, Puffin, Harmondsworth.

Preschool Playgroups Association (1991) *What Children Learn in Playgroup: A Guide to the Curriculum*, Preschool Playgroups Association, London.

Roffey, M. (1982) *Home Sweet Home*, Piper, London.

Rosen, M. and Oxenbury, H. (1989) *We're Going on a Bear Hunt*, Walker Books, London.

Rouse, D. (ed.) (1990) *Babies and Toddlers: Carers and Educators – Quality for the Under Threes*, National Children's Bureau, London.

Rouse, D. and Griffin, S. (1992) 'Quality for the under threes', in Pugh, G. (ed.) *Contemporary Issues in the Early Years: Working Collaboratively for Children*, Paul Chapman Publishing/National Children's Bureau, London.

Samuels, V. (1991) *Boxed In*, Red Fox, London.

Schickedanz, J. (1990) *Adam's Righting Revolutions – One Child's Literacy Development from Infancy through Grade One*, Heinemann, Portsmouth, NH.

Schiller, C. (1979) *Christian Schiller in his Own Words*, National Association for Primary Education/A & C Black, London.

Sendak, M. (1967) *Where the Wild Things Are*, The Bodley Head, London.

Shapur, F. (1991) *The Rainbow Balloon*, Simon & Schuster, London.

Sheffield Early Years Literacy Association (1990) *Reading Writing and Classroom Reality*, Sheffield Early Years Literacy Association, Sheffield.

Sheffield LEA (1988) *Dynamic Vertical Schema: Thoughts, Observations, Resources*, City of Sheffield Education Department, available from Early Childhood Education Centre, Stand House School, Queen Mary Road, Sheffield S2 1HX.

Sheffield LEA (1989) *Enveloping and Containing Schema, Thoughts, Observations, Resources*, City of Sheffield Education Department, available from Early Childhood Education Centre, Stand House School, Queen Mary Road, Sheffield S2 1HX.

Sheldon, D. and Smith, W. (1991) *A Witch Got on at Paddington Station*, Red Fox, London.

Sieveking, A. and Lincoln, F. (1989) *What's Inside?*, Frances Lincoln, London.

Smail, D. (1984) *Taking Care: An Alternative to Therapy*, Dent, London.

Smith, T. (1980) *Parents and Preschool: Oxford Preschool Research Project*, Grant McIntyre, London.

Stendler-Lavatelli, C. and Stendler, F. (1972) *Readings in Child Behavior and Development* (third edition) Harcourt Brace Janovich, New York.

Stenhouse, L. (1975) *An Introduction to Curriculum Research and Development*, Heinemann, London.

Tait, M. and Roberts, R. (1974) *Play, Language and Experience*, OMEP, London.

Tinbergen, N. (1976) *The Importance of Being Playful*, British Association for Early Childhood Education, London.

Vygotsky, L. S. (1978) *Mind in Society*, Harvard University Press, Cambridge, Mass.

Waterland, L. (1985) *Read with Me – An Apprenticeship Approach to Reading*, The Thimble Press, London.

Waterland, L. (1992) 'Ranging freely: the why and the what of real books', in Styles, M., Bearne, E. and Watson, V. (eds.) *After Alice – Exploring Children's Literature*, Cassell, London.

Watson, V. (1992) 'Irresponsible writers and responsible readers', in Styles, M., Bearne, E. and Watson, V. (eds.) *After Alice – Exploring Children's Literature*, Cassell, London.

Wild, M. and Huxley, D. (1990) *Mr Nick's Knitting*, Picture Knight, London.

Wilhelm, H. (1985) *I'll Always Love You*, Hodder & Stoughton, London.

Williams, M. (1988) *Noah's Ark*, Walker Books, London.

Williams, M. (1990) *Joseph and his Magnificent Coat of Many Colours*, Walker Books, London.

Williams, T. (ed.) (1991) *Stories as Starting Points for Design and Technology*, Design Council, London.

Willis, V. (1991) *The Secret in the Matchbox*, Picture Corgi, London.

Winter, M. and Rouse, J. (1990) 'Fostering intergenerational literacy: The Mossouri Parents as Teachers Programme, *The Reading Teacher*, Vol. 24, no. 2, pp. 382–6.

Wray, D., Bloom, W. and Hall, N. (1989) *Literacy in Action*, Falmer Press, London.

Zelinsky, P. (1990) *The Wheels on the Bus*, Orchard Books, London.

Zion, G. and Bloy Graham, M. (1960) *Harry the Dirty Dog*, The Bodley Head, London.

AUTHOR INDEX

SUBJECT INDEX

A KILLER'S
TOUCH

10650872

A KILLER'S
TOUCH

MICHAEL
BENSON

PINNACLE BOOKS
Kensington Publishing Corp.

http://www.kensingtonbooks.com

PINNACLE BOOKS are published by

Kensington Publishing Corp.
119 West 40th Street
New York, NY 10018

All Kensington Titles, Imprints, and Distributed Lines are available at special quantity discounts for bulk purchases for sales
promotions, premiums, fund-raising, and educational or insti-
tutional use. Special book excerpts or customized printings can
also be created to fit specific needs. For details, write or phone
the office of the Kensington special sales manager: Kensington
Publishing Corp., 119 West 40th Street, New York, NY 10018,
attn: Special Sales Department, Phone: 1-800-221-2647.

Pinnacle and the P logo Reg. U.S. Pat. & TM Off.

ISBN-13: 978-0-7860-2500-8
ISBN-10: 0-7860-2500-X

First Printing: October 2011

10 9 8 7 6 5 4 3 2 1

Printed in the United States of America

ACKNOWLEDGMENTS

Some of my sources for this book have asked to remain anonymous, and so I can only thank them privately. The others I would like to gratefully acknowledge here. Thanks to Assistant State Attorneys Lon Arend, Karen Fraivillig, and Suzanne O'Donnell; Tekla Benson; the Honorable Deno G. Economou; Laura Forti at Turner Broadcasting; Rick and Sue Goff; Jane Kowalski; James D. Martin, assistant general counsel, Florida Department of Law Enforcement; Trooper Edward Pope and Lieutenant Patrick Riordan, of the Florida Highway Patrol; Wendy Rose, community affairs manager for the Sarasota County Sheriff's Office; Alfred L. Thompson, correctional services assistant, Florida Department of Corrections; Tami Treadway, Saratoga County Animal Services supervisor; and Cortnie Watts, criminalistics specialist for the North Port Police Department.

Also, special thanks to my agent, Jake Elwell at Harold Ober Associates, super editor and man of ideas Gary Goldstein—and, as always, to my wife, my world, Lisa Grasso.

AUTHOR'S NOTE

Violent crimes exact their toll on cops and bequeath a painful residue—something akin to post-traumatic stress syndrome. Peace officers are a courageous and stubborn lot, proud by nature, and not many would admit to weakness of any sort—but this one did.

"I'm not going to be able to give you an interview," he said, a veteran of ten-plus years on the force.

"Why not?" the writer asked.

"I get nightmares. I don't . . . I don't want to relive this again. I want to get my point across about this—but I can't. I still get nightmares."

In all of the cases he'd handled, all of those crime scenes, two still stuck in his psyche and probably would never let go. One was the very first unnatural-death scene he saw, a suicide by hanging. The other was the murder of Denise Amber Lee.

At night, he would close his eyes and return to that dungeon, that rape dungeon. *Creepy* wasn't the word for it. *Evil* was the word. There was evil there. His hands shook the entire time he was there. His hands began shaking now, just from thinking about it. . . .

* * *

The author has used a novelist's methods but not his license. Although this is a true story, some names will be changed to protect the privacy of the innocent. Pseudonyms will be noted upon their first usage. When possible, the spoken word has been quoted verbatim. However, when that is not possible, conversations have been reconstructed as closely as possible to reality based on the recollections of those who spoke and heard the words. In places, there has been a slight editing of spoken words, but only to improve readability. The denotations and connotations of the words remain unaltered. In some cases, witnesses are credited with verbal quotes that in reality only occurred in written form. Some characters may be composites.

CHAPTER I

A DRIZZLY DAY

Latour Avenue, like so many streets across America, had been whacked by the economy. In the town of North Port, Florida, the street boasted spread-out single-level stucco houses with two-car garages. When the homes were built, only a few years before, the plan was for this street, and many of the other streets in surrounding North Port Estates, to be a safe enclave for young families raising small children.

Stats told the story. In 2006, 4,321 new houses were built in North Port. In 2007, only 380 of them were purchased. Hundreds of homes were unfinished. Hundreds were in foreclosure. As the money left town, locals (most of them newcomers, strangers in town) lost their jobs, and crime seeped in. On Latour Avenue, there had been burglaries. Car break-ins. Vandalism. Crimes that would have been unthinkable only a few years before.

More stats: there were 130 burglaries in North Port in 2001. By 2007, that number had risen to 466.

Violent crime came to North Port in 2006 when a six-year-old girl was abducted and found murdered a few blocks from her home. For many months, that crime remained unsolved.

The community didn't *feel* like a community anymore. Longtime residents felt hopelessly outnumbered by strangers. There was a time when people knew their neighbors. There was a time when people in North Port trusted each other. No more. And it was even worse during the winter when the town's population was inflated by snowbirds, Northerners who migrated to the South to keep the chill of winter out of their bones.

Now the people on Latour, as well as the rest of the city, locked their doors—not just at night but during the daytime as well. . . .

Thursday, January 17, 2008, 2:30 P.M.

On Latour Avenue, twenty-three-year-old Jenifer-Marie Eckert was unemployed and temporarily staying with relatives. She'd only been living in that house for two weeks. At that moment, she was home alone, watching the living-room television and waiting for her boyfriend, Charles, who was late. Normally, she would have had the blinds closed, but she needed to simultaneously watch TV and look out the window.

Jenifer-Marie saw a green Camaro crawling down the street at pedestrian speed, like drivers do when they're lost or trying to read house numbers. It was a late-nineties model; she couldn't tell specifically what year. There was a white male driving, no passengers.

The car went up the street, used a driveway to turn around, and then drove back just as slowly. *What the heck is this guy up to?* Jenifer-Marie thought. Four or five times the guy passed by, always going slowest right past her house.

She'd never seen him before, but he looked normal enough. If he was really lost, she should help the guy out, give him directions. She went outside on the walkway a few steps from her front door and briefly made eye contact with the driver while he was still on the road.

As the Camaro slithered into the Lees' driveway next door, Jenifer-Marie could see the man had light hair. She never saw him standing, but she thought he was tall. The top of his head was almost to the ceiling of the car.

Later she would try hard to remember the car in greater detail. She didn't notice any dents or bumper stickers, but she was pretty sure it had one of those black things on the front that covered the snout.

The Lees' home next door was much like the four others on the street—three-bedroom, two-bathroom, single-story, two-car garage—except there was a pillared overhang above the front entrance. This way, the young couple and their sons could sit or play outside the front door without being exposed to the strong Florida sun or equally harsh rain. A curving sidewalk led from the small front patio to the driveway. Since it was the corner house, it had kempt lawns on three sides. At the back of the house was a screened-in patio from which the occupants could gaze at the thick woods beyond their lawn.

The car usurped the spot in the Lees' driveway usually occupied by the husband's car. For a moment, Jenifer-Marie made eye contact. The last she saw of him he seemed to be fumbling around with something in the front seat. She thought the man had located his destination, so she went back in her house. As she was reentering the house, she heard the car door slam, indicating the driver had gotten out.

Fifteen or twenty minutes later—her boyfriend *really* late now—she went outside again and stood in her driveway, just in time to see the car leave the Lees' house—in a hurry. She knew he'd gotten out of the car and then back in again, but she only saw him in the car. As far as she could tell, when the guy left, he was alone. The big difference between his arrival and departure was urgency. He crawled in—but he peeled out.

Just at that moment, another neighbor, Yvonne Parrish, a thirty-six-year-old mother of five who lived two houses from the Lees, looked out the window and saw the Camaro speed by.

"It looked like he was trying to get away from something," she later said.

At just after two-thirty, thirty-nine-year-old Dale Wagler was leaving a friend's house in the drizzle, on his way to the brand-new Walgreens to pick up a couple of prescriptions. He was about to pull his white Dodge onto Cranberry Boulevard in North Port when he saw a dark Camaro with a black "bra" on the front coming around the curve, weaving all over the road.

"No directional signal or nothin'," Dale later said.

The Camaro slowed down, like the driver was looking for a street to turn off on. The car swerved right in front of Dale, cutting him off. Dale looked at the guy, a blond, and the guy looked back.

"Gave this evil look, a don't-mess-with-me look," Dale said, "and then he floored it. Stomped on it."

Normally, Dale Wagler would have been provoked, might've followed a guy like that, might've flipped him off—but not this guy, not after that look. That was a look that said, "Follow me and I'll kill ya."

After the car zipped by, Dale saw hands in the back window. He thought they were waving around, but he couldn't be sure because of the rain.

At the time, all he could think was "There's a couple of drunks."

Dale was heading in the opposite direction on Cranberry, but he continued to watch the swerving car in his rearview mirror. The car was all over the road, crossing the white line and the yellow line.

He thought: "Now there's some people that are going to get pulled over." Later he'd realize the importance of what he'd seen, but at the time, "it just didn't soak in enough."

The first indication to law enforcement that something was desperately wrong came at 3:29 P.M. when the local 911 center received a call from Nathaniel "Nate" Alan Lee.

Operator: "North Port Emergency."

Nate Lee: "Uh, yes, I'm at **** Latour Avenue. I just got home from work and my wife . . . I can't find her. My kids were in the house and I don't know where she is. I've looked everyplace."

He'd come home from his job as a meter reader for the electric company to find his two sons—a two-year-old and a six-month-old—in the crib together, but their mother was gone. She would never leave them home alone, no matter what.

There was the usual disarray that comes with having small children. Toys were everywhere. On the floor, on the furniture, in the tub. One closet was filled to capacity with nothing but disposable diapers.

Nate said there was no sign of theft, no sign of forced entry, but Denise's keys were on the couch, another indication that she had left the house under duress.

She left her purse behind—with her cell phone on. Women *never* leave their purse behind. That meant she either left on foot, or was in a car with someone else.

"The only thing that isn't normal is she isn't here," Lee said. He thought about the ease with which his wife could be overpowered. She only weighed 102 pounds.

Lee also told the operator that the missing woman was the daughter of Rick Goff, of the Charlotte County Sheriff's Office (CCSO).

After hanging up on the 911 operator, Nate called his father-in-law. Rick had called Denise's cell just minutes before and had gotten no answer. He wanted to invite "the kids" over for dinner that night. When he saw Nate was calling him, he assumed that it was in response to the invitation.

Rick answered with, "Hey, you guys want to come over and eat?"

"I can't. Denise is missing," Nate replied.

"Nate, you've got to explain what you mean by that."

"I'm telling you. She's missing."

"I'll be right there," Rick said.

If Denise had been stolen by someone hoping no one would notice, he couldn't have chosen a worse victim. Denise Lee was a member of the Goff family—a family to be reckoned with. They had been the first settlers of Englewood, Florida, in 1887. Denise's father had been with the CCSO since September 1982. He started in corrections, spent two years there, then three on road patrol, and fifteen years undercover. Since then, he'd been in charge of the

Marshal's Fugitive Task Force, tracking wanted suspects. Denise's mom, Susan, had been the supervisor in the Tax Collector's Office in Englewood, where they lived, for more than twenty years. Rick and Sue were married in January 1983 and had three children: Denise, born in 1986, Amanda—who, contrary to her dad's advice, wanted to be a cop working with children—born in 1989, and Tyler, a promising baseball player, born in 1991.

While on his way to the Lee house, Rick Goff called his sheriff's department. He knew that reports of missing spouses tended to be handled with nonchalance by police because so frequently the spouse returned on his or her own and their partner had been quick to panic. Goff wanted to make sure that no one took that attitude in this case. He told his people he wanted dogs, and he wanted helicopters. This was not a domestic squabble that would work itself out. This was a genuine emergency. He wanted immediate action. As is true when police feel one of their own is in trouble, the call to action went out without hesitation.

"Anything you need," Goff was told.

Rick Goff, like Nate before him, ran through the possibilities in his head, and didn't like the conclusions he was coming to.

"I knew right away something happened to her bad," he later said.

Among the officers who reported to the scene of the apparent abduction was a criminalistics specialist, Cortnie Lynn Watts, who thoroughly photographed the house inside and out. Not knowing what was evidence and what wasn't, she photographed everything, every room from every angle. The keys that the missing woman had left behind, the contents of her purse carelessly spilled out. The most heartbreaking of those photos were of the high chair on the back patio and the little clumps of hair on the floor.

The missing woman had been giving her son a haircut not long before she disappeared.

In response to Nate's 911 call, two units were dispatched to the Latour Avenue home. They arrived at 3:44 P.M. Nate gave a statement to Officer Scott Smith. He told Smith the same things he'd mentioned to the dispatcher: wife gone, two babies left behind, left her car, purse, key, cell phone, all behind. It was just past three-thirty. A neighborhood canvass was instituted to gather info regarding the lost woman.

Jenifer-Marie Eckert next door volunteered the information she had regarding the green Camaro she saw creepy-crawling the street at two-thirty. The neighbor now told her story with fear in her voice. The woman next door had been snatched, and there she was, all alone, only a few feet away. It could have been her.

The first detectives reached the scene of the possible abduction at four-sixteen. There were two cars in the drive-way, a 2006 Toyota Corolla (the missing woman's) and a 1994 Dodge Avenger (her husband's). At four thirty-three, a request came into the CCSO from North Port for a "K-9 search team"—that is, a bloodhound and trainer. Deputy First Class (DFC) Deryk Alexander and his dog responded to the call.

Both Charlotte and Sarasota sheriff's departments were sent requests for search helicopters.

Road Patrol sergeant Pamela Jernigan was the first officer to report to the Lee home. The missing woman's husband, Nate, and father, Rick, were there.

"Can you think of anyplace Denise might have gone? Someplace nearby where she could walk on foot? A neighbor's?"

Jernigan was well aware of police philosophy based on

years and years of experiences. When a wife disappeared or—heaven forbid—was killed, it was her duty to take a long look at the husband before considering other options. Despite the fact that the man's father-in-law was a cop and the husband was not sending up any red flags whatsoever, there were a few questions she needed to ask.

"When was the last time you spoke with her?" Jernigan asked.

"Um, a little after eleven o'clock this morning," Nate Lee replied. Phone records would later reveal that the call was placed from him to her at 11:09 A.M. The call had lasted approximately five minutes.

"What was said?" In other words, was there a fight?

The conversation couldn't have been more normal. Since it was cool, he advised her to open the windows and kill the air-conditioning, and Denise said she'd already done so.

"She told me she planned on giving our oldest son a haircut today." Again, no red flag.

The first note of concern came at three o'clock when he got off work. He called her cell phone as he left work, to see if there was anything she needed him to pick up on the way home. No answer. That was odd—but there were plenty of reasons why she might not answer. Maybe she was changing a diaper. She would call back. It was a twenty-five-minute drive from his job to his home. He expected her to call back, but she did not.

Phone records would indicate that Nate was growing worried already. He called Denise's cell eight times during the twenty-five-minute drive.

That worry grew to out-and-out concern as he pulled his car onto their street. Even before he pulled into the driveway, he could see that the windows—the ones she'd said she'd opened—were now shut.

"What time did you get home?"

"About three-thirty. The boys were in the crib together, and Denise was gone." He tried to stay calm, not to freak, but he couldn't help it. She'd never left the boys alone before, and there was no good scenario that explained the facts.

No red flags, but procedures still needed to be followed. Nate had to wait outside while the house was searched.

Inside the house, it was hot. With the windows closed, and the air turned off, the place had heated up. The windows had been pushed down but not latched, as if someone had closed them in a hurry.

A high chair had been moved onto the back patio and there were wispy tufts of blond hair on the floor in front of it, a sign that Denise had been playing barber just as she said she would.

Then the husband saw that she'd left her purse, keys, and cell phone behind; he immediately called 911.

Sergeant Jernigan noted that the front door had two locks. The top one was a dead bolt, the bottom one a regular lock. The bottom lock could be locked from the inside by turning a latch. The dead bolt could be locked only from the outside and required a key.

When Nate Lee had arrived home, the front door had been locked from the inside and pulled shut from the outside. Denise's key had not been used. Jernigan then looked at Denise's cell phone, checking for outgoing and incoming calls, to see which people Denise had been in touch with that day. There were several calls back and forth with her husband. She had called one friend, Natalie Mink, that morning. (It turned out Denise left a message and never got through to Natalie.)

Having determined that Denise was no longer there, and that she was gone under suspicious circumstances, Jernigan called a criminal investigator to the scene. He turned out to be Detective Christopher Morales, who would become the case's lead detective.

At 4:38 p.m., the following message went out over law enforcement's computer system: MISSING 21 YRO FEMALE DENISE AMBER LEE THIN BUILD BLUE EYES DIRTY BLONDE HAIR 5-2 UNK CLOTHING HER HUSB ARRIVED HOME AT 1530 HRS FOUND THEIR 2 TODDLER CHILDREN ALONE, VEH AND KEYS PURSE STILL AT HOUSE CANNOT LOCATE HER REQUESTING BLOODHOUND.

Morales took a look around the house. No signs of a struggle. No indications of a sex crime. The woman was simply gone. He spoke briefly to the woman next door, and took a look behind the Lee house, where there was a heavily wooded area. There was a lot of scrub, palmetto brushes looking like Oriental fans. There were few nearby houses. The area was kind of desolate.

Morales then returned to the North Port police station, where he organized the search for that Camaro.

At 5:02 P.M., a BOLO (be on the lookout) was dispatched for the late 1990s-model green Camaro and Denise Lee, a twenty-one-year-old white female. The BOLO also included a description of a "possible suspect," a white male, thirty to forty years old, tall, with light brown hair.

The possibility that the crawling Camaro and the woman's disappearance were separate and unrelated had to be taken into consideration. Eyewitnesses had been wrong before, and some became overzealous when relating their memories, caught up in the drama of the moment. So, four minutes later, all Sarasota County all-terrain vehicle (ATV) operators were requested to report for duty because of the vast wooded areas surrounding the missing woman's house. There was still a chance that she'd merely wandered off.

A Charlotte County bloodhound-and-handler team arrived on Latour Avenue at 5:21 P.M. DFC Deryk Alexander's dog started his search at the front of the house. Finding no trail, he circled the house and sat down in the driveway—very close to the spot where Jenifer-Marie Eckert saw the green Camaro park.

With all of the police activity, neighbors who were home came out of their houses to see what was going on. With her heart pounding, Yvonne Parrish told police about the car she saw speeding away.

"It's really, really scary that this happened just two houses away," she later explained.

At 6:14 P.M., two and three-quarters hours later, another 911 call was received. Kathy Jackson, brand-new on the job, answered the phone at the Sarasota County Sheriff's Office. She had just passed the dispatcher-training course. Little did she know that the call she was about to handle would change her life, and not at all in a good way.

"911. What is your emergency?"

On the other end of the line was a frightened young woman, whose words seemed disconnected, not quite in response to the operator's question.

"I'm sorry. I'm sorry. I just wanna go—"

"Hello?" the operator said.

There were unintelligible sounds on the other end, sounds of feminine anxiety and terror. The woman was speaking, but not into the phone, not to the operator.

The operator then heard words that could be understood, the words of a man saying, "Why'd you do that?"

"I'm sorry," the woman could be heard to say. "I just want to see my family."

It took the operator a moment to figure it out. The woman was speaking to her attacker, or abductor, or whatever he was.

"Hello? Hello?" the operator said.

A sound could be heard from the man, perhaps unintelligible words, perhaps just an animalistic growl.

The woman said, "Oh, please. I just want to see my family again. Let me go."

The operator: "Hello?"

The man: "What the fuck is going on?"

The woman: "Please let me go. Please let me go. I just want to see my family again."

The man: "No fuckin' problem."

The woman: "Okay."

The operator: "Hello?"

The man's accusatory tone could be heard, but his words couldn't be understood.

"I'm sorry," the woman said, her voiced reduced by terror into an infantile whine.

The man said, "I was gonna let you go, and then you go and fuck around."

"I'm sorry," the woman repeated. "Please let me go."

The man: "Now we got to go in the next street because of him."

The man was unaware that the phone had been connected to the emergency operator. He was scolding the woman for alerting people in their vicinity of her distress. Perhaps they were in a car.

"Now I want to bring you in there again," the man said. "I didn't want to do that."

"Please let me go, please. Please—oh, God, please."

The man could be heard scolding more. Only the end of

the statement could be understood: ". . . in front of my cousin Harold!"

The operator tried again: "Hello?"

The man: "I told you I would."

The operator: "Hello?"

The woman: "Help me!"

The operator: "What's the address?"

"Please help me!"

"What's the address where you're at? Hello?"

"Please let me go. Help me. I don't know." Perhaps she was trying to answer the operator's question without her attacker knowing it.

The man said, "Calm down."

The operator: "Hello?"

The woman: "Please let me go."

The operator: "What is the address that you're at? Hello, ma'am?"

The woman, now talking to her attacker: "Where are we going?"

The man replied, "I got to go up and around now because of him."

The woman asked, "Up and around where?"

The man answered incredulously, "Didn't you see?" Then, after a phrase the operator couldn't make out, the man added, "Exactly right four or five streets over from your house."

"I couldn't," she said, meaning she hadn't seen. "Tell me where?"

She was very clever, trying to get the man to state their location and destination while the 911 operator listened in.

The operator: "What's your name, ma'am? Hello?"

The woman: "Please . . ."

The operator: "What's your name?"

"Please, my name is Denise. I'm married to a beautiful husband and I just want to see my kids again."

The operator: "Your name is Denise?"

Denise, again talking to her attacker: "I'm sorry."

By this time, the operator had things figured out. Denise had called 911, but her attacker didn't know it. She was trying to give the information the operator requested without her attacker realizing what was going on.

"Please, God, please protect me."

The operator: "Are you on I-75?"

Then the male on the other end of the line could be heard saying, "What did you do with my cell phone?"

Denise replied, "I don't know. What do you mean?" There was an unintelligible phrase, followed by her saying, "Protect me."

The operator: "Where are you at? Can you tell us if you're on I-75?"

Denise said, "I don't know where your phone is. I'm sorry."

The man: "You be honest with me. . . ."

Denise: "Can't you tell me where we are?"

The operator: "Are you blindfolded? If you are, press the button."

Denise: "I don't have your phone. Please, God."

The man: "Look around and think. Well, not that . . . that's too little."

Denise: "I don't have it. Sorry."

Operator: "Denise, do you know this guy?"

Denise: "I don't. I don't have it. I'm sorry. I don't know where your phone is. I'm sorry."

More words from the man, but the operator couldn't understand what he was saying.

Operator: "Denise, do you know this guy?" Then, aside to someone at the dispatch center: "She might have the phone laid down and not hear a thing I'm saying, too. He keeps saying about the phone and she . . ."

Denise: "I don't know where it is. Maybe if I could see I could help you find it. No, sir."

Operator: "Denise . . ."

Denise: "I'm looking for it. Uh-huh."

Operator: "How long have you been gone from your house?"

Denise: "I don't know."

Operator: "Do you know how long you've been gone from your house? What's your last name?"

Denise: "Lee."

Operator: "Lee?"

Denise: "Yeah."

Operator: "Do you know what street?"

Denise: "I don't know where your phone is."

Operator: "Your name's Denise Lee?"

Denise: "Uh-huh."

Operator: "Can you tell at all what street you're on?"

Denise: "No."

Operator: "Do you know this guy that's with you?"

Denise: "No."

Operator: "What's your address? What's your home address? Do you know?"

The man's voice could be heard again: "I told you (unintelligible) cell."

Denise: "I don't know. Please just take me to my house. Can you take me to my home? On Latour, please."

Operator: "Can you see, or do you have a blindfold on?"

Denise: "I can't see. Where are we?"

There was more unintelligible anger from the man.

Operator: "Can they turn off the radio or turn it down?"

Denise: "I can't hear you. It's too loud. Where are we?"

Man: "Give me the phone."

Denise: "Are you going to hurt me?"

Man: "Give me the phone."

Denise: "Are you going to let me out now?"

Man: "As soon as I get the phone."

Denise: "Help me."

And with that, the connection was broken. Denise had stayed on the phone six and a half minutes. Caller ID told police that the call came from a phone belonging to a Michael "Mike" Lee King. A listing of registered vehicles almost instantaneously corroborated Jenifer-Marie Eckert's info—King drove a green Chevy Camaro. A new BOLO included King's name and the presumed license plate number on his car.

When Nate heard about Denise's 911 call, his brain scrambled for comfort with wishful thinking: *It might be a teenager playing a practical joke.* Oh, if only that were true.

A recording of the 911 tape was played for Rick Goff, who confirmed, with his heart breaking, that it was the voice of his daughter. It was the most horrible thing he'd ever heard, his beautiful daughter, screaming in terror, trying desperately to give clues that would help them find her. Unable to help her, he almost couldn't listen to her terrified voice.

And she'd been *so smart* and done such a good job. She gave her name and the street on which she lived. She managed to give the operator all of that info, while making her kidnapper think she was talking to him.

Plus, she managed to stay on the phone for *so long.* He was convinced they were going to find her and rescue her. Because they'd had so long to track the call, they would know just where she was. As police would soon realize, however, the kidnapper had a cheaper than cheap cell phone, one that was practically disposable, and it was not equipped with a GPS, which would enable police to track it to a precise location. All they had to sleuth with were the cell phone towers that handled the call. They knew she was close by. Precisely where remained a mystery.

The name Michael Lee King meant nothing to either Denise's father or husband. Nate was nearly overwhelmed by the randomness of the abduction. They didn't know him at all, and yet this guy might've been stalking his wife for a long time, waiting for the right moment to snatch her away.

Rick started making phone calls. He didn't know what else to do. He called every cop he could think of, and the Latour Avenue scene became crowded with law-enforcement personnel. Rick even called Howie Grace, a news guy from the local NBC affiliate, WBBH-TV. Grace had known Rick Goff for years, and knew him as a guy who never displayed emotion. But now, he was frantic, almost sobbing.

The Lees' neighborhood was freshly canvassed; police were now armed with a Department of Automotive Vehicles Identification (DAVID) photo of the suspect.

Not everything the neighbors had to say was immediately helpful. One neighbor said the man in the photo resembled a man who had visited during the summer of 2007 and inquired about the For Sale sign in front of her house.

Only a couple of minutes after the call from Denise ended on an ominous note, at 6:23 P.M., another call came into the emergency center.

Operator: "Police Emergency. Operator Bonnell. . . . yes, what's the problem?"

The call was from a woman identifying herself as Sabrina Muxlow, who said she had solid information that her dad's cousin Mike King had a girl tied up in his car. The dispatcher asked Sabrina for her address and she gave it, a home on Junction Street in North Port.

"How do you know this information?" the operator inquired.

"My father just called me and told me."

"Now, what would your dad's cousin be doing with this female?"

"The man [came] over to my dad's house and borrowed a shovel, a gas tank, and something else." She knew there was a third item, but she couldn't remember what it was. After that, King got back in his car and drove off.

The operator began asking for names, but the woman stopped cooperating.

"My father wants to remain anonymous," she said.

"Where does your father live?"

"In North Port."

"How did your father know there was a woman in the car?"

Sabrina didn't know, but she did know the captive woman had tried to escape. "The girl came up out of the car, but my dad's cousin put her back in the car." For a moment, her father had seen enough of the woman to see his cousin had her tied up.

Did her father have any idea where his cousin was going with this female?

Sabrina said no.

"Okay, we've been looking for this female."

"You have."

"Oh, yes, we have a helicopter up looking for her. You are just so wonderful to call on this information."

"Yeah."

Seven minutes later, at six-thirty, the emergency operator in Charlotte County received a call from a woman who was driving in her car along a local thoroughfare. She was on her way to visit her sick grandmother in Fort Myers. It was raining, she drove a small car, and she was staying off the interstate as she coursed North Port. There were too many people on I-75 who drove like maniacs. So she was on the parallel road and had to deal with stoplights.

"911. Where is your emergency?"

"I'm on [Route] forty-one going south, and I'm at a cross street right now. I'm on Chamberlain. I just crossed Chamberlain, and I'm on forty-one going south. I was at a stoplight and a man pulled up next to me, and there was a child screaming in the car."

"What type of vehicle was he in?"

"It's a blue Camaro, like in the nineties or early 2000s or something."

"Okay, it was a baby or—"

"No, it was a child."

"How old?"

"You know, it's dark, and I turned to look at him. He's a white male. Sort of light-colored hair. Sort of plump. He's behind me now, and I tried to slow down so that he can pass me and I could read his license plate."

"Ma'am, don't hang up."

"I'm not."

"Okay." There was a pause in the conversation, fifteen to twenty seconds, as the dispatch operator relayed the information she had already received. Then she was back on the line. "Okay, where are you now? Forty-one south?"

"I am. I'm going to pass a cross street, and I believe he is still behind me. It's Jenks Drive. I'm just crossing it and I'm going very slow, like thirty-five miles an hour, on forty-one."

"And he's behind you?"

"I believe he is behind me. He has not passed me. And he's going slower than I am, which is not like, I mean, we're holding up traffic and stuff. I think he saw me look at him. I don't want to be overdramatic here, but he's going even slower now. Is he pulling over? No. There is something going on because he is going even slower now. He is right behind me. I don't know if the kid was, I don't know . . ."

"What is your name?"

"My name is Jane—Okay, he's pulling over into the other lane now. Jane Kowalski. *K-O-W-A-L-S-K-I*."

"And give me your cell phone number in case I lose you."

Kowalski complied hurriedly so she could resume describing what was going on.

"Okay, he's going to turn. Oh, shit. He is going to turn left on Toledo Blade. He is turning left right now. I—I—I'm in the other lane."

"You're going southbound and he's turning left on Toledo Blade."

"Right, and it's like a blue, I want to say like a Camaro type of car. White male. And there's a kid in the backseat and they kept banging on the window."

"Left on Toledo Blade. About how old is this child? Can you tell me?"

"I didn't see the child. I'd say less than ten. Definitely not an infant. Old enough to bang on the window."

"Okay, seven to ten?"

"I don't know. Five to ten. Okay, now it's green. There are green arrows, and he's going now."

"He's turning left on Toledo Blade?"

"Yeah, do you want me to . . . Do you want me to turn? Try to follow him? Or . . ."

The operator could be heard saying, "Okay. Does he want her to follow him?" Returning her attention to the caller: "Can you turn?"

"Oh, oh, he just turned left on Toledo Blade. I don't know if I can catch up. There's a bunch of traffic and I can't get over. Um, oh, boy."

Again the operator could be heard relaying a message: "There's a child in the car somewhere between five and ten that was banging on the window."

"And screaming," the caller added.

"And crying," the operator said.

"And screaming!" the caller corrected. "Like *screaming* screaming. Screaming. And not a happy scream. It was a 'Get me out of here' scream."

"Left on Toledo Blade, and you say it was a blue Camaro?"

"Blue or black. Very dark. He's a white male. And I want to say sort of light-colored hair. Maybe a little plump in the face—not, I don't think, obese. I am way past him now. For me to go catch him, I don't know if I'd ever be able to go back. I mean, I would never stop him. I'm not going to put myself at risk."

The operator asked the caller to repeat her name and cell phone number. Jane Kowalski once again said her name, clearly enunciating, then spelling it.

"I mean I hope they weren't just playing around," Jane said. Then, looking at the big picture, she revised that statement. "To me, it sounded like the kid was frightened and panicky."

"Okay."

"But, um, I don't know..Instead of taking a chance, I just wanted to make sure I called it in."

The operator was typing: CALLER LAST SAW A BLUE OR GREEN CAMARO TURN LEFT ON TOLEDO BLADE FROM HWY 41 SOUTHBOUND CAMARO WAS DRIVEN BY W/M WITH LT HAIR AND THERE WAS A CHILD ABOUT 5-10 YRS OLD SCREAMING IN THE VEH AND BANGING ON THE WINDOW COMP CALLED IN THINKING THIS CHILD MAY HAVE BEEN INVOLVED IN A POSS AMBER ALERT SINCE THIS VEHICLE WAS ACTING VERY STRANGE.

Yes, the witness had said "blue" or "black" and the operator typed "blue" or "green." The car was actually green, of course, but this happy accident had no effect on what followed.

"Well, I'm very glad that you did, ma'am. That's exactly what you should do. Okay. Well, you lost him, and thank you now, and we really appreciate you calling us."

"Okay, can someone follow up with me? I mean . . ."

"Hold on, ma'am."

"Okay."

"Okay, hang on, ma'am."

"Okay."

The operator relayed the caller's question and then could be heard saying, "The vehicle turned left on Toledo Blade from forty-one southbound. She is no longer with the vehicle. White male driver. Blue or black Camaro. Male had light hair and there was a child screaming in the car and . . ."

"And banging on the window," Jane Kowalski prompted.

"And banging on the window," the operator relayed. She returned her attention to the caller and said, in an apologetic tone, "I've got everyone hollering at me, and . . . just a second. Okay, I may need you to pull over, so bear with me."

"That's fine. Okay. I'm going to pull over now, let me get over," the caller said.

"Yeah," the operator said, again sounding as though she was apologizing for the inconvenience. "That would be great." There was a moment of silence broken by the operator: "I am glad that you called in."

"Yeah, me too. I mean, I don't know if there is an AMBER Alert out or something like that, but—"

"Bear with me. And where are you pulling over?"

"I just pulled over into the Toys 'R' Us."

The operator placed the landmark immediately: "Okay, the Town Center Mall?"

"Town Center Mall. Yeah."

"Okay, that's excellent."

"I'm from Tampa. I'm going down to Fort Myers to visit my sister, and I don't even know where I am actually, but okay."

"You're going where?"

"I'm going down to Fort Myers to visit my grandmother and my sister."

Conversation could be heard on the operator's end. Where was the caller exactly? Anywhere near the Chili's restaurant? What make of car was she driving?

"Tell me what kind of car you're in?" the operator asked.

Jane Kowalski said that she was driving a silver Mercedes.

"Okay, if you'll just sit there—and your doors are locked, right?"

"Well, yeah."

"No, no, I mean . . . I always have my car doors locked."

"That's probably a good idea, actually. Yeah, okay, all

right," the caller said, now understanding that the operator, despite her assurances to the contrary, thought there was a possibility that she was in harm's way.

Now there was a long pause and all that could be heard was typing on the computer as the operator input the information she knew so far.

The typing stopped and the operator could be heard saying, "Do they want to make contact with her? She's pulled over." More typing. To Jane, she repeated, "Hang on, bear with me here. Forty-one south, yeah, he'd be heading toward the interstate." A loud sigh could be heard, but it was unclear if it came from the caller or the operator. "I appreciate you holding on, Jane."

"I just . . . Well, actually, I hope it turns out to be nothing, really. I mean, I would never . . ."

"She's pulled over in the Toys 'R' Us parking lot. Do they want contact with her?" On the operator's end, a female voice could be heard giving the operator instructions, a list that brought a frustrated response. "I have that. I already gave that to you." More instructions. "Okay, I'm asking you. Do they want to make contact with her? Okay, Jane, we have your phone number. If we need you, we'll call you. You'll be at that cell phone number if we need you, right?"

"Absolutely. And don't hesitate. I will give you whatever information I can give you."

"Okay, and we really appreciate you calling in."

"Yeah. Oh, God, I hope—man, oh man, okay."

"Thanks, Jane."

"Okay."

"Drive careful."

"Oh, I shall. Thank you."

"Bye-bye."

The communications supervisor tried to establish a

patch between North Port and Sarasota and Charlotte Counties so there could be interagency communication regarding the disappearance of Denise Lee. One dispatcher thought the patch needed to be completed before she should "air the call." Only minutes after Jane Kowalski hung up, there was a shift change, and the new people on duty didn't even receive the partial messages that the old shift had gotten. Eventually the information from the Kowalski call was put into the Lee file, when someone realized that the struggling child could be a diminutive woman, and the blue Camaro could be green. But still, deputies on the road were not told to respond to the Kowalski call.

Jane Kowalski sat in the parking lot, and sat and sat. She began to fume. She knew a little bit about 911 systems. She had, in fact, worked in the 911 industry. She'd worked for a company that developed 911 software and had been responsible for the software's implementation.

"I had personally installed the system with my engineers," she remembered. "I'd spent a lot of time in call centers and seen how they handled calls." One of the reasons she'd been so precise in the information she gave was the time she spent in emergency call centers. She knew the information that was needed and had given it to them in a calm, concise, and accurate fashion.

She understood the philosophy of keeping the victim talking until the police arrived, which was a good rule if someone was breaking into your house or if you've been in an accident. Jane Kowalski was not the victim here, and the perp was miles away by the time she pulled into the parking lot and stopped.

If the dispatcher who'd taken her call had been using a computer-aided dispatch (CAD) system, one used by emergency systems everywhere, she wouldn't have had to ask the same questions over and over again. (In reality, Charlotte County did have a CAD system. It simply hadn't, in this instance, been used properly.)

"I was giving her exact locations," Jane Kowalski later explained. There were five cop cars within a mile of her. If a CAD system had been in place, they would have been there by the time she hung up the phone.

Instead, she sat in the parking lot. When Jane called a second time, they didn't know who she was, and the best she could get from the dispatcher was "if we need you, we'll have someone contact you." Rightfully feeling that she'd done all she could do, Jane started her car and continued on her trip to see her grandmother.

Later, piecing together what had happened, one deputy sitting in his patrol car estimated that he was sitting at one intersection just as Michael King drove past with Denise Lee in the car.

At 6:50 P.M., a man called 911—apparently, the father of the woman who had called earlier about Michael King borrowing a gas can and a shovel. Because he did not want to get involved with any investigation, the man did not give the operator the whole truth. Caller ID at the police station revealed that the man was making the call from a pay phone, which, he hoped, would further assure his anonymity.

Operator: "911. What's the location of your emergency?"

Man: "I'm not sure what the emergency is exactly, but I think there's somebody that's been taken and they don't wanna be where they need to be, and they're in a '95 green Camaro in North Port somewhere."

Operator: "Okay, and how do you know this?"

Man: "I don't know. Just . . ."

He told the operator that the man dropped by to borrow

a shovel, a gas can, and a flashlight. He asked what the items were for and the man said he had a lawn mower that had broken down and was stuck in a ditch. While they were pulling the requested items out of a tool shed, the caller saw the woman try to escape. She said, "Call the cops" before the visitor struggled with her for maybe thirty seconds and finally managed to push her back into the car and "took off."

"Did the man say anything to you about the girl?"

"Yeah, he said, 'Don't worry about it.'"

"Okay, the car was a green '95 Camaro?"

"Yup. With a black 'bra' on the front of it."

"A black 'bra'?"

"Yup. So . . ."

"But you saw them, right?"

"Yes."

"And where was she?"

"In the car."

"Do you know where they are now?"

"I have no idea."

"Who did they take?" the operator asked.

"Some girl."

"Do you know who the guy is?"

"No."

"Anything else you can tell me?"

"Nope.

"Okay, hold on, okay? . . . Okay, do you know anything else?"

"Sure don't."

"Do you know when you last saw them?"

"Off of Biscayne."

"Where?"

"Biscayne and Price. It's hard to tell now."

"Is he gonna hurt the girl?" the operator inquired.

"I have no idea."

"You saw them, though?"

"Yeah."

"And where was she?"

"In the car."

"Was she okay?"

"She didn't seem like she wanted to be there. Let me let you go."

"Can you give me anything else?"

"No. If I find something out, I will."

"Can I get your name and number?" the operator questioned.

"No. I want to be anonymous."

"Okay."

"I'll call you back if I hear anything else."

"Okay, let us know if you hear anything," the operator concluded.

The caller hung up. The man's attempt to remain anonymous was in vain. During Denise Lee's 911 call, police heard King refer to his cousin Harold. As it turned out, King only had one cousin by that name, Harold Muxlow—and sure enough, he lived in North Port.

Early that evening the nearby Lee County emergency operator received a call from a man who identified himself as Shawn Johnson. Earlier in the day, he'd been leaving his job in North Port and heading to Fort Myers, where he was living at the time.

He was at a stoplight on U.S. Route 41 when he heard a cry for help. The intersection was Cranberry Boulevard (about three-quarters of a mile northwest of the spot from which Jane Kowalski called 911). Shawn said he'd rolled down his window and heard the cry again, several times.

The weather was nice, although it had rained earlier, and even though it was late afternoon there was still light enough to see.

Shawn didn't know what to think at first. He thought maybe it was a joke. He looked over at the car next to him, where the cries seemed to be coming from. For a moment, he and the driver of that car were looking right at one another.

There was something about the sounds of the subsequent screams, and there were as many as eight of them, that made him think this wasn't a joke. It wasn't an angry parent yelling at a kid or anything like that.

The screams were female and sounded genuinely desperate. Most of it was just sounds, but he heard "help" and "help me" in there as well. By the time the light had turned green and he took off, the screams had stopped.

At 6:59 P.M., a North Port cop named Sergeant Patrick Sachkar arrived at King's house on Sardinia Avenue, near the corner of Big Leaf Street in North Port, about two miles away from where the Lees lived.

The home was directly across the street from the Lamarque Elementary School, a disturbing proximity, to say the least. The single-level stucco house was painted white, with gray trim. It came with a two-car garage and a single-vehicle carport, which had apparently been added after the original construction. There was almost as much space allotted for motor vehicles as for living.

Behind the carport was a small trailer with Michigan plates, containing a couple of gas containers, a compressed-air machine, a jack, and a spare tire. The carport itself was practically empty, containing only a glass display case, a folding baby stroller, a dark wooden bookcase, a minibike, and several other items. The large garage was also mostly empty, containing only a few cardboard boxes and several pieces of broken-down furniture.

The blinds to the front windows were down and closed. At the side of the house, where only the meter readers went, the blinds were up. In back, the blinds were pulled closed on the sliding back door.

A wooden fence separated the property from that of the next-door neighbor. In the back was a swing set. The lawn consisted of sparse grass, cut short and growing from a sandy soil. Thick weeds and a row of palm trees provided privacy from the houses on the next street over.

The front door was just to the right of the garage. Because of the urgent circumstances, Sachkar kicked open the door. The wood splintered beside the doorknob and lock, and small pieces of wood fell into a pile on the walk in front of the door.

Entering the house, Sachkar heard loud music, which he quickly determined was coming from a television in the living room, which had been left on with the volume turned all the way up—as well as from another source elsewhere in the house.

Four full-length mirrors were mounted, side by side, along one wall. A fifth mirror had once been mounted next to the others, but it had been removed. Its outline was still visible. A large painting of a reclining tiger was mounted on the opposite wall. There was light gray wall-to-wall carpeting throughout the house, and the walls were painted the color of eggshells. A broom rested against a corner of the foyer. Nearby were two pairs of sneakers—one size eleven and a half, one size twelve—and a pile of laundry, all clothes for an adult male. On the floor in a hallway, near the bathroom door, was a balled-up pair of jeans. Except for the bathroom light, all other lights were off.

Sachkar and others wasted no time searching the house, believing Denise might still be there. But the house was empty, even, for the most part, of furniture.

Along with a newspaper, an empty Little Caesars pizza box, and an empty plastic bottle of water, there was a roll of duct tape sitting on the kitchen counter—brand Manco Duck. The newspaper was an edition of the North Port *Herald-Tribune,* dated Monday, January 14, 2008. The sections had been pulled apart, with one open to the want ads. Resting on top of the front page was a printout of computer-generated travel instructions in Michigan—from Marlette to Westland, 127.4 miles away.

Also on the same counter were various squirt bottles of cleaning fluid, a tin box half full of wooden matches, the business card of the *Herald-Tribune*'s Community Sports editor, and a Motorola cell phone. There were notes written on scraps of paper indicating that the occupant was looking for a job. A couple of unwashed Tupperware bowls, two plastic cups, and a plastic fork were in the sink.

The garbage was in a yellow plastic shopping bag attached by the handle to the doorknob of the kitchen closet. Another pizza box, many empty soda and water bottles, and a balled-up piece of duct tape with blood—and long dirty-blond hair adhering to it—were in there.

The bedroom was darker than the other rooms. Sheets had been stapled up over the windows to keep out light. A plug-in radio sat on the floor, volume cranked. A pillow with a plaid pillowcase, a Winnie-the-Pooh and Tigger sheet, a dark red blanket, and a black shirt were next to the radio, all on the floor. The missing mirror from the living room had been moved to the darkened bedroom, where it now leaned against the wall. A plastic laundry basket, with bedding inside, and a vacuum cleaner were next to the mirror. The only real furniture in that bedroom was a swivel desk chair on wheels.

Between the radio and the makeshift "bed," the police officer spotted something that turned his stomach: a hair tie, and another ball of duct tape. Like the one in the garbage, this one had long dirty-blond hairs adhering to it.

He looked at the blanket. It was stained. There also appeared to be bloodstains on the carpet next to the sheet. This was a sex crime scene, a rape dungeon.

Sachkar cleared the residence and secured the house's exterior, including the lawn, with crime scene tape. The avenue was closed at either end of the block. He would await the crime scene investigation (CSI) technicians.

Michael Lee King's full name and date of birth were added to the existing BOLO.

Many locals—natives and snowbirds alike—first learned of the missing woman at one of the roadblocks set up across North Port, tying up the evening commute. A helicopter flew low over the back roads, north of Interstate 75. All main roads right up to the county line had a cop car on them searching for Camaros.

Many places were searched—but they weren't the right places. A Code Red call was issued to residents who lived in the vicinity of Sardinia. There was at least one false alarm, as one of King's neighbors reported a green Camaro, which turned out not to be the right one.

At 7:32 P.M., in response to Jane Kowalski's call, which came in more than an hour earlier, Laurie Piatt, the supervisor of the 911 center, put in a request for the A Child

Is Missing program to be activated. That program offered a prioritization of activity for cases in which the missing person was a child or a student living on campus. Seventeen minutes later, the program still was not activated, as Piatt was waiting for a callback.

Because varying colors had been reported, police were stopping all Camaros. At 7:33 P.M., a patrol car stopped a purple Camaro on the outskirts of North Port. At 7:43 P.M., a lime green Camaro was spotted parked in a driveway on Goodrich Avenue. The owner quickly verified that the car was hers and explained that it hadn't moved in a long time because there was something wrong with the engine.

A half hour later, a more detailed description of Denise Lee went out, noting that her dirty blond hair came down just below her shoulder blades, that her eyes were blue, and she had a small mole under her chin. The BOLO contained precise info regarding the Camaro as well, noting that it was a green 1994 model being driven by Michael Lee King.

At 9:01 P.M., another dark Camaro was stopped on Cornelius Boulevard. A vacant house near the corner of McDill Drive and Chamberlain Boulevard was searched, to no avail.

At 9:17 P.M., the CCSO dispatch registered a call from one of their patrol cars. Florida Highway Patrol (FHP) had made a stop. SUBJECT X15, it said.

That meant suspect in custody.

CHAPTER 2

THE ARREST

Trooper Edward "Eddie" Pope was born and raised in Mount Vernon, New York, right across the border from the Bronx, until he was ten years old. Then Eddie moved to West Babylon, on Long Island. With dreams of one day being a state trooper, Pope had his first job in law enforcement with the CCSO in Florida.

Right from the start, Eddie Pope had a knack for being where the action was. Crimes sometimes came to him. Pope recalled, "I was working a security detail at Fishermen's Village, a mall where the road runs through the center. A guy came running out of a bar, got in his car, and tried to hightail it out of there. There were two little kids in front of their mom getting ready to cross the road. I grabbed the kids and threw them out of the way. The car hit me and dragged me about fifty feet." The accident tore up both of Pope's knees—which had to be surgically repaired—and derailed his career for a while.

He was going to school at the time and took a job

teaching special education at the Liberty Elementary
School in Port Charlotte. The doctors told him he should
abandon any notion of working for the state police, but he
refused to let go of his dream.

The teaching job turned out to be perfect rehab for his
damaged legs. "Special education kids are always on the
move. A lot of time they are trying to *escape*," he recalled,
adding that his nickname at the time was "Kindergarten
Cop." When he first began, he would trot in pursuit of es-
capees. Over two school years, he began "getting to the
fence before they did."

His legs as strong as ever, he applied for a job with the
Florida State Police (FSP); in 2003, he was accepted. He
graduated from the police academy at the top of his class,
earning both the Athletic and Presidential Awards.

During his time as a trooper for the state of Florida,
Pope grew accustomed to being in the right place at the
right time, partially because he was lucky, but mostly because he was a clear thinker and had the uncanny ability
to position himself where he could do the most good.

His skills had not gone unnoticed. He earned the
Trooper of the Month Award for the first time, in January
2006, when he both recovered stolen property and seized a
half pound of pot.

Pope set a record when he was named the Trooper of
the Month three more times in 2007. He was honored for
three acts: another case involving recovery of stolen property, a life-saving effort in an attempted suicide, and the
rescue of two motorists from a submerged vehicle in
alligator-infested waters. He received the 2007 Trooper of
the Year Award from the governor, and he got to throw out
the first pitch at a Tampa Bay Rays game versus the
Boston Red Sox.

* * *

During the search for Denise Amber Lee and her abductor, the forty-year-old Eddie Pope was working "aggressive driving" patrol on the 3:00 to 11:00 P.M. shift. He knew the Goff family well and realized this case was special. It was like trying to save his own sister.

At just after nine o'clock, Road Deputy Christian Wymer's car was parked on a grass median near Toledo Blade and Interstate 75, watching each car as it went by. After a while, Pope parked next to Wymer in his souped-up unmarked Mercury Marauder.

Facing opposite directions so they could watch traffic coming both ways, Wymer and Pope rolled down their windows and talked about the BOLO, the type of car they were after, and the description of the wanted driver.

Wymer later recalled that picking out Camaros from a stream of traffic was difficult. It was next to impossible, for example, to tell a Camaro from a Firebird in the dark.

At 9:16 P.M., a "definite possible" approached. Pope looked in his rearview and saw the car come off a side road about three hundred yards away and pull into the northbound lane of Toledo Blade. It was on Pope's side, the northbound side. It *was* a Camaro—correct year as well.

The car passed by and pulled onto the interstate. Pope quietly put his car in drive and followed. It had been dark since seven-thirty, but the streetlights were bright along that stretch. The weather had cleared. Visibility was excellent.

Pope pulled onto the road behind the Camaro. At first, there were about six cars between them, so he couldn't read the plate. A quarter mile later, Pope had maneuvered immediately behind the suspicious vehicle.

Pope tried the radio, but, as was not uncommon, there

were transmission difficulties. "From the 179 to the 170," Pope recalled, "we get intermittent radio trouble. Sometimes it sounds like a muted trombone, like grown-ups talking on those old Charlie Brown shows. *'Waaah, wah-wah-wah, waaah.'*" Pope had to speed to keep up with the subject's car.

"When I saw the first three letters on his tag, it was just like the old expression, I really could feel the little hairs standing up on the back of my neck," he said. "I also had that kind of warm sensation you get in your mouth, like you're going to throw up. I knew I had the right vehicle."

Should he continue to follow the car and risk losing it? Or, take it on his own initiative to make the stop? Denise Lee might've been in the car, so it was a no-brainer. Pope put on his lights and siren. The Camaro pulled over almost immediately, easing onto the interstate shoulder. The trooper pulled right up on his rear bumper in his Marauder. Because he was in an unmarked vehicle, he didn't have a spotlight and couldn't illuminate the interior of the suspect's vehicle. Pope executed what was called a "felony stop." He used his "loud Italian New York voice" to order the driver out of the car.

No response.

The trooper could see the driver inside the car moving around a little bit. Was he trying to dispose of evidence? Was he arming himself for a shoot-out?

Pope commanded the suspect to get out of the car with his hands up. Typically, when a cop ordered a driver out of his vehicle, the driver's-side door swung all the way open. Here, the driver's-side door opened only a few inches and then stopped. No one got out.

"He was trying to manipulate the door so he could find me in the rearview mirror," Pope said, possibly so he would know where to aim if he came out firing.

For his own safety, Pope had to *assume* he was armed, even though there wasn't enough evidence at that point to tell if a weapon was in play.

"I had to change my location," Pope said. During this sequence, no cars came down the southbound interstate, so it was easy for Pope to dash across the road, crossing four lanes. He took up a tactical position near a tree so he could look into the Camaro's driver's side.

Five times, Pope ordered the driver out of the car. "I shouted myself out" was how he later explained it. The Camaro had a high console between the front seats that stuck up. Pope knew this because he'd owned a '94 Camaro.

The driver moved so that he was bent over that console, his head pointing toward the passenger seat.

The fifth time Pope barked the command, he said, "Get out of the car with your hands in the air, or I'll fire!" That got a response. The driver's door finally swung all the way open. The driver was kneeling on the driver's seat, doing something on the passenger side. Then he started to back out, ass first. Pope didn't like the notion that the driver was exiting so that his hands came out last.

But he emerged with his hands on his head, his back still turned to the trooper. Pope charged. The suspect didn't have a weapon in his hands, but that didn't mean he didn't have one in his waistband or something.

"Turn around slowly," Pope ordered.

The suspect complied.

The guy had a goatee and was wearing a camouflage shirt and jeans. Pope heard him utter something. Pope noticed two things. First, no gun in the waistband. Second, from the waist down, the subject was soaking wet. A closer look revealed that his pants and shoes were muddy as well. Pope ordered the man to move to the rear of the vehicle, then to lie down on the asphalt.

"He was a little resistant about getting down on the ground," Pope remembered. But eventually he obeyed.

"Where's the girl?" Pope yelled. "I don't care about anything else. I just want to know where the fucking girl is."

"I was kidnapped, too," the suspect said as the cuffs tightly snapped in place. "I was a hostage, too."

"You're full of shit," Pope replied.

Only after the man was down and restrained did Trooper Pope call for backup, which arrived three or four minutes later.

Pope patted the suspect down and found a wallet in his left rear pocket. A quick look at the wallet's contents and his photo ID verified that this was indeed Michael Lee King.

In King's front pocket, Pope found a black phone, with a silver emblem on it, which had had the battery and SIM card pulled out. Also in his pants pockets were foam earplugs, like those used by people who operate noisy machinery or who fire weapons at a range.

With the suspect's body searched, Pope turned his attention to the car. There was a blue metal flashlight and a red gas can on the passenger seat. On the backseat was a yellow blanket. When that was moved, officers found a woman's ring shaped like a heart. (Nate Lee would later identify the ring as belonging to his wife.) On the floor was a piece of paper with a footprint on it, a pencil, a phone battery, a post from a headboard, and a blue-handled Phillips-head screwdriver.

Then Pope felt a sinking feeling—as he put it, it was like waking up on Christmas morning and discovering Santa hadn't come. There was no Denise, but there was a long-handled military-type shovel, which, like the suspect's pants, was wet and dirty—recently used.

Looking over the exterior of the car, Pope found strands of hair adhering to the rear spoiler. The back of the car was also spattered with what he later referred to as "pellets" of blood. The car's driver's seat was wet and muddy—a sandy mud. After backup arrived, Pope kept a log of those entering and exiting the crime scene.

Because of the nature of the developing case, Pope was compelled to take King's car keys and open up the trunk. Frustratingly, the missing woman wasn't there, either.

The passenger-side window was rolled down halfway. Was this what King was doing when he leaned over the passenger seat? Was he rolling down the window, possibly to toss something out—maybe a weapon? Throwing it like a Frisbee, a person might be able to toss a gun or a knife twenty to thirty feet into the weeds alongside the road. Probably couldn't reach the tree line, forty feet away.

(The weedy area beside the car was not secured that night, not until three or four days later. The car was considered a crime scene, but not the area surrounding the traffic stop. During that time, the grass near the shoulder of the road had been cut, and a crew went through the area picking up garbage. A highway worker could have found the weapon and wordlessly pocketed it.)

Sheriff's deputies now had Michael King bent over the front of the car. Pope asked one more time where the girl was.

"I'd never seen an expression on a man's face like the one King had then. It was cold, completely devoid of compassion or remorse," Pope explained.

King uttered something nasty—"Pure evil," the trooper recalled—and a couple of officers had to get between Pope and the suspect, who was promptly taken into protective custody.

* * *

The location of the arrest was communicated to the search helicopter—which was on the ground being refueled. The pilot agreed that he'd go back up as soon as he could and search the vicinity of the arrest for "hot spots."

Pope knew that Denise had to be someplace close to the arrest. There was wet blood and DNA-type material on the car—material that would have flown off or dried if King had driven very far before being stopped.

With a report that a wet shovel had been found in the Camaro, the search for Denise Lee donned a grim heaviness. In addition to searching for the missing woman by air, a dive team was readied to search nearby bodies of water.

Alive or not, Denise was someplace where it was wet. Trouble was, after a rainy day, that could be almost anywhere.

Moments after the traffic stop, Detective Lieutenant Kevin R. Sullivan, of the North Port Police Department's (NPPD) Criminal Investigations Bureau, arrived at the scene. By the time he got there, the suspect was already out of the car and had asked for a lawyer. Sullivan thought he looked familiar.

"Do I know you from somewhere?" Sullivan asked.

King replied that they had previously met through family.

"Are you okay?" Sullivan asked.

King assured him that he was. "I'm a victim here, too," he said. He explained that he, like Mrs. Lee, had been kidnapped, and he was eager to do whatever he could to help law enforcement.

"Tell me what happened," Sullivan said. He decided to play along and treat the man as a victim.

Observing the scene was Detective Christopher Morales, of the NPPD, who had also just arrived.

King agreed to a ride-along, sitting in the back of Sullivan's car, to look for Denise. Sullivan hoped to keep the man talking. The man was in custody, so no harm could come from the little game they were playing. During the ride-along, a fog lowered over North Port, cutting visibility. King said, "A guy took me and that girl, and I was tied up and had a hood over my head. . . . He let me go at my car and I just drove off."

The game did not bear fruit. In an attempt to throw the investigation a curveball, the suspect took the officers on a wild-goose chase, clear on the other side of town, as far from the scene of his arrest as they could get. Up and down. Back and forth. Till past 11:00 P.M. King had no idea where they were most of the time.

While they drove around, King was silently hopeful that his cousin Harold would keep his mouth shut. One statement from Harold Muxlow, and King's lies were exposed. He didn't know both Harold and his daughter had already spoken to police.

Trooper Pope was beat, but the adrenaline was still flowing. He couldn't get rid of the driving voice in his head. He needed to get back out there and look for Denise.

Just before 11:00 P.M., the aerial search had to be called off because of the now-heavy fog.

Cops were sent out to locate and interview friends and relatives of the arrested man. One such person was Jennifer Robb, King's ex-girlfriend, who lived in Homosassa, Florida, about fifty miles north. She was hoped to be a good source for info regarding King's relatives. Jennifer wasn't home, so patrols in Citrus County were informed that she was probably driving a red Nissan Frontier pickup, with black trim. It had a soccer ball bumper sticker on the back just above the license plate, and a decal at the top of the windshield that read ANGEL IN DISGUISE.

Police were also looking for a forty-one-year-old friend of King's named Robert "Rob" Salvador, who lived in Venice.

Cortnie Watts, who had already participated in the processing of the Lee house, was now called to the scene of King's arrest to photograph and collect evidence from the green Camaro. Watts had a routine that she followed. She always started at the outside of a scene and worked her way inward in ever-diminishing concentric circles. She created evidence swabs of the blood spatter on the car's spoiler, collected and bagged as evidence long, dirty-blond hair found both on the hood and rear of the car, and swabbed a mucus-like glob of material on the hood.

The passenger-side door handle, Watts noticed, was covered with a sandy mud. She photographed the car's interior—in particular, the red gas container, which sat on the passenger seat.

While she was doing this, Detective Michael Saxton was dusting the car's exterior for fingerprints. On the outside of the driver's-side window, he discovered a partial palm print, which he lifted with tape and placed on a white card.

The Camaro was secured with crime scene tape. That is, tape was placed over the space between the car doors and the rest of the car so that the doors could not be opened without breaking the tape. It was towed back to the NPPD and parked in the "evidence garage." Watts followed the tow truck in her own vehicle. The decision to move the vehicle at that time was made because the wind had picked up, and there was concern a new rain might wash away evidence.

Watts stayed with the car until quarter to one in the morning of January 18.

She returned to the car on January 19 and took tire ink standards from all four tires, using Sirchie fingerprint slab ink, with a roller and a glass slab. She put ink on the roller and rolled ink onto the tires. She put brown craft paper under each tire and, with the help of Sergeant Scott Graham and Property Evidence staff assistant Deb Hill, rolled the Camaro over the paper so an ink impression of the tire treads was made. Still using Graham and Hill's assistance, she pushed the vehicle out of the exam room and into a gated area in the police department's parking lot. A vehicle cover was placed over the car and locked into place with a padlock to secure the evidence.

Seeking a motive, police asked Denise's family and friends if they knew Michael King. They all shook their heads. No one had ever seen or heard of him before.

Michael Lee King was brought to the NPPD at 11:30 P.M., and put in an interrogation room. He sat in a corner, his hands cuffed in front of him, and told Detective Morales that he was born on May 4, 1971. King described the traffic stop and how Trooper Pope had repeatedly screamed, "Put your hands on your head" and "Where's the girl?" The trooper, King noted, was angry, pushing King's head up against the car, telling him that police had already been inside his house and had seen stuff.

King said he'd asked for a lawyer "all the way through" his apprehension, but he had been ignored.

Morales said, "When I got there, you were saying that you were the hostage."

King said he remembered saying that to somebody and complained that he hadn't been read his rights or given a chance to lawyer up.

Morales did read King his Miranda rights at that time, pausing after each line to verify that King understood what he was being told. King said he did, adding that he did not want to give Morales a statement. He just wanted an attorney—and he needed to use the bathroom. He was escorted out.

When King returned to the interrogation room, he was left alone until, around midnight, a cop King knew wandered into the interrogation room to "shoot the breeze." When was the last time they'd seen each other?

King said, "About three years ago."

"Still doing plumbing?"

"Yeah."

"Here or up north?"

"Here. There ain't nothing up north."

"The last time I saw you, I think we ran into each other on the street. Didn't you say you had a live-in girlfriend or something?"

"Yeah."

"You were having some kind of issues that the cops couldn't help you out with. What was that all about?"

"She took off in my car, went to Tennessee. Knoxville. I had to go all the way up there and pick it up."

"How long did you date her?"

"Not too long."

"What was her name?"

"Oh, shoot. Jen . . . Jennifer, something like that. Amy, it was Amy Sue (pseudonym)."

"I remember a Jennifer. I don't remember an Amy," the

cop said, nice and chummy. He asked the name of King's ex-wife.

"Danielle." He had been married to her for ten years, but she didn't work. She just played games on the computer all day.

"Yeah, I remember when you first came down here, with the jet skis and everything. It was 2003. All the trouble and shit with your neighbors—that's how I remember that stuff. So what have you been doing lately?"

"Not too much. Just hanging in there."

"How's everybody treating you? It was a madhouse when I showed up. I didn't know what was happening."

"When I first got pulled over, the friggin' guy was mad or something. He wouldn't let me talk. He's just screamin', 'Where's she at? We found duct tape.' Like that. I tried to tell him my side, but he didn't want to hear my side. 'Just tell me where she's at?' I said I wanted a lawyer present."

"Who was the cop talking about? I'm kind of lost."

"I don't know. I said I wanted a lawyer present, and he said, 'You ain't gettin' one.'"

"He told you that? Wow."

"I got bad luck. I ain't pickin' up nobody anymore."

"Who'd you pick up?"

"Guy on the side of the road." King told his story: The second the guy got in the car, he pushed King's head down and threw a hood over his head. "I couldn't even freakin' move, man."

"You look like you put on a few pounds since the last time I saw you. This guy must've been pretty big."

"Between you and me, I've never been in a fight in my life. He was a jerk."

The cop changed the subject: "Yeah, I remember Jen. I don't remember no Amy."

"Yeah, Amy was something else. They said she was on

cocaine. I thought she was straight, turned out she was just out of detox. Met her through friends. I picked her up, went all the way up to Tennessee to pick her up. The only reason I got mad at her was she took the car."

He said the house on Sardinia was the only place he stayed when he was in North Port. Although for a while, he was living in Homosassa, and then he'd been back to Michigan a few times, visiting his family.

"When was the last time you were in Michigan?"

"Three, four days ago. I got back Saturday."

"So you just got back. How was it up there? Cold?"

"Ice-cold, yeah. I was looking for work up there, filled out a bunch of applications, but it's slow right now. I got to see my kid. He wanted to stay up there, so I let him stay with my brother." He explained that his house had no furniture. His furnishings were at an old girlfriend's house. He didn't want the drama, so he just left it. That was Jennifer, the one in Homosassa. "I figured I'd just keep walkin'." She and his son didn't get along at all.

After a pause, King said, "I was hijacked. Crazy shit. It was the worst thing."

"Are they helping you out? Is that what you're waiting on?" the cop asked.

"They read me my Miranda rights and explained what it meant."

"You can do whatever you want. What is it you want to do?"

"I can just sit here all night. I can't tell them nothing. I don't know anything. I wouldn't mind going home."

"You got a girlfriend now? Got anyone waitin' on you?"

"Yeah, Tennille. Met her because she played bingo with my mom. She wanted to move in, but I said I don't want that right now. She's pretty nice. She's got no kids. But I been through a lot of shit. I just want to work."

"You still having problems with your neighbors? I remember you used to have a real feud going."

"No, when I wave, they wave. Just hi/bye. No problems anymore." There had been someone coming into his house while he was away. There wasn't anything to steal, so he didn't call the cops; however, someone was going inside and doing whatever. The front door was always jimmied open. Probably kids.

The cop left. For a time, King was alone to ponder his dilemma. He sat motionless, with head bowed. When the cop returned, he brought King something to eat and some water. King was thirsty, but he didn't feel like eating.

In the meantime, police had picked up Harold Muxlow and had questioned him at greater length about his cousin borrowing a shovel, and about the bound woman attempting to escape in front of his house.

Harold said he didn't intervene because he didn't think it was any of his business, that it was just another one of good ol' Mike's "crazy relationships."

Then police had an inspired idea. They put Harold in the interrogation room—just the two of them—and taped the conversation with a surveillance camera.

"What the hell you doin'?" Harold asked King.

King said, "I got hijacked. I couldn't, I tried to put 911 on the phone and everything. And here I am. I couldn't do anything, couldn't say anything, or he'd've took everybody out."

"Who was it?"

"I don't know, man. He was saying, 'I'm gonna kill them all.'"

"You were afraid of this guy?"

"Dude, he was big. It don't make no difference. I don't fight."

"They say somebody on the street seen you and somebody called. I got cops at my house, and I'm like, what the f***? What am I supposed to do, you know?"

"No, you did the right thing. I couldn't have called without him knowin'."

"Was he colored? Mexican?"

"He had a ski mask on. I don't know."

"How did you get involved with these people? You just got back into town, right?"

"I pulled over. I thought they were broke down or something. As soon as the door opened, something hit me in the head with the heel of his palm—so hard I saw white specks. Then something got pulled over my head, tight here," King said, gesturing with his cuffed hands toward his neck. "I think he knew somethin'. Karate or somethin'. One time, he hit me in the gut and I couldn't even breathe."

"When you were at my house you should've written something down, let me know what's going on."

"I should've thought of something, dude. He said, he promised, if we did everything, he said he was going to let this girl go."

"I don't get it. What would he gain? Holding on to you. Holding on to her. What would he gain? I can't see what gain there would be."

"Maybe he was sick, man. Maybe his was a totally different world from ours. You could tell by the way he talked and the shit he said."

"Just one guy?"

"Well, there had to be somebody else. He was talking to someone on the phone. 'Where you at now? Where you at now?' I couldn't hardly hear him. They put earplugs in my ears."

"Why'd they let you go and not her?"

"I don't know. I don't know what's going on. They probably let her go, too. Shouldn't they? I don't know."

"If they do find her . . ."

"Then I can get out of here," King said with a note of hope.

"If they find her—I mean, I hope they find her alive. . . ."

"Thank God!" King exclaimed.

"But if something did happen to her, they got forensics now, and they can tell."

"That's good. That's good. That's what I need, man. They find her—I'm good to go."

"What did you need the flashlight for?"

"He told me. That and the shovel and the gas can. I don't even have a f***in' riding mower. He just told me to say that."

King began to describe what his abductor did to him, making him lie on the ground, take his shoes off. Put cuffs on him.

"The guy or the cop?" Harold asked.

"It was the same," King replied.

They talked about King's problems with women. It was one thing after another.

Harold said, "They say this girl got snagged. They took her right from her house. She had two kids, two little ones. They didn't take money. Nothin'."

"That's crazy," King said.

"How this girl get in your car, though?"

"I pulled over and they weighed me down, and that was it, you know. Stupid, man, just stupid." King complained about the rough treatment he'd received when arrested.

"Can you blame him? Twenty-one-year-old girl kidnapped and you're the last one seen with her. When the guy let you go, you should've flagged down a cop right away."

"There's a lot of things I should've done," King said with a sigh.

"What would your brother Gary have done?"

"He thinks faster than I do. He'd've taken the guy. He was in the military."

"What did the guy have? A gun? A knife?"

"I couldn't tell. I wasn't paying attention."

"It's not good, dude. You're not in a good situation. So what did this guy want with a shovel for?"

"I don't know. I didn't ask him, and he didn't tell me."

"You'd better take a lie detector test, dude. If you don't, you are going to be screwed. It looks bad. I keep thinking what if it was my daughter that got snagged. How would I feel? Now, if they find her alive—"

"Thank God."

"But if they don't, the parents are going to need relief. They got to find her body. Otherwise, you got to live with that—live with that for a long time. Otherwise, her parents always be wondering, 'Where she at? Is she still alive?'"

"Right."

"Is she buried somewhere? You would want to know. I would want to know. It would haunt you for the rest of your life until you find out exactly. . . ."

King told Harold how he'd tried to use his cell phone, to call Tennille, his girlfriend, but the guy caught him and threw the phone into the backseat where the girl was.

"She made a call," Harold shared.

"She did? Thank God. Because that was what I was trying to do, you know?"

"Her dad works for the sheriff's department. That's bad for you. They got to find where she's at."

"Exactly."

"There ain't nothin' you remember that might help them?"

"I tried," King said, shaking his head. "It was like a roller coaster."

"If you told them where the part of the road was where you pulled over, maybe somebody would recognize something."

"It doesn't help when you got that stupid thing on your head. Everything was black. Why me?"

"Were you wearing that shirt earlier?"

"Yeah."

"You weren't wearing something white?"

"No, I do have a nice white T-shirt, short sleeve, but I only wear that once in a great while."

"You got to piece it together and get 'er done, man. Eventually they will find her, but till then, her dad and her husband are probably going nuts, not knowing. I would be that way," Harold said.

"I would, too—you know," King replied.

Harold tried to get King to remember landmarks. After all, there was no hood on his head when King came to his house looking for a shovel. All King could remember, he said, was he thought he was at his house at one point because he heard his garage door open and close.

What kind of car did his abductor drive? King thought he might've said something about it being a Sebring, but he couldn't be sure. Earplugs, you know.

"You got to take a lie detector test because this ain't going away. She called 911 on your phone. It don't look good. You better figure out something, dude. You got to take the test soon, before you get a lawyer. Once you get a lawyer, he won't let you take the test. Your mom and dad ain't too happy," Harold told his cousin.

"I understand that."

"What about the lie detector test?"

"They stick needles in you for that, right? I don't like needles."

"No needles. They just put a thing on you [and] ask you questions. The machine says if you're telling the truth. It won't hurt you. Can only help you. God knows what really happened. Nobody else." Harold Muxlow shook hands with his cousin and left. It was almost 5:00 A.M. Again, Michael King was alone in the room.

"He makes it sound so real," Harold said to the police outside, "but I don't think so. He may lose his house, he doesn't have a job, and then some of the relationships he's had with women . . . he probably just snapped."

Harold told police he was surprised when his cousin showed up at his house, even before he realized there was a captive in the Camaro. "I've scarcely seen him for months," he said.

The woman had begged him to "call the cops," but Harold hadn't. Why?

"Well, he had a history of psycho girlfriends. Drama wasn't necessarily unusual." Harold said that despite the frantic woman in his car, King seemed calm. At one point, Harold told police, he was about fifteen feet from the Camaro, and he and King were having a calm conversation about King's life. "I guess he had some problems, but he seemed pretty calm about it."

As for the woman, Muxlow said, he didn't really get a good look at her. Just a glimpse, really. The windows were "kind of" tinted. "He got the stuff he borrowed. I heard a bang when he put the stuff in the side door. I heard somebody say, 'Call the cops,' and then he said, 'Don't worry about it,' and took off. I didn't hear much. I thought it was that psycho broad he was with. I hadn't seen him in so long. It just didn't compute."

One reason it didn't sink in right away was his cousin was such a laid-back guy. King didn't seem like the type to kidnap someone—didn't drink, didn't do drugs. Didn't cause trouble.

King *did* have a tendency to spin a tall tale now and again—"Mikey had a big imagination"—so you always had to take his stories with a grain of salt.

Still, after Harold pondered it a bit, it didn't sit right—the "call the cops" part—so he phoned his daughter. Then he got in his car and drove to the 7-Eleven gas station on Price Boulevard and Sumter Boulevard, where he called 911 himself. By the time he got home, a state trooper was at his house waiting for him.

Harold Muxlow's emotions overcame him as he talked to police, and he began to weep.

"It's hard talking about it," he said. "When I think about it, I feel so bad for the girl and the family."

A search warrant was acquired for Michael King's clothes and person. Pamela "Pam" Schmidt, a criminalistics specialist, who wore a dark blue T-shirt, with a big white C.S.I. on the back, took fingernail scrapings and clippings. King's clothes were confiscated. Schmidt photographed him while he was naked from the waist up; then she photographed and swabbed spots on his right elbow and back where the skin had been broken.

Schmidt asked King how he had suffered those injuries. King said, "He had duct tape all over me. I know that."

He was ordered to remove his jeans, which were placed in a large paper bag. New photos were taken as he stood in his black boxer shorts. He was instructed to lean on a chair as the bottoms of his feet were photographed one at a time.

"Now your underwear," Schmidt said. King removed his shorts, and these were placed in another bag. Present was Detective Michael Saxton, who was somewhat surprised to see that King's pubic hair was completely shaved off. More photos were taken, particularly of "fresh marks" near his groin. King said these might have been caused by him trying to use the bathroom while handcuffed.

Michael King was issued an orange jumpsuit; then he was escorted from the interrogation room to be booked formally on charges of kidnapping with intent to commit or facilitate a felony. He was listed as five feet eight inches tall, two hundred pounds, hair blond, eyes blue. His mug shot showed him glaring—a mean man, his soul consumed.

Without allowing the two to see each other in the hallway, police took Michael King out of the interrogation room and brought in Nate Lee. Two CCSO detectives—one male, one female—did the questioning. They informed him that they intended to take a sworn statement and that he could be charged with perjury if he lied. Once sworn in, Nate said he'd been married to Denise since August of '05. Her birthday was August 6, 1986.

They met when he was a senior at Lemon Bay High School and had taken a law class together. They knew of each other at that point, but they had never communicated. Their first face-to-face meeting came while sharing a calculus class at Manatee Community College—she was a math whiz—spring semester, 2004. He was in college with a job working for a construction company called J.L. Concrete, but she was still a high-school senior, taking a college course, and making extra money babysitting. They began dating almost immediately. Denise spoke to Nate first, which was surprising, since she was so shy. She said, "Hey, weren't you in my law class?" Their first date was a study date, in January '04.

By February, they were pledging their love. He gave her a $40 ring, with a heart on it. She wore it even after they were engaged and then married. He met her family. Rick Goff and Nate had things in common and got along. Nate played baseball in high school, Rick coached baseball—so they always had something to talk about.

When Denise graduated, she and Nate moved to Tampa, where they attended the University of South Florida (USF). They both lived with a friend of his in the Lakeview Oaks apartment complex. They were there for a couple of months over the summer before the semester started; then they moved to another apartment right across the street from USF. They shared the apartment with a friend, the same from Lakeview Oaks, and his girlfriend.

In Tampa, Nate didn't have a job at first, but Denise had a credit card that her parents had given her. He was going to school full-time, and his parents were paying for his living expenses, so he wasn't in "a real hurry to get a job." They had two cats, enjoyed going out to dinner, and occasionally had Nate's friends over to play poker.

"She didn't really have any USF friends, just the friends she had in high school," Nate told the detectives. She did have college study groups that "got together" and discussed school online.

Denise took a job at CVS; soon thereafter, she learned she was pregnant. That was a stressful time. Telling their parents that they were expecting was tough. But the stressful period didn't last long. Once they decided to wed, everyone relaxed, although neither set of parents had pressured them.

Was she neat? Was she a slob? She was neat, but it wasn't like she needed everything to be spotless, Nate explained. "Obviously, our house now is a mess, but that's a different situation." She liked things being clean, but she wasn't obsessive-compulsive about it. The detectives asked if she had hobbies. That was a stumper. No, not really. They enjoyed going to the movies. She enjoyed TV shows—cop shows. One day, she wanted to be part of that world. Not the show business version, but in real life. She liked her cats. Before she had real kids, her cats were her kids.

Nate and Denise would go places, not often—the zoo, the aquarium, places like that. They didn't have a lot of money, but she liked to shop, go to the mall.

What were Nate's hobbies? Sports, playing them and watching them. Golf. He would like to play more often, but he couldn't afford it. He played the trumpet. He played cards every Friday night. Someday he would like to build a model train set.

Nate and Denise had known from very early in their relationship that they wanted to get married someday, but their plans were to finish school first. Pregnancy just moved up the date. They wanted to be married when the baby was born; so they exchanged vows in August 2005.

Nate stopped going to classes and took a full-time job at a Best Buy that fall, and the baby, Noah, was born January 8, 2006. For a little more than a year, Denise and Nate lived with his in-laws, and he considered taking a job in the sheriff's office. He wasn't sure why the CCSO turned down

his application, but it might have been because he lied
during his polygraph exam about smoking pot as a kid.
Denise never smoked anything. She hated smoking. Nate
would have a cigar now and again while playing poker, and
his wife hated it. So, instead of being a cop, he worked for
a company that built docks and seawalls.

They lived with Denise's parents for a year, and that was
okay. They had their privacy; the house was big; the garage
had been converted into a bedroom. But as soon as Nate
was making enough money for them to rent their own
place, they did.

Since March '07, he'd been a meter reader for Florida
Power and Light (FP&L). That same month, they began
renting the house on Latour. Four months after that, Adam,
another surprise, was born.

The couple hated the house on Latour. It was one of a
bunch of North Port houses that had been built but had not
sold, so they were put up for rent at $800 a month. It was a
good location for him to get to and from work. However,
trouble started right away. They'd only been living there for
a couple of weeks when someone stole $600 worth of CDs
and a pair of Oakley sunglasses out of Nate's car, which
he'd left unlocked in the driveway. They'd been there for
two weeks and already they were trying to figure out how
they were going to get out of their lease. They would have
had to pay the rent there until they got someone else to
move in, and nobody else was going to want to rent that
house. They couldn't put a security system in the house because it wasn't theirs. He worried because Denise didn't
work and she was home alone with the babies every day.

Nate followed the same routine every morning, up at
six-ten, out the door by six-twenty. He showered at night,

had his clothes laid out—in the morning, he did nothing. Didn't eat breakfast. Put his clothes on, grabbed his phone and wallet, then headed out the door. Monday through Friday, weekends off.

For a time, he had a second job at a Winn-Dixie. He dropped it just that past December because he never got to see his family. The boys would be asleep when he left, asleep when he got home.

They paid the bills—rent, car, insurance, phone, Internet— just barely each month. It always came down to the last penny.

This most recent Christmas season, he'd had a few gigs playing the trumpet with the Venice Symphony, in churches and things like that.

He admitted to a small amount of tension at home, just because Denise wanted to go out all the time—because she was stuck in the house—and he wanted to stay in, because he was out all the time. When they did go out, it was usually so the boys could see their grandparents, both sets, or to go to the mall or Walmart.

He knew her routine pretty well. He talked to her every day, several times throughout the day. He would put her on speakerphone and talk to her as he worked. Noah got up between seven and eight every morning. That's when Denise would get up. Adam woke up not long after that. Adam could talk to himself in his crib for hours and be fine; but the second Noah woke up, he needed attention. She would breast-feed Adam and give Noah oatmeal and chocolate milk. She watched TV a lot, went on the Internet, talked with her friends on Myspace. She put pictures of the kids on there, but she only communicated with people she knew.

The boys napped in the early afternoon. They had lunch

midafternoon. She'd make Noah a sandwich—grilled cheese. The only time she would leave the house was to go to the store—and only then when they actually needed something, if they were out of juice or something like that. She would have to take the boys with her. They did not use a sitter much.

"Nobody wanted to drive all the way out to North Port to watch them," Nate said.

She didn't go shopping for fun with the boys because Noah would want to run around, and it was too stressful. They'd gone to the park maybe once since they moved to North Port. Maybe once they went to Walmart to get a money order. She couldn't even go to the gas station with the kids because she had to pay in cash, and it was a hassle. They did those things together. He drove a '95 Dodge Avenger. Denise drove a Corolla.

One thing that made Nate nervous was that she would walk around the house wearing nothing but a shirt and underwear—and she didn't necessarily always have the blinds closed. He would tell her to close the blinds and she would say, "No one can see," because the house was so secluded. He said it was true that there were no neighbors who could look in, but a driver on the street could see "right in."

For the past month, the weather was nice and Denise had been opening windows, and raising the blinds so they wouldn't blow in the wind. There were screens, but that was it. He knew for a fact that the windows were open on Thursday because he'd talked to her that morning and she'd said so.

There were two locks on the front door—one on the handle and a dead bolt. They locked both at night; but during the day, usually just the handle was locked.

One potential security problem with the house was the garage door—the door from the garage into the house, which didn't lock all the time. They'd had a problem with it since they moved in.

The detectives asked Nate about events of the recent past. Tuesday night, he'd had rehearsal. Wednesday night, they'd had dinner with his parents. During that night, she'd gotten up a couple of times in the middle of the night because she was having her period. He thought she was wearing a white shirt, but he couldn't be sure.

On Thursday, he'd called Denise about 7:55 A.M., which was early, and he'd been afraid she would still be asleep. But she was up and they had a five-minute conversation.

He also talked to her around eleven o'clock. She said she'd taken a shower. He asked her what was for dinner. She said she had chicken out or they could have pasta, but they were out of ingredients for that. She also said they were out of milk and juice—and he had the money.

He talked to her less than normal that morning. It was raining and he wanted to get his route done as quickly as possible because he wasn't enjoying getting wet. When he did finish, he called home to see if he still needed to go to the store and to let Denise know he'd be home by three-thirty.

No answer.

The phone was ringing all the way through, so he knew it was turned on. He called again, and again. Six, seven times. He figured she must have gone to the store and left her phone at home. When he got home, the first thing he noticed was that the windows were shut, garage door shut,

Denise's car in the driveway, and front door locked. He opened it with a key.

When he got inside, he saw Denise's phone on the reclining chair near the front door. It was plugged into a charger and said: **Seven missed calls.** Then he heard Noah, who was in Adam's crib with Adam. Very odd. Denise would never allow that. Noah was so much bigger than Adam, and he didn't completely know how to be gentle. Nate picked up Noah; then he checked the bedroom and bathroom. No Denise. He began yelling her name. Checked the whole house, opened all the closets, pulled back the covers on the bed, went outside and checked all sides of the house, called 911, went to a neighbor's house and knocked on the door. Seen my wife? They said no. Both kids had full diapers. He changed the diapers and asked Noah where Mommy was. Noah pointed in the bedroom, but she wasn't there. She wasn't anywhere. The windows were shut but not locked. That wasn't right. They were either open or closed and locked. Nothing was broken. It was 82 degrees in the house, so Nate turned on the AC.

At some point, he tried calling his mother-in-law—no answer. Then he called Rick, who said he was on his way. It started hitting Nate then, and he began to cry. The next time he looked out the window, the first police car was pulling up. Two police cars came. A few minutes later, Rick arrived. Nate dressed the boys. Police kicked everyone out and shut down the house as a potential crime scene.

The search for Denise Lee utilized the combined strength of the areas' multiple law enforcement agencies. Canine search-and-rescue were active. Sheriff's deputies from two counties, North Port cops, Fish & Wildlife agents,

Animal Services, and Florida Highway Patrol all had people searching.

There were even civilian volunteers; some working in coordination with officials, some out on their own. All off-duty officers reported for duty.

Trooper Eddie Pope, the arresting officer, appreciated the numbers. It was a hell of a search team, but the game plan missed the mark. The evidence on the car was *still wet*. They should just draw a circle around the point of the arrest—or better yet, three or four hundred feet south on Toledo Blade, where he first saw the Camaro.

The trooper joined up with a corporal and went to a search command center at Sumter. He talked to some big-wigs he hadn't seen before. They had it wrong.

Three hundred searchers all over the grid. No disrespect, but Pope was pretty sure Denise was close to the arrest site. They should concentrate on that region.

"Hey, we appreciate what you did. Good job—but we've got it from here," they told Pope, who felt dissed. He was invited to join a new search team being put together just outside the trailer. The trooper and the corporal opted out of that detail and forged off on their own. Pope pointed his Marauder toward the corner of Cranberry and Toledo Blade. At that site was the staging area for the canine units, Fish & Wildlife, and the Sarasota Response Team.

Pope talked to a captain and told him his story. Turned out the search teams had not been told where the arrest was made, nor had they heard about the evidence found on the car. Pope and a team, which included dogs, headed for the spot he had in mind.

The initial reports in the local papers befuddled resi-dents. One typical comment from a North Port woman was

"Maybe I need more coffee, but this story doesn't make sense. Surely, no one would give him a shovel after seeing her in that situation." She wasn't the last person to question Harold Muxlow's actions.

Harold Muxlow had not been quick to act, but his daughter had. She, too, seemed confused about her dad's hesitance when she said, "It's common sense. The woman needed help. She was yelling, 'Help!' If someone needs help, then you get help. You don't stop and think about it."

CHAPTER 3

JANUARY 18, 2008

At 1:38 A.M., police officers in South Venice knocked on the door of Robert Salvador and woke him up. When was the last time he'd seen Michael King? Did he know the whereabouts of Denise Lee? Robert said he knew no Lees and hadn't seen King lately.

He talked to the officers for about five minutes and then they left. He and his wife went on the Internet and found out what it was all about. Robert thought about it, and decided he might be deeply involved in this. His best bet was to tell the law everything he knew.

In the morning, he called the Venice police, the agency closest to him. They said the case was not in their jurisdiction and was being handled by the North Port Police Department. They gave him the number to call.

So Robert Salvador went to see Detective Morales, and Salvador had a very interesting story to tell about the captured suspect. He apologized for the delay, but he'd been a little slow on the uptake as to the importance of events. It took a while to sink in that anything quite this horrible could be real.

Robert was a married man with six kids, a self-employed construction worker. He knew King as a plumber. They'd worked jobs at the same site. Robert remodeled or renovated. King did the pipes. Sometimes King tore up a wall to get at the pipes and Salvador came in immediately after to patch up the holes. He'd known King for a couple of years, and really got to know him when he did a job at King's house on Sardinia. After that, Salvador and King hung out.

Once King asked him to go deep-sea fishing with him, and Robert took his wife with him. King was with an older couple, whom he introduced as his girlfriend's parents.

There was a period of time when Robert didn't hear from Michael King. He thought maybe King had lost his job. He heard from a third party that King had moved back to Michigan, where he was from. Then King called him, said he was back in Florida, and was wondering if Salvador knew of work. He claimed he was "trying to get his house back in order." He needed furniture. His place was empty. Robert offered an old TV he could have.

That was the last he heard from King until the day before. At 11:00 A.M., King called him and asked if he could pick up the TV. Robert told King it was raining, so he didn't have to work—he'd been doing a lot of outside work lately. He was on his way to a gun range, where he enjoyed target shooting.

"I went two, three times a month, usually on days when I had no job—or there was no work because of weather," Robert told police.

He had to admit, he was becoming addicted to target shooting. His wife knew that he went to the gun range on occasion, sure—but she had no idea how often. He had four guns: a nine millimeter, two small twenty-two pistols, and a Russian pistol.

Salvador politely asked King to shoot with him. Surprisingly, King said yes. Robert asked him if he still had his .357 and King said no. Now King had a nine—but no nine ammunition.

No problem. Robert had plenty of nine ammo, in the box where he kept all his ammo, a sealed plastic box, a dry box, important for when he went boating.

So they went to Knight Trail Park & Gun Range in Nokomis. Salvador could tell that King had never been to this range before because he didn't know where it was. After trying to give King directions, without success, Robert suggested that they meet at a nearby gas station and then go to the range together. King said fine.

Robert drove his white minivan. King his green Camaro. Later, Robert wondered if King had ever been to *any* gun range. He didn't know the rules. When they got to the range, King was wearing a black T-shirt, memorable in that its sleeves were longer than normal.

Robert had given King ammo for his gun. Salvador said to police, "He could have pocketed one or two more."

He handed over all four guns that had been used at the firing range the previous day. No, he didn't have King's gun. As far as he knew, King had King's gun.

Jane Kowalski woke up at her grandmother's house and had a cup of coffee in her hand when she turned on the TV. There, full screen, was a picture of Michael King.

"Oh, my God, that's the guy in the car," she exclaimed. "Holy crap!"

A picture of Denise Lee came on the TV. She realized

that it hadn't been a child whom she had heard screaming and pounding on the glass, but rather a young woman.

She called the hotline number that flashed on the screen and explained, "You guys probably want to talk to me. I'm the one who made that 911 call."

"Okay, we'll get someone to get back with you," they said.

No one called back.

On the afternoon of January 18, Channel 10 News in Tampa Bay located Michael King's parents, James and Patsy, in their mobile home in the Tidevue Estates, just north of U.S. 301, in the town of Ellenton, Florida.

James said that he was "worried and scared" for his son. He had not seen Mike in twenty-four hours, and didn't fully understand what was going on. The entire family had just returned from Michigan on Tuesday afternoon, January 15.

He was asked how the arrest was affecting the family and responded, "We are still trying to figure this out. It has been hard."

"What is the relationship between your son and the missing woman?" a reporter asked.

"I don't know. I only hope she is found alive and in good health."

Patsy chimed in that she heard about it on the TV news. "It is totally out of character for Mike," she said.

At around that same time, only a few miles to the north from the Kings' mobile home, the search for Denise had moved to Manatee County after a woman's sandal was found. Police dogs, officers on foot, and a helicopter were called to the site south of U.S. 301. False alarm.

A pile of women's clothing was found on the north end

of Salford Boulevard, south of Interstate 75, not far from Michael King's home, but police dogs determined that these did not belong to the victim.

The search team of Trooper Pope was in the woods in the vicinity of King's arrest; it was tough going because of the thickness of the brush. There were many areas where searchers could barely see the ground.

Among those actively searching for Denise was her father. Rick Goff told Chief Deputy Bill Cameron that he wanted to "stay involved," and was allowed to do so.

For North Port police, there was an eerie and grim sense of déjà vu. Less than a year and a half before, six-year-old Coralrose Fullwood was abducted from her North Port home in the middle of the night. She was discovered several hours later, raped and murdered, behind a construction site only a few doors down from her home.

Now a new search was under way. Some specialists boarded kayaks and johnboats to navigate canals and survey large ponds. Nothing. Police chased down twenty-five leads. The first twenty-four were false alarms.

Then came number twenty-five.

CHAPTER 4

CANINE SEKOU

Tami Treadway was a SCSO Animal Services supervisor, a civilian employee, who trained dogs to conduct search-and-rescue missions. The dogs, once trained, could no longer live in a normal home, and they needed to be placed with a search-and-rescue specialist or a member of law enforcement. She made sure everyone was trained properly—humans and dogs alike—and safeguarded the dogs' health.

She had her own dog, of course. Canine Sekou was his formal name; he was a golden retriever she'd handled for six years. *Sekou* was a South African word for "great warrior" or "learned one."

"He was my husband's dog," Treadway later said. "He got him from his nephew in New Orleans, where my husband is from. We weren't together at the time, although we were both members of the team. He got Sekou to be a search dog, and trained him initially in wilderness searches. We got together when Sekou was young."

When her husband went to school to become a firefighter and a paramedic, Tami Treadway took over Sekou's training. The dog was trained in human remains detection, and Treadway had been his handler since.

"He's still my husband's dog in the family sense, but I'm the one who has worked him," she noted.

Treadway and Sekou were a team, she and that dog, two halves of a whole. She could read his body language like a book, and he "told" in a million ways just what he was doing and thinking. He was her partner. They lived together. They slept together.

Golden retrievers made great search dogs, but they were by no means the only breed capable of doing the work. German shepherds, Labs, Australian cattle dogs, and even mixed breeds were also suitable. Aptitude varied more from dog to dog than from breed to breed.

A dog trained in human remains detection followed the scent of decaying human body parts, so Sekou's searches almost never had a happy ending. Most were just flat-out heartbreaking.

"The one that sticks out in my mind was a case in Tampa, to the north of us. They had some intelligence that a girl might have had something bad happen to her with a guy who lived in the house, and they wanted us to search this empty house. Stripped-to-the-walls empty. It had a concrete floor, and they thought he might have buried her under the concrete." They never went in with just one dog, always with three or four, because a "dog will be a dog" and they don't have 100 percent success. All three dogs in this case came up with nothing in the house. In fact, they didn't even want to be in the house. They kept trying to go outside. So they moved the search to the backyard, and the dogs hit on a spot near a shed. There, about six feet down, they found the girl's body.

The girl's name? Treadway didn't know. She might never know. "We try to be disconnected," she said.

But there was no way to be disconnected in this case. She lived in North Port and the search for the missing Denise Lee was all over the local news, even before she and Sekou took up the search.

Even if you weren't watching TV, you knew something was up, with so many roads closed by police. To make it even more personal, Denise was the same age as Treadway's daughter; and her daughter had two little boys, just like Denise.

The dogs don't know, of course. They are just happy that they got their toy or their reward for a successful search. Sekou had a clownish personality, and that didn't change just because he was searching for a cadaver. He never picked up on the grimness of the task.

On January 18, 2008, Treadway and Sekou were called in to assist with the search for Denise Lee. She was given her orders by the sheriff, and they were one of six-to-eight canine teams involved in that day's desperate activities.

The initial plan was to search a wide variety of areas, in the vicinity of the Lees' house, around King's house, and the area around Harold Muxlow's home.

But Trooper Pope said their best bet was to search in the area of King's arrest, and that was where Sekou and Treadway were happily doing their thing.

CHAPTER 5

THE DISTURBED EARTH

The search continued into the early-morning hours. Tami Treadway and Sekou strode with purpose into a remote swampy section off an unfinished road. The dog was particularly curious around a large pile of sand, the grains of which resembled those found in the Camaro and on the suspect.

There was an unfinished development off Toledo Blade, and the site was part of that. Construction had stopped in the middle when the economy fell; this part of the road had gone undeveloped. The location was just off Cranberry Boulevard.

The search was interrupted briefly when a fire chief on the scene called it a night and ordered the search resumed in the morning. Many searchers, including Pope, left, but Treadway remained on the scene. She and Sekou returned to the area near the large pile of sand.

Sekou wandered into the wooded area and then came

back out. He went back in; this time, Treadway followed him.

"Whatcha got, boy?"

There were pine trees and a gully. At one point, both woman and dog had to go under a fence to proceed. Treadway saw a spot where pine needles had fallen, where perhaps there had been standing water, where the ground was darker. It was a sandy area, and it was a spot where the vegetation differed from the surrounding area. There was clay mixed in with the sand at that spot, indicating the surface was recently tilled.

Plus, it was this spot that had Sekou reacting. A barbed-wire fence bordered the scene at its rear. Without touching anything, Treadway set out to call law enforcement to the scene, which was taped off and slowly excavated.

No, it wasn't that easy. The first police officer she encountered out on the street paid no mind to her. "He wasn't interested and left," Treadway later recalled with frustration in her voice.

Luckily, there were other officers in the area, and eventually the area was sealed off. Looking at the ground at that spot carefully, armed with flashlights, police saw what appeared to be blood in the sand. The large sand pile nearby was missing shovelsful of sand on one side. The sand was very light, the kind Floridians called "sugar sand." On the ground between the pile and the disturbed earth, there was bloody sand in two dinner plate–sized piles. It hadn't been caused by someone bleeding over a sandy spot. The sand was on top of the blood, placed to hide the blood. The blood had already been there, pooled in spots.

SCSO crime scene technician Lisa Lanham arrived on the scene. First order of business for her was to preserve the evidence. A tent was erected over the site to accomplish that. Because the ground was wet and sloped, sandbags were piled up on one side of the suspicious location, to help prevent water from seeping in.

All of this was starting to paint a picture. The disturbed earth was now being referred to as the "potential grave site." Lanham bagged blood, sand, and sandy blood. She noticed that there were some blades of grass in the area that were naturally red. Back at the lab, they would determine what was and wasn't blood. Excavation would begin the following morning, under natural light. Lanham left the site and reported to another emergency; then she returned to the white tent on the morning of January 19.

CHAPTER 6

JANUARY 19, 2008

On Saturday morning, Jane Kowalski again called the hotline number. The reaction was still lukewarm.

"We probably need to talk to you," the operator said. "We'll have someone call you back."

"Okay, I'll be home all day," Jane said.

She never went far from her phone, but again the authorities didn't call.

Under the supervision of a professional archaeologist named Lewis "Skip" Wood, working for the SCSO, the excavation began at dawn. When Wood got there, he described the site as a shallow swale behind piles of palmetto root. For comparison purposes, Wood paced off fifty feet from the suspicious site and dug with a shovel a bit, overturning earth in a patch that measured two feet by two feet. He discovered that, as expected, the soil under the earth was similar in color to that found on the surface at the suspicious site. A quick visual analysis of the soil at the site revealed sand such as would be found at the beach; charcoal, the result of some past forest fire; and a brown soil that included degraded roots. The yellow sand found on the surface of the suspicious site had been twenty-two inches beneath the surface at the test patch that Wood had dug. What they had here was a hole that had been dug out, then filled back in.

Material was removed from the potential grave site a wafer-thin layer at a time.

With Wood was another archaeologist, Maxine Miller, who searched in vain for items that might yield a readable fingerprint. She took fresh photos of the site after each slice of earth was taken away. She placed measuring sticks on the ground before taking photos to provide a scale.

Both archaeologists avoided contaminating evidence by donning gloves, caps, booties, and white jumpsuits. Pine needles and pinecones were found beneath the surface, another indication of digging and refilling. The edges of the suspicious site were obvious. The soil was hard-packed all around, but it was looser and softer at the site itself.

As the digging continued, Wood and Miller could see "scallop marks" at the edges of the site, evidence of digging with a round-nosed shovel.

When the hole was still only inches deep, a human shoulder became visible.

As expected, it was the remains of Denise Amber Lee.

The medical examiner was called. Body found.

Wood and Miller used a variety of small shovels at first, but they switched to brushes once the body became visible. There would come a time when digging from the top of the hole was no longer practical. They would need a way to get at the earth at the sides of and underneath the body without hanging upside down. This, in essence, opened a door to the grave site and allowed them greater access to the soil under the body. The shallow grave ended up being four feet deep. Photos and videos were taken throughout the excavation. After a time, a plastic sheet was placed over it to prevent contamination from any trace evidence, possible wind-borne, that might blow into the hole.

The medical examiner was off duty, so his backup, Dr. Daniel Schultz, a competent forensic anthropologist in his own right, came to the scene and took charge. He officially pronounced the body dead, and the remains were wrapped in a plastic sheet, then lifted from the hole at 3:56 P.M.

There was soil still stuck to the body's face, but Dr. Schultz didn't remove it. He could see that there was also blood on the face, and he didn't want to disrupt that.

The body had been packed in moist soil, a factor when he tried to determine time of death by taking the body temperature. The remains were wet for a while. The hands were a washerwoman's hands. He'd seen hands like those before, on bodies pulled from swimming pools.

Once out of the hole, the cadaver was briefly unwrapped. Dr. Schultz noted fixed lividity—that is, a bruise-like discoloration—on the left side. With death, the blood stopped circulating and became subject to little else but gravity. Blood pooled on the bottom. Rigor mortis had set in. The woman had survived only a matter of hours after her abduction.

Dr. Schultz didn't want to jump to conclusions as to cause of death, but the woman had suffered a potentially fatal gunshot wound to the head. He ordered her rewrapped and taken to the morgue. Everything he could see here, he could see better in the perfect light of the autopsy room.

After the body was photographed and removed, the archaeologists noted that some water seepage had gotten into the bottom of the grave site and the trench they'd dug.

Work continued at the grave site even after the body was gone. More layers of dirt were removed, sifted for hidden evidence, and bagged for laboratory analysis.

As soon as the victim's body was found, and it was determined that a single gunshot most likely killed her, crime scene specialists examined the area with that in mind. They found a ring of dirty blond hair around an apparent bullet hole in a palmetto leaf only a few paces from the hole in the ground. Along that same path, police found a patch of shredded bark close to the ground, where the bullet apparently grazed a tree trunk. By running a string taut between the hole in the leaf and the groove in the trunk, they accurately determined the path of the bullet, which hit the ground just a couple of feet on the other side of the barbed-wire fence.

Well-wishers tied yellow ribbons around trees near the Lees' home. Denise's family was notified of the body's discovery; they gathered at the Goff home for the grim wait, until the remains were positively identified.

Police, however, didn't have to wait. They were allowed to assume. They theorized immediately that Michael King took Denise Lee to the remote location, dug the grave with a shovel he'd borrowed a few hours earlier, shot Denise to death, and then jumped into a pond or drainage ditch in an attempt to wash blood from his clothes and skin. The search continued for the victim's clothes and the murder weapon.

The sad duty of telling the press of the discovery went to North Port police chief Terry Lewis, who said, "Today, forensics experts from the Sarasota County Sheriff's Office and the medical examiner's office did a very detailed, long search, and we've discovered the remains of an unidentified white female buried at that location. It will take several hours to make a positive identification of the remains."

Still, the assumption was there, and everyone knew it.

Any connection between the suspect and the victim? No, Lewis said. "We have nothing to believe this was anything other than a random act of violence."

When King's neighbors heard about the murder, they almost exploded with frustration. Everyone knew there was something wrong in that house. Brian and Dana Lewis, King's next-door neighbors, had called police on King twelve times since 2003, but police said they could never do anything because of lack of evidence. The Lewises complained that he'd thrown battery acid in their pool, pelted their car with eggs, and had slashed their tires, among other things. They said that until the previous year, Michael King, who was divorced, had been living with his grade-school-aged son. One neighbor complained that King had been stalking his daughter from the bus stop.

Sitting in his jail cell, Michael King was informed that a body had been found, more than likely that of the woman he'd been with.

"I'll never go to prison," he said. "I'll kill myself first."

* * *

In short order, the remains were identified as those of Denise Lee. Murder charges were added to those already filed against King.

Rick Goff tried to make a public statement but broke down. Nate Lee managed to say, "I'm going to miss her so much. And I don't know how I'm going to go through the rest of my life without her."

Investigation revealed that their suspect had been having financial troubles due to unemployment. He was under threat of foreclosure on his Sardinia Avenue home.

Florida Department of Law Enforcement (FDLE) Crime Laboratory analyst Steve Balunan processed the Lee home in search of previously undiscovered evidence. The residence was freshly photographed, documented, searched, and sketched.

The living-room carpet was vacuumed for trace-type evidence, and carpet standards were obtained. The house was thoroughly dusted for fingerprints. Among others, three prints were lifted from the interior of the sliding glass doors at the rear of the house.

Collected as evidence from the home were three pillowcases and a sheet from the master bedroom. A feminine pad from the bedroom garbage can was also seized. Three toothbrushes were taken from the master bathroom.

Other items taken were the cell phone resting atop a dresser in the southeast bedroom, and a tissue from the floor in front of the nightstand in the master bedroom.

That same day, just past noon, police tracked down Jennifer Robb, King's ex-girlfriend, at her home in Homosassa, Florida. The lawn had been mostly burned away, revealing a near-white sandy soil. There were children's toys in the back, and a rusted burn barrel on the side.

As were all of King's women, Jennifer was diminutive. She weighed 102 pounds, and was born January 29, 1976. She admitted to knowing King, and ID'd his photo. Cops asked, "When and where did you meet Mike?"

"February 2006, at a wedding in Ocala," she said. "We were both alone and they had dancin'." She approached him. He said he didn't dance, but they got to talking.

Mike introduced himself, said he lived in Sarasota, was divorced, had a son. She said she was a single parent also—two kids, a ten-year-old boy and a three-year-old girl. They exchanged numbers.

After the wedding, three weeks went by, and she called him. They spoke regularly on the phone over the next month before arranging to get together.

No e-mails. She didn't do computer. She had one, but they said it didn't have enough megabytes to get on the Internet, so she just played games on it. Mike didn't have a computer. Well, his son did—but it only was used for game playing as well.

For their first date, Mike drove up to Homosassa. She didn't travel well. He arrived about 10:00 P.M. They met in a video store parking lot, each driving his and her own car. From there, he drove her—in his red Corvette—to Denny's, where they had dinner. Afterward, they went to a dock, where it was dark and they were alone. Jennifer made jokes about being in such a vulnerable position with a "practical stranger."

She couldn't swim, but she didn't let him know that. She told him, for all he knew, *she might be the psycho* and she could push *him* into the water. She asked if he could swim. The jokes made Mike nervous. He was so quiet.

They moved off the dock when a bunch of rowdy kids

showed up and ruined the ambiance. They went to a different spot, on the other side of the parking lot, where they talked till dawn.

"Talked about this and that. I don't know about what all—but I did most of the talking," Jennifer explained.

Mike told her he was a "master plumber," made good money. She said she worked at her dad's pet store. She said he probably wouldn't like her neighborhood, as it was all "trailer trash." He said his mom lived in a trailer. She told him her son was biracial and asked if that was an issue. Mike said he had no problem with that. He and his family were familiar with biracial couples. With the morning light, he drove Jennifer back to her car. He had a long drive back down to North Port. He tried to give her fifty bucks. "I don't need no money. I'm not strugglin' that bad," Jennifer said. He told her to spend it on her kids. She couldn't argue with that, so she took the money.

They had a couple of dates after that, one at a flea market; then they got together at a park with their kids, so everyone could meet. He said he wanted to make sure Jennifer and his son, Matthew, got along because the kid had had issues with the women in his life.

Matt and Tyler were about the same age, so they hit it off. Mike and Jennifer did weekends together after that, including a trip to Disney. He picked her and her son up at her house. Her daughter stayed home with a sitter.

He couldn't find her house. "I had to give him directions *many times,*" she said.

They all rode around in his white van and stayed in one hotel room; the boys in one bed, Mike and Jennifer in the other. "Lights were left on. Nothing happened," she added.

But he was so calm—and he made her comfortable. Next day, Mike drove Jennifer and her son home. The babysitter, a friend of Jennifer's sister, met Mike and told Jennifer, "He's a cute one. You better hang on to him."

In another circumstance, Jennifer might have been suspicious that Mike was still married or had another girlfriend, but she could tell by the way Matt talked that there was no one.

Still, he had everything going for him, and she couldn't figure why he'd be interested in a poor mother of two— especially one who lived fifty miles away. She never would have a good answer for that one.

The relationship grew. Mike met her parents and they all went together to the aquarium in Tampa. Jennifer's mother got sick, had to be on a ventilator, and Mike came to visit Jennifer at the hospital in Ocala. "He'd come sit with me," she said.

That was when they became lovers. They were at her house. The kids weren't there.

"I don't know who came on to who," she said, although she considered herself the dominant one. The sex was normal—very, very straight. She remembered having to tell him to loosen up. He said he was not "involved that much" with sex. When he was married, there wasn't a lot of sex involved, and she believed him. The only unusual thing he liked was having his feet rubbed, and she didn't think it *that* strange. He was "just shy," when it came to stuff like that.

"Of course, there were some things I told him right off the bat I wouldn't do, so don't ask. Nothing with toys, nothing that wasn't the natural way. He said no problem to that," Jennifer remembered.

She tried to buy him a pornographic magazine once, but he said he didn't want it. The only magazines he was interested in were about cars. "Cars, cars, cars," Jennifer said. He was still quiet, unless the subject was something he knew about. "If it was plumbing or cars, he'd run his mouth," she recalled.

Her mom complained that Mike didn't know how to make conversation, but her dad had better luck. Jennifer told her mother she had to talk about a man subject. "That was what Mike could do."

Mike was more affectionate toward her daughter than her son, she noticed. She was the more affectionate child. It never made Jennifer uncomfortable, though. He didn't handle her in a weird way or anything, and he was never left alone with her.

Mike was with her parents a lot more than she was with his. Jennifer met his parents a total of four times, tops. He drove her down there and she had dinner with them. "His mom was different. She was okay. His dad was a really nice guy," Jennifer opined.

She asked Mike what was the deal with his ex-wife; did he think he'd ever get back with her? He said no way. She was out of state. *Maybe* they spoke twice a year.

In July 2006, Jennifer's mom got out of the hospital and she left her kids in Homosassa and moved in with Mike at his house in North Port. The first time she saw the house on Sardinia was when she was moving in. She remembered he had a stomachache. Turned out to be ulcers or something. His kitchen was done up nice, because his mother had done that, but the rest of the house was sparsely furnished, with little or nothing on the walls. The school across the street was under construction, but scheduled to open for the next school year. She admitted she was a little worried about money. She doubted her father was going to keep paying her if she stopped working at his store. Mike said not to worry and gave her a small diamond ring. She had no friends in North Port, and the only friend of his that she knew about was a guy named Rob. They had dinner at his house once, with Rob and his wife.

The police showed Jennifer a photo of Rob Salvador, King's friend from the shooting range—and she said that was the guy. She remembered Rob and his wife had a lot of kids (six, police knew) and were deeply religious. Before they went over there, Mike warned his son to watch his language in front of them. Jennifer remembered thinking, sure, it was okay for Matt to curse around *her*.

There was also a guy named Carlos Saenz (pseudonym), who worked with Michael King. He was a funny guy, but not the type you'd want to hang around with, Mike said. He skipped work a lot and pulled the Hispanic card if they tried to fire him.

Did King mention any family living in North Port? Jennifer said he said something about having a cousin who lived nearby, but she never met the guy. (Police concluded this was a reference to Harold Muxlow.)

King didn't want Jennifer to work, so she stayed home and cleaned. "That was the cleanest I ever had a house," she said, "because I didn't have anything else to do."

He told her they would never break up. There was no reason for her to keep her home in Homosassa. He allowed her to pick up some of her stuff, but the washer and dryer stayed behind. If they did break up, he'd buy her a new one.

Jennifer went along with it, but she didn't completely buy it. She'd been around the block once or twice, and had heard this story before. She left a lot behind, and he never took her back to get it.

She didn't even call her parents. She had her cell phone but not the charger. King, she later learned, knew her family was looking for her, but didn't relay the message.

It wasn't right to call her a captive. She had her car and she could leave. Mike, in fact, would tell her to go out, go to a store. She didn't know her way around, so she stayed in the house. The only road she knew was the one that went to Super Walmart.

They did get her kids, and her son went to school across the street. King wasn't stingy with money and always made sure they had enough to eat.

When bored she'd go for walks during the day, but Mike said don't, there were a lot of construction workers up and down the street and he didn't want them looking at her.

Eventually Jennifer started talking to her dad again.

When that little girl was murdered in North Port, King told Jennifer that she and her daughter should be extra vigilant regarding strangers, and should always keep the door locked when he wasn't around. King said they shouldn't go to the grocery store. In fact, he didn't think Jennifer should take her daughter outside at all. When he got home, he said, he would take them to the grocery store.

One time, a neighbor lady came to visit and Jennifer fixed her a cup of tea. When Mike heard about that, he was unhappy and told Jennifer he didn't get along with his neighbors.

She was a big help to him when it came to paying his bills. He had trouble writing checks—getting the numerals in the right order and writing the amount in words—and Jennifer helped him. His mortgage payment was huge, she recalled, and she also had trouble writing a number that big in words.

Stuck in the house all day, Jennifer had plenty of time to snoop through his stuff. To her relief, she learned that he really was divorced. There was also evidence of previous girlfriends. One of his ex-girlfriends, in particular, left a bunch of stuff at his house. As far as Jennifer knew, she never got any of it back.

It was when they talked about his exes that they began to quarrel. The arguments with King got worse and worse.

In October 2006, the blowout fight started when Mike lied about going to a tanning place. He called her a nasty name and she threw macaroni and cheese at him. He said she was looking for an excuse to go back, and she said maybe she was. She grabbed her kids, some of their stuff, and hightailed it back toward Homosassa. As she was headed out, he got on the phone, making like he was calling the cops on her.

She didn't make it all the way, but called her dad from a cheap hotel and told him she was broke. Dad said they were always welcome back home. Mike called Jennifer's dad after a few days and said he just wanted to make sure she and the kids were safe.

During the last months of 2006, Mike continued to call. For weeks, she ignored the calls, but finally she talked to him. She said if they were ever going to live together again, it had to be up there. She couldn't be in North Port anymore. It just wasn't home.

And she was working again for her dad, and that wasn't going to change. She knew Mike didn't want her to work, but she had to. Life was too boring, otherwise.

He began to visit her frequently and talked about buying a house in Homosassa. By January 2007, they were back together, at least on weekends. It was at this point that Jennifer first realized that money was an issue for King. What up until then had appeared to be a bottomless well of funds started to dry. He admitted that he couldn't afford to buy a house and needed to rent. He sold a couple of his cars. He tried to sell his house in North Port, but it wouldn't sell.

By the end of January, she and Mike had rented a house—the same house where the police were currently asking her questions. He moved his furniture from the house on Sardinia up to the rented house in Homosassa, which was why the house down there was empty. Jennifer watched Matt, who went to school in Homosassa. Mike was still working at Babe's Plumbing in Venice and had to get up at 3:30 A.M. to get to work on time.

Eventually he quit his job at Babe's and went to work for the local Homosassa Roto-Rooter. When he lost that job during the summer of 2007, he took his son and they left for Michigan. Jennifer had no clue how long he was there. A long time. Longer than a month.

When he did come back, he didn't try to get a regular job but instead hatched a buying-and-selling cars scheme. They were together until Thanksgiving, 2007, when they broke up for good.

On that day, he needed to wear one particular pair of jeans, even though he had many identical pairs, and was taking forever to wash and dry them. She knew he was just stalling. He didn't eat any Thanksgiving dinner and wouldn't help clean up. She told him to get the heck out of her life and he started to scream, so much that she was embarrassed that her father was hearing it. Since they came in her truck, he and Matt walked the four miles home. When she finally returned home, Mike and his son, along with his car and a lot of their belongings, were gone.

There was another car at the house, a green Camaro. It was part of King's buy-and-sell scheme. The car had damage on the front end, so King put the black "bra" on it to cover the damage up, and hoped to sell the car for a profit.

Jennifer searched her hiding spots, where she kept the money bags from her father's store, and discovered King had stolen cash. The bags had been moved. Inside, the big bills were gone, but the small bills were left behind—so the bags still appeared full. More than $1,000 was missing.

Jennifer called King's mom, who was in Michigan at the time, and told her about the stolen money.

"If you hear from Michael," Jennifer said to Patsy King, "tell him to return the money, no questions asked, and he can be on his way."

She waited and waited, and nothing happened. She called her father and asked him what to do. Jennifer's dad said she should call the Citrus County sheriff's department. She explained to a deputy that she had to go to work the next day and was fearful King would return and clean her out. The next morning, as expected, King showed up with a U-Haul rental truck and began to load up his stuff. Lawn mower, propane tank. Three or four 4-wheelers. Later he called and denied taking the cash from the money bags.

"Somebody must've broken in," Mike said, adding that he would help her pay the money back. She talked to the deputies again. They told her King said she made the story up about the missing money, that she'd probably taken the money for herself. They wanted her to take a lie detector test.

The last time she *saw* King was two weeks after Thanksgiving. She told him he was a pathological liar, but there was still hope for them. All he had to do was go to her father, admit that he took the money, and make arrangements to pay it back. He again denied it and left—and that was that. He called her at midnight on the dot, New Year's, but she didn't pick up. He didn't leave a message. The last time she spoke to him was January 12, five days before the murder.

She said, "What do you want?"

He said, "Do you still love me?"

She repeated, "What do you want?"

He said he wanted to thank her, you know, for the good times. She asked where he was working. He said he was still plumbing. She asked where, and he said some odd name she'd never heard before. She didn't ask from where he was calling.

Did he have a gun? Sure, she replied. He had a little brown pistol. The box for it was in the house somewhere, but he never kept the gun in the box. He was afraid the kids would get at it. She'd seen him clean it. He had it wrapped in a towel and in a closet. She was pretty sure he took it with him when he left for North Port.

Could they come in and take photos of her house? Sure, no problem. To get into the house—which was white but needed a coat of paint, or at least a hosing off—they had to climb up five rickety wooden steps. Although the house itself wasn't of the best construction—a mobile home attached to a small structure of permanent construction, with a living-room ceiling on a slant—it was nicely furnished, and the living room featured a large flat-screen TV.

In a storage area in the corner of a bedroom, they found a set of weights for lifting, an electric keyboard, which looked like it hadn't been played in a while, and a box for a single-action semiautomatic nine-millimeter Parabellum pistol. When they opened the box, they found no gun, just a single shotgun shell and the nine's instruction and safety manual. The box indicated that the gun had been purchased from Kassnar Imports of Harrisburg, Pennsylvania.

There were lots of photos of King, holding and kissing a little girl, fishing and lounging on a boat in the ocean, and one of him just standing there wearing what appeared to be the same sleeveless camouflage-colored shirt that he'd been arrested in.

Jennifer had learned about Denise Lee's murder when her aunt called her up.

"Your Michael, what was his last name?" the aunt asked.

"King."

"In that case, you'd better turn on the TV," the aunt replied.

She couldn't believe it. How could the man she knew and cared for behave this way? There must have been some mistake. She couldn't believe that Michael would just randomly pick a woman to rape and kill.

Jennifer Robb still had feelings for Michael King—no matter what he did. She always would have feelings for him. He did so much for her family when they were together. He was a family guy. If Michael had been with her right then and there, she wouldn't even feel nervous. She would feel completely safe. If anything, she felt guilty; it was clear to her that Michael needed help. There was something wrong with him to make him do these things. He needed help, and no one recognized that fact.

She'd never heard him mention any Denise. When she saw the photo of the slain woman on TV, she knew right away that she'd never seen her before.

Did King ever mention the name Coralrose?

Jennifer thought for a moment, failed to recognize the murdered little girl's name, and shook her head.

The cops noted that when King was arrested, he had dyed hair. Did he do that when he and Jennifer were together? She said that he did. King went to the "hairdresser's" and had it done. Jennifer didn't like it and told him so. "I said he looked like a guy who likes other guys," she said.

Wasn't it true that he also shaved his chest and pubic hair? Yes, but she didn't think that was odd because she shaved down there also. She told him it was cleaner, so she figured he was just trying to be like her.

* * *

Police located and interviewed Michael King's current girlfriend, Tennille Ann Camp, who said she and King had been seeing each other off and on for about a year. They started dating in December 2006, but they broke up and King went back to his old girlfriend, a woman named Jennifer Robb, who lived in Homosassa. Then they got back together, late in 2007.

Although she and Mike were both from Michigan, that was just a coincidence. They hadn't known each other "up north." They met because she, like King's parents, lived in Ellenton, and she played bingo with his mom. His parents were snowbirds, and they only lived in Florida during the winter.

She had stayed with Mike the previous Tuesday night. She called him on the phone on January 17, at 11:00 A.M. She asked him how his appointment with the lawyer had gone that morning and he said fine. He was filing for bankruptcy, hoping to keep his house. He said he was watching TV at his house with his friend Rob [Salvador]. She asked him if he wanted to go to the Fifties and Sixties dance the next week, and he said he'd like that. He seemed normal.

She talked to him again, at 3:45 or 4:45 P.M. (a time that police knew was during the abduction and attack of Denise Lee). Tennille asked him what he was doing and he said his parents had dropped off a trailer full of stuff at his house and he'd been going through that. He said he'd talk to her later. Again, he seemed perfectly normal. When she called back a couple of hours later, her call went straight to his voice mail.

Mike had been in Michigan for Christmas, and Tennille flew up there to be with him at that time. On the evening of King's arrest, Tennille talked to his mom, who, apparently unaware of what had occurred, said she had a bed and a mattress for Mike, and to let him know if Tennille saw him. Tennille believed that King last saw his parents on Wednesday, the day before the murder.

She said Mike was a quiet guy, and he didn't seem to be the type to do something "like this." "Not that I know of," Tennille added.

She described a typical date as going out to dinner—he liked Applebee's—or shopping at Walmart or something like that. Sometimes they'd "cuddle up together and watch movies."

He liked to fish and to work on cars. She knew that King had been married when he was in his twenties and that his ex-wife lived in Las Vegas with her boyfriend. Mike had a son, Matty, who turned twelve on Monday and lived up north with an uncle.

Tennille said sex with Mike was frequent but not unusual. Sure, oral—but no bondage, no role-playing. They'd had sex twice during the previous week—Sunday night and Tuesday night—both times at his house. He didn't use a condom, but that was okay because she had her tubes tied. Plus, she was on the pill to be sure.

CHAPTER 7

JANUARY 20, 2008

Dr. Daniel Schultz began the postmortem procedure on the remains of Denise Lee at 8:30 A.M., January 20. In attendance were NPPD criminalistics specialists to process any discovered evidence.

The only thing she wore was jewelry: a gray-metal necklace with a heart-shaped pendant around her neck, and a wedding ring on her left ring finger. Her ears were pierced, but she was missing an earring, which would at some point be discovered near the grave site.

Two pieces of duct tape were removed from the back of the victim's head. Those pieces were stretched out and placed on a board so they could be photographed, then bagged as evidence.

Once everything was removed from the body, it was measured and weighed. Five feet two inches, 109 pounds. Speaking aloud for the record, Dr. Schultz listed the wounds he found on the body's exterior.

There was a bruise and abrasion on the back of the left

arm and on the wrist. These looked as if they might have been caused by someone squeezing the arm and wrist with a powerful hand.

There were other bruises as well, apparently from hard impact with objects. On the legs, there were more bruises, shaped like handprints, in places where the killer had gripped her cruelly hard to control her during the attack. Four bruises that were lined up along the victim's inner thigh represented fingers that had dug deep into the flesh.

The bruises were not healing—and, of course, would never heal. The pathologist could tell by their purplish hue that they had been suffered short moments before the woman expired.

The body was flipped over and the back observed. There was an abrasion to the scapula and a yellow discoloration that might indicate this wound was caused postmortem.

The body exhibited blunt-force trauma to the chin, along the angle of the jaw; plus, there was a contusion and abrasion on the left side of the face.

Also on the cheek was a pattern of abrasions that ranged in size from five millimeters to one centimeter. The bruises were parallel to one another, along a line, and separated by a three-millimeter gap.

The abrasions were surrounded by a maroon contusion, the color indicating that the wound was caused several hours before, but probably on the day of death.

Dr. Schultz now took a look at the gunshot wound. The entrance wound was on the right side of the face, and the exit wound, which was larger as expanding gases exited along with the bullet, was on the back left of the head.

He could tell that the killer had not just fired the gun from point-blank range, but had pressed the gun firm against the woman's temple before pulling the trigger.

The entrance and exit wounds were carefully photographed, measured, and described. The bullet had done collateral damage. The shot had been fired so it traveled parallel to and directly behind the left eyebrow. The bullet passed immediately adjacent to the left eyeball with such force that the left eye had been exploded outward. There were fractures of the skull at the exit wound, and also at both sides of the left eye socket.

A sexual assault kit was used to take internal and external swabs from the victim's mouth, vagina, and anus. The doctor created the swabs and then handed them off to a technician, who in this case was NPPD criminalistics specialist Pamela Schmidt.

Dr. Schultz described aloud the condition of the victim's private area, a sad necessity because of the crime's sexual nature. Looking at the vagina, the pathologist noted bruising on both sides of the labia minora. There was also bruising along the lower left portion of the vagina. Being a veteran investigator of sex crimes, Dr. Schultz recognized that these wounds were caused by insertion trauma, either the rough penetration of the vagina with a foreign object, or were caused when the victim struggled as she was about to be raped. They were a clear indication that a sex crime had occurred, as such bruises were extremely rare in cases of consensual sex. There were also injuries around and in the anus. There was a skin tear at the edge of the anus, measuring ten millimeters by two millimeters, with a contusion. This wound, like those on the vagina, was caused by insertion trauma—again, a wound that would have been extremely unlikely if the anal sex had been consensual. The wounds to both vagina and anus were caused before death.

DNA testing on the autopsy evidence received top priority. A test that normally might have taken weeks was done pronto. Those tests revealed that Denise Lee had indeed been raped, and the rapist was Michael King.

Back at the site of the shallow grave, Sarasota County deputy Anthony Egoville was searching with a metal detector. Squatting down and carefully moving the grass out of the way with his gloved fingers, he discovered a shell casing only a few feet from the sand pile. At first glance, he guessed it was either a thirty-eight caliber or a nine millimeter. (It turned out to be a nine.) He didn't touch the casing, but rather he placed a marker at the spot and someone from forensics collected it.

At the NPPD, an SCSO polygraph expert administered a lie detector test to Robert Salvador, the man who'd gone target shooting with Michael King only hours before Denise Lee's abduction. Robert said he had no knowledge of Denise's ordeal and passed with flying colors.

It was also on Sunday that law enforcement finally returned Jane Kowalski's phone calls. The call came from the case's lead investigator, Detective Christopher Morales himself.

She intended to be fully cooperative, but first she was going to give him an earful. Considering her importance as an eyewitness, his callback was way past overdue.

Her memory was pretty good as it turned out, but they didn't know that. For all they knew, precious details might have been lost due to the delay.

She was still at her grandmother's, but . . . "I'm

coming home today," she said. "I'll stop by in North Port on my way."

Morales said that would be fine.

Once the police had her, they did do a thorough job with her. With videotape rolling, Jane Kowalski sat down with two detectives and discussed "every little thing" she had seen on the evening of the murder.

They showed her a photographic lineup and she picked Michael King out of the pack without hesitation.

"Is that because you saw him on TV?" they asked.

"No, that's the guy in the car," she replied.

CHAPTER 8

THE VICTIM'S CLOTHES

On January 21, 2008, NPPD detectives interviewed Joe Dalton, who was Michael King's boss at Babe's Plumbing Inc., in Venice. According to Dalton, King began work there on September 14, 2004, and quit on June 20, 2007. He quit because he was going to take over a Roto-Rooter franchise in Port Charlotte, he claimed. He came in one Monday morning and said he'd met a guy over the weekend who was going to give him a Roto-Rooter franchise. Dalton didn't want to stand in the way of a man making better for himself and said "Good luck to ya."

King was rehired by Dalton on September 13, 2007, and worked until October 15, 2007. The Roto-Rooter deal apparently was fiction, because between June and September of 2007, Dalton knew, King worked at another plumbing company called Hill & Hill, which was just on the other side of the bridge, and owned by a guy named Seth Hill. When he came back looking for his old job, Dalton said sure. King had always been a good employee. Dalton always received positive feedback regarding King. He was clean and courteous, was willing to work at night if a job came up, always volunteered, never complained. Never once was there a complaint about Mike King.

One of the detectives asked about the time a woman said Michael King had exposed himself to her in September of 2006. Dalton said he never heard anything about that. When King left the company the second time, he said he had some estate business to take care of up in Michigan. Then he never heard from him again. Dalton said that he was surprised to see King's mother interviewed on TV after the murder. One of the times Mike went back to Michigan, he said, was to attend his mother's funeral.

"He was a BSer like a lot of these guys. He would always have these deals, you know?" He got a special deal on his house in North Port; he knew a guy involved with car auctions; he was always getting deals on cars—that sort of thing. Dalton never got involved in any of that because it had nothing to do with his plumbing business. "I sort of had to separate myself," he said.

The policemen said they'd heard King got in trouble moonlighting on his own, using one of Dalton's trucks. Dalton said that wasn't true. He never took the truck home, unless he had a job to do at night, and the lot was locked up by the time he was finished. Even then, a lot of times he would park the truck nearby and go home in his own vehicle. He drove a red Corvette for a while, and a motorcycle; then he dated a girl in Ocala and she had a "hopped-up" black Mustang.

The policemen went through King's personnel file. One of the last papers in there was a phone message from a woman named Kelly, asking Mike to call her back.

* * *

On January 22, Lieutenant Ed Fitzpatrick supervised a search of heavy brush on either side of Plantation Boulevard. A large truck containing a crime scene command center was parked by the side of the road.

Incongruous to the desolation was a manhole cover, a fire hydrant, and a fresh and even sidewalk along the road, only a few yards from the crime scene, an indication of tract housing planned for but never built.

Fitzpatrick and the officers under his command performed what was called a "line search." The men stood shoulder to shoulder and moved slowly through an area, methodically covering every square inch. In this case, they started close to the grave site and moved outward. There were two teams of six and seven officers working simultaneously.

At some point during the search, Fitzpatrick was alerted that the other team had a possible hit on something—an item that could be seen on the other side of a fence from where they'd been searching. Approximately a quarter of a mile from the burial site, on the other side of the street, pieces of clothing were discovered. Something white was snared to a tree limb.

The lieutenant did not approach the items but rather ordered the area around the items secured as a crime scene, a process that took approximately ten minutes.

The items turned out to be a pair of light blue men's boxer shorts and a pair of red panties. The item on the tree branch turned out to be a bra strap. A close look at the strap revealed dark red stains that could have been blood.

Fitzpatrick called in Pam Schmidt, who photographed the site thoroughly and then collected and processed the evidence. A thorough search of the area was impossible because of the thickness of the foliage in places. Heavy equipment was needed.

That equipment—an excavation shovel with claw—arrived a week later, January 29, and was used to pull out the vegetation. While the machine was "skimming" the earth, it unearthed a half-buried piece of cloth. Pam Schmidt was called back to photograph the item, a woman's shirt with one strap broken. Schmidt dug up the shirt, also removing a big hunk of the dirt in which it had been embedded. During this process, the rest of the bra was also recovered.

A blond woman named Anitra Fritz told police that sometime the previous week—she wasn't sure what day it was—when she was either coming back from her babysitter's or the post office, she was driving east on Tropicaire Boulevard in North Port when she passed a slow-moving westbound green Camaro with a "bra" on the front, which was going in the opposite direction from her.

The car must have made a U-turn, because the next thing she knew, it was right behind her. She feared the driver was stalking her. She had her baby in the car and didn't know if her husband was home, so she didn't go there. Instead, she turned off Tropicaire onto Imbe Street and decided to go to the home of a friend whose husband was a cop. The Camaro followed. She made a second turn, onto Leryl Avenue; this time, he didn't follow, so she returned to Tropicaire.

When she got home, she told her husband she thought she'd been followed. He was not concerned. She didn't think it was the day of the murder, but it was close to that day. When she learned about the murder, she was frightened to see how much she resembled the victim. She could have been the one who got abducted.

Anitra added that she had psychic abilities and felt the

killer had a girlfriend who was a petite blonde who'd been pregnant but had an abortion, and he flipped out.

A man named James Navin (pseudonym) told police that he believed he might have witnessed the moment when Michael King chose Denise Lee as his target for the day. It happened at five minutes before two in the afternoon, about thirty minutes after Rob Salvador last saw King at the firing range, and about twenty-five minutes before a neighbor saw a man in a green Camaro at the Lees' house.

The witness claimed he saw both King and Lee waiting in line at the North Port Post Office. Police asked him how he could be so sure, and he said he recognized them from photos he'd seen on television the day after Denise Lee disappeared.

"I turned around and looked at the girl behind me and it was her, and she was holding a good-sized box." James said King was farther back in the same line. "He caught my attention because he was, I don't know, grisly. He had strange-looking eyes when he looked at me, a lot of white in them."

Doubt was cast upon James Navin's observations, however, when it was pointed out that, as far as anyone knew, Denise mailed no box, and she went nowhere without her kids.

The police quickly filed this information in the round receptacle labeled "urban legends."

How Michael King chose Denise Lee as his victim remained a mystery.

News of Denise Lee's murder sent reporters mining for background information. One fruitful dig occurred at the online social network Myspace, where Denise's account painted a picture of her busy life as a young mom, an occupation not just mentally challenging but physically demanding as well. In August of 2007, Denise wrote: **Something so simple as going to the mall to buy a pair of sunglasses is a thousand times harder when you have two boys under tow.** They shopped a little, retreated to the car so she could breast-feed Adam, and returned to a mall bench for a break. Noah ran around a play area and twice was knocked down by older boys. Adam needed a new diaper, but changing it became tough. Every time she took her eyes off Noah, he ran across the mall. She ended up changing the diaper, with Noah sitting on the hanging table. In jcpenney, she tried on sunglasses, but Noah again made a run for it. An old man told her she sure had her hands full and checked the bottom of her stroller to make sure she didn't have a third kid in there. **But it was still fun, she** concluded. **Any time I get to leave the house is a treat for me.**

CHAPTER 9

FUNERAL

Denise Lee's funeral was handled by the Lemon Bay Funeral Home in Englewood and held on Wednesday, January 23, at the First United Methodist Church in Punta Gorda, the same church where Nate and Denise were married three years earlier.

As expected, there was quite a crowd—friends and family, of course, but also many strangers, attracted by the media attention. Every police officer in the area was there. It was the biggest funeral in the region's history.

As the Reverend John Bryant, the church's pastor, read "The Lord's Prayer," Nate Lee and Rick Goff sat in the front pew, each holding one of Denise's two boys.

The pastor said, "Today I extend my heartfelt sympathy and love to Nate, little Noah, and Adam, who probably don't know what I'm saying now, to mom Susan, to Rick, to Amanda and Tyler, grandparents, and to the extended family and friends of Denise."

Rick Goff kissed a large photo of Denise on his way to

the pulpit, then said Denise was a wonderful, special, downright extraordinary person. She was so smart—honor roll in tenth grade—but also so nice. Not a mean bone in her body, always a bright smile; when she smiled, everyone else smiled, too. Her happiness was contagious, a physical manifestation of positive vibes. She could have used her charm to get what she wanted, but she didn't want that. She was too concerned with how she could be helpful in a situation and was always a willing worker. As a teenager, she behaved like a girl beyond her years, and it didn't surprise her father when she became a wife and mother so quickly after she graduated from high school. She always seemed like a fully mature woman who was ready for responsibility. As a student, she couldn't have been more organized and prepared. Rick was familiar with his daughter's study habits because she took a course he taught in law enforcement, during which his lectures touched upon a myriad of controversial subjects. Yet, the papers Denise wrote were thoughtful and contemplative. Plus, she was humble. You could try to tell her how great she was, but she would laugh it off with a delicate touch of self-depreciative humor.

"She's the most wonderful person I've ever known. She's my baby girl, and I'm going to miss her," he said. He didn't know how the family would get along without her. They would need enormous strength. "The Lees are an awesome family, and thank you. I love you, baby girl, and I know you're home," he concluded.

Goff was thinking things he hadn't said aloud. He'd seen trouble coming. It was that damned neighborhood the kids had moved into—a new housing development that was only partly filled. Many of the houses around theirs were empty, as the developer had failed to anticipate a shrinking market. There were even empty lots where houses were planned but never built.

One of the reasons the Lees had decided to settle in that section of North Port was rents were cheap. The relatively low cost of living had made North Port a rapidly growing community, population fifty thousand and getting bigger every day. But who were these newbies? A big question mark, that was who.

When it was his turn, Nate Lee called his wife amazing and selfless. His father-in-law stood by his side and placed a hand on his shoulder when his voice filled with emotion. He recalled moving into the house in the North Port Estates section of North Port, about forty miles from Sarasota, more rural than suburban. Nate and Denise called it "living in the sticks." They were close to their parents—but not too close. Nate had three jobs; Denise was home with the boys. Times were tough, but certainly not bleak. They were happy together in their new rented home—three bedrooms, two baths—in North Port.

They just didn't have much money. All in all, affluence was a secondary concern when you have as much love in your hearts as Nate and Denise had.

Besides, they were poor now, but that didn't mean they were going to be poor forever. They were smart and eventually life would grow easier. They knew. There was no hurry. They were very, very young—time was their security blanket. They had all of the time in the world.

"We were going to grow old together," Nate recalled.

As 2008 dawned, Denise found herself a woman with her hands full. Taking care of a two-year-old and a six-month-old was a full-time job, 24/7. She could never take her eyes off either one of them. Plus, she was still breast-feeding the little one.

Nate trusted her completely and could concentrate fully

on the things he needed to do because he knew that the boys were safe and happy with their mother.

And they were a handful. The oldest was two when the youngest was born. He remembered her going online and googling "potty training."

"It didn't work," the widower recalled.

Those boys were going to be the smartest kids in pre-K and kindergarten, Nate knew. That was because, when she wasn't feeding them, she was teaching them: the ABC's, counting from one to ten.

She could never be alone. "She even had to bring the boys with her when she went to the mailbox," he remembered.

Plus, he was well taken care of. When he got home at night, Denise was busy fixing dinner. And, in addition to all of that, she'd gone back to school and had plans to become a speech therapist.

"We were living the American Dream," Nate said. He used to joke and say that he didn't notice her in that first class they had together at school, but it was a fib. "I knew exactly what seat she sat in," he said.

He concluded by making a promise to his wife: "I will be as strong as I can be. I love you so much, Denise, and I will talk to you every day. Your boys will know who their mother was. They will know you."

Reverend Bryant concluded the ceremony by offering "The Wind Beneath My Wings" as a final song in remembrance of Denise's spirit. As they recessed, mourners filed past Denise's royal blue casket.

A half hour later, a thirty-mile funeral procession began, 150 cars long, headlights on, to the easternmost section of Gulf Pines Memorial Park, where Denise Lee would be interred.

There were rose petals in the road. Fire trucks led the way, their lights going around. Spectators lined the road and saluted as the hearse carrying Denise's coffin drove by. Elementary schools emptied so students could stand outside and watch.

State troopers pulled up in front of the cemetery and parked so that they were blocking the southbound lanes of traffic on State Route 776. The long parade quietly entered.

Nate Lee's mind was haunted by memories. Nightmares. Alternate realities. What if? What if? After the ceremony at the cemetery, he found himself thinking about how the bad thing had started.

The creep showed up at the house and somehow managed to get in. He must've had a gun, threatened to hurt the boys. Denise would have done anything to protect those boys—even leave with a man with a gun.

But how had he gotten into the house?

Then he had a thought, a horrible thought. The killer drove a '95 green Camaro. Lee drove a '94 green Dodge Avenger. The cars resembled one another. Maybe Denise saw King's car pull into the driveway and thought Nate was home.

Someone had shut the windows but not latched them. Two possibilities: the creep did it so neighbors wouldn't hear screaming, or she did it so the boys wouldn't be able to wander off while she was gone. She knew she was going away and leaving them behind.

Part of him didn't want to focus on what Denise must have been thinking during those desperate last hours. But the bigger part of him couldn't help but dwell there.

He was always blown away by how competent she was, even during that horrible crisis. She left so many clues—

evidence to both facilitate her discovery and to help catch the creep if she was never found.

All during that time, she must have been bolstered by confidence, thinking her father, the cop, would make sure that the search for her was as massive and efficient as possible.

Leaving the ring in the back of the killer's car was pure genius. That was the first ring he ever gave her and it had grown tight. The ring didn't accidentally fall off into the Camaro's backseat, that was for sure.

Part of him would have liked to shrug and say, "It was fate, and these things happened, and it must have all been part of God's master plan." But the bigger part of him knew she should have been saved but wasn't. And he knew who was to blame: certain employees of the CCSO.

CHAPTER 10

THE PROSECUTORS

Assistant State Attorney (ASA) Lon Arend would helm the prosecution of Michael King, with a supporting cast of his colleagues Karen Fraivillig and Suzanne O'Donnell.

Arend did his undergraduate work at Florida State University, and earned his law degree at the University of Florida. He'd been a prosecutor for fourteen years, including eight as chief prosecutor in the DeSoto County office. He became the Sarasota region's chief homicide prosecutor.

The trio of Arend, Fraivillig, and O'Donnell were no strangers to big cases, having successfully countered the insanity defense in the disturbing murder trial of Elton Murphy.

Elton Murphy—now there was a sick dude. "One of the scariest individuals I've ever encountered," O'Donnell recalled.

Fraivillig added that to understand that thoroughly weird case, you needed a little background on the fabric of the area. Sarasota County was a beautiful little section of Florida, but it did have its pretensions. Nothing sinister, of course, but Sarasota was a community that liked to cast itself as artsy. There was opera, ballet, and a formation of art galleries on the main drag. Just how artsy Sarasota really was could be argued, but art and culture were important facets of its self-image.

So it hit the town where it lived when downtown Sarasota art gallery owner Joyce Wishart was found hacked to death in 2004 on the floor of the Provenance Gallery on Palm Avenue—posed to shock, and missing her vagina.

The killer had apparently taken the victim's female parts with him, maybe to dabble in cannibalism or necrophilia, or maybe just to remove DNA evidence from the crime scene.

Didn't work.

Cops found DNA foreign to the victim at the crime scene—a piece of skin under the body, and blood droplets—and inevitably that was what solved the case. The vagina was never found.

At first, police thought there might be a connection between the grisly murder and the Sarasota Film Festival, which had attracted upward of thirty thousand strangers into town.

The case broke eight long months later when Elton Murphy was caught in Texas, where he had fled, committing a burglary. There was a DNA hit, and they had their man.

During interrogation, Murphy was deemed to be a little wacky and was examined by four psychologists, one of whom worked for the state. Murphy was found incompetent to stand trial.

The case lingered and lingered, until Arend decided he wanted to bring the case to trial—even if it meant butting horns with a formidable insanity defense. Arend concluded that Murphy was seriously mentally ill but not legally insane, and he was fairly certain a jury would see it the same way.

"In the state of Florida," O'Donnell said, "you can be schizophrenic and still be able to tell and appreciate the difference between right and wrong."

All of the things Murphy had done at the crime scene—cleaning up, for example, and his other attempts to avoid detection—could be used to argue he was sane.

During the trial, Arend—with the supportive help of the two other assistant state attorneys—was masterful. He impeached all four doctors and convinced the jury to return with a guilty verdict.

In May 2009, Murphy received a sentence of life in prison. Unlike the Murphy case, the King case was clearly capital murder, and Arend planned to pursue the death penalty aggressively.

When Arend put together his team for King's prosecution, he went straight to the short list. He asked the same two women who had done such a slam-bang job in the Murphy case to help him. They worked well together, and they were already a well-oiled team.

First to be asked was Mary-Catherine Fraivillig, whom everyone knew as Karen. Her name *was* Karen, as far as she was concerned. Her parents were Catholic, and apparently, there's no Saint Karen.

"A priest went crazy," she explained. "I had to be baptized as Mary-Catherine. I probably should have legally changed it years ago, but never got around to it."

Fraivillig was sixty-two years old, but didn't have nearly as many years of legal experience as people assumed. Truth was, she started law school unusually late in life.

"I am a land surveyor," she explained. Her husband, Lee, was a civil engineer and had a family business back in Bethlehem, Pennsylvania, where they lived until 1993.

He worked in the office—she outside with the crew, handling cases involving water, sewage, and pavement; performing topographic surveys; gauging the sturdiness of a piece of land before a construction project began.

When their last child went off to college, her husband announced his intention to retire and move to Florida. She loved her work and didn't want to stop, but she gave in to her husband's plan with one caveat: "I'm going back to school," she told him. "I had always wanted to be a lawyer. It's just that circumstances always intervened." Life always got in the way—but not this time.

Fraivillig completed her undergraduate work at the New College of Florida, a school that didn't have grades. However, in order to graduate, you had to write a thesis, give a dissertation, and then defend that dissertation in front of your professors. No pressure. From there, she went to Stetson Law, in St. Petersburg, graduated in 2002, and had been prosecuting cases ever since.

Fraivillig was a large woman, with long blond hair, who moved deliberately and erect—as if balancing an invisible book atop her head. The effect was downright regal.

She enjoyed taking on the bad guys. Sometimes she wondered about the human condition, but she felt better when tenaciously combating its darkest corners.

She was ambivalent about the death penalty. Sometimes people had this image of prosecutors, that they wanted to hang and behead everyone. It wasn't philosophically true. Prosecutors were educated people and knew that the death penalty was reserved for the worst of the worst.

"But in the King case," Fraivillig declared, "there was no question."

Fraivillig would be responsible for questioning the state's eyewitnesses.

Suzanne O'Donnell, the third member of the prosecution team, was a graduate of the University of Florida School of Law. Unlike some lawyers who'd seen things from both sides of the courtroom, O'Donnell always wanted to be a prosecutor. After school in 1999, she started as a prosecutor in St. Petersburg, Florida, and shortly after that came to Sarasota.

Her forte was forensic evidence. When Denise Lee's body was discovered, O'Donnell went to the burial scene and scoped things out.

For four years, O'Donnell had been the state attorney's specialist in sex crimes against children. Her work on the Murphy case had been invaluable, and Arend expected nothing less when it came to Michael King's prosecution.

Her job would be to introduce the evidence in the case, and to question the crime scene technicians who worked at the various crime scenes, as well as the scientists "back at the lab" who analyzed that evidence.

She would handle all of the evidence, except for the DNA, which Arend was saving for himself.

Lon Arend began strategizing immediately. He knew that the eyewitness and lab stuff in this case was very strong. His worry: what would King's defense do?

Arend thought of possible defenses and made efforts to combat them—indeed, to nip them in the bud.

He informed law enforcement that he wanted the members of King's family interviewed immediately before they had a chance to put their heads together and come up with a feasible psychiatric defense.

Officers flew up to Michigan to conduct the family interviews—hopefully, before a defense attorney could get to them and tell them what to say. King had three brothers, Jim and Gary older, and Rodney who was younger. They could not pin down brother Gary to make a statement.

When they went to see the mom and dad, the dad said he was too ill with heart problems to give a statement, but Michael's mom volunteered to answer questions. They asked her about her son's psychiatric background: any head injuries?

"No," Patsy King said.

CHAPTER 11

INTERNAL AFFAIRS INVESTIGATION

By Sunday, January 20, 2008, just three days after the murder, it was clear that the mishandling of the Kowalski 911 call by personnel of the Charlotte County Sheriff's Office Communications Section, specifically the dispatch center, had hindered law enforcement's gallant attempt to save Denise Lee's life.

To see that nothing like this would ever happen again, Charlotte County sheriff John Davenport ordered a "professional standards Internal Affairs investigation" into the actions of two dispatchers: Susan Kirby Kallestad and Elizabeth Martinez.

The investigation was conducted by Captain Donna H. Roguska, of the CCSO Internal Affairs Section, assisted by FDLE resident agent in charge Yolanda Carbia.

On Monday, Captain Roguska interviewed Kallestad, who remembered well the call in question. At approximately 6:30 P.M., CCSO call taker Mildred Stepp realized the importance of the Kowalski call and stood up to say that the information needed to get out on the radio. Stepp wrote the key information on a piece of paper and brought it over to the dispatch area. According to Stepp, she advised CCSO communications supervisor Laurie Piatt of the situation. Piatt said she was trying to patch the radios, and dispatcher Kallestad said she did not believe that she could use her radio. Kallestad told CCSO dispatcher Elizabeth Martinez that the information *had to get out*. While call taker Stepp was still on the phone with the caller, she was also talking to both her and Martinez with updated information. It was approximately 6:40 P.M. that Stepp posted the information regarding the Kowalski call into the dispatch computer.

And here came the sad coincidence, the key factor. It was just about at that same time that the shift change occurred. Afternoon dispatchers knocked off for the day and the night dispatchers started. According to Kallestad, CCSO dispatcher Kattie Beasley was assigned to take over the Mid-County (dispatch two) radio. Kallestad made sure Beasley was aware of the Kowalski information and advised her that it needed to get out. Kallestad said she later heard Beasley say that she "assigned it," but was uncertain if Beasley was referring to the Kowalski information or something else.

"Who replaced you on dispatch one?" Captain Roguska asked.

"Brandie Schaefer," Kallestad said.

"Did you pass the information from the Kowalski call on to her?"

"No."

"What else, if anything, did you do?"

"Around this time, I recall putting out a BOLO about the green Camaro."

"Who directed you to do that?"

"I don't remember."

Captain Roguska checked Kallestad's story and subsequent investigation, in the form of the radio traffic log. It revealed that Kallestad had been contacted by Sergeant Floyd Davis to put out a BOLO to all units regarding the green Camaro. The radio log showed that Kallestad did as she was told, and the BOLO went out at 6:35 P.M.

On the same day as the Kallestad interview, Roguska took a statement from dispatcher Elizabeth Martinez regarding the handling of the same emergency call. She said that on the day of Denise Lee's murder, she had been working dispatch channel two, otherwise known as Mid-County. She knew that an important call had come in to Stepp.

"Was a call to service entered?"

"Not to my knowledge."

Martinez said she saw Stepp discussing the call with Kallestad and she thought she was rightfully out of the loop, since "the units responding to North Port were mostly on dispatch channel one.

"I was busy on the radio and phone."

"Did Kallestad tell you to get the information out?"

"She might have. I didn't remember her saying that, but I talked to her later and she said she had."

What Martinez did remember was that even before the Kowalski call, two BOLOs had been received from North Port and subsequently put out regarding the missing woman and the suspect's car, based on information gathered from the victim's husband and elsewhere. This volunteered comment might have implied that dispatchers were aware that the crime being reported by Kowalski and the one reported by Nate Lee were one and the same. However, their actions made it clear that no such connection was made. Kowalski had reported an abducted child, and Denise Lee was a grown woman. The missing woman investigation involved a green Camaro. Kowalski reported a blue or black Camaro. There were similarities, for certain, but there was just enough difference to keep the connection from being automatic.

Captain Roguska's investigation ran into February, and everyone associated with the 911 center in Charlotte County was interviewed, some twice. After analyzing the data she'd collected, Roguska wrote her conclusion, which was released on February 13. She cited all of the failures to communicate in the communications center, blaming the bulk of them on personnel who were preoccupied when Stepp took the call from Kowalski. Piatt was on the phone with both the SCSO and NPPD trying to patch radio channels for better communications, an effort that was successful with the SCSO but not with the North Port police. Piatt was also answering the Nextel and the supervisor's unrecorded line, while making calls out for additional resources. The preoccupation was with the disappearance of Denise Lee, a police sergeant's daughter. Everything else was put on the back burner, so to speak; a tunnel vision existed, which served to eliminate the Kowalski call from consideration. Kallestad not only failed to put out the Kowalski info, but when she was advised by Davis to call North Port and get more info, she failed to do this as well.

Based on the evidence in this investigation I recommend the . . . charges against . . . Kallestad be sustained, Roguska wrote. The charges were failure to send units to Toledo Blade and Route 41, and failure to follow Davis's instruction. Kallestad stated under oath that she advised Martinez that the Kowalski info needed to go out. Martinez vaguely recalled Kallestad saying this to her, but couldn't recall the details. Bottom line, info didn't go out, and Roguska recommended the charges against Martinez—that she failed to send a unit to Toledo Blade and Route 41—be sustained as well.

As Rick Goff put it, "We blew it—and I say 'we' because I'm part of that sheriff's office."

Susan Kallestad was eventually suspended without pay for sixty hours, would participate in twelve hours of remedial training, and would be on six months' disciplinary probation. Elizabeth Martinez was suspended for thirty-six hours, and received the same twelve hours of remedial training, and six months of probation. Martinez was also ordered to attend a Critical Incident Stress Management Debriefing.

Jane Kowalski was asked her opinion and she said she was blown away. She had been on the phone with the dispatcher for—what?—something like nine minutes. She was reporting an incident with obvious serious consequences—indeed, even grave consequences—yet the call was "lost in the mix."

Nate Lee felt the two punished dispatchers should have been fired, and the woman who fielded the Kowalski call should have been terminated as well. Nate listened to the Kowalski call on tape and he heard incompetence. The point of the call was that a possible kidnap victim was in a car on Toledo Blade, and the operator—Mildred Stepp— seemed more concerned with the caller, her whereabouts and her safety. "Are your doors locked?" *Please.*

Sheriff Davenport was aware of Nate's feeling, but the sheriff defended his own actions. He believed there was no punishment he could dish out that would compare with the way Kallestad and Martinez were punishing themselves. Those women were going to have to consider the tragic consequences of their inaction for the rest of their lives. "They felt terrible about this. Terrible," Davenport said. "We feel terrible about it." The entire department had made a mistake. The sheriff also pointed out that for both Kallestad and Martinez, working under pressure was nothing new. This time, they made a mistake, but it wasn't part of a pattern. They had each handled thousands of emergencies over the years, and they didn't "choke."

Just a month after his wife's death, Nate Lee granted a reporter an interview and said that, even though Denise was gone, she was still finding ways to surprise him. Just the other day, he was going through some stuff and found some things she had put in the back of their wedding album—cards and a note he wrote to her while they were dating. Nate said that he was only just getting an opportunity to grieve. "The past three weeks I haven't had a chance to think about her as much as I want. I haven't had a chance to pull out the camcorder and look at the videos." For the past month, he had spent a lot of time wondering how it all could have happened, how someone could snatch away a woman with two little babies in the house. "I know what he did, the ruthless cruel nature of what he did. I laid in bed a couple of nights ago and was trying to say, you know, 'I need to forgive him.' And I couldn't."

Glitches in the area's law enforcement system kept emerging. On February 28, 2008, the *Herald-Tribune* reported that a delay in updating a state computer database might have cost authorities their chance to save Denise Lee. That database contained vehicle registration and other records; in this case, it failed to ID the Camaro as belonging to Michael King. In December 2007, King submitted a registration for his Camaro that included his North Port address, but that info was not entered into the database.

According to local officials, there could be a ninety-day lag before the database picked up changes. If the database had been up-to-date, there was a chance that police might have arrived at King's Sardinia home while King and his victim were still there. As it turned out, police didn't learn of King's name and address until Denise used his cell phone to call 911. Because of this case's notoriety, the FDLE and the state's Department of Highway Safety and Motor Vehicles worked to shorten the lag time for updating database records from ninety days to no more than one week.

Records showed that within a half hour of Nate Lee's 911 call, after information was taken from the Lees' neighbor about the suspicious green Camaro, local police searched the state database, known as the Factual Analysis Criminal Threat Solution (FACTS), for a list of all green Camaros registered to owners in North Port. But King's name was not there. There were three other green Camaros on the list and police checked on those immediately, all before 5:30 P.M. on the day of the murder—of course, to no avail.

Police felt they had enough evidence to convict Michael King, but they continued to search for more. Discovery of King's nine-millimeter gun would have been great. The only way to search some areas was to kill and clear all of the vegetation.

To do that, herbicides would need to be applied; and before police could do that, they required Consent to Search forms signed by all of the involved landowners. Those forms gave police permission to search as much as they wanted for six months.

This being Florida, dive teams that would search the waters of the region had a special concern: alligators. So, for the owners of those lakes and other bodies of water, a second form was signed, giving the Florida Department of Fish and Wildlife permission to "trap and relocate" all alligators that might hinder the police search.

The evidence against King was presented to a grand jury, which indicted King on first-degree murder, a crime punishable by death.

Presiding over every phase of the Michael King case would be Judge Deno Economou, a thin man whose salt-and-pepper hair grew in thick waves. He was no stranger to newsworthy cases, dating back to before his time on the bench, to when he was an assistant state attorney. In 1989, for example, he successfully prosecuted the third-degree murder and child abuse trial of a Sarasota couple, William and Christine Hermanson, who tragically deprived their seven-year-old daughter of medical care because of their Christian Science beliefs. The girl died of complications from diabetes in 1986. His comment at the time was "If they wish to become martyrs for their religion, they have that right. But I contend to you that they do not have the right to make a martyr out of a seven-year-old girl."

Now, on March 6, 2008, Judge Economou sat on his bench and heard Michael Lee King's lawyers enter his plea of not guilty. The plea was a mere formality, and King did not appear in the courtroom. Also at the twenty-minute hearing, the judge denied a defense attempt to have the first-degree murder indictment thrown out because media publicity about the case might have tainted the grand jury. The defense attorneys didn't expect the judge to rule in their favor, but asking was necessary to preserve issues for eventual appeals.

* * *

On March 24, 2008, Susan Kirby Kallestad wrote a letter to Sheriff Davenport in response to the Internal Affairs investigation regarding the handling of Jane Kowalski's 911 call. She wrote that she "accepted her responsibility" for not passing on the information from Kowalski's phone call to the oncoming dispatcher. She wanted to note, however, that she did pass the information on to dispatcher Kattie Beasley, and asked that she air the info put into the computer by call taker Mildred Stepp. Kallestad wrote that she had only recently had the opportunity to listen to the tape of the Kowalski call in its entirety and was concerned by the fact that the internal investigation did not address inappropriate handling of the call by the call taker Stepp, who, Kallestad wrote, delayed in posting vital information. The call came in at 6:30 P.M., Kallestad noted, but it wasn't until twelve minutes later that Stepp posted information in the "Signal 59/Agency Assist" that had been opened into the computer-aided-dispatch for units responding to North Port. Kallestad wrote that Stepp spent a full nine minutes on the phone with Kowalski without entering any notes at all into the CAD system, which is the nucleus of CCSO dispatch operations.

All calls were supposed to be entered into that system in a timely fashion, she wrote, but for twelve minutes, Stepp entered nothing. She called that an "unacceptable amount of time" and "absolutely inexcusable," particularly considering the critical nature of the call. The twelve-minute delay in entering info in the system included the entire nine minutes of the call, plus three additional minutes. Listening to the call, Kallestad wondered if Stepp understood the "importance of this call." (She, for example, was told of a screaming child; yet immediately she relayed a verbal message that the call concerned a "crying child," diminishing the urgency.) Kallestad wrote that because of the conclusion of the internal investigation, her name and Elizabeth Martinez's name were "forever linked" as the dispatchers who mishandled the Kowalski call; yet, Stepp's failures were not addressed. She requested that her letter be added to the file containing the reports and documents produced during the internal investigation, and also that a copy be placed in her own personnel file.

Already flabbergasted and annoyed with the system that had failed to save Denise Lee's life, Jane Kowalski was further irritated when the 911 call she'd made was released to the press. That was because her phone number appeared both on the tape and on the transcript of the tape. Despite the ease with which it could have been redacted, everyone watching the news on TV or reading a newspaper suddenly knew Kowalski's cell phone number. According to law enforcement, they had no right to bleep out that information. All redactions in released materials were the responsibility of the media.

She expected half the kooks in the world to call, but it wasn't that bad. "I got some phone calls, but it wasn't horrific or anything," she said.

What *was* a pain was the media feeding frenzy that ensued. She had reporters at her door all day. She tried to do the right thing and make everyone happy, so she told the same story—the exact same story—about "a thousand times."

Nate Lee announced that he was starting the Denise Amber Lee Foundation, a movement calling for the revamping and improvement of 911 systems across America.

As winter turned to spring, the snowbirds migrated north and the natives of southwestern Florida sought ways to help the foundation. On the evening of March 30, 2008, Nate threw out the first pitch for a Port Charlotte High School baseball twin bill held at Pirate's Cove. Port Charlotte donated 100 percent of that night's proceeds, from both the gate and the concessions, to the charity, an amount in the vicinity of $1,000.

About the evening, Coach Bob Bruglio said, "I just thought, 'What a tragic thing.' I was born and raised in this town, and I want this community to be a community. When I grew up here, there was nothing. Kings Highway was a dirt road. You opened a gate to go to Arcadia and you closed the gate, so you didn't let the cows out."

CHAPTER 12

CRIMINOLOGISTS' REPORTS

On May 2, 2008, at 11:00 A.M., criminalistics specialist Cortnie Watts met with Nate Lee at the NPPD, in the property area. Watts was under orders from Detective Christopher Morales to show to the victim's husband items of evidence for identification. All of the items were clothing discovered down the road from the shallow grave, and they were in bags sealed with evidence tape. The first item was the pair of blue boxer shorts.

"Recognize these?"

"They're mine," he said. "She . . . She used to like to wear my boxer shorts."

A pair of red women's underwear. Lee said he believed they belonged to Denise.

A portion of a bra strap. "I can't be sure," he said.

When the items were rebagged and sealed, they were sent to the DNA Labs International to see if any DNA found on them was a match for either Michael King or Denise Lee.

Watts swabbed Nate Lee inside his mouth with a long Q-tip–like applicator for DNA.

Five days later, at two in the afternoon, Detective Morales instructed Watts to swab the nine-millimeter Luger shell casing found near the burial site. The casing was removed from its evidence bag, swabbed, then resealed in the bag. The swab was sent via FedEx to DNA Labs International (DLI) for testing.

DNA Labs International, located in Deerfield Beach, Florida, received, in all, thirty swabs for analysis. The first thirteen of those were swabs taken from the Camaro and its contents.

Only two of those contained sufficient DNA for analysis: One from the back of the driver's seat, near the bottom, was a match for Denise Lee. It was now impossible for King to claim Denise was never in his car. The chances of that DNA belonging to anyone other than Denise were 1 in 9 trillion. A hair found in the car also belonged to Denise.

A bloodstained yellow blanket found in the Camaro yielded a DNA mixture. Denise was the primary contributor to the tested material, and Michael King was almost certainly the secondary contributor. The profile on the secondary DNA was not complete; but still, chances that the DNA did not belong to King were 1 in 280.

The next four swabs to be tested came from King's attire when arrested. His shirt, jeans, and sneakers yielded insufficient data. However, his black boxer shorts had visible bloodstains on the right and left exterior waistband. According to the DNA Labs report, however, *No DNA profile foreign to Michael Lee King was obtained from this item.*

Seven swabs from King's "rape room" were tested, two successfully: one from the Winnie-the-Pooh blanket and one from a section of carpet that had been cut out and removed. Both semen and blood were detected on the blanket. The bloodstains were a mixture of male and female DNA. Neither the suspect nor the victim could be eliminated as possible donors. The chances that the combination DNA belonged to someone other than the suspect or the victim were 1 in 600,000. The carpet contained both blood and semen. There was a 1 in 19,000 chance that some of that blood didn't belong to the victim, a 1 in 310 chance that some didn't belong to the suspect. King was the donor of the semen. Long hairs found at the scene belonged to the victim.

Evidence gathered at Denise Lee's postmortem procedure was also sent to the FDLE for DNA analysis and given top priority. Those items included the vaginal, anal, and oral swabs, and those from the victim's breasts, and medial left thigh. Also among the items to be tested were fingernail clippings, head and pubic hair (hairs that included the root bulb), and duct tape still attached to the victim's head.

In early April 2008, Nate Lee and Rick Goff lobbied Florida State lawmakers to establish statewide standards for the training and certification of 911 emergency dispatchers.

A few days later, Nate came to the Charlotte County Justice Center, where he held a press conference and announced that he blamed the CCSO for not saving his wife. He intended to sue.

A tearful Nate Lee said, "If you have heard Ms. Kowalski's call, you heard severe incompetence [by the Charlotte County communications center]. That is unacceptable. Someday I'm going to have to tell our little boys, who will have very few memories, if any, of their amazing, courageous, and brave mommy. Despite all of this, I will have to tell them that she died needlessly. People need to be responsible for what happened. If that call was dispatched, we would never have wasted time looking and searching at all because Denise would have been rescued that night and would be with us today," he concluded.

Representing Nate Lee in the lawsuit was attorney Thomas D. Marryott, of Punta Gorda, Florida, who delivered the letter to Charlotte County Commission chairman Tom D'Aprile, informing the county of his client's intention to sue the sheriff's office for incompetence on behalf of himself and his two sons.

Marryott said, "The sheriff's office received sufficient information in a timely fashion in particular with Jane Kowalski which we believe, if they acted in the appropriate fashion, would have saved Denise Lee's life."

"We need to know if [the murder] could have been avoided and, if so, how. We have to make sure it never happens again," D'Aprile said.

Rick Goff called for the employees involved in the botched 911 call to be fired and added that he was still waiting for an apology from Sheriff Davenport.

On April 16, the Goffs, Nate Lee, and his sons went to the National Crime Victims' Rights Week ceremony in Port Charlotte. The event was organized by the Center for Abuse and Rape Emergencies (CARE) and the Charlotte County chapter of Parents of Murdered Children (POMC). During the ceremony, 101 local murder victims' names were read, and with each name a flower—a red, pink, or white rose—was pinned to a wreath of twigs. The ceremony was held in a movie theater and a spotlight lit the wreath.

Donald Mason, the head of the state attorney's office in Charlotte County, spoke at the ceremony. He said the ceremony's theme was "justice for victims, justice for all. For some, justice is revenge. For others, justice is acceptance and forgiveness. For others, justice is something that can never be rendered on earth. I urge you all to make the best that you can from this day."

Rick Goff also spoke, telling the audience about Denise: "I cried when she was born," he said. "I cried the day I dropped her off at school. I cry every day now. It's day by day. Some days are better than others. I have no good days. I just want to remember her for the special person she was. I just remember everything about her."

In October 2008, Deputy Daniel Cameron, of the SCSO, was working at the Sarasota County Jail, where Michael King was incarcerated. It was Deputy Cameron's job to supervise prisoner recreation, which was held on the jail's caged roof.

One day, Cameron and King began a conversation—the first time that the two had spoken to one another. It was just chitchat, at first. They were both originally from the Midwest and talked about the difference between Midwestern and Florida weather.

Then King said, "Do you know why I'm here?"

The deputy said no.

"They think I killed that girl in North Port," King said. Cameron felt a start. King added, "I met her, but I didn't kill her."

On December 12, 2008, Nate Lee appeared on *Dr. Phil* to discuss the flaws in the 911 system and how they might have cost his wife her life. Not everyone was pleased with his appearance.

Charles Cullen, president of the California chapter of

the National Emergency Number Association (NENA),
who also appeared on the program, called it a "setup."
Although he expressed the utmost respect and sympathy
for Nate Lee, he felt that using local mistakes to indict
all 911 systems was "a disgrace."

CHAPTER 13

PRELIMINARY HEARINGS

Preliminary hearings for the capital murder trial of Michael King were held in courtroom 4-A at the Twelfth Circuit Courthouse on Ringling Boulevard in Sarasota, which was also where the trial would be held. While in court, Michael Lee King wore a series of dress shirts in pastel colors with just the top button unbuttoned. The witness stand was in the center of the back wall, to the judge's right, directly in front of the centered lectern from which both sides would do their questioning. For an attorney to get any closer to a witness than that lectern, he or she would have to ask permission from Judge Economou to approach. The courtroom was modern, with individual padded seats for spectators, instead of the wooden pews that made older courtrooms resemble a church. Judge Economou's bench was at the rear right corner of the room; the defense was on the right side; the prosecution was on the left. The jury would sit against the left wall.

Ringling Boulevard! It was the perfect setting for the

media circus that was expected because of the notoriety that the case had garnered. An extra layer of security protected the courthouse for every Michael King hearing. Law enforcement's biggest fear was that a vigilante would try to inflict some instant justice on King. At all times, at least five SCSO deputies would be on hand, both to maintain order in the court and to protect the defendant.

Two of King's court-appointed lawyers were John J. Scotese and Carolyn Schlemmer—no strangers to capital murder cases. In 2007, both had been on the defense team of Blaine Daniel Ross, who, in 2004, murdered his mother and father with a baseball bat and then clumsily attempted to make the scene appear like a robbery. Ross was convicted and sentenced to death.

Schlemmer, without Scotese, was also part of the unsuccessful defense team for Richard Henderson Jr. in 2007. Henderson was charged with killing his entire family on Thanksgiving Day, 2005, and then sleeping in his parents' bed. Schlemmer did her best to paint Henderson as insane, but a jury didn't buy it. In that case, at least, Schlemmer convinced the jury to recommend life in prison rather than execution.

Schlemmer's career had not turned out at all as she had anticipated. When she was attending law school at Stetson, she had wanted to be a prosecutor, but fate pushed her onto the other side of the aisle.

"I had to take the public defender clinic while in law school because the prosecution clinic was full," she explained. She graduated in 1991 and began her career working for a friend's firm in St. Petersburg. After that, she worked as a public defender in the traffic division in Tallahassee. In 1993, for the first time, she defended a client facing the death penalty, and capital murder cases became her specialty.

How did she handle defending the worst of the worst?

"I do feel that, no matter guilt or innocence, everyone is entitled to good representation and a fair trial," she said. "Maybe that is why I can so easily represent the people accused of the worst crimes. I have a knack for separating feelings and work. You either have it, or you don't."

The third person on King's defense team was assistant public defender Jerry Meisner. One notch on Meisner's belt was that he had a few years earlier accomplished something very rare: he'd successfully argued that a client was not guilty because he was insane.

Jurors rarely buy insanity defenses—they don't like 'em. In February 2005, Meisner's client Larry Smith, of North Port, was acquitted of second-degree attempted murder charges because a jury found him insane. Smith had fired four shots at a gas station following an argument, but Meisner sold his theory that Smith was temporarily insane due to "involuntary intoxication," an adverse reaction to a prescribed antidepressant.

On April 16, Michael King himself appeared in court for the first time since his arrest. He was wearing a yellow prison jumpsuit. As would become the norm in court, King remained silent and stared straight ahead.

At the hearing, John Scotese argued that King's statements to police and civilians (i.e., Harold Muxlow) in the minutes and hours following his arrest should not be released to the media.

Scotese argued, "Everything the court has been provided is not a public record because it does speak of participation. There are statements of participation in the sense of being present at certain locations."

Judge Economou, however, reviewed the records and ruled that they did not contain admissions and should be released.

Fourteen months passed. King stewed in jail, not concerned with his grooming. On June 11, 2009, Michael King again appeared in court, now sporting long hair and a full beard. At the hearing, his lawyers noted that since community outrage over the case had been a predominant subject on online bulletin boards and in chat rooms, they should be allowed to ask potential jurors during voir dire if they had ever used the Internet to discuss the murder of Denise Lee. In the past, it was routine for potential jurors to be asked if they had written any letters to newspaper editors regarding a case. Asking them if they had ever blogged about a case was just an update of that. Questionnaires needed to be modernized. Did the potential juror online-chat? Tweet? Was he on Facebook?

Several mistrials had been declared in the recent past because of the common use of the computer as a research tool and as a way to express personal opinions. Nine jurors in a Florida drug trial admitted that they violated the judge's instructions and researched that case on the Internet. A federal corruption trial ended in a mistrial when jurors were found to be using Twitter and Facebook.

Judge Economou okayed the updating of voir dire. In addition to tweeting and blogging, potential jurors could be asked what they remembered about media coverage of the case. Of particular concern to the defense team was an appearance by Nate Lee on *Dr. Phil,* during which the widower asked that mistakes made in the aftermath of his wife's abduction become an impetus for improving 911 centers.

* * *

On Wednesday, July 22, 2009, Michael King appeared in court, clean shaven with neatly short-cropped hair, wearing a yellow prison jumpsuit and orange sandals.

Carolyn Schlemmer requested a change of venue, arguing that local notoriety rendered impartial jurors nonexistent. Almost everyone had read something about the case, Schlemmer told Judge Economou, and "when you read it, it is particularly disturbing."

The judge ruled that they would cross that bridge when they came to it. He was not going to assume that an impartial jury was impossible to seat in Sarasota County. If that did turn out to be the case, he would rule that the trial could be held elsewhere. For now, the judge said, the case would move forward.

It was noted that the courtroom was not large, and it might be too small to handle the number of spectators and media that were expected. The victim had many friends and loved ones who intended to observe every minute of the proceedings.

The judge ruled that "provisions would be made" for Denise Lee's supporters to sit in the courtroom. They would not, as some feared, be forced to watch the trial via TV monitor in an "overflow room."

Jury selection would prove to be particularly cramped. A pool of one hundred jurors was expected on the first day. Those people, plus the family members, would already fill the courtroom. Where would everyone else sit?

The judge said, "We will have to make arrangements." Before the jury was selected, the judge noted, some spectators might be allowed to sit in the jury box.

Schlemmer moved that evidence discovered at King's

home and obtained during a jailhouse conversation be ruled inadmissible. Detective Christopher Morales, Lieutenant Kevin Sullivan, and Deputy Daniel Cameron testified on these matters.

Sullivan said that on the evening of Michael King's arrest, he arrived at the scene on Interstate 75 moments following the traffic stop by Trooper Eddie Pope. The defendant had already exited his vehicle and asked for an attorney. Sullivan said he took King on a ride-along in hopes of finding Denise Lee, but the efforts were in vain. King said he hadn't been able to see during his abduction and didn't know locations. Sullivan said that King was not read his Miranda rights and that the defendant told him that he had also been kidnapped.

Detective Morales explained that King clearly did not know about the 911 calls from his cousin Harold Muxlow and Harold's daughter Sabrina, or else he would have realized that no one was buying his claim to be a victim. Morales said that many questions were asked of King during the ride-along, that no attempt was made to provide King with an attorney, although King asked for one on at least two occasions.

Deputy Daniel Cameron testified regarding the conversation he had with the defendant during October 2008 on the caged roof of the Sarasota County Jail during which King admitted to having met Denise Lee.

Denying the motion regarding evidence seized at King's home, Judge Economou said that after Denise King made her 911 call on King's cell phone, police were justified in entering his home. When police saw evidence of abduction in King's home, a search warrant *was* acquired, after which evidence was seized—evidence that police had reasonable cause to believe was pertinent to the victim's abduction.

The judge ruled that it was appropriate to suppress some postarrest statements made by the defendant. In his ruling, Economou said, "Neither Lieutenant Sullivan nor Detective Morales read Miranda rights to the defendant at the traffic stop or during the ride-along—the defendant was in custody at the time—nor did they provide the opportunity to have an attorney contacted." The ruling to suppress included any and all statements made by the defendant up until the time he was finally read his Miranda rights at the NPPD station late on the evening of January 17 and into the early-morning hours of January 18. This included the statements he made to Harold Muxlow, who was brought into the interrogation room to pump his cousin for information. The judge also ruled inadmissible the statement made by King to the deputy on the jail rooftop.

(Before faulting the officers for not reading King his rights or allowing him to get an attorney, readers should keep in mind that any eventual prosecution of this man was not the priority of law enforcement at that time. *Finding Denise Lee was their priority.* In that sense, they chose the best course of action.)

As the prosecution prepared its case against Michael King, it was Suzanne O'Donnell's job to be in charge of the hundreds of pieces of evidence.

"I was the evidence gal," she recalled.

From O'Donnell's POV, this was a complicated case because of the multiple crime scenes: the Lees' house, the Camaro, King's house, the burial site. She had to *edit* the evidence down to a manageable amount, prioritize, and eliminate the redundant.

A crime scene investigator's motto is "When in doubt,

bag it." Evidence had been taken from Harold Muxlow's house, for example, and none of it was pertinent to the crime. Not everything in the Camaro was relevant, either. King had paperwork in there that had nothing to do with the crime.

There was a bedpost found in the car's backseat, and O'Donnell wanted it to be relevant. But she couldn't tie it in, and the jury would never get to see it.

Her work was made easier by the "phenomenal job" done by the evidence techs, who had packaged and sealed each piece individually in clear plastic.

She knew of some trials where it took forever to introduce evidence. Each bag had to be cut open in front of the jury and the item removed so they could see what was inside. At King's trial, no scissors would be necessary. She could just hold up each package. Witness, jury, everyone, could see what was inside.

The techs prepared the evidence in other helpful ways. Denise's clothes found near the burial site were mounted on cardboard so that the jury could tell what they were. Otherwise, they would have just looked likes clumps of indistinguishable cloth.

CHAPTER 14

KING'S WOMEN

To best prepare for trial, the police and the state attorney's office wanted a complete picture of Michael King's sexual history. So, in addition to the already interviewed Jennifer Robb and Tennille Ann Camp, they sought out and interviewed every woman they could find who had been intimate with the accused.

Stephanie Sloan (pseudonym) was thirty-five when she met Mike King in the fall of 2005. As was true of all of King's women, she was diminutive—four-eleven—but in great shape, 117 pounds of nothing but muscle. Her sister had a Pilates studio and she took excellent care of her body. That autumn, she had just married her husband, John—and Mike was a friend of John's. Not close friends, but they used to work together—"side jobs, plumbing, automotive, stuff like that."

During the first six months of their marriage, the Sloans lived in Venice and didn't see much of King. After that, King started coming around—sometimes in his white truck, sometimes in a red sports car—to pick up John for jobs. He'd come in the house and talk.

The odd thing was that Mike was paying John really, really well. For one day's work, Mike would pay $300. She asked John why he was getting so much, but John was hard of hearing and uneducated and didn't know.

After a while, Mike started showing up at the Sloans' house with his new friend, a guy named Carlos Saenz. Stephanie wasn't thrilled because those two would show up when John was gone and she was home alone. Stephanie was usually drinking, because that was her lifestyle at the time.

On those occasions, Mike would say unpleasant things about John; that before he got married, he "bought prostitutes and was a bad person." Stephanie believed him and got mad at John. Then, when Mike went to the bathroom, Carlos would say, "He's very interested in you, Stephanie. He wants you as his girlfriend."

She and John were having some problems, and she agreed at some point to go over to Mike's house. Mike said he wouldn't try anything—*the liar.* Stephanie realized that hindsight was twenty-twenty. Mike had manipulated the situation from the start.

Mike had set John up, sent him to a job, so he wouldn't be around when Mike stole his wife away. She stayed over one night. Maybe two. While she was there, John called and talked to Mike. John said Stephanie was missing and asked Mike to help him look for her. Mike said he didn't know where she was.

Mike's son, Matt, and Mike's parents were there. Stephanie felt awkward. Mike and Stephanie rented movies. Knowing she was an alcoholic, he bought her beer. When they got back from the beer run, she went into the bedroom alone, drank, and watched the movies. Mike was in and out.

Mike kept going on and on about what a bad guy John was; the stories got worse and worse, until Stephanie couldn't believe them anymore.

No, that's not true, she finally told herself. She suddenly saw everything in a new light. Mike was obsessed with John and determined to tell lies about him.

Stephanie came out of the bedroom once or twice and chatted with Mike's mom a little bit. Once, she and Mike were in the bedroom and the son came in. That was *really* awkward.

She wasn't sure which bedroom she was in. It seemed small to be the master bedroom, but, on the other hand, it had its own bathroom.

Stephanie eventually got drunk and passed out. The next thing she knew, her pants were down and Mike was having sex with her. She was on her belly and he was coming at her from behind. She only vaguely remembered that part. It was brief—she knew that much. She couldn't tell at the time if he finished or if he stopped because she woke up. (The next morning, she discovered that he *had* ejaculated.)

The next day, or maybe the day after, she called John, crying and upset. "Please come get me," she said. And she went back home. Mike was at work. Later, her mother-in-law told her that Mike King was a weirdo, and she shouldn't believe a word he said.

After that, John and Stephanie didn't have anything more to do with Mike King for a long time, but they did see him again in January 2007. It was a matter of desperation. The Sloans were down on their luck, living in their car. John called Mike to ask if he could borrow a tent. John started hanging out with Mike and Carlos again after that, and another guy—she didn't remember his name, scrawny fellow, younger, maybe twenty, and usually stoned. Sometimes John wouldn't come home at night.

One time, John and Stephanie went over to Mike's house, and Mike, Carlos, and the scrawny guy were getting ready to go out. Stephanie remembered Mike bragging about this girl, who was *very* young, like fourteen or fifteen. They were all talking about little girls and sex and stuff like that, very graphic—talk that made Stephanie feel uncomfortable.

"It was gross," she recalled. She seemed to remember Mike saying that a bunch of young girls were coming over to his house and doing Ecstasy. There was a fifteen-year-old girl in particular that Mike talked about. A sexy strawberry blonde who was very mature for her age and dressed provocatively. The girl's parents lived up north somewhere, and they told Mike they were coming to take their daughter back. Stephanie couldn't remember the young girl's name, but she thought it might begin with an *A*.

A beauty salon in Venice, Florida, where Michael King was a regular, was the scene of some other noteworthy behavior. The owner, Patti Paull, said King was quiet and unassuming, but there was one skeevy moment.

King showed up at the beauty parlor one day accompanied by a young female, who he boldly claimed was only fifteen years old. Patti had never seen a man brag about being with an underage girl before.

It almost didn't compute.

She tried to reassure herself that all was not as it seemed, that the "fifteen-year-old" was his niece or daughter, something like that. However, those efforts went by the wayside when King began to passionately kiss the girl by the parlor's front desk.

King later bragged that the girl was from Tennessee and he'd met her on a dating service.

Now, as part of the murder investigation, cops looked

more thoroughly into the Venice incident and learned that the seemingly underage girl in the beauty parlor did indeed have a name that began with *A*.

She was Amy Sue Speranza (pseudonym). From her description, Amy was a Denise Lee look-alike. They found her because King himself had called the cops on her. She had stolen a car from him once and cops had to tow it back.

Police ran a check on Amy Sue. At first, they couldn't find her, but they did find the number of an ex-husband at his new residence in Kentucky. They gave the guy a call, to see what he knew about his ex-wife's fling with the suspected killer.

The husband, Robert Bryant (pseudonym), wasn't informed of what the call was about, and police got to the info they wanted in a roundabout way. Robert asked if Amy Sue was in trouble, and the officer said no. They had a situation regarding an acquaintance of hers and he couldn't get in touch with her directly.

Robert wanted to know if he was in trouble, and if it was about the car that was stolen. The cop said he wasn't in trouble, but it did have to do with the car.

He said he met Amy Sue three or four years before in a bar called the Starlite and they dated. She was a tiny thing. A blonde. Five-two. Hundred pounds.

At that time, she had two kids and lived in low-income housing. Bryant lived in Clinton, Tennessee. They dated for half a year, then split up.

"She had a habit of jumping from man to man," Bryant said. He couldn't handle the cheating, so they broke up. Still, he was in love with her.

She had a crummy childhood, she'd said—molested when

she was ten by her stepfather. She ran away when she was fourteen and got married when she was still underage.

The guy she married was named Speranza. She left Speranza and moved in with a guy named Bobby, with whom she had her first kid. That kid was now five and living with his grandmother. She subsequently had a little girl—despite the fact that she had stopped eating in hopes she would miscarry. She gave that baby away to her next-door neighbor so she could go out and get high. Father of the second child was a guy named David. Robert didn't know the last name. The girl was six months old when Robert met Amy.

She was okay at that point, had a job at a nursing home, and had both kids with her. After they broke up, she again hung out with the wrong crowd. In the summer of 2006, Robert had a hand amputated in a cabinet factory accident. They sewed it back on, but he never regained use of it and was disabled.

A month later, Amy Sue got back in touch. Thinking of her as broken, Robert decided to try to fix her. She got pregnant, and he married her in November 2006—although he suspected she might have been pregnant even before she got back in touch with him. He'd just gotten an insurance settlement and she quickly scammed him out of that. They were together until she started talking to a guy named Mike, a plumber from down in Sarasota, Florida.

She met Mike on a phone dating service line. He didn't know which one. Mike came up from Florida, drove all night long, and she was gone. This was two weeks after they got married.

"She's a scam artist," Robert said.

Robert and Amy Sue had been living in a hotel, and he didn't know she was gone until her grandmother and daddy came by to pick up her stuff. She called and said she was all right, but didn't leave her number. She said she was all set. Mike owned his own business and was going to buy her a car. Mike had a son she watched while Mike went to work. Robert was left over Christmastime, feeling lonely.

By the middle of January 2007, she was back.Because she was little and looked so young, she and her grandmother had concocted a story that she was underage. They used that as an excuse to get her away from Mike. She was actually a woman in her twenties.

Robert never met Mike but heard he drove a pickup, was heavyset, and had blond hair. Amy Sue moved back in with Robert. Then she called Mike again, and he either picked her up again or sent her a bus ticket. She went off with Mike for a second time, in February 2007.

The next time Robert saw her, she was driving a new car, which she said she had talked Mike into buying for her. She told him she was going to take the car, drive to Georgia to have an abortion, and then return. Mike gave her money for the abortion, but she took the cash and bought a large quantity of drugs.

She played some of Mike's phone messages for Robert. In these, he begged her to get in touch, just so he would know where she was, just so he would know she was okay. She also played a message from a man who sounded like a police officer, but Amy Sue insisted it was just one of Mike's friends and they were "trying to fake her out."

Robert was starting to think she stole the car. He eventually got so suspicious he called the Sarasota police. He guessed the car must've been reported stolen, because police came later that day and took it away.

* * *

Through Robert Bryant, North Port located Amy Sue in Tennessee. During an interview at the Campbell County Sheriff's Office, she told police her last name was Bryant. She figured that was her name, anyway, since Robert, the man who'd lost his hand, was her most recent husband.

She said she met Mike King on a dating phone line called Lova Light—like Lava Light, only with an *o*—that she'd learned about from a commercial on TV. The guys had to have credit cards and paid by the minute, but it was free for the girls. That was December 2006.

She looked like a little girl, a point she emphasized in both manner and appearance. However, when she met Mike, she was really twenty-five. She put an ad on Lova Light, set up a voice mailbox, and King called. She talked to him once, for maybe ten minutes. He said he was lonesome and needed someone to spend Christmas with. She told him she was sick of her husband, who hit her, and she just wanted to get out of there and teach everybody a lesson. King said he was in Florida and offered to come get her. She said that sounded pretty nice; she'd never been out of Tennessee.

He picked her up at her grandma's on December 18 or 19. King was driving a gold or brown Blazer. Once in Florida, he took her shopping, and they went for walks.

She thought he was strange. Not his looks. She kind of liked the way he looked. He had different personalities. He was controlling. Not violent, but domineering. She stayed at his house, for maybe a month. His son was there at the time. She got along with him okay. The kid just wanted to watch TV or play video games. Amy Sue tried to get him to ride his bicycle and go outside and "do the normal things that kids do."

* * *

Amy Sue became increasingly reluctant to talk. Maybe because talking to police was against her principles, maybe because she simply lacked the articulation to answer their questions adequately. They would ask what King was like and she'd say, "I don't know what you want me to say." The police emphasized that she was not in any trouble, wasn't going to get in any trouble. They wanted to know about Mike King.

"We're going to need to know about some personal things, Amy—like Michael King's sexual preferences."

"That's filthy stuff," she said.

"I think you should know that Michael King is under arrest in Florida. The charge is murder. We think he murdered someone, okay?"

This was news to Amy Sue. "He don't seem like that kind of a person," she said with a small nervous giggle.

They gave her the horrible details of King's crimes. They told her the victim looked *a lot* like her.

"That's why we're here. That's why we need you to co-operate with us totally on everything. We don't drive eight hundred miles just to say 'hey' and buy you a bottle of (Mountain) Dew."

"I really need a cigarette. You guys are stressing me out."

"I don't think you can smoke in here. There was a deputy out there. He had to step outside to smoke." She said she didn't have a cigarette; so one of the policemen went out to search for one, while the other continued the questioning.

She said Mike didn't let her have any money and she didn't have any way of getting around when she was living on Sardinia Avenue with Mike. The best she could do was walk around the school across the street and maybe sit on a bench. She didn't fight back when he tried to control her.

"I just stayed to myself," she told the cops.

After she went back to Tennessee for the last time, she tried to call King. He'd changed his cell phone number, though. She called him at his work, Babe's Plumbing, Inc., and she told him where she was. "I told him I had his baby here," she explained. One time she called and they said he was in Michigan because of a family emergency. They didn't know if he was coming back or not. She didn't leave her real name. She said to tell him "Kelly" called. (The police knew Amy Sue was telling the truth. The message from Kelly had been found in King's personnel file at Babe's Plumbing.)

She told the cops she was "pretty sure" her most recent baby was King's. So, yes, they did have a sexual relationship. They asked if he did anything odd sexually or asked her to do anything that made her feel uncomfortable. She said no, but in a barely audible voice.

"Any anal sex?"

"No, just vaginal. He might've tried anal, but nothin' ever come of it."

"How often did he want sex?"

"He liked it every day. But I didn't."

"Any bondage situations?"

"No."

"Did he have a favorite position?"

"No."

"Always in a bed?"

"Yeah. Or a couch."

At that point, the cigarette arrived. "You don't know what I had to go through to get this!" a cop said. She laughed. After the cigarette break outdoors, the questioning resumed.

She said she split from Florida twice. Three times, really, but once she didn't make it. She didn't stay in Florida long the first time. The fun only lasted a few days to a week. She said she had to go, and he bought her a Greyhound bus ticket and dropped her off at the station in Port Charlotte. It was December 24, because she told him she had to be home for Christmas. But she was only on the bus for a few minutes when he called her cell phone and talked her into getting off the bus in Ocala, where he picked her up. They made a stop at a nearby motel and eventually made it back to Sardinia Avenue. Soon thereafter, his meanness returned and she said she had to leave again. This time, he said he would drive her. She started to get scared. She didn't know anybody in Florida and she was completely under his control. He didn't hit her, but he'd get right in her face and yell. "He looked like he might hit me sometimes, but he didn't." So she told King she was underage and he had better take her home or else her family would call the police. King talked to Amy Sue's grandmother and aunt, and they backed up her story. She was underage and he'd better bring her home. And he did. He still wasn't sure, though. Three or four times, Amy Sue dozed off in the car during the ride. When she woke up, he'd turned the car around and was heading back toward Florida. He wouldn't stop the car to let her pee. Eventually he got her back to her grandma.

For the ride back to Tennessee, she didn't remember much because King bought her about thirty "totem poles," ten bucks apiece, and she was pretty zonked. The cops asked her what a totem pole was. She giggled and explained that they were like ten Xanaxes rolled into one. Did she know where he got the drugs?

"From Asian dudes, or sump'n," she said. "Not far from his house."

He never did drugs with her. When she told him that she needed drugs, something she didn't tell him right away, he knew exactly where to go to get them. She thought there might have been a connection through some guys with whom he worked.

The police wanted to know what she told King to get him to buy the drugs.

"I told him I can't sleep at night."

The cops tried to press her for more info regarding the drug dealers, but she cut them off.

"When it comes to drugs, I don't ask for names. Just give me my drugs and I'm out of here. They might've been good-looking guys. I don't know. They didn't look Mexican or black or white. They looked Asian to me."

At her request, Mike came back and got her a second time—at which time, she told him that she *wasn't* underage.

"He should have known better, anyway. I had a five-year-old son at home," she said with a laugh.

This time, not long after she arrived, she talked King into buying her a car so she and his son could go out and do things—and he brought one home for her that night. She thought he might have purchased it in Port Charlotte.

The next day, when he went to work, she got in her new car and split, spent a couple of days in Georgia, visiting her friend Brian, and then went back to Tennessee. While in Georgia, she got a call from a North Port cop regarding a stolen car. Brian didn't need the law at his house, so she had to leave—and took the hot car with her.

She stayed with her dad. A cop showed up at the door and took the car. She talked to King only one more time after that, maybe a month later. He told her that breaking up was her fault. She had a drug problem and he didn't think she would straighten out. He said he was moving to Ocala and was living with somebody, and they were very happy together.

She did text him once after that, to tell him she was pregnant and to request a sample of his DNA. He changed his cell phone number after that.

She was so confused about all of this. Mike King didn't seem like the kind of guy who would kill someone. He had a job and a nice house. But back home, her friend Randall said there was something wrong.

Randall said, "What's up with this guy? There are a lot of beautiful women in Florida. Why's he got to come all the way up here to Tennessee and get you?"

The cops explained that Michael King had lost his job, and was in the process of losing the house to foreclosure. A year earlier, he was doing better; but since then, he'd been digging himself a hole that he couldn't get out of.

She told the police she had never seen King with a gun, no weapon of any sort—and there was no gun in the house on Sardinia.

Amy Sue was concerned about what became of King's son and was pleased to learn the boy Matthew was in Michigan living with an uncle.

She repeated that she *really did* think her third child was Mike's, that Robert was taking care of the baby, but she didn't think her husband could have kids.

She and Robert had unprotected sex for years and she never got pregnant, and he'd had unprotected sex with other women, and none of them got pregnant, either. The baby must be Mike's.

The cops ended the interview by scolding Amy Sue, telling her how stupid it was to get in cars with strangers and drive away. It could have been her with a bullet in her head in that shallow grave instead of Denise Lee.

"We don't know if this is the only woman he ever killed. As soon as he got out of the car, he wanted a lawyer. He never told us where she was, never helped us in any way, and he was ice-cold."

One thing Amy Sue did notice was that he liked to stretch the truth, told a few whoppers, lied about things you didn't even need to lie about. She never let on that she didn't believe him, but in her mind she'd say, *Yeah, right*.

"I knew I was a little bit too far from home to be questioning him," she said.

CHAPTER 15

THE TRIAL

Jury selection commenced on Monday morning, August 17, 2009. As this was a death penalty case, members of the jury pool had to pass two levels of questioning. First they had to be "death qualified." People who believed that the death penalty should *never* be used were dismissed, as were people who believed the death penalty should *always* be used. This portion of the questioning tended to be repetitive and tedious.

On the prosecution side, the work was divided up between Lon Arend and Suzanne O'Donnell. They asked, "Can you listen to the evidence and make a determination? Will you consider the aggravating and mitigating factors?"

Once "death qualified," jurors were questioned a second time—voir dire, it was called—and prosecutors and defense attorneys asked questions regarding the general aspect of a murder trial, and about each potential juror's exposure to media reports on the case. Karen Fraivillig handled this task for the state.

Judge Economou scheduled a week for jury selection because of the exceptional publicity the case had received. And the process required all of that time. An unusually large jury pool, four hundred people, was eventually whittled down to twelve jurors and four alternates.

The prosecution had their game plan in place. Arend would deliver the state's opening statement, Fraivillig would examine eyewitnesses, and O'Donnell would handle the introduction of evidence.

The prosecution worked right up till trial time to maximize their presentation's power. Four days before opening statements, NPPD criminalistics specialist Cortnie Watts flew in the police helicopter taking aerial photographs of the various crime scenes that would serve as visual aids for the jury.

Nate Lee talked briefly about the upcoming trial. Yes, he planned to be there every day, as did many of Denise's friends and loved ones. He said, "In the coming weeks, I'm going to have my friends and family near me, and that's what really matters. Justice will be served, and that's what we're focusing on."

The trial began on Tuesday, August 25, 2009. Because of the case's emotional nature, security was tight. Double metal detectors were employed, at the courthouse and at the courtroom door.

Press presence was to be strictly governed. At any given time, only eight handpicked members of the media were allowed in the courtroom. The rest of the pack was corralled into a "media room" on the courthouse's main floor and allowed to watch on TV.

As he would throughout the trial, King wore a collared shirt in a "happy" color and dark pants, looking like he hadn't slept since his arrest. Beneath his sunken eyes were dark circles and heavy bags, the haunted eyes of a man plagued and then defeated by his own demons. He would display no emotion. He wasn't sad or angry or nervous or frightened. Tabula rasa. Could he even focus on his surroundings?

Michael King's utter blankness caught the attention of Judge Dena Economou—and troubled him.

Among those sitting in the spectator section was Amanda Goff, Denise Lee's younger sister, who was twenty and a student at the University of Central Florida. She would always sit behind her parents and her younger brother, Tyler.

Unlike her family members, however, Amanda took copious notes. A poli-sci major with a minor in legal studies, she'd already received an associate's degree from Valencia Community College in Orlando on what would have been Denise's twenty-second birthday.

Amanda had permission to take time off from school to attend the trial; but upon her return, she had to submit a long essay on the trial's "every detail."

Judge Economou told spectators that he wouldn't have a lot of coming and going in his courtroom. "If you leave, you may only return during a break," he said.

He gave the jury instructions: They were to have no preconceived notions, and there was no assigned seating in the jury box. Jurors could sit anywhere they wanted, as long as they were in the box. It was the jury's job to determine what the facts were, but it was his job to apply the law to those

facts. The charges against the defendant were solemn:
murder in the first degree, kidnapping with the intent to
commit murder, sexual battery by threat to use force. Outside court, jurors would not discuss the case. Not even
among themselves. They should weigh the testimony on
the last day the same as that on the first. If the defendant decided not to testify, that shouldn't be held against
him. Taking notes was optional. Pen and paper would be
provided—but all notes would be destroyed following
deliberation.

Lawyers briefly met in a sidebar to agree upon stipulations, things that didn't need to be entered into evidence
because both the prosecution and defense agreed they
were true.

A quick glance around revealed the spectator section to
be about one-third filled. Only those with a personal interest in the case were there in person. (Don't think the press
corps in the media room didn't notice that!) The rest were
content to watch the trial on TV, or read summaries of the
action on the Internet and in the daily newspapers.

The prosecution began its case by reading from a transcript of the horrifying 911 call the victim had made on her
own behalf. ASA Lon Arend addressed the jury, quoting
Denise Lee's words that she spoke during her 911 call:
"I'm sorry. I'm sorry. I just want to go. I just want to see
my family again, please. Oh, please."

The emotional response from the victim's family was
obvious. Denise's sister and mother wept. Her father lowered his head, his elbows on his knees. When he raised his
head, he gave Michael King a look that could kill.

Rick Goff would later say that sitting in the same room

with the man who killed his daughter was the toughest thing he ever had to do in his whole life.

ASA Arend said the state intended to prove that moments after that 911 call ended, the defendant took the victim to a secluded spot, took her life with a single bullet to the head, and, using the shovel he'd just borrowed, buried her in a shallow grave.

It was Arend's sad duty to relate to them the details of the crime, which, he assured the members of the jury, were almost unbelievably horrible. They would be hearing from crime scene technicians about those details. Denise Lee was abducted from her home, leaving her two young sons home alone, and then driven to the defendant's home, where she was raped. She was found with duct tape still in her hair, bruised thighs, and vaginal and anal injuries.

Using DNA evidence, the state would prove that the defendant transported her to the grave site in his car and killed her there. There was an eyewitness—the man from whom the defendant borrowed the shovel—who saw him struggle with the victim in his car and push her head down. A neighbor saw the defendant's Camaro drive back and forth in front of Denise's house several times that morning. To pull it together like a bow around a complete package, they would hear from the victim's husband, a man left alone with his two sons, who no longer had a mom. They would hear him identify boxer shorts found as his, a pair he knew his wife liked to wear.

Jerry Meisner delivered the opening statement on behalf of the defense. As he spoke, Denise Lee's mother, Susan Goff, wept. Rick Goff reached over to give his wife's hand a squeeze. Sitting behind them, Nate Lee also became teary.

Meisner said the prosecution was going, no doubt, to do a thorough and highly skilled job of presenting the evidence. His job, however, was to make just as obvious the evidence that was missing. Where was the murder weapon? Where were the bullets? Where was the blood on Mike's clothing?

"The medical examiner will tell you that the victim was shot point-blank by that nine-millimeter gun," Meisner said, "but will not be able to say who shot that gun. That question of identity will be left to you. The evidence will show that Michael King *did not* fire the shot that ended Denise Lee's life."

This was a simple case of mistaken identity, Meisner said. He told the jury that the defendant had gone pistol shooting with a business colleague that day. The defendant had never gone shooting at that gun range before; he did so on this day only at his colleague's invitation. It was the colleague who last held the presumed murder weapon.

The defense submitted that the prosecution, though perhaps well-intentioned, was—figuratively speaking— target shooting in the dark. There was every chance that it was that colleague, and not the defendant, who killed Denise Lee.

The prosecution had another witness, a cousin of the defendant's who knew him his whole life. The cousin would say he loaned Michael a flashlight and a shovel, but he wouldn't be able to tell you where the defendant went after he left, or that he saw Michael shoot Denise.

When the police stopped Michael that day as he drove his Camaro along I-75, there was no victim, no gun, and no bullets in the car.

Meisner said they would hear much about the shot that killed Denise Lee, but he was certain they would

find, when all was said and done, that there was more than
a reasonable doubt as to the identity of the shooter.

The first prosecution witnesses were members of the
North Port Police Department, Sarasota County Sheriff's
Office, Florida Highway Patrol, and Florida Department of
Law Enforcement, as well as crime scene technicians who
laid down the evidence against Michael King in an orderly
and methodical manner.

NPPD detective Christopher Morales said he'd been
nine years with the department, and he was the lead detective in the case. He summarized his activity in the case,
reporting first to the Lees' home, then to King's home. He
told the jury about the defendant's arrest and the subsequent sad search for Denise, which involved search dogs
and helicopters.

The detective used a series of maps to show the locations and the testimony that the jury would be hearing
about during later testimony: Latour, Sardinia, Muxlow,
Kowalski, grave, arrest, and the location where Denise's
undergarments were found dumped.

This gave the jury some perspective, a look at the relationship between the sites. All of the locations were in
North Port. Denise lived in the northwest corner of the city.
King's house was in a more crowded neighborhood, but
also off I-75, immediately facing an elementary school.

Photos of the locations were shown, the witness identifying and describing each. Morales said that each photo
shown was a fair and accurate depiction of how that site
looked.

The detective concluded his direct testimony by saying
that yes, it was he who prepared the search warrants for

King's home, and that as a result of that search, clothes were seized as evidence.

Under cross-examination, Detective Morales was forced to admit that despite an exhaustive search of roadway sewers and ditches, the murder weapon was never found. When Michael King was arrested, there were no guns or bullets in the car. None were found at King's home, either. Retention ponds were drained, but no luck. Dive teams searched area lakes. Nothing. The search did turn up an old rusty gun unrelated to the case.

Morales admitted that one of the guns turned in by Robert Salvador was a nine millimeter, but it was never tested to see if it was the murder weapon. And a nine-millimeter gun was found at Harold Muxlow's home as well. No, that one wasn't tested, either. Why? Both men had alibis; so neither gun could have been involved.

On recross, Christopher Morales admitted that Rob Salvador gave police two statements, one on January 18 and one on January 20, and that there were discrepancies in those statements involving receipts that Salvador was asked to show to prove his whereabouts during the key hours.

During his first interview, he said he had no receipts. But on January 20, he submitted to cops a timed-and-dated receipt from a Checkers restaurant indicating that he'd purchased a hamburger. During his first interview, he said he went straight home after the firing range. But on his second, he said he'd gone to Checkers and then to a storage facility between the range and home. Rob Salvador had initially denied seeing Michael King on January 17, but rather quickly admitted that he had. At first, he didn't admit that he'd visited King's house about a week before the crime. Later he admitted he had.

"When he came in on the twentieth, he admitted he lied on the eighteenth. Is that correct?"

"Yes."

"No further questions, Your Honor."

"Prosecution calls Sergeant Pamela Jernigan."

Jernigan testified that she had served with the North Port Police Department for eleven years. She was the first responder at the Lee residence on the day of the murder. Because the mother had left without her kids, purse, or keys, she determined that a suspicious circumstance existed, and a criminal investigation detective should be called in. That day, she next traveled to Harold Muxlow's home. Harold wasn't home at first, so she canvassed his neighbors to see if anyone had observed the Camaro, with the apparent hostage inside. When Harold Muxlow returned home just shy of seven o'clock that evening, Jernigan and Todd Shernier, another police officer, interviewed the witness and obtained a written statement. Jernigan visited area gas stations to see if any had serviced a green Camaro. When this bore no fruit, Jernigan participated in a meeting at which the methodical search for Denise Lee was organized. At about nine o'clock that night, she was notified that Michael King had been apprehended. She participated in the search of a sod farm and other isolated areas near Toledo Blade, north of the interstate, but found nothing of importance.

On cross-examination, the defense poked here and there, not expecting much. Was Jernigan aware that Denise had more than one purse? Yes. Were fingerprints found on the Lees' front doorknob or dead bolt? She didn't know. Was

DNA evidence found on the doorknob or dead bolt? She didn't know. Witness excused. Judge Economou said it had been a full morning and called for the lunch recess.

After the break, the jury learned that sperm found inside Denise Lee's body was a DNA match for King's, blood spattered on the front of Michael King's car was found to belong to the victim—and they were reminded that the victim made an emergency call during which she could be heard begging for her life from the defendant's cell phone.

As the defense cross-examined each witness, a pattern emerged. The defense was not refuting the kidnapping and rape charges. They were only interested in putting doubt in the jurors' minds regarding the murder charge.

Twenty-four-year-old Jenifer-Marie Eckert looked tiny as she sat anxiously on the witness stand. She lived on Long Island now, but on January 17, 2008, she resided next door to the Lees. The state flew her down to testify. Jurors sensed her nerves. She was afraid—afraid of what she had been so close to almost twenty months before, afraid of the monster in the room right now looking at her. (She knew she was "his type," blond and diminutive.)

She also felt pangs of guilt. Nothing rational, but real nonetheless. She'd seen the guy pull up. If only she had known, or sensed, that he was bad. If only she'd *done* something. That poor lady would still be alive.

Karen Fraivillig asked questions in her most soothing voice: "Were you a friend of the Lees'?"

"No."

"How would you describe your relationship?"

"Acquaintance."

"Before I start asking about the events of that date, I want to ask you a couple of questions about your background, so nobody thinks we're hiding anything," said Fraivillig.

"All right."

Fraivillig established that Jenifer-Marie Eckert, while living in North Port, was arrested and charged with petty theft. Subsequently, when moving to New York State, there had been a problem with completing her mandated classes and she got in trouble again. The witness agreed that "trouble" was an excellent summary of her status.

"And despite that, no promises have been made by me or anyone else that you would be given anything in exchange for your testimony, correct?"

"Correct."

She told the story of that day, how she was watching TV, and waiting for her boyfriend. Her boyfriend, as it turned out, never did show up, and they later broke up. But while she was waiting, looking out the window and watching for his car, she saw that green Camaro *creeping* down the street.

Fraivillig showed her a map that showed the proximity between her house and the Lees' house. The witness said it looked like a fair representation. The map was projected so that everyone, especially the jury, could see it. Jenifer-Marie used a laser red dot to show where her house was, where Denise's house was, and the path the car took as it went back and forth in front of the houses, four or five times.

She told how she went outside and saw the man parked in the Lee driveway and made eye contact with him. Fifteen minutes later, she watched as he pulled the green Camaro out of the Lees' driveway and drove away hurriedly.

Fraivillig asked the witness if she remembered what the driver looked like, and she said sure: heavy, blondish hair, light eyes. Did she see him in the courtroom? Jenifer-Marie Eckert was brave. She said yes and pointed at the defendant. Fraivillig made sure the ID got on the record.

On cross-examination, Jerry Meisner used transcripts of previous statements Jenifer-Marie Eckert had given to make it appear that the number of times the green Camaro passed her house seemed to be increasing with time. He implied that as stories sometimes do, hers was getting a little better with each telling. He wanted the jurors to infer this.

Meisner then made the witness reiterate the key points to her statement: though she saw the Camaro pull in and pull out, she didn't see anything that happened in between.

"You never saw Denise go in the car?"

"No."

"You never saw a struggle take place?"

"No."

"Did you hear screaming?"

"No."

On redirect, Karen Fraivillig had the witness look at another part of her initial written statement to the police, to a place where she said the Camaro might have gone past the house four times. To change from four times to five or six times wasn't much of an embellishment, more of a molehill compared to the mountain Jerry Meisner tried to make out of it.

Fraivillig later called Jenifer-Marie Eckert a "good witness. She did a really good job for us, helping us lay down our foundation. Considering how scared she was, she held her own. Her testimony showed his premeditation. King had a plan. He didn't just pull up to the house. He drove up and down the street, trolling, choosing."

"Prosecution calls Harold Muxlow Jr. to the stand."

With many spectators gazing upon him with distaste, Harold entered the courtroom from the back, took the oath, and sat in the witness stand. He told Karen Fraivillig that he was forty-six years old and made his living in lawn maintenance and house painting. The defendant was his cousin. He wasn't sure of Michael King's exact age, but he remembered he was about ten years older than King. King must've been somewhere in the vicinity of thirty-six.

"Before you lived in Florida, where did you live?"

"Michigan."

"Did the defendant live in Michigan before he moved to Florida?"

"Yes."

"Have you spoken to him since he moved to Florida?"

"We've spoken hundreds of times—phone and in person."

On January 17, 2008, sometime between five-thirty and six o'clock, Michael King drove up to Harold's property. He parked his car on the other side of the street, with the passenger side facing the witness's house. No, Harold was not expecting him.

King explained that he had a lawn mower stuck in a ditch out in front of his house, and he needed to borrow tools. "He asked to borrow a shovel, a can of gas, and a flashlight," Harold said.

"And you got him the items?"

"Yes, they were in a storage trailer."

"Did you have any conversation with the defendant as you got the items out of the trailer?"

"Yes—same conversation we always had. Talked about jobs and stuff."

The three items, all of which were found in King's car at the time of his arrest, were presented to the witness, who identified them as his. The items were then entered into evidence.

The prosecutor projected a map of Harold Muxlow's house and property so the witness could show where the green Camaro parked, and where he and the defendant stood and went. Cousin Mike remained outside when Harold went into the trailer.

"Regarding the car, earlier we heard Detective Morales describe the Camaro as having a black 'bra' on the front. Do you know what he meant?"

"Yes, the Camaro had a black thing on the front of it to protect the paint from bugs."

As soon as Harold handed over the items, his cousin said he had to go. King put the items in his car. Harold had his back turned to the car when he heard a sound that he, at first, thought might be the shovel hitting the car. Then he heard a woman's voice crying out, "Call the cops."

"You are certain it was a female voice?"

"Yes."

"What did you do?"

"I began walking down the driveway, toward his car."

"Did you say anything to the defendant at that time?"

"Yes, I said, 'What the fuck are you doing?'"

"And what did he say to that?"

"He said, 'Don't worry about it. Get back inside.'"

"He told you to get back inside your house?"

"Yes."

"Did you go back inside?"

"Yeah, I did. I figured this was a boyfriend/girlfriend thing, and it was none of my business."

"Did you stay inside?"

"No, curiosity got the best of me. I needed to see what he was up to, so I went back out to the driveway."

"And what, if anything, did you see?"

"I saw a silhouette of someone in the middle of his car, and I saw him shove her head down and then take off."

Harold Muxlow indicated on the map where he and the car were when he saw this. King was in the front with his back to the steering wheel, and he was leaning into the backseat.

"Could you see her?"

"I could only see that she had shoulder-length blond hair, and I caught a glimpse of a knee as she was pushed."

"What happened then?"

"He got behind the wheel and drove off."

"And what was on your mind after the defendant drove off?"

"Something didn't seem right."

"So what did you do?"

"I called my daughter, Sabrina." He was on his cell phone and walked outside as he was talking to her, telling her what he saw, and what he thought it meant. He got in his truck and drove off, in the direction of King's house. Harold was starting to think there was no lawn mower stuck in a ditch. When he got to King's house, there was no lawn mower—and there was no green Camaro, either. He pulled into his cousin's driveway and got out.

"I checked to see if his door was locked. It was, so I banged on the door. No one answered." He pulled out his cell phone. He wanted to call 911, but he wanted to remain anonymous. If he used his cell phone, the automatic caller ID would immediately give him up. So he tried dialing *67 before 911, which was supposed to mask the call. That didn't work; so he got back in his car and drove to a gas station pay phone, where he dialed 911. That call wouldn't go through, either—at least not until he deposited fifty cents.

"Now, you said something to the 911 operator, but you weren't that forthcoming."

"Well, I still didn't want to get involved, and I wanted to remain anonymous, and this was my cousin. So I gave a description of the car and said that if I found out anything else, I would call back."

"And did you ever get back to the police?"

"By the time I got back to my house, there were three cop cars on my street." He gave a statement right then and there, and was questioned at least three more times that night. He told them he owned a gun and kept it in his bedroom. He was worried about his cousin coming back. He was concerned enough about his safety to take the gun out of his bedroom. There were knocks on the door, but it was always the cops. He showed his gun to a cop at about eight-thirty on the evening of January 17.

"Did you hear the 911 call made by Denise Lee that day?"

"Yes."

"Did you hear in the background of that tape a male voice?"

"I did."

"Could you identify that voice?"

"Yes, it was the voice of my cousin Michael King."

"Are you certain?"

"No doubt in my mind."

Harold was asked if he saw King in the courtroom, and he said he did: he was the defendant, the fellow in the blue shirt.

"No further questions, Your Honor."

* * *

"Mr. Meisner?"

"Thank you, Your Honor." Jerry Meisner established that Harold Muxlow lived alone. He had a daughter, who lived with her mother. He was Michael King's first cousin. Their mothers were sisters. Their families spent a lot of time together—every Thanksgiving together. The witness moved to Florida eighteen years earlier; the defendant moved to Florida six years before.

"You have a lot of different jobs. Is that right, Mr. Muxlow?"

"Yes."

"You don't have a schedule?"

"Not really."

"Have you ever known Cousin Mike to have a nine-millimeter gun while he lived in Florida?"

"No."

"You've been over to his house before. Do you know if he owns a gas can?"

"No, I don't."

Meisner took the witness through his testimony regarding King's visit: "After he left your house, you didn't call the police, did you?"

"No."

"You spoke to your daughter and told her not to call the police, didn't you?"

"She said we needed to call police, but I said we didn't know what was going on."

"But she called the police, anyway?"

"Yes, I was proud of her."

"You got mad at her?"

"Not really."

"You didn't get into ten arguments over that call?"

Harold Muxlow admitted he'd raised his voice, but only because his daughter's mother was speaking to her simultaneously and she wasn't able to hear everything he was saying.

"When you went to 7-Eleven and you did call 911, you didn't tell the truth, right?"

"I didn't say who I was. I gave a description of the car."

"On the other 911 tape, you said you recognized King's voice?"

"Yes."

"Wasn't there a lot of noise on that tape?"

"Yes."

"Music was blaring?"

"Yes."

"You can't hear everything that voice is saying, can you?"

"I can hear enough," Muxlow replied, standing his ground.

Karen Fraivillig had a few questions on redirect, starting with: "The fact that you wanted to remain anonymous, does that change anything that you saw the defendant do, like pushing the head?"

Muxlow said it did not.

"On that 911 tape, did you hear enough to recognize your cousin's voice that you've been talking to for thirty-five years?"

"Yes, I did," the witness replied confidently.

When Harold Muxlow stepped off the witness stand, Fraivillig breathed a sigh of relief. Harold had not been an easy questioning to prep for. He was essential to the state's case, and yet he came loaded with baggage. It was anticipated that the jury—just like everyone else—was going to judge Harold. They would hear his story and think, *He could have done more.* The trick to eliciting his testimony in the most effective way, Fraivillig realized, was to get him to talk about the things he did without asking him too much about the things he did *not* do. Reacting to an emergency immediately and correctly might have been beyond his behavioral scope. Michael King was his cousin. Harold Muxlow was a man who would think long and hard before calling the cops on a relative, regardless of how troubling the circumstances. Even if King hadn't been related, Muxlow might have reacted slowly, Fraivillig believed. He was from a segment of society that didn't want to get involved. There are Good Samaritans, and then there are those who wouldn't stop if they saw a baby crawling across a highway.

Plus, Harold Muxlow had a chip on his shoulder. He felt that he had been mistreated and scrutinized with unwarranted suspicion by police during the first hours and days after the murder. So he had an attitude, too. Add to that mix the victim's family, who were extremely resentful toward Harold. They felt Denise would still be alive if he had done the right thing immediately. He was a tough witness all around. Fraivillig was glad she'd finished with Harold Muxlow.

Shawn Johnson testified that he lived in Fort Myers and for the past few years owned his own restoration company. On the afternoon of the murder, while driving south on U.S. Route 41, on his way home from work, he'd seen the green Camaro. He heard the screams of the captive inside it, heard her cry "Help! Help me!" He could tell it was no joke. He called 911 when he got to Fort Myers, and he was invited to the NPPD to look at photos. From an array of photos, he picked out one. That was the guy. He signed the photo. Now, in the courtroom, Karen Fraivillig showed him that photo array, one photo signed.

"That's the photo you chose?"

"Yes."

"Do you see that person in the courtroom today?"

"I do. He's sitting right there, in the blue shirt."

"Are you sure?"

"Without a doubt."

"Nothing else, Your Honor."

On cross, Jerry Meisner asked if Shawn Johnson was certain the cries came from a female. He said he was. Could he tell if the cries came from a child or an adult? He said he knew it wasn't a child.

"This encounter didn't last very long, did it, Mr. Johnson?"

"Just as long as it took for the light to turn green."

Meisner emphasized that the police had not asked him if any of the photos looked familiar, but rather to "pick one"—thus indicating they *wanted* him to choose one of the photos.

On redirect, Karen Fraivillig asked, "Did law enforcement coach you before you identified the photo?"

"No."

"Did you pick out King's photo as a result of any suggesting or coaching?"

"No one in any way coached me. They asked me, can I pick someone out, and I said I could."

"Was it a long process?"

"Very quick. I looked at each photo for about five seconds and made my pick."

"And there is no doubt that it is the defendant you saw driving that car?"

"None at all."

Judge Economou said, "Any recross, Mr. Meisner?"

"Just one question, Your Honor. Mr. Johnson, you don't think the phrase 'pick someone out' is suggestive?" (After all, the perp's photo might not have been there at all.)

"No," Johnson said.

Christian Wymer testified that he was a road deputy for the CCSO and was driving alone, no partner, on the day of the murder. Wymer described the events just before the defendant's arrest, how he was staked out on a grass median watching cars, looking for the suspect's Camaro. He told the jury that Trooper Eddie Pope pulled up next to him. When the suspect's car passed, it was Pope who chased it down and stopped it. Wymer testified that less than a minute later, a second state trooper pulled up next to him on the grass median and informed him that the stop had been made and the car was the correct vehicle.

On cross-examination, Jerry Meisner asked if at any time he saw anything being thrown out of the vehicle. No, he had not. Yes, Christian Wymer had proceeded to the place where the Camaro had been stopped. When he got there, Michael King was still in the car. Did Wymer look at the ground around the Camaro? Yes. Did he see a nine-millimeter gun? No.

Trooper Eddie Pope took the stand and said he was a six-year veteran on the force. At the time of Denise Lee's murder, his routine duty was "aggressive driving" patrol. His beat was comprised of the interstate highways in Charlotte County. On January 17, 2008, he knew Michael King was wanted and Denise Lee was missing. He was looking for the defendant's Camaro.

Lon Arend showed Pope a photograph of the I-75 Toledo Blade intersection and he correctly identified it. He said he was headed southbound on I-75, heading toward North Port, when he saw a NPPD car parked on the grassy median. He pulled up next to it in his unmarked Lincoln so they could watch the traffic heading in either direction.

It was a little after nine o'clock when he spotted the Camaro. He pulled over the green Camaro on Interstate 75, near that thoroughfare's 177-mile marker. He ordered Michael King out of the car five times before he got out. During the first four commands, Pope could see the driver bent over the console and he couldn't see his hands. The fifth command came with an addendum: *". . . or I'll fire!"* That did the trick. As soon as the driver exited the car, Pope could see that the subject matched the description of the wanted man.

Arend asked if maybe the defendant hadn't heard him. Was his radio on loud? Was there much noise from other cars? No and no.

"Do you see the man who got out of that car in court here today?" Arend asked.

"Yes, the man in the blue shirt."

"Does he look the same today as he did on the night of his apprehension?"

"No, his appearance has changed some. His hair was a little longer, for one thing."

"Did you eventually get close enough to touch the man?"

"Yes."

"And was there anything unusual about his condition?"

"Yes. From the waist down, he was soaking wet and muddy."

Trooper Pope described the arrest and initial search. A crime scene was established. The car and immediate surroundings were taped off to prevent evidence contamination. No one, including himself, entered the car until the crime scene technicians arrived.

On cross-examination, Jerry Meisner asked Eddie Pope if when he patted Michael King down as he lay on the asphalt, with his hands cuffed behind his back, had he found any weapons? No. No nine-millimeter gun? No. No bullets? No. Unfortunately, it wasn't until days later that he helped with a thorough search along the side of the road. No gun. No bullets.

No further questions.

CHAPTER 16

DAY TWO

Day two began with the jury out. The state requested, on behalf of the victim's family and loved ones, that TV stations be banned from playing Denise Lee's 911 tape. Also, the family was concerned that photos of Denise's remains would be shown on TV.

Judge Deno Economou said because the request would have needed to be made before the trial started, he couldn't change what the media could and couldn't do at this late date. The judge did say, however, that he would request that the media show appropriate taste and consideration. The judge ruled the tape would be played in court, but not until the afternoon. There would be a warning in case anyone needed to leave.

The prosecution's first witness of the day was Jane Kowalski, who told Karen Fraivillig that she was a computer consultant from Tampa.

Jane felt prepared to give her testimony. She had already met with Fraivillig and together they listened to the 911 tape. There was more on there than Jane had remembered. All of the repetition, giving the same answers over and over again, it drove her nuts. Fraivillig had been very specific with Jane Kowalski about what she would be asking, and there had even been a run-through. Fraivillig called it a "dress rehearsal." Jane said it was a "prep." Fraivillig told Jane not to be scared, and Kowalski laughed. Being scared wasn't part of her personality.

Now, on the witness stand, Jane Kowalski was brimming with confidence. Some witnesses might have had trouble looking at the defendant, but not Jane. He was the one who should be scared.

The witness testified that she called 911 that day from her car, reporting disturbing noises coming from a car stopped next to hers at a red light in North Port.

Asked to describe the noises, she testified, "It's not going to sound like glass, but *bang! Bang! Bang! Bang!* But even harder than that."

"Do you recall the weather and the time of day?"

"Yes, it had been raining, and had just stopped. It was dusk. There was still light. It had just started to get darker."

"What, if anything, did you hear coming from the car?"

"I heard the most horrific screaming."

"Where were you when the screaming started?"

"I was already stopped at the red light."

"Where was your window?" Karen Fraivillig asked, referring to the driver's-side window being up or down.

"Cracked," she said, just open enough to let a little air in.

"Was there anything obstructing your view?"

"No." The car was definitely a Camaro. She admitted, however, that at the time, in the gloaming of the waning day, she thought the car was blue.

Using a map of the location, the witness showed the jury exactly where she was, and where the Camaro was, when she heard the sounds.

"Could you describe the screaming?"

"Horrific. Terrified. I had never heard anything like that in my life."

"Loud?"

"Loud. You would think at first—it's only natural to think at first that someone is goofing around, but that was not the scream of someone fooling around. It was panicky and terrible."

"Did you hear words or just screams?"

"Just screams."

She looked in the defendant's direction in his car and made eye contact. He turned around and started pushing something down in the backseat. A hand appeared in the window, banging at the glass—the same banging noise she'd heard earlier. Jane was on the handless cell phone with her sister at the time; the banging was so loud, her sister thought someone was banging on Jane's window.

"I told her to get a piece of paper and a pen in case I had a chance to get the license plate number."

Jane hung up on her sister and called 911. The suspicious car pulled in behind her and slowed way down; so did she. Soon they were forming an uncomfortably slow parade. Twenty to twenty-five miles per hour. The Camaro pulled away from her tail and turned left. She had to go straight, and that was the last she saw.

The witness identified a recording of the 911 call she had made, in which she described the action in real time. Fraivillig asked her how she knew this was the same tape she heard, and she noted that she had signed and dated the tape after listening.

As the recording played, jurors squirmed. They heard

the focus shift from the screaming captive to the safety and whereabouts of the caller herself, who had pulled over in a mall parking lot miles from the Camaro.

Jane testified that several days after the incident, she spoke to Detective Christopher Morales, of the North Port Police Department, and was shown a photo lineup. Police gave her no instructions, didn't coach her in any way, and she was able to make an identification.

"And is the person whose photo you identified in that lineup in the courtroom today?"

"Yes. He's sitting right there in the blue shirt," the witness said, pointing at the defendant.

She then identified a photo of the defendant's Camaro and ID'd it as the car she'd seen on the day of the incident.

"Since the incident, have you received any requests for interviews from the media?"

"Yes."

"Did you at any time receive any compensation for those interviews?"

"Never."

On cross, Jerry Meisner took a tact that might have insulted some jurors' intelligence. He sought to weaken Jane Kowalski's testimony by establishing that she could not positively ID the screaming person as the victim. She saw only a hand, no face.

How much did it really mean when she ID'd a photo of Michael King's Camaro, when she thought it was blue at the time? She admitted that all Camaros from that time period looked alike—and it was true, she never did get an opportunity to read the license plate number. Was the Camaro alone, or was it being followed by another car? She hadn't noticed. She admitted that she'd seen a photo of

Denise Goff was a beautiful child who grew into a beautiful woman. *(Yearbook photo)*

Denise was a bright but shy young woman who married her first and only boyfriend. *(Courtesy Rick and Sue Goff)*

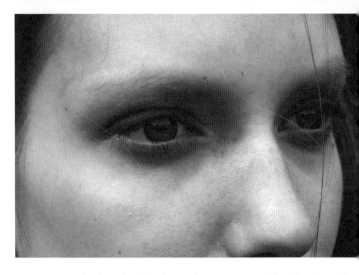

Everyone who knew her found in Denise a maturity and wisdom beyond her years. *(Courtesy Rick and Sue Goff)*

A barefoot Denise negotiates a crystal clear stream while on vacation in Tennessee. *(Courtesy Rick and Sue Goff)*

Denise, pregnant with Noah.
(Courtesy Rick and Sue Goff)

The entire region was heartbroken when they heard that beautiful 21-year-old Denise Lee, a loving wife and mother of two small sons, had been murdered. *(Courtesy Rick and Sue Goff)*

Denise, the daughter of a cop, was courageous and quick-thinking to the end, saving her sons and leaving the clues necessary to capture her killer. *(Courtesy Rick and Sue Goff)*

Denise's teacher, Mrs. Kari Burgess, described Denise as "bright as a shiny new penny. A girl who lit up a room with her smile." *(Yearbook photo)*

A check of Denise's phone showed that her last call before her abduction was to her best friend Natalie Mink. *(Yearbook photo)*

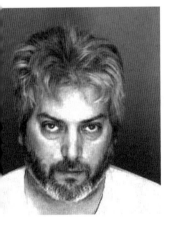

Mug shots of Michael King, with and without hair.
(Florida Department of Corrections)

King in handcuffs only hours after his arrest. *(NPPD)*

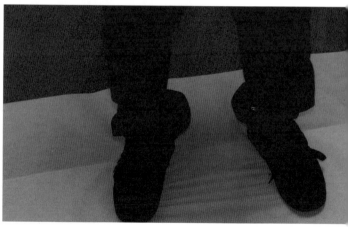

King was arrested while wearing wet pants, his shoes covered with sand.
(NPPD)

The Lees' home from which Denise was abducted. *(NPPD)*

The view of the driveway from the Lees' living room. Did Denise mistake Michael King's Camaro for her husband's car? *(NPPD)*

The victim's husband knew something was desperately wrong when Denise was gone, leaving her sons and her keys behind. *(NPPD)*

The North Port house on Sardinia Avenue where Michael King brutally assaulted Denise Lee. *(NPPD)*

Inside the Sardinia Avenue home police found Michael King's rape dungeon. At the left is a radio with volume all the way up and a clump of duct tape with long hairs attached to it. Note the window has been covered with a blanket to provide maximum privacy. *(NPPD)*

In Michael King's garbage was another clump of duct tape with Denise Lee's hairs attached. *(NPPD)*

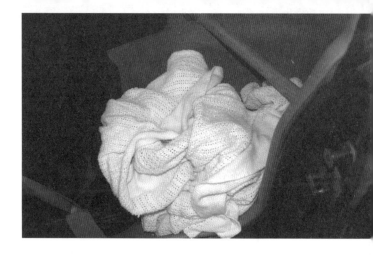

The bloodstained yellow blanket found in the back of King's Camaro yielded Denise Lee's DNA. *(NPPD)*

Police give an initial once-over to the green Camaro belonging to Michael King. The car is on the shoulder of I-75 at the spot where King was pulled over and subsequently arrested. *(NPPD)*

In the backseat of the Camaro was the shovel that King borrowed from a friend and used to dig his victim's grave. *(NPPD)*

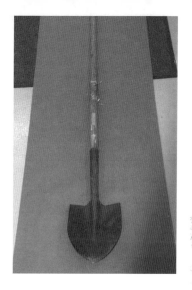

The daughter of a cop, Denise left clues behind, assuring that her abductor would be caught. In the back seat of King's car police found Denise's ring, a present from her husband, which she managed to remove despite her bondage. *(NPPD)*

The gas can King borrowed from a friend was found on the Camaro's passenger seat. *(NPPD)*

The phone Denise Lee used to call 911 during her abduction was found pulled apart and on the floor of King's Camaro. *(NPPD)*

North Port CSI Pam Schmidt photographs a fresh abrasion near King's private parts. He said he got it trying to use the bathroom while in handcuffs. Police had other ideas. *(NPPD)*

Saratoga County Animal Services supervisor Tami Treadway and her search dog Canine Sekou discovered the location of Denise Lee's remains. *(Photo by Linc Hay)*

A nine-millimeter shell casing was discovered in the grass near the spot where the fatal shot was fired. *(NPPD)*

The suspicious area before excavation began. Sandbags were placed to keep water flow from affecting the site. *(NPPD)*

The area was excavated by archaeologists, a fraction of an inch at a time, and slowly revealed the remains of Denise Lee. *(NPPD)*

Among the items of clothing found near the burial site were a pair of blue boxer shorts, a bra, and a pair of red panties, all worn by Denise Lee at the time of her abduction. *(NPPD)*

Prosecutor Suzanne O'Donnell laid out the evidence against Michael King for the jury. *(Photo by Dawn Buff)*

The Honorable Deno G. Economou presided over Michael King's murder trial with a cool steadiness that prevented raw emotions from overflowing in his courtroom. *(Courtesy Judge Economou)*

Michael King on the TV news before she ID'd him in the police lineup. However, she insisted she was IDing the man in the car, *not* the one on TV. And though she hadn't received payment from any media outlet for any of the interviews she had given, she did once get free airfare and hotel accommodations when she was booked to appear on a show in Los Angeles.

In retrospect, Karen Fraivillig felt Jane Kowalski had been a fabulous witness. Feisty. She knew what she knew, and she wasn't going to let a defense attorney convince her otherwise. It was so rare, Fraivillig opined, to put a witness on the stand as articulate as Jane was. The same heightened communication skills apparent on her 911 tape had also illuminated her trial testimony.

With her testimony given, Jane Kowalski took a seat in the courtroom, right behind the defendant. She couldn't believe how still and blank he was. "They must have had him on some serious drugs," she later said.

Kathy Jackson—a short, soft-spoken woman with curly hair—was called to the stand. She snuck a quick glance at the nearly motionless defendant. Only his icy blue eyes moved, flicking upward and from side to side nervously. He surveyed the courtroom without moving his head or neck.

Karen Fraivillig questioned Jackson. After a couple of false starts, trying to speak loudly enough for everyone to hear, Jackson testified that she was forty-six years old and lived in Iowa City, Iowa. In 2008, she had lived in Sarasota, where for eighteen months she had worked as a 911 operator for the Sarasota County Sheriff's Office.

"What do you currently do for a living, Miss Jackson?" Fraivillig asked.

"I work for the University of Iowa's police department."

Jackson testified that yes, she was the one who talked to the victim when she used her attacker's cell phone to call emergency. She'd been given an opportunity earlier in the day to listen to a recording of that call. Yes, the recording was genuine and reflected the events as they occurred. Yes, that was her voice on the recording.

The recording was accurate, but not as clear as it might be. Jackson remembered the call being much clearer and the voices easier to understand than as recorded.

She knew the recording in Fraivillig's hand was the same one she'd listened to, because she had initialed it. Everything was just as she remembered it, unfortunately. There were no additions or deletions. She had also read the transcript of the call, and it, too, was accurate.

She remembered the call drawing much attention at the 911 center. By the time it was over, "every 911 dispatcher in the room" was involved, feeding Jackson questions to better determine the caller's location.

After six minutes of screams, there was nothing. The call had terminated. "When the call hung up, it was devastating. We still had hope, but you just had a feeling that the chances of saving her went way down. Denise's voice haunts me. I'm just hoping this trial will bring some closure to that."

She said the stress she felt over what had happened forced her to completely change her life, to remove herself as best as possible from all memory of Denise Lee's pleas for help.

She developed emotional problems, falling into what she called a "deep depression." Within days of Lee's murder,

Jackson was looking for another job. The woman's voice as she begged to be allowed to see her family again was stuck inside her head. She feared it would never leave, and she would carry Denise Lee's last moments with her forever like a scar.

She eventually quit her job and moved more than a thousand miles away, to be back with her own family for a fresh start.

"It was a call you get once in a lifetime and never want to get again," she said.

Jackson had words of admiration for the victim, who had been a very brave woman indeed, trying to steer authorities to her location without alerting her kidnapper.

"She did everything right to save herself," Jackson said, now weeping on the witness stand. "It breaks my heart to think how she tried so hard, and we still couldn't save her."

Her testimony given, Jackson dabbed away her tears with a handkerchief and threw her purse strap over her shoulder. She exited the courtroom, a small smile on her face, relief that the ordeal she had been dreading was over. Outside, she was overheard saying she felt better. At least part of the weight had been lifted.

"It feels like justice is going to be served," she said.

The jury left the courtroom right after Kathy Jackson, and the subject inside turned to the heart-wrenching Denise Lee 911 call that the jury was scheduled to hear that afternoon.

The prosecution moved that, because of the low quality of the tape, and the fact that much of it was unintelligible upon first hearing, the jury be supplied with a copy of the transcript. Testimony had verified the transcript as accurate.

There was argument regarding the transcript. The defense did have some items deleted, such as when the transcription characterized sounds on the tape as "screaming" and "crying." Judge Economou agreed to delete those words. The jury would have an opportunity to judge for themselves what the sounds were and what they meant.

At one point, the transcript read, *Man grabs phone from her.* That was deleted as an assumption on the transcriber's part. The judge also agreed that when the time came, he would instruct the jury that the transcription was only a guide, and that they were to rely on what they heard, not on what they read.

The jury returned and another witness was called.

Sean Karnitz said he was a translations engineer at AT&T Mobility, a custodian of records, who had examined the defendant's phone and the calls generated by it. The witness had blond hair cut short in a flat top and wore a dark blue suit. Karnitz said he could identify which specific cell phone made any AT&T call.

The witness determined through forensic cellular means that the phone Denise Lee's 911 call came from was Michael King's cell phone—the one that was found and seized at the time of the defendant's arrest.

When a 911 call came in, a search for the phone's precise location commenced immediately and automatically.

Following the phone expert's direct testimony, the defense chose not to cross-examine.

As Karnitz left and the call went out to the witness room to send in the next witness, the court's audio-visual people hurriedly readied an overhead projector in front of a white screen.

* * *

Tami Treadway had shoulder-length black hair and wide, sincere eyes. She wore white pants and a green golf shirt, with an official canine logo on the left breast.

With Lon Arend questioning, Treadway said she was an Animal Services supervisor, twenty-two and a half years as a civilian employee, who used trained dogs on search-and-rescue missions.

She described her dog, Canine Sekou, as an eight-year-old golden retriever. They had been a team for six years. The dog lived with her and slept with her.

It was Sekou who discovered the suspicious spot that turned out to be the victim's burial site, forty feet from the road, in a clearing but provided cover by a line of thick vegetation. Treadway was shown an aerial photo of the site. She testified that it was an accurate depiction.

The site was suspicious because of disturbed earth, darker than that all around it, a pile of sand off to one side, and uprooted plants. She left the spot to tell police in the area that there was a suspicious location. Oddly, she'd had to contact two searching officers because the first one *ignored* her.

Along with the burial site, the dog also sniffed out several dinner plate–sized piles of sand that were covering up a dark red substance, apparently blood.

On cross, defense attorney John Scotese asked Tami Treadway how many agencies were involved in the search. She said she wasn't sure of the exact number, but a lot. Even Fish & Wildlife had people searching.

"All in all, there were about one hundred people involved in the search," Treadway said.

After years of experience, she knew when Sekou picked up a pertinent scent. He sniffed first along the barbed-wire fence, on both sides. "Used to" barbed wire, the dog went under the fence without difficulty.

When her dog hit on the site, she knew better than to try to disturb the scene in any way. Someone far more qualified than she would do the digging.

Nothing to gain, Scotese cut his cross-examination short.

The state called Lisa Lanham, a Sarasota County crime scene technician, a position she'd held since 1996. Her job was to report to crime scenes, and to collect and preserve evidence.

On the night of January 18, 2008, she was called to report to a scene off Plantation Road, to assist North Port police, who were already there. She described the spot located by Tami Treadway's trained dog. First order of business was to preserve the entire site. The location was taped off, photographed from every angle, and covered. A white tent was put up between the road and the site, beside the large pile of sand. This would serve as the "staging area" for law enforcement personnel. A blue tent was put up over the suspicious site, to protect it from contamination, especially if it rained again. The tent also gave the excavation process privacy. Lon Arend showed Lanham an aerial photo of the site and she positively identified it as the spot to which she had reported on that day.

Photographs were introduced. The witness remained in her seat and indicated locations on the projected photograph with a red laser pointer. The jury could see how the palmetto brush grew and grew and then stopped at the spot. Reeds stood up, up, up, and then were flat.

Between the road and the suspicious site were the dinner plate–sized piles of white sand—the witness called it "sugar sand"—that had apparently been taken from the big pile nearby, to cover up blood.

The defense objected to this statement. Since this witness had not personally tested the substance, and had no way of knowing what the dark red substance was, she was coming to a conclusion when she called it "blood." From that point on, then, she referred to the substance as "apparent blood." Whatever the substance was, it was clear that it was there first, and the sand had been placed there after, covering it up.

Lanham explained that they had to be very careful when photographing the apparent blood. There were tufts of red-bladed grass in the area that greatly resembled the green grass and palm fronds stained by blood.

Objection.

"Apparent blood," the witness said.

Close-up photos of the smaller sand piles were shown. Each had been marked by a numbered flag. Some of those piles covered up droplets of blood, but one covered up "pooled apparent blood."

"Ms. Lanham, could you tell us what you mean by 'pooled'?"

"When something that is bleeding rests in one position for a length of time, the blood pools around that item. If you spill it, milk would pool in the same way."

Also found in the area, and marked with a flag, was apparent blood that the killer had missed—apparent blood without sand covering it.

"Did excavation begin that evening?" Arend asked.

"No," the witness replied. "The operation resumed in the daylight."

To prevent water seepage from affecting the suspicious site, sandbags were placed on either end. Once excavation began, the site was revealed to be—as suspected—a burial site.

Lanham remained at the site as the victim's body was discovered, removed from the grave site, and taken to the medical examiner for autopsy. At that point, her responsibility at the site ended. She packed up her equipment and left.

On cross-examination, John Scotese wanted to talk about evidence contamination. What types were there? Water damage, things falling off the trees onto a site that weren't there previously, trace evidence placed by well-meaning police examining the area. To prevent the latter, a log was kept; and everyone who entered and left the crime scene logged in and out. And the people inside the police tape were kept to a minimum. While working, Lisa Lanham wore gloves, booties, a plastic suit, and a cap.

"You are aware that before the area was sealed off, there were ways for the evidence to be contaminated?"

"Yes."

"Do you have any way of knowing whether or not this scene was contaminated by police before you got there?"

"No."

"Are you aware that contamination of evidence can be purposeful?"

"I haven't seen that."

"Do you realize this site was at risk for purposeful contamination?"

"I suppose. . . ."

"Should precautions be taken with regard to storage of items of potential evidentiary value?"

"Sure, most urgently to prevent evidence from disintegrating in the Florida heat."

"When you made your thorough search of the area, did you find a nine-millimeter gun?"

"I did not personally, no."

"Find any bullets?"

"Not at that time, no."

On redirect, Lon Arend asked, "At the time you were at the crime scene, were you looking for shell casings?"

"I was not," Lisa Lanham replied.

Judge Economou noted the hour, quarter to twelve, and gave everyone an extra fifteen minutes for lunch.

"It's a beautiful day. Eat, go outside," he suggested to the jury, knowing what was in store for that panel of peers.

When the jury returned, Judge Economou solemnly warned them that they were in for a rough afternoon. Following a viewing of a crime scene video, they would listen to a 911 call, and it had been stipulated that the voice on the tape was that of Denise Lee.

The videotape showed the grave site—before, during, and after excavation. As it started, the photographer (Lisa Lanham) was looking north. The large pile of sand was on the left; the thick line of foliage was to the right. Visible were places in the big pile where shovelsful of sand had been recently removed. The camera panned right to a spot where the foliage was not as thick, and the barbed-wire fence was visible.

Michael King watched the video unblinkingly.

The vegetation near that fence, one could see, was made up predominantly of palmetto leaves. The camera panned back and to the left, until it had returned to its starting point. The next shot was a close-up of the spots of apparent blood partially covered with sand and marked with numbered evidence flags. The spot of pooled blood was shown last.

The camera showed all of the blood spots before moving to a spot closer to the fence where the weeds were beaten down, where the earth was disturbed, and then covered with loose vegetation. There were sandbags at the north and south ends of the spot. The video did not have sound, but it was clear that this was the spot where the excavation would be done.

That spot was next shown with the vegetation removed, and then at various stages of excavation. According to an earlier ruling by the judge, the jury was not allowed to see the portion of the tape that showed the body as it was unearthed. Instead, a single still photo of the ghastly scene was inserted in the video, replacing the moving images. Finally the video showed a hole—the body of Denise Lee already removed.

"Now I know there are some family members that would like to leave at this point," the judge said. Among others, Denise's mother and sister got up and left.

Denise's husband and father remained. Rick Goff rocked with nervous tension. He'd heard the tape before—back before they'd even found Denise—to confirm that it was her voice.

Nate Lee had heard it before as well, at the recommendation of the prosecution, which didn't want Nate to be hearing the tape for the first time in the courtroom.

The jurors were each given a copy of a transcript of the tape, which had been stipulated as accurate. They would be able to read along as they listened, but they would not be allowed to keep the transcripts, or use them as reference during deliberation.

The judge also emphasized that the transcript was not evidence; the tape was evidence. If they heard something different from what they read, they were to believe their ears, *not* their eyes.

It is impossible to put into words the effect a tape such as this has on a listener—a woman begging for her life. The word that best describes the effect is "traumatic." People in that courtroom would later experience insomnia, anxiety, and even depression. Rick Goff rocked rhythmically and shuddered, working just to stay inside his skin.

In a room filled with good posture, the defendant's slouch made him conspicuous. He wasn't following along with the transcript, as were his lawyers, the judge, and the jury. It wasn't interesting to him. He'd heard it before. He was *there.*

Jerry Meisner and John Scotese kept their eyes on the transcript throughout the tape, but Carolyn Schlemmer twice lifted her head and looked back and to her left. Clearly in pain, she was perhaps making sure there were no imminent physical threats to her client.

Emotionless, Michael King kept his eyes lowered, but he did look up to flick his eyes from side to side a couple of times. As Denise Lee was heard pleading for her life, begging to be allowed to return to her beautiful husband and sons, this was a courtroom consumed with hate—hatred for him. He could stand to see it only for a flash before returning his eyes to the table in front of him.

When the tape was over, the state called Deputy Anthony Egoville to testify. He was a fourteen-year veteran of the SCSO and worked in the warrants division and on the emergency response team (ERT).

Deputy Egoville was the one who'd discovered the nine-millimeter shell casing near the sand pile. Egoville, who seemed himself on the verge of tears, explained that he had been at the site the night before Denise Lee's body was discovered, as well as the day after. It was during his second search that he made his important discovery.

Of course, he had not been the only searcher. He was part of a team of thirty that were "line searching" the area—searching tight together and in a line so every square foot was scrutinized.

It was just happenstance that he had been one of the searchers to grab one of the ten to fifteen metal detectors that his team had available to them. His beeped as he was searching a spot just northeast of the big pile of sand. At first, he couldn't see what had made the metal detector react. But when he reached down and pushed blades of grass out of the way, he found the nine-millimeter shell casing.

"I flagged the spot and continued searching," Egoville testified.

On cross-examination, John Scotese, as was becoming the norm, was concerned with what the witness *didn't* find. Any other casings discovered? No. Bullets? No. Gun? Nope.

(No one knows how much of Deputy Egoville's testimony the jury registered. They were partially in shock—had to be—so soon after hearing state's exhibit 102, the victim's 911 call.)

The state's next witness was Lieutenant Ed Fitzpatrick, who'd been a North Port police officer for sixteen years.

Now, as in 2008, he was a district commander. On January 22, two days after the discovery of the shell casing near the grave site, Fitzpatrick supervised a search of thick brush along both sides of Plantation Boulevard. He was informed that items of clothing had been discovered and so ordered the area around the items sealed off.

On cross-examination, Jerry Meisner asked if Fitzpatrick's team turned up any nine-millimeter guns during their search. It had not.

Sergeant Patrick Sachkar testified that at a few minutes past seven o'clock on the day of the murder, he had reported to an address on Sardinia Avenue, which turned out to be the home of the defendant. It was a "well-being" call. Denise Lee's fate was unknown, and rescuing her was a priority. There was no one home, so he looked around and saw a roll of duct tape on a counter and a wadded-up ball of duct tape, with long dirty-blond hairs sticking to it, on the floor next to a makeshift bed in a room devoid of furniture. He was only in the house for a few minutes before retreating outside so that the entire house could be sealed off for the CSI technicians, a process that would begin as soon as a search warrant for King's home was secured. A log was kept of everyone who entered and exited the house during the well-being call.

Sachkar testified that he had also been in on the apprehension of the defendant, and he noticed Michael King's jeans were wet and had light-colored sand or clay on the knees.

Following Sachkar's testimony, a number of new stipulations were read for the jury, among them that the victim had been menstruating at the time of her death.

* * *

Cortnie Watts took the stand and, questioned by Suzanne O'Donnell, testified that she was a criminalistics specialist and a ten-year NPPD veteran. She reported to the Lees' home on the day of the murder. While searching the house, she saw a woman's purse that had been upturned, its contents apparently "gone through." On the back porch, she found hair clippings, apparently from the victim giving her son a haircut before she was abducted. Watts was there from 4:45 to 8:00 P.M.; then she returned to the police station with her bags of evidence taken from the house.

At 9:45 P.M., she was called to the scene of the arrest to process Michael King's Camaro, where she swabbed and bagged blood and hair evidence. She also gathered one sample of a milky gelatin-like material that at the time she referred to as "sap." Others collected evidence at the scene as well, under her supervision. She was shown photos of the evidence as it existed when she found it, and positively identified those photos as fair depictions. She was shown a hair that had been found on the front of the Camaro; because of the chain-of-evidence procedures, she could state under oath that it was the same hair she'd found on the car at the scene of the defendant's arrest.

She described how she took blood samples, using a long Q-tip and distilled water.

"I would gather up some of the substance and then put the substance on a piece of cardboard, where it was allowed to dry," Watts said.

She positively identified photos she took of the interior of the Camaro after it was transported to the NPPD— photos that showed the borrowed red gas can inside the car.

Next to the can was a box of baby wipes, which Watts checked for fingerprints, using black powder and superglue processing. Partial prints were lifted.

O'Donnell projected a photo of a partial print onto a screen and asked if this was one of the prints she'd lifted from the box of baby wipes. Watts said it was.

"Could you explain how a fingerprint is lifted?" O'Donnell asked.

"Of course. I sprinkle special black powder over an area, which makes fingerprints more clearly visible. I then use a piece of clear tape, which I press down over the print. Carefully pulling the tape back off the surface, the print comes with it. I place the tape on a card, which is dated and signed, and write on the card the exact spot where the print was discovered."

The photo was entered into evidence.

Other pieces of evidence were introduced and Watts identified all—shovel, heart ring, flashlight, blanket, and jacket—as those found in the Camaro. Yes, they were in the same condition as when she first saw them. Well, the shovel was a little different. There had been more dirt adhering to the spade, but some had flaked off.

When introducing the ring into evidence, O'Donnell reminded the jury that it had been stipulated that the ring belonged to Denise Lee.

Was anything else found in the car? Yes, a cell phone battery, presumably pulled from its home to prevent the victim from further communication with the outside world.

Yes, the phone and battery were checked for fingerprints, yielded more partial prints. Once again, Watts used black powder, superglue, tape, and a card to collect the evidence.

"Okay, let's shift gears for a moment and talk about trace evidence," O'Donnell said. "What exactly are we talking about when we use that term, 'trace evidence'?"

"That refers to hairs or fibers that might be pertinent to who committed a crime."

"And how is trace evidence collected?"

"We use a sheet of clear plastic. One side is sticky and we tap it down over an area. It is then lifted—the trace evidence adhering to it—and taken to the lab to be examined."

"And did you collect trace evidence from the defendant's automobile?"

"Yes, from the backseat."

O'Donnell switched subjects again. After collecting evidence from the car, when was Watts next involved with this case? It was 12:45 A.M., January 18, when she photographed the defendant on the second floor of the NPPD. The witness positively identified photos as those she had taken. They were projected so the jury could see. These photos showed Michael King wearing a camouflage shirt, jeans, and black sneakers. There was dirt on the jeans, especially at the knees, and across the bottoms.

At 8:45 A.M., January 18, Watts reported to King's house and was briefed on the incident and scope of the search warrant by Detective Christopher Morales. She made a videotape of the house, thoroughly capturing the exterior. After entering through the sliding door at the back, she videotaped the interior of the house as well. That tape was shown for the jury, with Watts offering narration. Between the exterior and interior shots, the camera was paused for a moment as Watts put her "detective equipment on"—booties, gloves, and plastic suit—to prevent crime scene contamination. She noted that with the exception of a television in the front room and a chair in the master bedroom, the house was without furniture. On the videotape's audio, one could hear considerable background noise. She explained that the TV was on, with the volume turned way up. To further create a cacophony, a clock radio on the bedroom floor played music with the volume cranked.

This had been done presumably to mask any suspicious noises—screams for help, for example.

A floor plan of King's house was shown to the jurors so the jury panel could better visualize where things in the home were in relation to one another. There were several mirrors on one wall, but one had been removed. There was a bar area in the kitchen, and on that bar was a roll of duct tape.

The videotape showed the drawers and the area under the sink in the kitchen being searched. On the kitchen counter was a pizza box, as well as a small pile of mail addressed to King.

"Did you find anything of interest in the kitchen area?" O'Donnell inquired.

"Yes, inside a garbage bag in the kitchen pantry, I found a ball of duct tape with long hairs adhering to it."

O'Donnell introduced that duct tape into evidence, explaining that it was no longer balled up because it needed to be flattened for crime lab testing. It had been white and gray when the witness first saw it, but it had picked up blackish spots during testing. Despite the change in appearance, Watts could positively ID it as the same tape she discovered in the garbage bag, because she had dated and initialed the bag it was stored in. The chain of evidence from discovery until the present was intact.

After processing the defendant's kitchen, Watts did the master bedroom, where the items she observed included the previously mentioned chair and clock radio, another wad of tape, a blanket with Winnie-the-Pooh on it, and another blanket that had been tacked up over the window. One long-sleeved shirt was also bagged as evidence.

Next she processed the bathroom, which had a walk-in

closet. In there, she found a circular piece of elastic such as what might be used to tie a woman's hair back, and a mirror that was not attached to the wall, but rather rested on the floor and against the wall at an angle.

Judge Economou reminded the jury that it had been stipulated by the prosecution and defense that the hair ties found in Michael King's house were "the same type" as those usually worn by Denise Lee.

The witness was shown the Winnie-the-Pooh blanket, which she identified as the same one, in the same condition as when found, with the exception of some crime lab markings.

Next evidence was a piece of carpet that had been cut out from the defendant's floor. Watts ID'd that piece of rug, and it was entered into evidence.

"Why was the rug taken as evidence?"

"I noticed on that section of rug what appeared to be bodily fluids of some sort," the witness said.

"Were those stains visible to the naked eye?" O'Donnell asked.

"No, we looked at the rug first with an alternative light source, which made the stains easier to see."

"When you say 'alternative lighting'?"

"Black light. It makes hairs, fibers, and stains more visible. We look through a pair of orange glasses when using the alternative light source."

"And using the glasses and black light, the fibers and stains fluoresced?"

"Yes."

"And after seeing these things on the rug and cutting the carpet up for removal, this evidence was sent to the crime lab?"

"Yes."

"After seizing and processing evidence at the defendant's home, what was your next involvement with this case?"

"On January twentieth, I was called to a location off Plantation Boulevard very near to where the body was found. A shell casing had been discovered," the witness replied. When she got there, she had no trouble finding the casing, as a small flag had been placed there to indicate the location.

O'Donnell projected a photo in which the casing and flag were visible. Watts said yes, that was just the way it looked. The casing was partially covered by dirt, which Watts took to mean that it had rained since the casing was dropped at that spot.

"Did you lift prints from the casing?"

"No prints were found."

"While you were at the scene, did you see a tree you found interesting?"

A sidebar was immediately called and the witness was never allowed to answer the question. O'Donnell tried to undermine the defense's now predictable cross-examination with her next line of questioning. Did the witness search King's entire house? Yes. Find a nine-millimeter gun? No.

That concluded Suzanne O'Donnell's direct examination of the criminalistics specialist, and the day's testimony. Judge Economou ordered everyone back first thing in the morning.

Following the second day of testimony, Nate Lee said he was concerned about Denise's legacy. "I want her to be remembered for the person she was and all of the things she did to get this person caught. Hopefully convicted. I don't want her to be remembered for the horrifying 911 call that she made."

Ah, but Denise Lee had left a trail of bread crumbs that led police to her killer, and the 911 call was the biggest crumb of all.

CHAPTER 17

DAY THREE

Come morning, Cortnie Watts returned to the stand, where she was cross-examined by Jerry Meisner.

"You are aware that there is such a thing as contamination of evidence, right?"

"Yes."

"Transfer contamination?"

"Yes."

"Walking from here to there, I might pick up hairs and fibers, or deposit them. Isn't that correct?"

"Yes."

"And trace evidence I might have picked up in my home this morning, I might now deposit here in the courtroom?"

"Yes."

"Now, when you reported to the house on Latour Avenue, there were already police there when you arrived?"

"Yes."

He showed the witness a fingerprint recovered at the Lee home and asked if she recognized it. She didn't, as it wasn't one she personally lifted. Meisner asked how that could be, and she replied that at the scene were criminalistics specialists from several law enforcement agencies, including the FDLE.

"Who lifted this print? Was it someone named Justin Rogers?"

"I don't know. I would have to look at the card."

"Okay, here."

"This print was lifted by FDLE employee Justin Rogers," she said.

Meisner asked her about another print, not lifted by her, and she had to read the card to know who lifted that one as well. Another was signed by a P. S. Bauman. Meisner asked Watts how many FDLE employees were at the Latour Avenue scene and she said she did not know.

Meisner then set out to show that even given the evidence that she herself discovered, her search for fingerprints was less than exhaustive. She had dusted the gas can, but not the flashlight; a wooden banister from the car, but not the shovel.

"Before entering the home on Sardinia, you say you donned protective equipment, correct?"

"Yes."

"Were you the first member of law enforcement to enter that home?"

"No."

"Did the members of law enforcement who entered the house before you don the protective garb?"

"I don't know."

Meisner forced the witness to admit that not all of the search for evidence was timely. The cell phone and battery found in the Camaro, for example, were not dusted for prints until months after the murder. Watts had to check notes to recall that the cell phone was processed for prints on April 9, 2008; the battery was on June 11.

"Okay, I'd like to go back to January seventeenth again, all right?"

"Yes."

"On that day, you took photos of tire marks outside the Latour Avenue home, correct?"

"Yes. There was a sandy area on the driveway and road where prints were visible."

Yes, she'd also made ink tire prints of the defendant's car not long after it was seized. Yes, the photos, ink prints, and the actual ties from the Camaro were sent to the FDLE.

"During the course of this case, was there ever an occasion when you went to the home of Harold Muxlow to process that scene?"

"No."

Did she go to the home of Robert Salvador? No. Did she ever search for evidence in Robert Salvador's storage unit? No. Did she at any time search for and process evidence in and on Robert Salvador's car? No.

"No further questions, Your Honor," Meisner said.

The state had no questions on redirect, and the witness was excused.

The state called Pamela Schmidt, who was questioned by Suzanne O'Donnell. Schmidt testified that she'd been a criminalistics specialist since 2003. To earn that position with the NPPD, she had taken seven hundred hours of training, learning how to collect and preserve the integrity of evidence. Regarding this case, it had been her duty to process the defendant's body. This process had taken place at five-thirty in the morning on January 18, 2008, in interview room number 2 at the NPPD. Also in the room were two detectives. The defendant's clothing, which she seized, included a green camouflage shirt, jeans, underwear, and sneakers. The jeans were muddy and dirty from the knees down; while not dripping, they were still cold and damp. There was mud on the sneakers, especially at the toes and on the laces. She was shown the jeans and identified them as those that the defendant wore. Although they were now dry, the mud on them was still visible.

Schmidt, along with others, participated in the search and seizure of items at Michael King's house, beginning at 9:30 A.M. on January 18. It was also her sad duty to attend the victim's autopsy at 8:30 A.M. on January 20. She processed the swabs made by Dr. Daniel Schultz from the victim's mouth, vagina, and anus—inside and outside. That evidence was catalogued carefully and placed inside envelopes provided by the medical examiner's office. She photographed the body during various stages of the autopsy, and she noticed that when the victim's head was lifted so the back of the head could be photographed, there were pieces of gray duct tape still sticking to the hair. One was longer than the other and went from ear to ear across the back. That tape was carefully removed and was photographed before it was packaged. O'Donnell now showed this evidence to the witness, who identified each piece. They were all in the same condition as when she first saw them, with the exception of certain markings that were made by the lab and the remnants of black fingerprint powder clinging to the tape. During the autopsy, Schmidt fingerprinted the body, so her prints could be easily identified when found at the various crime scenes. The prints, once taken, were packaged and sent to the Integrated Automated Fingerprint Identification System (IAFIS). The witness was shown those prints and identified them as those she'd taken at the autopsy.

Schmidt's next involvement with the case came on

January 22, 2008, when she reported to the site, not far from the burial site, where a bra strap, men's boxer shorts, and ladies' red underwear had been discovered. When she arrived at the scene, those clothes items had not yet been touched or moved. Officers were standing around the scene, but none had disrupted the evidence.

The jurors were shown an aerial photograph that showed both the burial site and where the clothes were found, so the jury panel could appreciate the proximity.

"Lieutenant Fitzpatrick was there?"

"Yes, he's the one who asked for me."

Schmidt had photographed the items from every possible angle. The jury was shown a sampling of the photos, and Schmidt verified that she created those images. The item that was hardest to see was the bra strap, which was slung over a tree branch.

"At that time, did you know that these items of clothing belonged to Denise Lee?"

"No."

Schmidt was shown the bagged items of clothing and identified them as the same as those she'd seized on January 22. Judge Economou informed the jury that the prosecution and defense had stipulated that though Nate Lee did not identify the red panties as belonging to his wife, he did say they were of the same size and type as those she wore. The boxer shorts he did identify as a pair of his that his wife enjoyed wearing.

Later, when Schmidt was called back to the site, there was excavation equipment there "skimming" the area, clearing the brush, to make any evidence easier to find. This process bore fruit. One time the claw came up and a shirt was visible, still half under the ground.

She ID'd photos of the shirt sticking out of the ground as those she took. She'd used a small spade to dig out the shirt, seizing and bagging, along with the shirt, a large chunk of the dirt around it. She was shown a bag with a shirt and soil in it and positively ID'd it.

The bra was found last. More photos, more identifying, plus a stipulation that Nate Lee had ID'd the bra and shirt as belonging to his wife. Schmidt found the serial number and size of the discovered bra and contacted the manufacturer to acquire a photo of a pristine version of the same bra, which was then shown to the victim's husband for identification. O'Donnell concluded her questioning.

John Scotese handled the short cross-examination, in which he implied that rape kit results were subject to contamination and that law enforcement was so tunnel-visioned regarding Michael King's guilt that they failed to collect hair samples from other men who might have been involved.

The prosecution recalled Harold Muxlow, this time to ask only one question: what type of shirt was King wearing when he saw him on January 17? Muxlow said it was a white shirt with some sort of design on it. There was no cross-examination.

Detective Michael Saxton testified that he was an NPPD trainer and a CSI who began working crime scenes in 2001. From 2003 through 2009, he'd headed up his own CSI team. In July 2009, he became a CSI trainer. As a rule, he only reported to crime scenes when Cortnie Watts and Pamela Schmidt were off duty. Yes, he did work this case. He was called in to process the Camaro while it was still pulled over on the shoulder of the interstate. He dusted the exterior and discovered a partial palm print on the outside of the driver's-side window. He carefully used tape to lift that print and put it on a card, which was sent to the lab.

On the evening of January 18, Saxton took samples from the defendant's person. A warrant had been secured allowing law enforcement to take swabs of DNA samples from Michael King, who was completing his first full day of residence at the Sarasota County Jail. Saxton took evidence from the insides of King's cheeks, from both sides of his hands, and from his groin area. Asked if he saw in the courtroom the man from whom he took the DNA samples, Saxton said he did. He pointed out the defendant, identifying King as the "man in the yellow shirt."

After that jail visit, Saxton went to a firing range, where he met with a man named Robert Salvador.

"What did you do when you arrived?"

He'd asked Robert Salvador to show him the area where he and King had been target shooting before the murder. Once there, he picked up shell casings. He took the casings from an area on the far side of a sidewalk from the targets, where casings are regularly swept. He discovered at that location casings for a nine-millimeter Luger Winchester.

"Did you pick up all of the shell casings you saw?"

"No, just the nine-millimeter [ones]."

Saxton was shown an evidence bag containing shell casings, and the witness identified them as the casings he had discovered at the gun range.

During cross-examination, Saxton admitted that he had no way of knowing how long the nine-millimeter shell casings from the gun range had been there.

Judge Economou called the midmorning break.

The prosecution called Jennifer Setlak, who identified herself as an FDLE lab analyst, Biology Division. Suzanne

O'Donnell asked the witness for a summary of her background. The witness said she had a bachelor's degree in science—major biology, minor chemistry. She'd done postgraduate work at the University of Florida in genetics and had been with the crime lab for three years.

She explained that she worked in DNA, the nucleic acid in a person's body—half provided by the mother, half by the father—that made everyone (except identical twins) unique. She described the manner in which she did her testing. She took a sample found at a crime scene and created a DNA profile, and then she compared that profile to that of samples of known origin. In this manner, for example, a semen stain at the scene of a rape could be matched with 100 percent certainty to a suspect. She explained that she had taken classes in biological statistics, and received continuing education in DNA statistics. Statistics were important in cases in which DNA cannot be matched to an individual. In such cases, the characteristics of the DNA can be used to determine the characteristics of the unknown subject.

"What things from the human body can be used to create a DNA profile?"

"Every cell in the human body contains DNA unique to that individual. Most commonly, we use hair and skin samples. Various bodily fluids are used as well."

As part of her work on this case, Setlak explained, she had developed a DNA profile for the victim, using a cheek swab made at the victim's autopsy. She also created a profile for Michael King, using the DNA samples collected by Michael Saxton from the defendant at the Sarasota County Jail.

She tested the vaginal swabs taken from the victim during her postmortem procedure. The witness quickly determined that there were sperm cells mixed in with that sample.

"You can distinguish a sperm cell from other types of cells?"

"Yes. Part of my training is to know the unique shape and size of sperm cells."

"In this case, were you able to create a DNA profile from the sperm cells found in the victim's body?"

"Yes. The DNA profile for the sperm cells found in [Denise] Lee matched the DNA profile of Michael King."

"In terms of statistics, how frequent would that particular DNA profile be?"

"In Caucasians, that profile would occur once in every one quadrillion Caucasians."

"One quadrillion. That is one followed by how many zeroes?"

"One followed by fifteen zeroes."

The witness was shown a bag holding duct tape that was found on the floor of King's home. She was asked if she recognized this evidence. Setlak said she did. She had taken a swab from the tape, and successfully developed a DNA profile from it that matched King's DNA.

On the duct tape discovered in King's trash can, she tested the adhering hairs and found them to have a DNA profile matching that of the victim. The odds of that DNA belonging to anyone else were 1 in 110 quadrillion. Hair and blood found on the hood of the Camaro also proved to belong to the victim.

"The evidence that you tested all arrived to you in sealed bags?"

"Yes."

"Did any of it appear to be tampered with in any way?"

"No."

"When you were done with the evidence, did you reseal it in its bag?"

"Yes."

"If a seal had been broken, you would have been able to tell?"

"Oh, yes."

"And none of the seals were broken on any of the evidence you analyzed?"

"None."

"No further questions, Your Honor," O'Donnell said.

Jerry Meisner said, "Thank you, Your Honor, and good morning, Ms. Setlak."

"Good morning," the witness replied.

"Was there among the evidence you received an anal swab taken from Denise Lee during her autopsy?"

"Yes."

"Did you obtain a profile from that swab?"

"Yes."

"Was there any DNA foreign to Denise Lee found on the anal swabs?"

"No."

"No semen?"

"No."

"Did you ever obtain a known sample from a man named Robert Salvador?"

"No."

"About how many people are there in the world?"

"Around 6.5 billion people."

"What is the highest frequency of occurrence of DNA typing in an unknown that you attributed to King?"

"One in one quadrillion."

"How many zeroes?"

"Fifteen."

"And how many people are in the database that you use to create these numbers?"

"About two hundred individuals are tested to make up the database."

Meisner's face said it all. A quadrillion was an unimaginable number—it was so huge—and to base such an estimate on two hundred test cases! The numbers were meaningless.

Meisner continued picking away at DNA technology, trying to make it seem like it didn't produce the certainty that the prosecution was trying to make it out to be. He made the witness describe the process in the most scientific of terms, better to sell the whole package as scientific mumbo jumbo.

The prosecution team was not terribly concerned with this tact. Juries either believed in DNA or they didn't. Although it had only been around for a generation, most people saw DNA identification every bit as damning to a defendant as fingerprints.

"You tested a red-and-black jacket, correct?"

"Yes."

"Find any blood on it?"

"No."

"You tested scrapings from Denise Lee's fingernails, correct?"

"Yes."

"Did you find any DNA foreign to Denise Lee in those scrapings?"

"No."

Christina Sanders testified that she, like Setlak, was an FDLE employee. In fact, she worked in the same crime lab as Setlak, but with a different focus: trace evidence. She used a range of microscopes to distinguish and identify varieties of soil, vegetation, fibers, etc.

Sanders had a bachelor's degree in forensic science from the University of Central Florida. As an undergraduate, she completed a sixteen-hour-per-week internship in the crime lab. The first phase of her training consisted of background with a lot of hands-on training, and she also took a basic textile course. The second portion involved supervised casework. She was supervised by experienced analysts, who ensured she was doing everything properly. She was what was called a "testifying analyst" in that she had been deemed qualified to testify in court about the results of her analyses. This would be the eighteenth time she had testified in a criminal trial.

Suzanne O'Donnell drew Sanders's attention to the duct tape that had been earlier entered as state's evidence.

"Is duct tape the sort of thing you analyze?"

"Yes."

"What sort of analysis do you do?"

She explained that she would observe the tape carefully, both with the naked eye and using a low-powered microscope, searching for fibers or other small items adhering to the tape that might help link a crime scene to a suspect. Also, she'd look at the physical makeup of the tape: "the number of yarns, and the spaces between those yarns." She did this to determine if separated sections of tape came from the same roll.

Then she would look at the end of each piece, the pattern created by the tearing or cutting of the tape, to determine if the sections had once all been one piece.

"That's called making a fractured match," Sanders said, explaining that fractured matches were difficult to determine with duct tape because the ends became distorted.

O'Donnell asked the witness to focus on this case's duct

tape. Yes, Sanders analyzed it. No, she couldn't make a fractured match, but she did examine them thoroughly. She separated the pieces and laid each one out individually on pieces of acetate. These pieces were very similar, sharing all of the same class characteristics—same number of yarns, yarns running north-south, space between yarns.

O'Donnell took Sanders through the rest of her work on the case. She'd been given a bra strap and a bra that was missing a bra strap, and asked if they had once been a complete bra. The bra with the missing strap was in bad shape, having been found, apparently buried, by a grater that was scraping earth away at the search site, one inch at a time. Again the items were examined thoroughly, visually and microscopically. She spent particular time studying the strap that was still attached to the bra. It wasn't, in the strictest sense, a strap at all. The strap, instead of being sewn, fit inside two pieces of cloth. That meant that the strap could be pulled asunder from the bra without tearing, thus making it impossible to find a fractured match. There was no fracture. The witness stood and used a laser pointer, showing the jury what she meant. So instead she listed the similarities. She looked at the dot pattern. The smoothness and roughness of the sides, patterns in the material, and how far from the edge it stopped.

"And how did the separated strap compare with the strap still on the bra?"

"There were similarities, yes," the witness said.

She had not compared the strap to the found bra, because that bra was too old and had been exposed to the elements. There was no way to determine what alterations the weather or animals might have made.

"So what did you do?"

"I used the characteristics of the bra to purchase a new bra of the same type from the same manufacturer." Sanders went shopping at several stores before finding the bra she was looking for at Kmart.

O'Donnell showed the witness a new-looking bra, and Sanders ID'd it as the one she'd purchased at the megastore. The witness again gave the jury details of her analytical process. Back in the lab, the newly bought bra was placed on a foam torso-only mannequin for testing. To simulate the bone at the top of the shoulder, the handle to a pair of rubber mallets was placed under the straps at the top. Similarities were found, but no absolute match could be made.

On that tepid note, Christina Sanders's direct testimony ended. Jerry Meisner was eager to cross-examine, to emphasize for the jury how vague Sanders's conclusions had been. She'd been asked to find a fractured match in the pieces of duct tape found in King's house—in the kitchen garbage bag, on the counter, and in the victim's hair at the autopsy. No matches.

Regarding the bra: "Did it occur to you that, because this evidence was discovered by a *piece of heavy machinery,* pulled at and dragged by an earth grater, that this process, the very discovery of the evidence, might have been the cause of the missing strap?"

"The heavy machinery could have been responsible for the missing strap," the witness agreed.

"You compared at some point the duct tape found at the autopsy with the duct tape found in the garbage bag?"

"Yes."

"Did you find visual differences?"

"Yes."

* * *

On redirect, Suzanne O'Donnell asked if all of the duct tape could have come from the same roll of tape. Christina Sanders said that although she couldn't say for sure, the tape *could have* come from a common source.

Judge Economou called the lunch recess and ordered everyone back by 1:45 P.M.

The afternoon session began with a short field trip for the jurors. They were escorted to a well-guarded portion of the courthouse parking lot, where they were allowed to observe the defendant's Camaro. No witnesses were called or questions allowed while the jury and lawyers were outside. Jurors could bring their notepads with them if they wished, but they were under no obligation to do so.

To establish the defendant as a man in possession of a nine-millimeter handgun and the ability to use it, Suzanne O'Donnell called Robert Salvador to the stand.

The witness testified that he was a friend of the defendant's and, only hours before Denise Lee's abduction, had made arrangements with Michael King to meet at a pistol range. Robert, in his white minivan, and King, in his Camaro, met up at a gas station and then drove to the range together. They parked in the range's lot, with one parking space between them; Robert Salvador on the right, Michael King on the left.

"When you got there, did you have your weapons in a case with the ammo?"

"Yes."

"Did you observe King get his weapon?"

"He opened the [car] door, got out, and pulled it out from under the passenger seat, and that's when I told him, 'You can't just walk up there with your gun out of a case.' I told him they were pretty strict about that." The witness said he felt stress when he saw King do that. He thought they were going to come and get him for pulling his gun out in the parking lot like that. "So I put it in my case for him."

"It is required to have your gun in a case?"

"I don't know if it's required. I do know that it's an expected thing."

Yes, the witness saw King firing at the gun range, using a semiautomatic nine-millimeter gun. Yes, he got a good look at it. "It was mostly black, had a clip," he said.

"Do they charge for using the gun range?"

"Yes, but I had sessions paid for in advance, so I told them to take two sessions off my account."

"Did you have to sign in?"

"Yes."

The witness identified the sign-in sheet from the gun range for the day of the murder. Yes, there were the defendant's and the witness's signatures. The time was recorded as 11:57 A.M.

"How long did you practice?"

"About an hour."

"Were there a lot of other people there?"

"It wasn't as crowded as I've seen it, but there were other people."

"What was the layout like?"

"It's all a pavilion, and they have tables all along, and then there's a divider, and then you walk to other pavilions that are in the one-hundred-yard range."

"Is there a range master to make sure everyone is doing the right thing?"

"Yes."

"What range were you in?"

"I usually go to the short ten-yard one, and sometimes the twenty-five-yard [one]."

"You weren't at the one-hundred-yard range?"

"No."

"Did you fire all of your weapons?"

The witness said he did not, just the nine-millimeter gun and the two .22s. He didn't fire the Russian pistol.

"Which weapons did King fire?"

"He fired his own, and then he asked to shoot my nine a couple of times."

"Where do you buy your ammunition?"

"Wherever I can find it cheapest. Walmart. I buy reload."

"The nine-millimeter ammunition you brought, was it reload?"

"Some of it was new, some reload."

"As you were shooting, did someone occasionally come by and broom away the shell casings?"

"Yes."

"What time was it when you and the defendant left the gun range?"

"Sometime around one o'clock."

"And as you left, you had the defendant's gun?"

"Yes, I gave him his gun back when we got to his car."

"And you saw the defendant put his gun back under the seat of his car?"

"No, I put his gun under his seat for him."

"And then?"

"We parted, and I went back to work."

"On that day, on January seventeenth, did you know what was going on in regard to this case?"

"No."

"When did you find out?"

"When officers rang my doorbell at two, the next morning."

"When they started asking questions, did you know what they were talking about?"

"No. They told me he'd been apprehended and why."

"How long did the police talk to you at that point?"

"Just a few minutes."

"And what did you do after the police left?"

"My wife and I went on the Internet and we verified that what the police were saying was true. At first, we didn't think it was that big of a deal, that this was just some domestic dispute with a girlfriend he had." When the witness realized that there was more to it, he voluntarily went to the police and gave them his story in detail.

As he wasn't sure which law enforcement agency the officers from the previous night were from, he called the Venice police, the closest police to where he lived. They gave him the phone number for the NPPD, which was handling the case. Later on that day, he went to the NPPD and gave them a detailed interview.

"How were they treating you?"

"They were hard on me. Looking back, I understand now. They were still trying to find her. So they were not being nice, but I guess they were being as nice as they could, under the circumstances."

Robert gave the police some receipts he kept in his wallet. He was certain they lacked relevance to the case because he only kept receipts that had to do with his work, for tax purposes. But police didn't know that and checked the receipts out.

"No further questions, Your Honor."

* * *

"Mr. Meisner?"

"Thank you, Your Honor . . . ," Jerry Meisner said. Under cross, Robert Salvador said he'd met Michael King three or four years earlier. He'd worked with him. Hired him. Paid him. Made a lot of referrals.

"You drove by his house?"

"Yes. Once. To see if he knew of any work. I knew where his house was because I worked there." Yes, they'd gotten together socially as well, a fishing trip being the best example. Under defense questioning, the witness rehashed his testimony, now framed the way the defense wanted it in jurors' minds. He testified that, as he said before, it was not uncommon for him to go to the gun range, that he liked to think of himself as a gun enthusiast. He owned upward of twenty guns in all, and it had been his idea to go shoot together. He met King at a gas station and led him to the range. King didn't even have any of his own ammo.

When the practice shooting was done, there were still nine-millimeter bullets left unfired, and Robert offered those to the defendant—but the offer was only for firing then and there. He *did not* offer bullets to King to take home with him or to use later. When King demonstrated that he was done shooting, Robert took back the bullets. As far as he knew, King had not pocketed any.

How did he know King was done shooting? Because there was a process that shooters went through when they were finished firing. With a semiautomatic, they would put the gun down, take it apart, and inspect it to see that there were no bullets in the magazine.

"You took the bullets with you?"

"Yes."

"As far as you know, King left with no ammunition whatsoever?"

"Correct."

"Let's skip ahead. At two the next morning, you get up because there's a ringing at the door. An officer asks to speak with you, and this is your first contact with the police?"

"Yes."

"You lied to them at that point? You said you hadn't been practice shooting with him?"

"They never asked if I saw him. I told them about seeing him the next day."

"So you lied."

"Well, I spent a lot of that night thinking about it. Technically, it was a lie. They asked me if I knew him and I said yes. They asked if I'd seen him, I said no. My wife didn't know I'd been to the gun range, so I didn't volunteer it in front of her. But it bothered me all night."

"You didn't just deny seeing him, you also deleted calls on your cell phone from King. Isn't that right?"

"Yes. I wasn't up front with my wife about how often I went to the gun range, so I took those calls off my phone so I wouldn't have to tell her why." As it turned out, he'd done a sloppy job of it. Even though he tried to erase all records of his calls to King, he missed one.

"After you left the gun range, you went to a customer's house?"

"Yes."

"And after that, Home Depot?"

"I don't remember. It's possible. I have a lot of info to remember and it happened a long time ago." After reading a written statement that he'd made on January 20, 2008, Salvador agreed that he'd gone to Home Depot after the customer's house. After Home Depot, he went to Checkers and got something to eat; he had a receipt to prove it.

"That would have been about four o'clock?"

"If that's what I said."

"You told the police between four and five o'clock."

"Then, yes."

"Isn't it true that when you first talked to police you didn't mention Home Depot?"

"Yes. I was running all around, didn't remember where-all I went."

"I'm sure you were very careful about telling the truth, right? When police question you about a possible homicide, you want to make sure the information you give them is accurate."

"Yes."

"But you didn't give them accurate information on the first day, did you?"

"I didn't mean to."

"You purposefully withheld information from the police, didn't you?"

"If I did, it was not on purpose."

"Before you left the pistol range, before you parted ways with Michael King, you arranged to meet him later in the day, didn't you?"

"No, sir."

"And didn't you go over to his home on Sardinia that day, January 17, 2008?"

"No, sir—I did not."

"And wasn't the purpose of going over there to bring a lawn mower and a gas can?"

"Absolutely not."

"To help him cut the grass?"

"No, sir."

"And didn't you meet him out on Plantation Boulevard during the evening hours of January 17, 2008?"

"No, sir."

"Didn't you fire the shot that killed and took the life of Denise Lee?" Jerry Meisner asked.

"Absolutely not."

"You said you wanted to 'burn' King. Isn't that right?"

"I didn't say that."

"No further questions, Your Honor," the defense attorney said with disdain.

On redirect, the prosecution found the quote in Robert Salvador's written statement in which he'd used the phrase "burn King." When the sections before and after the quote were read, it became clear that what the witness actually meant was that he felt as if he'd been taken advantage of, that King took his bullets at the gun range without his knowledge for the purpose of killing a person. Salvador was angered and felt that *justice should be done as far as King was concerned, if what police were saying about him was true.* "Burn" in this case being the opposite of "protect." *He should burn.*

"Did your wife like you being around King?"

"No."

"Did your wife like his number being on your phone?"

"No."

The witness said it was routine for him to visit his storage unit after shooting, as that was where he stowed his guns and his gun-cleaning equipment.

"And you subsequently took the police to your storage unit and gave them your guns?"

"Yes."

"When you were at the range, when someone takes a clip out, can you tell if there is ammo in the magazine?"

"If you look hard enough."

"Could you tell if King had ammo when you and he finished shooting?"

"No, I had no reason to."

"Did you keep your ammunition next to you?"

"It was between us."

"And there were times when your eyes were not on the box?"

"Yes."

"Is it possible that he took some of your ammo without you knowing it?"

"Yes."

"Do you know whether or not he left the gun range with any of your ammo?"

"No." But, the witness added, with the machinations of the range being what they were, there were "many opportunities" for King to take bullets and pocket them without his seeing him.

"While at the range, did you and King ever trade nine-millimeter pistols?"

"No."

"Now you admitted that when you first talked to police, you didn't say everything. . . ."

"I didn't make a point to lie. I was terrified—plus, it was difficult for me to remember everything that went on."

"Did the police treat you like a suspect?"

"I didn't realize it at the time, but yes, they did."

"Did you ever see Denise Lee?"

"No."

"Did you shoot her?"

"No."

* * *

On recross, the witness admitted that the Checkers receipt was the only thing he had in terms of an alibi.

"When Michael King left the range, you thought he didn't have bullets with him, right?"

"Yes. Correct. I had no reason to think otherwise," Robert Salvador said.

Before the next witness was called, there was a ten-minute break followed by an argument that started when Lon Arend complained about the defense's cross-examination techniques. They seemed to be asking questions out of the blue, and not based on facts in evidence, just to place a notion in the jurors' heads.

Okay, the last witness wasn't completely candid with law enforcement when he was *first* questioned. How do you get from there to *he killed Lee*?

That was quite a jump.

Jerry Meisner said he had statements to back up his questions, but the only statement he would name was a previous statement indicating Robert Salvador had indeed agreed to meet with the defendant later on after practicing at the gun range.

The implication was that Jerry Meisner was basing his questions for Robert Salvador on statements that had been made to him by Michael King, statements that Meisner did not have to quote in court because of lawyer/client confidentiality rules.

Judge Economou didn't think this provided adequate foundation for asking if he was a murderer. The defense was, in law school vernacular, trying to walk through a door that hadn't been opened.

There was no "good faith" basis for asking those questions. The "agreed to meet" statement came from the defendant himself during an early police interview—the same interview in which he claimed that someone shooting from a helicopter murdered Denise Lee.

Meisner said that questioning Robert Salvador about what really happened was allowable once it was established that he'd lied to police, and the defense attorney itemized the differences between his earlier statements and this day's testimony. There were all sorts of reasons to suspect the witness. He lied about being with Michael King. He lied about ever being in King's home, and about the extent of their friendship. Plus, there were indications of deception—i.e., he deleted calls from King on his phone. And because his client never admitted anything involving Denise Lee's death, the defense could question this known liar without contradicting King.

The judge ruled that the questions involving Robert Salvador knowing and killing Denise Lee did not have proper foundation and constituted improper cross-examination.

When the jury was brought back in, the judge informed them to disregard that portion of Robert Salvador's testimony, and that that portion of the Q&A had been stricken from the record.

Judge Economou read for the jury the specific questions and answers they were to disregard, so everyone would know exactly what they were supposed to forget.

The question and answer regarding whether Robert Salvador and Michael King ever traded guns at the range would be allowed in, however, as it did not imply guilt on Salvador, and the handling of the guns and ammunition during the hours before the murder was clearly relevant and proper cross-examination.

John Romeo, a Florida crime lab supervisor/firearm expert, testified that he had a bachelor's degree from South

Florida, completed a two-year course in ballistics, been tested annually for fifteen years in his proficiency and never failed, and had testified in court about one hundred times before.

After establishing his firearms expertise, Romeo was shown a gun like the one Robert Salvador said Michael King was practicing with at the range. Romeo described the nine-millimeter gun as a semiautomatic pistol made to resemble a Glock. He demonstrated for the court how the gun was loaded, using a detachable magazine. When fired, the gun automatically ejected the spent shell casing, which would go up and to the right, landing about three to five feet from the shooter.

"Would it be possible for an ejected shell casing from this gun to travel ten feet?"

"That is not unheard of."

Romeo said he'd been given forty-seven shell casings taken from the gun range—near the spot where the two men were practicing—and, for comparison purposes, the shell casing recovered near the burial site. He looked at each shell through a microscope and placed shells next to each other to compare them. He looked for any tool marks, impressions, or scratches on the case.

"Tool mark?"

"The metal of a gun is harder than that of a bullet casing, so the gun makes marks on the casing through all stages, from loading to firing."

"Tool marks help you identify the weapon?"

"Yes, the tool marks left by every gun are unique."

Another key method of determining if two shells had been ejected from the same gun was the impression made by the firing pin.

"And what did you discover during your analysis of these casings?"

"I found that four of the casings from the gun range were ejected by the same gun that ejected the casing at the crime scene."

"Are you certain of this?"

"One hundred percent."

John Scotese cross-examined the witness. He directed his attention to the four range shells that he'd ID'd as coming from the probable murder weapon. Did he collect those shells? No. Did he bag them? No. Did he have any control of the collection and packaging of the evidence up until the time it was delivered to his lab? No, he did not.

The implication was that this was manufactured evidence, that the fix was in. Michael King was being railroaded.

Scotese induced testimony that various ballistics experts will sometimes use different terminology, and then he used that to imply that there was a subjective component to the witness's science.

The witness acknowledged that in some cases this might be true, but that there was *always* a great deal that *was* objective. John Romeo admitted that the same gun might not always make the same tool marks on the casings it ejected, and that those marks might vary slightly depending on the manufacturer of the ammunition.

There were also misfires to take into consideration. In some cases, the gun itself proved faulty, in which case the tool marks on an ejected casing might vary from a casing ejected from the same weapon when it was functioning properly.

He also noted that unlike fingerprint analysis in which a certain number of common features officially made two fingerprints a match, no such magic number existed with shell casings from semiautomatic pistols. The number of identical markings that would constitute a match varied from scientist to scientist.

Yes, there could be a situation where one ballistics expert might call two shell casings a match, while another would determine that the evidence was inconclusive.

Romeo fought back, however, emphasizing that it was not the number of identical marks on two shell casings that determined a match, but the uniqueness of the shapes. And the identical nature of two marks' shapes was very objective and "used scientific principles." It was very rare for well-trained examiners to disagree.

On redirect, John Romeo said that although it was conceivable that variant manufacturers could hinder a scientific match with two casings fired from the same gun, the various manufacturers of the ammunition in this case did not affect the comparison.

On recross, Romeo said that no, he didn't know the metal content and composition of the casings he'd compared in this case.

Romeo was excused, and the third day of testimony came to an end.

CHAPTER 18

DAY FOUR

Court began on day four with Jerry Meisner moving for a mistrial because the evidence regarding Robert Salvador had been disallowed. Judge Deno Economou denied the motion.

Lon Arend asked the judge to add to the state's witness list the name of Robert Salvador's wife, whom he wanted to question regarding the specifics of Salvador's alibi.

The state argued that it should be allowed to bolster Robert Salvador's testimony by calling his wife to the stand. He was where he said he was, and his wife, Betsy, would back him up on that.

The defense didn't like that idea, arguing that if the state wanted to call Mrs. Salvador to the stand they should have put her on their pretrial witness list. Besides, such an addition to the list would necessitate a delay as the defense would need an opportunity to prepare cross-examination. And thirdly, Mrs. Salvador had been a spectator in the courtroom during her husband's testimony. By rule, witnesses had to be kept out of the courtroom until after they were done testifying.

Arend argued that because Michael King's DNA, and only King's DNA, had been found during Denise Lee's autopsy, there was no evidence that Harold Muxlow, Robert Salvador, or anyone else for that matter were present when Denise Lee was murdered.

The judge agreed with the defense and ruled that Betsy Salvador should not be added to the list of prosecution witnesses. With that, the jury was brought into the courtroom and testimony resumed.

The prosecution's first witness of the morning was NPPD officer Todd Choniere, questioned by Suzanne O'Donnell. He testified that at 6:35 P.M., on January 17, 2010, he and Pamela Jernigan went to the home of Harold Muxlow, knocked on his door, and found no one home. They canvassed the neighborhood, asking people if they'd seen anything suspicious. They gave the Muxlow property the once-over. Behind the house, there were two structures: a workshop and a storage shed. There were also a couple of vehicles back there on blocks. In the front, an unhitched trailer was parked on the lawn next to the street.

At 6:56 P.M., Harold Muxlow returned home in his white Chevy pickup, so the witness and Jernigan questioned him. They talked to him for ten minutes outside, and then they went into his home. Crossed Confederate flags were featured in his decorating, along with the slogan "Git-R-Done." He had his own slot machine. Choniere took photos.

Harold didn't bother to hide his weapons. Immediately upon entering, Choniere and Jernigan observed a black nine-millimeter Wesson pistol.

"I told Muxlow not to touch the firearm while their investigation was under way, and Muxlow said okay." The officers left; and for the rest of the evening, until midnight, the Muxlow house was under surveillance, thus verifying that he and his white truck did not leave.

There was no cross-examination.

Suzanne O'Donnell questioned William Dunker, a twenty-five-year-veteran fingerprint expert with the SCSO. He had received every conceivable training in latent prints, and tested other fingerprint experts in their proficiency. He'd developed and taught a course in South Dakota.

Dunker proudly testified that fingerprints were still the best way to connect a criminal with a crime, and they had been globally used in that capacity for more than one hundred years. Fingerprints, he said, were permanent and remained unchanged. And in history, no two different people had been found to share the same fingerprint. The quality of a fingerprint was variant depending on the amount of oil or dirt or other substance—such as blood—on the fingertip, and the smoothness or roughness of the surface being touched. Another factor was how a touch was made. If the fingertips dragged across a surface, a fingerprint could be smeared.

Dunker went over the methods used to make fingerprints easier to see. Old-fashioned dusting and lifting was still the most common method.

The rules were that a certain number of similarities had to be present before two fingerprints could be called a match, but only one difference was necessary to distinguish them.

During his work on this case, Dunker was provided a set of "known prints" for comparison purposes. He received a set of the victim's prints made during the autopsy, but eight of the ten fingerprints were inadequate for identification purposes. The victim's remains had been underground and wet. Her fingerprints were shriveled, but the palm prints were adequate for matching purposes.

He was also provided with a set of the defendant's prints taken after his arrest. All of these were of top-notch quality, perfect for identifying mystery prints.

Dunker positively matched the defendant's fingerprints with a left thumbprint found on a box of baby wipes discovered inside the Camaro. A fingerprint found on the cell phone battery pulled from King's phone and found in the car matched the defendant's left index finger.

The key piece of evidence was a palm print found on the outside of the driver-side window that matched the victim's right palm print.

John Scotese cross-examined, picking at the chain and quality of evidence. William Dunker was not there when the crime scene prints were found and lifted. There were prints that could not be matched because they were smeared or prohibitively incomplete. These came from the front door and sliding glass door to Lee's house, the passenger side of the Camaro, and King's cell phone.

On redirect, Dunker said that the mystery prints found at the Lee home could potentially be those of the defendant, and those found on and in the Camaro could potentially be those of the defendant.

The state called Kevin Noppinger, the lab director at DNA Labs International. Questioned by Suzanne O'Donnell, Noppinger testified that his lab was internationally accredited and functioned under the guidelines of the FBI. It was audited every two years to make sure it remained under those guidelines.

Noppinger defined DNA as the readable code of a person's biological makeup, a code provided half by each parent. The DNA in cells from the bottom of a person's foot is the same as that in his or her hair.

Noppinger had a master's degree in forensics and received DNA training from the FBI. Noppinger said that he was in on the ground floor of DNA technology, which had only been perfected and used to catch criminals since the 1990s.

For this case, he was given organic material known to have come from the defendant and the victim to use for comparison purposes. He was also given a hair found in King's Camaro and was able, using DNA, to identify positively that hair as belonging to Denise Lee. He also positively ID'd the blood found on the outside of the Camaro as that of the victim. The odds of another human having a DNA code that matched the victim's were 1 in 1 trillion.

"Was the bloodstain solely Ms. Lee's, or did it involve a mixture?"

"A mixture." But the quantity of secondary blood was insufficient for testing.

"Were the results of your testing such that Mr. King could be excluded as the secondary donor?"

"No."

All in all, the witness testified, thirteen bloodstains were found on the Camaro. Of those, eight were pure and five were mixtures of the blood from two individuals. None of the blood could be matched positively to King, *but*—and it was a big *but*—jut one dissimilarity in DNA code would have been enough to exclude King as the secondary donor of blood, but no dissimilarities were found.

"What are the odds that King wasn't the secondary donor?"

"About two hundred eighty to one."

"Let me now show you a blanket found on the floor of the King residence. Did DNA Labs International do DNA testing on this blanket?"

"Yes."

"Multiple areas on the blanket were tested?"

"Yes."

"Was there a bloodstain on the blanket?"

"There was."

"Sole donor or mixture?"

Noppinger said it was a mixture, and as had been the case with the stains on the car, this one predominantly came from the victim, but the defendant could not be excluded as the donor of the secondary blood. The odds were stronger that the blood was his, however, as the DNA code the lab was able to extract made it a 1 in 600,000 chance that the blood belonged to anyone else.

Noppinger testified that there was also a semen stain on the blanket. The semen *could* be positively ID'd as King's using DNA technology to the point of certainty. Chances the semen belonged to another man were 1 in 1 quadrillion, which was a 1 followed by fifteen 0s.

The witness was shown the piece of carpet removed from the King residence. It, too, had a semen stain on it, and the odds were 1 in 1.1 quadrillion, an even larger number, that it wasn't the defendant's. A small quantity of blood was found on the blanket, a mixture. Odds were 1 in 19,000 that the victim was not a contributor, and 1 in 310 that the other blood didn't come from King.

A bloodstain on the piece of bra strap, to a strong degree of certainty, belonged to Lee. A stain found on the boxer shorts turned out to be a combination of "sperm cells and regular cells." Using a chemical process, Noppinger was able to separate the cells and found that the sperm most likely belonged to King while the other cells were probably those of Denise Lee.

John Scotese cross-examined: "When trying to match DNA samples, you use the same database as used by the Florida Department of Law Enforcement, correct?"

"Yes."

"Could you tell me what PCR stands for?"

"It stands for polymerase chain reaction."

Kevin Noppinger acknowledged that PCR was a technique used by his lab to "amplify DNA in order to analyze it further." The process caused the DNA to make copies of itself, so that there was more DNA to test.

"I've heard the analogy that PCR is like a copying machine, a biological Xerox. Would that analogy be correct?"

"Yes." PCR could make a million copies very quickly, Noppinger added.

"Such a technique would be highly sensitive to contamination, wouldn't it?"

"Yes." If a contaminant was present, the process would make copies of it as well as of the DNA that the lab was attempting to identify. Noppinger acknowledged that. Though it was highly unlikely that a sample would be contaminated once it arrived at his lab, he had no control over how a sample was handled up until that point.

"In your lab, you use a DNA analysis system known as Identifiler, correct?"

"That's one of the DNA profiling kits we use, yes." That system, the witness said, was better because it recognized two more DNA markers than other analysis kits.

Noppinger acknowledged that others had helped with

the lab work on the blood and semen samples he'd testified to. Others, for example, had extracted and amplified the DNA samples.

"Isn't it true that your job today is to testify to results found by other people?"

"No, it is not."

"Could you explain what a reference sample is?"

"A reference sample is also sometimes known as a 'known sample'—such as a cheek swab or blood sample taken from a known individual for comparison purposes."

No, Noppinger's lab had nothing to do with the collection of the reference samples in this case, and he could not testify to their purity. He also had nothing to do with the DNA analysis of the reference samples, the results of which were e-mailed to him by FDLE and then printed out on a piece of paper. If there were mistakes in those results, he would have no way of knowing it, Noppinger admitted.

"Let's talk about that bra strap for a moment. If I understand your testimony, you tested that bra strap and found a partial DNA profile, correct?"

"Yes. You cannot exclude Ms. Lee as a contributor to that profile."

"So you would agree that in that case, there wasn't necessarily a match, right?"

And on and on, the cross-examination went. Yes, there was a chance that the DNA did not match the victim and the defendant with all of the tests he'd done. But, also in every case, it was a very, very slim chance.

Scotese, making the most of what he had to work with, hoped that the slim chance that the DNA testing was wrong might constitute reasonable doubt in the minds of a juror or two.

"Are you a director of DLI?"

"Yes."

"You have an ownership interest?"

"Personally, I do not. My wife owns the company."

"Do you know how much it costs to amplify DNA?"

"I do not. I am on the science side, not the business side."

He was knowledgeable enough to make an educated guess, saying he figured it cost about $600 or $700 per sample. The witness then acknowledged that in April of 2008, three months after Denise Lee's murder, he offered Detective Christopher Morales a deal, saying he was willing to do a DNA analysis for free on the shell casing found near the burial site.

And further, didn't Noppinger tell Morales that it would be worth it to the lab if word got around that they'd done the testing that cinched a guilty verdict for such a notorious case?

Noppinger said he didn't remember; at which point, Scotese produced an e-mail Noppinger had written. After reading the e-mail, Noppinger admitted that he had made the offer to Morales to test the shell casing for DNA for free.

"Did you offer to type Mr. King's and Ms. Lee's profile for free?"

"No."

"Why not, because it wasn't good for business?"

"I would strongly disagree with that."

Scotese quizzed Noppinger about how long various aspects of the lab work took, painting a picture for the jury of long and tedious work. From beginning to end, the process would last three days if scientists worked a twenty-four-hour day. Wasn't it a grueling effort that could be easily lightened by cutting corners?

The witness, again, strongly disagreed.

Scotese brought up some items from this case that Noppinger tested, but about which the prosecution had not asked. These items included the blue jeans, black boxer shorts, and black sneakers that King was wearing at the time of his arrest. Of these, blood was found only on the shorts—blood that most likely came from the defendant. Nothing connecting the defendant to the victim was found on those items.

On redirect, Suzanne O'Donnell asked Kevin Noppinger what type of testing he did on the shell casing found near the burial site. The witness replied that the search for DNA on the shell was done with a DNA profile kit known as MiniFiler, which was a relatively new kit—"cutting-edge," Noppinger called it—designed specifically for degraded samples.

"Were you able to obtain any DNA profile from the shell casing?"

"No, I was not."

In addition to receiving reference samples for the victim and defendant, DLI also received samples from Carlos Saenz, Harold Muxlow, Robert Salvador, and Nate Lee.

"Did you find any matches on any of the items you analyzed with any of these other reference samples?"

"No."

Lewis "Skip" Wood took the witness stand and testified that he was an SCSO employee who currently reported to the supervisor of the Forensic Services Unit. He reported to crime scenes and submitted written reports regarding his findings. He'd worked for the sheriff's office since 1992 and had worked in the Patrol/Bomb Unit and on the dive team before being assigned to forensics. He attended classes at the graduate level at the University of Maryland and was a professional archaeologist.

"What is an archaeologist?"

"I'm a dirt detective. In non–police work, I evaluate soils and cultural remains to determine what types of people lived in an area in the past and what their culture was like."

In January of 2008, he assisted the NPPD with the recovery of Denise Lee's body. The process had to be done very carefully, since the body needed to be unearthed and eventually removed from the site without destroying any potential evidence.

He told the jury about protecting the site with sandbags overnight, and how he and archaeologist Maxine Miller began the actual digging on the morning of January 19. Photos were taken after each small layer of earth was removed. Eventually scallop marks could be seen indicating that someone had dug a hole at this spot with a round-nosed shovel. No, the archaeologists could not have made these marks as they only used much smaller hand tools. The victim's shoulder became visible first; then, slowly and carefully, the rest of her.

That ended the direct examination of the archaeologist. There was no cross-examination. The witness was excused, and Judge Economou called the lunch recess.

That afternoon, Maxine Miller testified that she was a crime scene analyst and nine-year veteran of the SCSO. Like Lewis Wood, Miller was an archaeologist who helped with the excavation of the victim's remains. Just like Temperance Brennan, the protagonist in the *Bones* TV show,

Miller was an anthropological archaeologist who also used her considerable skills to help solve crimes.

It had been her job to search the grave site for finger-prints. She had also been the photographer who memori-alized the hole at each stage of the dig, after each layer, or stratum, of earth was removed.

When emptying out the already-loosened earth with the grave site, they were careful not to excavate new earth for fear that they would inadvertently alter the position of the body. They wanted to be sure that they found the body just as the killer had left it. Wearing her booties, cap, and jump-suit at the scene, Miller continued to work after the body was removed.

The witness was shown the photographs taken during the excavation process. She said those were the photos she took. The images were on a screen and Miller used a laser pointer to demonstrate her points: the darker soil and the scallop marks of the round-nosed shovel.

"What type of tools did you use as you dug?"

"We used a variety of small shovels. When the body became visible, we switched to brushes."

"What were the shovels made of?"

"Plastic. I should add that, like any good archaeologist, we did a lot of digging with our hands as well."

She described for the jury the removal of the body from the grave, and the official transfer of the remains to the medical examiner, who took them to the morgue for au-topsy.

No further questions, no cross, witness excused.

Following the natural order of the prosecution's case, the next witness was forensic pathologist Dr. Daniel Schultz. He was also the medical director at LifeLink, a nonprofit organization that helped facilitate organ and bone marrow transplants. He was not the medical examiner, but rather his backup, a role he served now and at the time of the murder. When the call came in that remains were found, it was he who came to the scene and supervised the removal of the body from the shallow grave.

For the jury's sake, he felt it was okay to refer to him as the medical examiner. He was qualified, and that was the role he served in this case. Enunciating upon those qualifications, he told the jury about his bachelor's degree in chemistry, his medical degree from the University of Michigan, and the pathology residency he'd completed.

"What was your first task after you took possession of the remains?" asked Lon Arend.

"To determine the cause and manner of death."

"You performed the autopsy. Is that correct?"

"Yes. It began at eight-thirty A.M., January twentieth."

"You had performed autopsies before, Dr. Schultz?"

"Oh, yes, somewhere between four and five thousand autopsies."

"Had you ever before done one involving a gunshot wound?"

"Yes. Hundreds."

"Ever dealt with cases that involved vaginal and anal damage?"

"Yes."

"Any cases that involved blunt-force trauma?"

Dr. Schultz said he had, and defined what "blunt-force" meant for those who might not know. Any blow to a body that didn't involve a pointy stabbing object was considered blunt-force trauma. The most common injury that resulted from blunt-force trauma was bruising or contusions, in which blood vessels broke, creating a purple area. People were familiar with bruises. They turned a variety of colors as they healed. Abrasions, on the other hand, were usually caused by contact with rough surfaces, and involved tearing of the skin.

Arend asked the witness to take the jury through the process of determining the cause and manner of death in an apparent homicide.

The witness replied that evidence came in different ways. There was what he could observe during the postmortem operation, the results of evidence collected during the autopsy and sent to the crime lab, and photographs and eyewitness statements regarding the conditions in which the body was found. All of those things together hopefully made the medical examiner's conclusion an easy one—which was true in this case.

He'd arrived at the grave site as the body was slowly uncovered. The body was found thirty-nine inches from the surface, naked, on its left side, in the fetal position. He described how he and another man had wrapped a plastic sheet around the body before it was lifted from the makeshift grave.

"Did the depth of the hole have an effect on any of your analyses?"

"The victim had been buried in moist sand, and that was a factor." This was because it could speed up the cooling of the body and affect his ability to determine the time of death. The moisture of the earth was such that the hands were pruney, like hands belonging to drowning victims.

There was a pause in the questioning as Judge Economou read aloud for the jury a stipulation that the body found in the shallow grave was indeed that of Denise Amber Lee.

Dr. Schultz described the autopsy. They began by removing her jewelry, which consisted of a gray-metal necklace with a heart-shaped pendant, one earring—the other was found near the grave site—and a wedding ring. Arend showed the pathologist photos of these items and he identified them as those removed at the autopsy. Arend asked if the items were the same as when he saw them, and Dr. Schultz replied that the wedding ring had been cleaned before the photograph was taken.

The judge announced a stipulation that the jewelry did belong to Denise Lee.

The body, the pathologist testified, was measured and weighed, and the wounds to it were itemized.

Arend showed Dr. Schultz photos of a bruised arm and wrist, and the witness positively ID'd them as those taken at the autopsy. The jury could see for itself—the bruises resembled handprints, caused by someone squeezing the woman hard, like a vise grip.

There were bruises on the legs, up and down, crotch to ankle. You could almost see the handprints. The bruises were caused by four fingers and a thumb, here, here, and there. Then there was the yellow bruise on the back, perhaps caused after the victim was dead.

There were injuries to the face and head, of course. These were particularly difficult to view on the screen, as Denise was recognizable in some images. But it had to be done. The jury had to *see* what the defendant had done.

Dr. Schultz noted at the grave site that the body had fixed lividity on the left side and rigor mortis was complete, all of which was consistent with the murder taking place during the early evening of January 17, only hours after the defendant stole Denise Lee from her home. Arend asked if there was any evidence inconsistent with the murder taking place at that time, and the pathologist said there was not.

Dr. Schultz described the gunshot wound, a little

entrance wound above the left eye and a larger exit wound behind the opposite ear, through the head, from left to right.

"From how far away was she shot?"

"The gun was pressed directly against her head when the trigger was pulled," the pathologist replied.

"Could the gun have been an inch away?"

"No. It was in contact with the skin."

Arend asked how Dr. Schultz could determine which direction the bullet had traveled. He replied that the internal beveling in the skull positively proved direction, but the fact that one wound was small, and the other large and outwardly explosive, was also a strong indication that this was the way it happened.

Dr. Schultz testified that the bullet had traveled directly behind and parallel to the left eyebrow. The force of the shot exploded the left eyeball outward and fractured the bone at either side of that eye socket.

Arend asked what happened when an eyeball exploded, and Dr. Schultz said a thick gooey fluid that looked like mucus emerged from inside the eyeball.

Arend drew Dr. Schultz's attention to the gooey mucus-like fluid that had been found on the defendant's Camaro and asked if this could have come from the inside of the victim's exploding eyeball. The pathologist said it could.

"Were you able to determine the angle at which the bullet went through Denise's head?"

"Not the exact angle. I give estimates. It went left to right, front to back." The exit wound was slightly below the entrance wound. The bullet had ranged slightly downward.

Arend gave the witness a facsimile of the murder weapon and asked for him to get up and demonstrate how, in his opinion, the shot was fired.

Dr. Schultz stood next to Arend, placed the muzzle of

the nine-millimeter pistol against the attorney's left temple,
and said, *"Bang."*

"And it is your testimony that the gunshot was what
killed her?"

"Yes."

Dr. Schultz explained to the horrified jury that he had
successfully swabbed the woman's vagina and anus for
semen, and that there was bruising in both places caused by
insertion trauma that was inconsistent with consensual sex.

Lon Arend concluded his questioning, and Jerry Meisner cross-examined.

Yes, Dr. Schultz viewed the burial site and its surroundings. No, he saw no drag marks.

"Did you see injuries consistent with being dragged
along the ground?"

"No. There were injuries on the back that theoretically
could have been caused by dragging. Let me put it this way,
I saw no postmortem injuries consistent with dragging."

Jerry Meisner then attacked the demonstration the witness had made of how he envisioned murder. Dr. Schultz
admitted that there were various ways the killer could have
stood in relation to his victim and still cause the bullet to
enter and exit the victim's head along the same path. He
could have been standing behind her on the right, or in
front of her on the left. Another variable Meisner forced the
pathologist to discuss was the position of the victim's head
at the time of the shot, whether she was looking toward or
away from the gun, and whether the duct tape found stuck
to her head might have influenced this variable.

Meisner asked if the witness was an expert in blood
spatter.

"No. Gunshot wounds, yes—blood spatter, no." He did, however, know that blood spattered in a concentric fashion outward from the open hemorrhage—but of the distance the blood might go under various circumstances, he had no idea.

Meisner returned to the uncomfortable subject of the victim's exploded eyeball and induced the witness to say that, given the circumstances, it was possible that a mixture of blood and inner-eye fluid would spatter outward; yet, there was no blood mixed with the mucus-like material found on the defendant's car.

Given the data in this case, Dr. Schultz admitted that he could not determine if the killer was right-handed or left-handed, how tall he was, his identity, or the type of gun he used. He could exclude certain guns as the murder weapon, but he could not pick out a particular gun and say this was the one. The weapon could have been either a nine-millimeter or a thirty-eight caliber. He could exclude all other guns.

"No bullet was recovered. Is that correct?"

"Not by me."

"While you were at the scene, did you observe a firearm?"

"No."

The defense attorney asked if any of the wounds the victim suffered, other than the gunshot wound, were life-threatening. Dr. Schultz said they were not—apparently setting up a defense that claimed that, while the defendant abducted and raped the victim, he did not kill her.

Regarding the bruises on the victim's body that were consistent with hand marks, Dr. Schultz admitted that he couldn't state for certain that a hand caused them.

Switching to the bruising found on the victim's private parts, Meisner asked if it wasn't true that some individuals were more susceptible to bruising than others. Dr. Schultz admitted that was true.

Couldn't the bruising have been caused by rough yet consensual sex? Dr. Schultz's sour expression conveyed his opinion of the question, but he answered in the affirmative.

"No more questions, Your Honor."

On redirect, the prosecution asked if a killer could hold a gun to a victim's head, pull the trigger, and not get blood spatter on themselves in the process. The witness answered that a killer could get blood on himself, but not necessarily. Dr. Schultz couldn't say for sure unless he knew more about the situation.

That concluded the day's testimony.

Judge Economou asked everyone to get home safely, and ordered everyone back in their seats at nine the next morning.

CHAPTER 19

DAY FIVE

The morning began with the state announcing that it had presented its case and was about to rest. Before officially resting, however, Lon Arend wanted to get a couple of things into the record to counter any future appeals, in case the defendant was convicted.

First, if allowed, they would have introduced as evidence a statement made by Michael King to police officers immediately following his arrest, as well as statements made later to Harold Muxlow. King had said, among other things, that someone firing from a helicopter had killed Denise Lee. Those statements had been ruled inadmissible, as they constituted a violation of Miranda laws. Arend said it was the state's belief that those were voluntary statements and not subject to Miranda.

Jerry Meisner moved for a mistrial on a variety of grounds, but mostly that the prosecution had failed to prove its case, being that the defendant was found with no gun, no bullets, and no blood. Judge Economou denied the motion; at which point, Meisner said that Michael King would not be testifying on his own behalf and that the defense, too, rested its case.

The judge talked directly to the inanimate defendant, making sure that he understood that his representation was putting forth no case in his defense and that he would not be given an opportunity to testify.

Speaking in his high, reedy voice, Michael King said he understood. The defendant answered the questions quickly, clearly, and correctly.

And so the trial moved briskly to closing statements, with Lon Arend going first. The prosecutor reminded the jury of the male voice they had heard on the tape of the 911 call made by the victim, and emphasized the defendant's vulgarity.

"Do you remember what he said?" Arend asked the jury. "He said, 'Why did you do that? What the fuck is going on? No fuckin' problem, go fuck around, do that in front of my cousin Harold, now we go to the next street because of him.'" This was the last voice the victim heard, the way she spent the last day of her life.

Arend had a pattern to his movements. When he was speaking his own words, he stood behind the lectern, his hands gripping tightly at the sides of the podium. When he was reading other people's words, he stepped to one side so the jury could see he was holding the paper from which he read.

He reviewed the points the state had proven. Using a map, he navigated the panel through Denise Lee's ordeal. As it began, she was home alone with two kids. She wore panties and boxers, a shirt with spaghetti straps, a bra and jewelry, including a wedding ring and another ring.

"Sometime between one-thirty and two-thirty in the afternoon, he arrived at Denise Lee's home in a Camaro. We know the defendant has a green Camaro, and we know he had a gun, because he had one when he left the gun range earlier. We know he was wearing a long-sleeved black T-shirt with a design on it. She placed both kids in the crib, and left without her phone or purse. The defense will say there was no sign of a struggle, and we remind you the defendant had a gun. She left with him to protect her children. From there, the defendant took Denise to his home on Sardinia Avenue. . . ."

Arend described vividly how Michael King forced the diminutive woman into a "dungeon-like rape room," and raped her—a fact they knew because of the medical examiner's testimony.

When the eyewitness Jenifer-Marie Eckert saw the defendant, she said he was wearing a black shirt—and a black shirt was found on the dungeon floor. Evidence showed that King changed his shirt a couple of times that day.

Arend's face showed his distaste when he gave the details of the sex crime. There were marks, wounds, on her vagina and anus simply inconsistent with consensual sex. The defendant played music loudly, so no one would hear the sounds of the brutal attack.

He put her on the floor and bound her with duct tape. They knew this from the duct tape found in the room, from the victim's hair and the marks on her wrist.

Sperm wasn't found only on Denise Lee, but it was found all over the rape room. There was a mix of the victim's and defendant's DNA on the carpet.

Arend paused and shook his head. The jury read his mind. He was sorry he had to say these things aloud, sorry they had to hear these words, but it was necessary. They had to know everything—all of the cold-blooded sadism, calculation, and brutality—if they were going to deliver the correct verdict.

From the house on Sardinia, the pair was next spotted at Harold Muxlow's house for the borrowing of the gas can, flashlight, and shovel.

Regarding Harold Muxlow, Arend said, "I won't defend him. He could have been more of a man. But this is about Michael King." Harold said King was wearing a white shirt at this time. That shirt was important. The tools were also critically significant to determining what happened. Clearly, the defendant already knew what he was going to do, already knew how the nightmare would end. He was gathering up his "burial tools."

They knew from the 911 tape that at the Muxlow house Denise attempted to escape, tried to get out of the car, but the defendant squelched her attempt, an act witnessed by Harold Muxlow.

Brave Denise Lee made the 911 call and eventually Michael King realized what was going on. He took the phone away from her and removed the battery so she couldn't do it again.

The defendant's fingerprint was on the battery. True, one couldn't tell when a fingerprint was made, but "how often does a person touch their phone battery?" Arend urged the jury to let common sense be their guide on that one.

They knew by the timing of the 911 calls that the defendant talked both to her captor and an emergency operator from 6:14 until 6:20 P.M. They could next place Denise Lee on Highway 41, where Shawn Johnson and Jane Kowalski saw her. She was still struggling, still trying to get out of the car, or—at the very least—draw attention to her terrifying predicament.

True, Kowalski never saw Denise Lee's face, but there was plenty of proof that it was Denise Lee in that car: hair, fingerprints. There was certainly no evidence that it was anyone else. There were ten minutes between the end of the victim's 911 call and the start of Kowalski's, which was placed at 6:30 P.M. Three minutes later, Kowalski lost the suspicious car she was reporting.

After that, the defendant was not seen again until later in the evening, when he was stopped and arrested by Trooper Eddie Pope. What happened at the grave site? There were no eyewitnesses, obviously, but the evidence told a story. The defendant took her there, to that secluded spot, and there he shot her dead. According to the autopsy, the killer pressed the barrel of the gun right up against her head.

He dug her grave with the shovel he'd borrowed. How deep? Deep enough so that he struck water. He buried her clothes at a separate location, five hundred yards away from the body.

They knew where the shooting occurred because there was a concentration—a pool—of the victim's blood there. The defendant tried to sprinkle sand over that blood to hide it.

The defense might argue that if all of this was true, then why wasn't any blood found on the defendant's clothes when he was arrested? Truth is, they don't know if he got blood on his clothes or not. He changed his shirt again, and the white shirt he wore to the murder site, like his gun, had never been found. But that didn't hurt the people's case any. There was plenty of evidence. There was plentiful DNA evidence on the defendant's car, blood spatter and other fluids released from Denise when she was shot. When the victim's boxer shorts were found, they had Michael King's sperm on them.

Arend then refocused the jury's attention on the arrest. No more white shirt. Now wearing a camouflage shirt.

Pants wet and dirty. There was a line of dirt across the back of his pants as if he'd stood in a hole and leaned back.

His shoes were muddy. He had a shovel.

"My God, the horrible picture it painted," Arend said. "He dug the hole, and was in it."

The prosecutor had alluded to it before, but now returned to the eye fluid on the Camaro. If the defense was going to insist on the defendant's innocence, they were going to have to explain away that condemning fact. He pressed the gun against her head and pulled the trigger. Her blood came out two ways, through the exit wound and through her destroyed eye. There was no back blast of blood. That was why there was no blood on his pants. It had all spattered out of the victim in other directions.

True, no gun. But they had proven he had the gun earlier in the day, and the matching shell casings showed that the victim was shot with the gun; so the fact that the defendant lost the gun after the murder, lost it so it could never be found, was no indication of innocence at all. There were a couple of other men that the defense wanted to point fingers at, but those men still had their guns. *The only one with a missing gun was Michael King.*

The defense would try to put reasonable doubt in the minds of the jury, but how could they? All of the evidence supported the scenario that Michael King abducted, raped, and murdered Denise Lee. Nothing else made sense.

"In light of the overwhelming evidence against the defendant, the question for the defense is 'Who to blame?' Robert Salvador? 'Let's take a look at him.'"

They would say Robert Salvador lacked an alibi, but that wasn't true. Detective Christopher Morales was asked under oath about Salvador's alibi, and he said it existed. Receipts and videotapes.

The defense objected, saying that the prosecutor was

basing this conclusion on facts that were not in evidence. The receipts and the videotapes didn't even exist, as far as the defense was concerned. There was one receipt, from Checkers, and that was it.

In response, Arend read from the trial transcript, quoting Detective Morales: "'Through the course of our investigation, receipts and videotape provided him an alibi.'" Because of this, the investigation into Robert Salvador was discontinued.

That—Morales's testimony—was evidence, the prosecutor proclaimed. "Everything else is speculation."

The defense would call Robert Salvador a liar, and it was true that he'd been less than forthcoming at first with the police, and he did delete those calls from his phone.

But this was a man who wasn't sure how much trouble he was in and was divulging the full truth tentatively— which isn't being a liar at all. That initial interview took place unexpectedly in the middle of the night, policemen pounding on his door and asking him if he knew Michael King without explaining exactly why they wanted to know. It only made sense that, at first, Robert played his cards a little close to the vest.

He not only had to worry whether or not he was in trouble with the law, he also had to worry about his wife. Here was a man who knew his wife didn't like the defendant and he didn't want her to know that he was taking King's phone calls. He didn't want her to know he was going to the gun range, where she felt her husband spent too much time.

The defense would use the "burn" quote to imply Robert Salvador was out to frame the defendant, but the evidence showed that this was not the context in which he used the word at all. When Salvador found out the horrible things Michael King had done to Denise Lee, he said the man "should burn." Arend paused for a breath to let that sink in.

He was pretty sure that by this time, more than one juror agreed with Robert Salvador's assessment.

If Salvador was out to frame King, it would have been *so easy* to do a better job. He could say that King borrowed a bullet from him. Instead, he said he didn't know if King took any of his bullets or not—which was no doubt the truth. If framing King was on Salvador's mind, he could have said that King was acting "strange and nefarious" at the gun range. But he didn't say that. He said there was nothing noteworthy about King's behavior. What kind of a frame job was that? And it wasn't like Robert Salvador was incapable of being crafty. He'd hung around with Michael King because he thought it would help him get work. He could scheme—so there was every reason that if he'd set out to frame King for murder, he would have shown signs of craftiness. But he didn't. He showed hesitance at first, followed by full disclosure.

Lon Arend continued to argue against the closing argument the defense had yet to make. They would argue different scenarios: One, Michael King was never at the murder scene, and there was a "mountain of evidence" refuting that. Two, Denise Lee and King had consensual sex, and someone else then killed her. That couldn't be true. Third scenario was that, okay, King abducted and raped Denise, but he didn't kill her. Someone else did it, while standing near King's car. So which would they believe? That King did it and did it alone, or that the defendant would voluntarily leave her two children so she could go to King's house and have torturous S/M rough sex with him? Was she still playacting the whole S/M scene when she pounded on the window while next to Jane Kowalski's car? When she cried with terror into the phone? Was Harold Muxlow's shovel obtained for some reason other than to dig a grave? He said it was to get a tractor unstuck, and that was a lie. Was there a third option? No. Did the jury believe that Michael King and Robert Salvador had a conversation at the gun range: "Hey, I've always wanted to shoot somebody." "Cool, meet me off Plantation Road at six-thirty." The prosecutor asked the jury to recall what was said during the defense's opening statement. "I have a transcript," Arend said. "It says, 'Ladies and gentlemen, that this case is simply a "question of identity, that the evidence will show on January 17, 2008, a person played with a gun and fired a single shot. The evidence will also show that the person who fired the single shot was not Michael King. The evidence will show King did not fire the shot that ended life." '" The prosecutor paused to let that sink in. Didn't the statement of the defense seem ridiculous, now that they'd heard the evidence? "I submit to you to hold them to the statement they made."

The defense objected vehemently at that moment and demanded a mistrial. Mr. Arend was trying to confuse the jury, the defense said, as to who bore the burden of proof in an American criminal trial. The defense didn't have to prove a damn thing. That was the prosecution's job. Judge Economou overruled the objection.

Arend continued: "You've heard the evidence they claim illustrates and demonstrates their client's innocence. You've heard it all. They asked some questions of the crime scene technicians. All of the evidence might have been 'contaminated.' You heard that. Maybe the contamination was accidental, a mix-up in a transfer, or intentional, police officers looking to railroad Michael King. Is that what you think happened, ladies and gentlemen? That all of the evidence is contaminated? I submit to you that it is contaminated, all right, but not by law enforcement that was diligently wearing gloves, caps, and suits. It was contaminated by Michael

King! Michael King contaminated that Winnie-the-Pooh blanket when he left his sperm on it. Michael King contaminated the victim when he left his sperm on her."

To suggest that someone other than the defendant killed Denise Lee, Arend maintained, was a forced, imaginary, and speculative doubt. Not a *reasonable* doubt.

Arend called the shovel "one of the most vivid examples of premeditated murder that I can recall during my time seeking justice. It was, by definition, murder in the first degree."

Michael King did it. He did it alone. His white shirt, with or without blood on it, along with his nine-millimeter gun, were at the bottom of some pond, someplace, where they might never be found. He placed the gun to Denise Lee's head and he pulled the trigger. He consciously decided to do it, and he did it. He also met the criteria for the most extreme charge by committing the murder during another criminal act—in this case, kidnapping and sexual battery. The prosecution also proved that he stole Denise Lee away from her home and raped her. Through testimony, it had been established beyond doubt that Michael King, before killing her, raped her. His semen was found inside her bruised vagina. She had defensive wounds. There was an indication of choking by ligature.

Arend told the jury that the defense had rights—the right to question the evidence, to a vigorous defense, even to accuse another person of committing the crime if they had the evidence to back it up. But to merely accuse someone else out of the blue, they didn't have the right to do that.

"Ladies and gentlemen of the jury, Thursday, January 17, 2008, was the worst day of Denise Amber Lee's life, the last day of her life. Wednesday, August 26, 2009, was the worst day of [Robert] Salvador's life, accused without evidence of murder. Today, August 28, 2009, is the day Michael King will be held accountable for the rape and murder of Denise Lee." Arend thanked the jury and returned to his seat.

Jerry Meisner placed his own visual aids on the easel, and said, "Ladies and gentlemen of the jury, I started this trial with a question of identity. Who tragically ended her life? The prosecution has failed to answer that question. And, more importantly, it has failed to prove it was Michael King. For that reason, he is not guilty of first-degree murder. Instead, the prosecution has offered you an invitation, probably the most elaborate you have ever received, brutally packaged. You have been invited to *guess* that Michael King killed Denise Lee. You have been invited to guess, but your answer to that invitation must be no. You cannot guess, you should not guess, you must not. This matter is far too important to be resolved by guessing. The standard of proof in a crime case is to the exclusion of reasonable doubt. That standard was not met in this case."

Meisner's pattern of movement was similar to Arend's. He stood behind the lectern, gripping tightly at its sides, as had the prosecutor, but he wandered out to the side of the lectern when he made his conclusions. Point made, he would return to the lectern to begin a fresh argument.

Meisner explained to the jury that he'd asked them not to presume guilt. They had promised not to do that, and now he was asking them to honor that vow.

He reminded them that some of them might have heard things about the case from outside the courtroom, and they were to disregard all of that, and consider only the evidence presented there in court when making their decision.

"I am going to go over the details of the case with you now, but I want you to keep in mind the burden of proof, that the prosecution must prove its case. The defense is not required to prove anything."

Indeed, they were not even obligated to present a case of their own—and the defense had not in this case—if they felt the prosecution had failed to prove its case.

"If the matter of guilt or innocence in this case vacillates and wavers in your mind, then you must declare the defendant not guilty."

Meisner recalled voir dire. He remembered talking to them when they were being considered to serve on the jury; they told him that—before they could call a defendant guilty—the evidence would need to be *clear,* that they would need to understand it *thoroughly.*

"'I have to be sure,'" Meisner quoted one eventual juror as saying. "'It must be incontrovertible.'"

Those were the standards that they said they'd use, and those were the standards he wanted them to use now, because the state had *failed to prove* Michael King had pulled the trigger.

He reviewed some of the evidence, the statements the jury had heard with its own ears, to demonstrate his point—starting with Trooper Eddie Pope, the arresting officer.

Pope said that when he pulled up behind the Camaro, with the siren on and lights flashing, the defendant pulled over.

"He didn't try to evade the stop," Meisner emphasized. "He pulled over!"

The trooper executed what police called a felony stop, ordered him from his car, put him on the ground, patted him down—did he find a gun or bullets? No. While behind the Camaro, did he see any items thrown from the car? No.

It wasn't just that Pope found no gun, no bullets—*no one* had. How many types of searches had been executed? Individual, canine, line searches. Both sides of the interstate, in the grass, along the tree line, canal, the sewers! According to Detective Christopher Morales, the search for the murder weapon was ongoing. It continued to this day. And, the fact that there was no firearm for this shooting opened up the possibility that someone other than Michael King had fired the fatal shot.

"The prosecution wants you to guess that Michael King stood next to Denise Lee, placed a gun to her head, and fired. You remember Dr. Daniel Schultz's testimony. Yet, when King was arrested, the authorities confiscated his pants, his shoes, all of his clothing. They even confiscated his body. They looked and looked and looked, yet they found no blood. Not on him, his shoes, or his clothes."

Meisner reminded the jury of what Dr. Schultz had said about blood spatter, how blood exploded outward from a high-velocity gunshot wound. The blood would generally go out the exit wound, he said; in this case, out two exit wounds, taking into consideration her wounded eye. But Dr. Schultz also said the spatter wouldn't spatter exclusively in those directions. Blood, he'd said, could be thrown out in *all directions*.

There were elements of the prosecution's scenario that did not make sense. Denise Lee, they said, was shot in front of the Camaro—because of the spatter on the car.

"If Michael King's Camaro was there at all, it was parked out on the street, far from the grave site," Meisner said—and yet there were no drag marks on the ground. With the exception of one wound on the victim's shoulder, there was no indication that the victim's remains had been dragged. So the prosecution would have them believe that Michael King stood next to his victim and then carried her to the grave site, and did it without getting a single drop of blood on him. "How can there be no blood on his face and hair? That lack of blood also suggests that someone other than Michael King killed Denise Lee," Meisner said. "And *that* person has the gun and the bloody clothing."

Meisner shifted the jury's attention to the testimony of Harold Muxlow, who said he thought his cousin was wearing a white shirt when he saw him—the implication being that Michael King changed his shirt, since he was wearing a camouflage-colored shirt when arrested. Yet, no white shirt had ever been found. For all anyone knew, Harold Muxlow could have been mistaken about the white shirt. Michael King, perhaps, had worn a camouflage shirt all day, and still hadn't gotten any blood on it. "The prosecution wants you to *guess* that Michael King changed his shirt," Meisner said. "They want you to believe that Michael King used the shovel he had borrowed to bury his bloody clothes, but the facts don't back it up." No white shirt was found. The red underwear, boxer shorts, and bra strap were not buried.

The fact that no white shirt had been found called into question the believability of Harold Muxlow. Could they really believe anything the man said? Even if you believed he was sincere, it wasn't hard to imagine he was just flat-out wrong.

Harold Muxlow had revealed himself on the witness stand as a man who paid little attention to detail: "When Michael King came to his house, did he knock on the door or did he ring the doorbell? Muxlow didn't know."

The defense attorney admitted that the doorbell/knock detail was a small one—even minute—but it was an indication that Muxlow's testimony regarding the details of King's visit was suspect. This was a first-degree murder trial. If he got the small details wrong, who was to say whether he got the big ones right?

Meisner then started in on Robert Salvador, whom he referred to as a "suspect" in the case. Salvador admitted to having a nine-millimeter gun on him on the day of the murder. He admitted to firing it. Later the police confiscated his guns, including his nine. Had the jury heard John Romeo, the Florida crime lab supervisor/firearm expert, talk about testing Robert Salvador's nine to see if it was the murder weapon? No, they had not. That was *missing* evidence.

"Here's some additional *reasonable doubt* for you to consider," Meisner said, and summarized what "we knew" about this suspect Robert Salvador. He was King's "business partner." When business slacked off, he would go to King's house on Sardinia, looking for work. He was a gun enthusiast, owned twenty guns, handled his guns expertly, went to the gun range so frequently that he purchased twenty sessions at a time, owned a nine, fired it expertly. Contrast that with Michael King's attitude toward guns: didn't own one, didn't go to the gun range—indeed, didn't even know the rules of the gun range. Robert Salvador said he had to talk him through the whole process, even how to get the guns from the parking lot to the range. According to Salvador, King was acting like a man who had never been to a gun range before. King struggled. He even struggled with the directions on how to get to the gun range. Salvador was convinced that King would only end up getting lost, so they'd driven to the range convoy-style.

According to Salvador, he and King had traded off weapons. Shell casings fell to the ground. In other words, there was *no proof* that King had fired a nine-millimeter gun at all that day, even at the gun range. The murder weapon—the jurors were expected to conclude—might have belonged to King, but Salvador could have easily framed King.

Robert Salvador testified that when he last saw Michael King that day, he did not think that King had any bullets.

"I questioned him about that," Meisner recalled. He said he was certain that there were no bullets in the gun when he put it in the Camaro. He knew because—for safety reasons—he had removed the magazine from the gun. No bullets. It was Salvador who left the gun range with his own nine-millimeter firearm, at least, and a box of bullets.

"Now, let's take a look at Salvador and his contacts with the police. Salvador's first interaction with police came at two on the morning after the murder." His statements at that time were a combination of *"evasion, concealment, and lies."*

Meisner repeated that phrase slowly, letting the words linger in the air.

Robert Salvador was rousted out of bed, admitted to knowing King but offered not a word about being with King for an extended period of time the previous day. They told him that they were dealing with a possible kidnapping; still, he made no mention of his experiences at the gun range.

"Is this not a material omission?" Meisner asked.

When Robert Salvador finally did start talking about the gun range, police asked him if he'd been lying earlier. He admitted he had. He should have been treated as a suspect, but he was not. Precious time, when Salvador's guilt could have been proven, slipped away.

Was Cortnie Watts ever called to Robert Salvador's house? She never checked Salvador's clothing, never checked his storage compartment. Nobody from the police ever searched any of those areas.

Did police ever take a good look at how flimsy Robert Salvador's alibi was? He said he had a receipt from Home Depot, a video showing him in Kmart. Meisner said he hadn't seen them. The jury hadn't seen them. That was because they *didn't exist.* Only the Checkers receipt existed. His alibi only covered the middle of the after-noon, and yet Denise Lee was seen by eyewitnesses hours after that.

Meisner said, "Judge Economou is going to give you in-structions before [you] begin your deliberations in this case. He is going to tell you that you are on your own when it comes to weighing the importance of statements made by the witnesses. I ask you to consider now just how much weight you want to give to Salvador's testimony."

There were questions Meisner wanted the jury to ask themselves: Did Robert Salvador have an accurate memory? Was he honest and straightforward? Was he inconsistent? Was he wrong? Did he try to deceive?

Jerry Meisner took off his glasses and spoke slowly. "Robert Salvador was a suspect. He remains a suspect."

The defense attorney reminded his audience once again that the burden of proof was entirely on the prosecution. And what did the state prove? *Nothing.* It had been their job to prove that Michael King put the gun to Denise Lee's head and pulled the trigger, and they had failed. They could have thoroughly investigated Robert Salvador, but they chose not to.

The prosecution had used a mocking tone, Meisner said, when claiming they proved their kidnapping/sexual battery case, a tone inappropriate for proceedings such as this.

"It is up to you to consider every possibility, every sce-nario. We simply do not know what happened. And no matter what scenario we consider, we should never forget that a woman's life was ended—that it was tragic—and we must acknowledge her loss and the grief of her family."

But, he added that when it came to making a decision during deliberation, the jurors should keep that grief out of their minds. It was not fair to decide a case based on sympathy. Facts mattered. Emotions did not.

Meisner now dealt with the results of the rape kit administered to the victim. "There was no semen on the anal swab taken in this case," he said. "No foreign DNA." The defense attorney sensed that this wasn't his strongest point and moved on. The boxers, panties, and bra strap were not found buried, he said.

Bottom line: there was no blood; there was no gun—therefore, there was no case.

"You've received an invitation to guess—but you *must not guess*. You *cannot* guess. Your response to their invitation must be no. Thank you." He'd spoken for about forty-five minutes.

"Does the state have any rebuttal?" Judge Deno Economou inquired.

"Yes, Your Honor," Lon Arend said.

"All right. Let's take a fifteen-minute break first."

When the break was over, Lon Arend explained to the jury that this was his opportunity to respond to what the defense had just said. He sympathized with their impatience. He knew they were eager to get on with their deliberations so they could be done with it and get on with their lives. He promised not to repeat himself. He also wanted to comment on things the defense attorney had *not* said. He didn't talk about the kidnapping or the rape. That was because there was nothing he could say. All he could do was argue that the defendant would kidnap and rape a woman, but he drew the line at murder.

"Does he expect us to believe that his client would

kidnap and rape a woman, yet would never slip a bullet into his pocket when he had the opportunity?"

The defense had said the items of clothing were not buried. Well, they were buried—and in separate holes. The defendant had done a lot of digging with that shovel he'd borrowed from his cousin.

Jerry Meisner had implied that the evidence indicated that Michael King owned no gun. To the contrary, the evidence indicated that the defendant had a gun—a nine-millimeter one.

He implied that the Camaro had been parked far away from the grave site, if it was there at all. But the evidence showed that the Camaro had been pulled right up to the grave site, headlights forward so the defendant could see what he was doing.

The spot where the pool of blood was found—the pool of blood that someone had shoveled sand on top of—was the place where Denise stood when she was shot.

The blood spattered toward the car. There was no evidence that any blood spattered back toward the gunman, so it was *not* inconsistent that no blood was found on the defendant's clothes and shoes.

They would never know whether or not King had gotten blood on his white shirt because he'd disposed of it and was wearing a camouflage shirt by the time of his arrest.

Meisner had spoken about deception and lies, but it seemed to Arend that those deceptions and lies were not coming from Robert Salvador, but rather from Michael King.

"He tried to evade Jane Kowalski. He tried to evade Harold Muxlow when Denise was trying to escape. He concealed Denise in his car. He concealed her in his home. He concealed her in a four-foot hole. He ultimately concealed his gun and his white shirt in a place where they were never found. Michael King was the one engaging in evasion, concealment, and lies. The defense wants you to think Robert Salvador murdered Denise Lee, but does that make any sense? Which do you believe—that the defendant's sex with the victim was consensual, or that he raped her but didn't murder her? I do not ask you to guess. I simply ask you this question—is there any evidence that would create a doubt that King committed the three crimes with which he has been charged? Thank you for your time and attention."

Rebuttal lasted ten minutes.

The noon hour approached as Judge Economou gave the jury their instructions—which were long and repetitive. He explained that for each of the three charges, lesser charges were available to them, if they believed the prosecution had not proved the three charges. The alternate jurors were dismissed and thanked for their time. For the remaining twelve, the judge reminded them that they were to elect a foreperson who would supervise the deliberation, that all deliberation needed to take place in the jury room, and that a bailiff would be posted outside their door in the hallway at all times.

"If you have any questions, you are to write them down on a piece of paper, knock on the door, and give the piece of paper to the bailiff. We'll discuss whether or not we can answer it. If I can answer the question, I will do so. All of the evidence will be sent back to you. You have the right to see any and all of the evidence introduced.

"You may retire now and consider your verdict," the judge concluded. The jurors filed out of the courtroom. It was quarter after twelve in the afternoon.

After only fifteen minutes, there was a question from the jury: Would they be able to listen to both of the 911 audiotapes; and if they did, would the bailiff have to stick around inside the room to watch the evidence while the tapes were being played? Same question regarding the twelve-minute video of King's home.

Judge Economou ordered the jurors back into the courtroom and explained to them that they were deliberating in *their* jury room, their room for deliberation. No one else was allowed to be in that room except the jurors. No cameras. Mounted cameras were turned off. No one was allowed to stand outside the windows and look in. Bailiffs would keep people away from the back window. They were assured complete and utter privacy—complete and utter secrecy. After deliberation, they were free to talk to the media if they chose to. Up until that time, it was their room and they had it to themselves.

"One thing I should have mentioned earlier. Jurors and their bailiff should communicate by cell phone, exchange numbers. Do not bang on the jury room door. Bang on that door and an alarm goes off," Judge Economou warned.

With everything clear, the jury returned to their room. Just shy of two hours later, the jury's chairperson called the bailiff. They had reached a verdict. Within five minutes, all of the principals had returned to their places. Everyone rose for Judge Economou's entrance, and then sat again. The judge spoke to the entire courtroom with a warning tone. "The jury does have a verdict. If you cannot control your emotions, please leave now." No one left. "Okay, when the jury comes in, the verdict will be read."

The jury filed in and stood solemnly.

"You have a verdict. Is that correct?"

"Yes."

"Madam Foreperson, please hand the verdict to the bailiff," the judge instructed.

The bailiff did the reading: "'In this Circuit Court, State of Florida, versus Michael King, we, the jury, find the defendant guilty in count one, guilty of count two, guilty of count three. So say us all on this August 27, 2009.'"

Rick Goff breathed a visible sigh of relief. Denise's family quietly wiped away tears.

The judge polled the jury, asking them each if they agreed with the verdict on all three counts, to verify that the verdict was, indeed, by consensus. Because all of the charges had to be repeated by the judge verbatim for each juror, the polling took eight minutes—a very long eight minutes.

"Have I skipped anyone?" he said when the process was complete. "Shall I discharge the jury?" After a moment of silence, Judge Economou reminded the jurors that the first part of their task was complete, but there was still the penalty phase to come, and he ordered them to return to the courtroom the next Tuesday at nine-thirty in the morning. That gave them the required "cooling-off" period between the guilt and penalty phases of the murder trial. Plus, the judge emphasized, it gave the jurors a much-needed opportunity to spend time with their families and friends. They had to be extremely careful, however. They were going to be in contact with people who, in turn, had been in touch with the media, and it was essential that they not discuss the case in any way, shape, or form. Of course, they should watch no TV. Such a mistake could be grounds for a mistrial, and all of their work would have been for naught.

"Have a safe weekend," he concluded. The jury left. Judge Economou adjudicated the verdict, making it official. Beginning his life as a convicted murderer, Michael King was freshly fingerprinted, then led out. There was a brief moment of celebration as the friends and family of Nate and Denise Lee hugged—hugs muted with tears. That was one hurdle cleared, but the ordeal was still not through.

Outside court, Nate Lee told a reporter that he felt good. Justice was being served. He felt tremendous pride in Denise, who had been so brave and resourceful during her last minutes. "She got this guy caught and convicted," he said. She'd successfully protected her boys and had seen to it—absolutely *seen to it*—that this creep would never be able to hurt anyone ever again.

Nate felt Denise's presence throughout the trial. He believed she was in that jury room with the jurors, that she was sitting next to all of her loved ones who were wondering if they had the strength to get through this, and she had lifted them up and carried them through.

Any words for her killer?

"I believe he deserves a lot worse than he's going to get."

Did he send any messages to Denise in there?

Yes, just before the verdict. He told her he wished she were there so he could hold her hand, that he just missed her so much, and he was anxious to get home to the boys so he could give them big hugs and play trucks with them because that was what they liked to do.

Rick Goff also fielded media questions. He said the verdict had been "emotional—to say the least." They were a third of the way home. They'd gotten their conviction. Next the death penalty. Then the needle. He could envision the day they'd go to watch that needle enter Michael King's arm, sending him to the "place where he belongs," quite different—opposite, in fact—from where Denise was. Couldn't send him there fast enough.

Rick thanked the press for giving the family space during the ordeal, thanked the members of law enforcement who'd helped along the way. He singled out Chief Terry Lewis and Detective Christopher Morales. Regarding Morales, Goff said, "We love him. He's one of my best friends now. He's part of the family." He thanked the community for rallying around the cause, thanked the state attorney's office for giving the family rooms to stay in during the trial so they wouldn't have to drive the long commute every day.

He called Denise "our hero, our angel." She'd done things he wasn't sure he'd be able to do if put in that place.

Rick said he wasn't convinced Denise was King's first victim. A guy like that—it seemed extremely possible that he'd hurt women before. He was acting crazy now, hoping the act would make things better for him, but he could keep up the nutcase act right up until the needle penetrated his vein for all Goff was concerned.

If Goff was in the same room with him, what would he do?

"Good thing I didn't get a hold of him—simple as that. He is a coward, trash."

Did the kids know what was going on?

No, they'd done a good job of keeping the boys isolated, so they would only have good memories of their mommy. In fact, that was what he was doing right then, going to see the boys.

To combat an expected psychiatric defense during the penalty phase of the trial, the state had requested, and been granted, permission to evaluate Michael King's mental condition freshly. At a hearing on August 31, Carolyn Schlemmer tried to prevent that exam. She told Judge Economou that the evidence the defense planned to present during the penalty phase was narrow in scope. They planned to establish that King's IQ was very low, in double digits, and that he'd suffered a severe brain injury when he was younger. She added that the defense intended to demonstrate that "the capacity of this defendant to appreciate the criminality of his conduct, to the requirements of law, was substantially impaired."

After consideration, Judge Economou ruled that the prosecution's mental-health experts would be allowed to examine King that day, because those examinations were necessary for the prosecution to rebut King's defense.

At the same hearing, the defense noted as well that two victims were scheduled to give "victim impact statements" during the penalty phase, Rick Goff and Nate Lee. The defense had reviewed the written versions of those statements and asked the judge that some of the husband's statement not be read before the jury. Specifically, they wanted struck that he would be "haunted forever" by the fact that his children were to grow up without a mother, and that telling those children why their mother was gone was "a lesson that no father should have to teach his children."

Judge Economou ruled that those two portions of the husband's statement would be deleted. The judge also agreed that the word "murder" in one statement be changed to "death." These edits, he felt, prevented the statements from being unfairly inflammatory. It was a ruling that irritated friends of the victim, but it was made to ease the appeals process down the road.

CHAPTER 20

SEPTEMBER 1, 2009

The penalty phase began with the jury out of the room as the state accused the defense of discovery violations. Both sides were obligated to present the opposing side with all evidence they planned to introduce—witness statements, for example. Lon Arend complained to Judge Economou that transcripts of interviews the defense had done months before had been supplied to the prosecution only the day before, just after five o'clock. The defense, Arend maintained, would try to show that Michael King lived in a chronic catatonic state—and it was true, he couldn't have looked more dead-eyed during the course of the trial. Yet, there were interviews with doctors who examined him that stated he was acting normally. Arend suggested that the judge impose upon the defense an admonishment or a fine for their violation of the discovery rules. Arend criticized the defense's strategy, saying he had solid proof—the 911 tape, for example—that King was not catatonic.

In her own defense, Carolyn Schlemmer said she had been working "to get that stuff" to the prosecution, and added that the state had had plenty of opportunity to depose defense witnesses scheduled for the penalty phase. They had chosen not to do so.

Perhaps sensing that the prosecution was on solid ground, the judge told the defense to try harder in the future to obey the discovery laws but rendered no punishment. There followed some discussion on technology that was going to need to be in place because one witness was testifying remotely, from Michigan. A teleconference would need to be set up. There was a chance that, while the audio was solid, they might lose the video.

Judge Economou said they'd cross that bridge when they came to it and ordered the jury brought in. The judge explained to the panel that this part of the trial was solely to determine what punishment the state would give King. There were two choices: life in prison without chance of parole, or death. They were to include the testimony that they had heard during this part of the trial and combine it with the evidence they heard in the first part, to make their decision. Just as with the first phase, there would be opening statements; each side would be given a chance to make its case, and there would be closing statements. He explained the concept of mitigating and aggravating factors, and how they should make their decision based on the weighing of these factors on a scale of justice. Aggravating factors were those that leaned toward death, mitigating toward life.

Lon Arend gave the opening statement for the state. The prosecution, Arend explained, intended to prove four aggravating factors: 1) The murder was especially "heinous, atrocious, or cruel." This factor focused on the murder from the unique perspective of the defendant. 2) The murder was "cold, calculated, and premeditated," without any pretense of moral justification. This factor focused on the *manner* in which Michael King killed Denise Lee. 3) The murder was committed for the purpose of avoiding a lawful arrest. This factor focused on King's icy motive, which was to eliminate a witness who could have testified against him at a kidnapping and rape trial. 4) The murder was committed while King was committing a felony. This factor focused on the relationship between the murder and the commission of the other felonies.

Arend concluded his four-minute statement by saying he was certain the jury would find that the aggravating factors vastly outweighed the mitigating factors and that King should "forfeit his life" for the murder of Denise Lee.

Speaking for the defense, Carolyn Schlemmer reintroduced herself to the jury, explaining that she'd had the pleasure of speaking to them during voir dire, but not during the previous week's trial. It was her job to present the case supporting the mitigating factors.

Despite the fact that the defense was going to argue for the more lenient of the two possible sentences, that did not mean that they were not respectful of the jury's verdict, nor were they arguing in any way that the guilty verdict was wrong.

By arguing for the sparing of Michael King's life, they were not downplaying the terrible loss of a human being in this case. They were not making excuses.

She reminded them that they were about to make a decision of life and death, what might be the most important decision they made in their lives. The defense was going to be presenting evidence about King's life; but in doing that, they were not minimizing anything. She asked them to weigh and sift the evidence realizing that King's life was at stake.

She tried to force the jury to think of Michael King as a person. She gave his birth date, she spoke of his siblings—then she got to the crux of the matter: King was a guy with mental problems, stemming from an accident he'd had as a child. The defendant took a direct blow on his "frontal lobe and top of his head." Experts would testify about the physical proof that King's brain injury existed, and about certain behaviors that could be caused by a damaged frontal lobe. They would explain how injury left King with a diminished capacity for distinguishing right from wrong, and that King possessed slow mental function (a two-digit IQ) and paranoia.

He had a loud ringing in his ears and suffered from chronic, unexpected nosebleeds.

In addition to the physical and mental problems King suffered, Schlemmer explained that there were elements of his *circumstance* that comprised mitigating factors. There were observable causes for King to be on edge. In fact, his life was spiraling downward and out of control.

"His only wife left him for another man that she met on the Internet," she said. After that, King was granted sole custody of his son, Matt, who was now thirteen.

His girlfriend, Jennifer Robb, broke up with him on Thanksgiving Day. He was unemployed, losing his home to foreclosure. His house was pretty much empty because his furniture was all at Jennifer's—where he had been living before they broke up.

He sought work, but each failure contributed to his developing and growing depression and paranoia. He returned to Michigan, where things were no better, and then headed back to Florida. He could no longer take care of his son; so he left him with his brother and sister-in-law. He spent Christmas in Michigan, where it became increasingly obvious that he was a sick guy. He was facing bankruptcy, and was scheduled to see a bankruptcy lawyer on the morning of the murder.

Schlemmer summed up: "After listening to all of the evidence, ladies and gentlemen, after you weigh the aggravating factors with the mitigating factors, this most important decision you'll ever make, I hope that you will set aside your anger and emotions, I know that isn't an easy thing to do—and see that Mr. King *is not* the worst of the worst."

She noted that what she was recommending they do was not exactly merciful: "Michael King should be made to live the rest of his life in prison, away from his son, deprived of his freedom, where he will die in prison. The law allows you to do that."

Regardless of their findings with respect to the comparative weight of the aggravating and mitigating factors, they were never *required* to recommend death. She thanked them and concluded her eight-minute statement.

Reading from a written statement, the prosecution's first witness began, "'Good morning. I am Rick Goff, Denise's father.'"

On behalf of his wife and himself, he wanted the jury to know more about the daughter they lost, and to recognize how extraordinary she truly was.

He read aloud two statements written by Denise's former teachers. Her tenth-grade honors teacher, Kari Burgess, described Denise as "bright as a shiny new penny." A girl who "lit up a room with her smile."

Denise's law teacher called her "quiet," but always willing to contribute to classroom discussions. He found her to
be calm and imperturbable. No matter how hard he tried,
he couldn't "get a rise out of her" during lively classroom
arguments. She was a "rocklike presence" in his class.
When tempers flared, Denise had a calming influence. Her
words were a "salve" to relax the tension.

The law teacher noted that he got to know Denise best
through her writing, which was "thoughtful and contemplative." Because of the differences between her spoken and
written words, the teacher suspected that Denise did not
want people to know just how smart she was. He called her
"whip-smart, gentle, and compassionate with words."

Rick then spoke on his own behalf, discussing the
strength of his daughter's character, a strength that developed when she was very young.

"'She was a caring mother who always put her children
first,'" Goff read. She loved the TV shows *CSI* and *Law &
Order,* and never gave up her dream of one day attending
law school.

She'd been a great friend, student, wife, and mother. Her
life was bursting with potential. She breast-fed both children, and was still breast-feeding her youngest son when
she was murdered.

"'Denise was everything we could have wished for in a
daughter and more,'" he concluded. Goff thanked the jury
for listening, left the stand, and returned to his seat in the
spectator area.

Nate Lee took his place. Whereas Rick Goff's voice had
been strong during his difficult testimony, Nate's voice fal-
tered. His voice shuddered with the never-ending pain of
his ordeal, and he seemed on the verge of breaking down.

The widower described for the jury a videotape Denise had made of the boys. On the video, Denise's voice could be heard, alive and happy as she played with her children. She was taking the video of the boys and could be heard saying, "Look, Noah. Oh, good job, Adam." Her voice was soft and warm. The oldest boy took note of the camera and began to perform, bouncing up and down enthusiastically. "Are you dancing, Noah? You are silly."

Nate told the jury that the video captured the real Denise, doing the thing she loved to do most, playing with her boys. She'd devoted her entire life, "her every breath," to her family. Their two little boys were her life. He recalled her as a woman who could multitask. Breast-feed, change a diaper, do her homework, and fix dinner. Despite her hectic life, she maintained an even strain. She was task oriented, and no one who heard her voice on that video could question her nurturing nature.

Nate recalled one night when they were driving home from the Goffs' house and Adam was very upset. He was screaming at the top of his little lungs. Nate urged his wife to go into the backseat and nurse the boy so that he would be quiet. Denise became angry at this suggestion because driving with the child out of his car seat was prohibitively dangerous. Sure, his screaming was annoying, but it was nothing compared to the risk they would be taking, the risk to his health, if he was removed from the car seat. Nate remembered being angered by her point of view at the time. But now, looking back on it, he realized that it was so typical of Denise, to see past the little bothers of life and look only at the big picture. The safety of the boys, of course, had to be their top priority at all times.

Lee recalled that when Noah turned two, Denise decided it was time to start potty training. His birthday had been in January of 2008, the same month in which Denise was taken from them. Denise went online and found a set of potty-training instructions she liked. She wanted to print them out, but their printer was broken. Instead, she hand-wrote two full pages of instructions.

For Denise, taking time for herself was never an option. She was either fixing dinner, doing laundry, nursing Adam, helping Noah with his ABC's, or taking pictures of how cute they were. She wouldn't even go to the mailbox without the boys. She'd changed her mind about being a lawyer. Now she wanted to be a speech therapist for autistic children.

Being a wife and a mother was "what Denise lived for."

"'The love in her heart was so warming that I never wanted to be away. I was proud to call her my wife,'" Nate said to the jury. "'She was the love of my life, my soul mate. She was the perfect girl.'" Noah was now three and Adam two. They were amazing and knew that their mommy had gone to heaven and was an angel. The virtues that she already ingrained in them would forever radiate her love.

Finished, Nate Lee flashed a brief but meaningful glance at Michael King—if looks could kill—then returned to his seat.

"Prosecution rests its case, Your Honor," Arend said.

"Is the defense prepared to call its first witness?" Judge Economou asked.

"Yes, Your Honor. Defense calls Dr. Joseph Wu."

Dr. Wu had a round face, a mustache, and a thick Asian accent. He wore half-moon glasses, which he looked over as they sat perched on his nose. He told the jury that his full name was Joseph Chang-Sang Wu. He was a graduate of Stanford, an expert on psychiatric disorders and brain scanning, the associate professor in residence in the department of psychiatry and human behavior at the University of California at Irvine's Brain Imaging Center. He was a leading expert in using so-called PET scans to visualize brain function and/or activity. He'd published multiple articles on PET scans of neuropsychiatric conditions, and had received during the course of his career more than a million dollars in grants from the National Institutes of Health (NIH). He was a busy guy, teaching programs as an assistant professor, doing medical research, cutting-edge stuff. He'd been published many times.

"Articles?" Carolyn Schlemmer asked.

"Yes, and sometimes chapters in books." He had written more than fifty peer-reviewed articles on PET scans and their usefulness regarding a variety of brain ailments, including Alzheimer's, brain injuries, tumors, and epilepsy. In the leading book on psychiatry, *Kaplan and Sadock's Synopsis of Psychiatry,* Dr. Wu wrote the chapter on functional brain imaging.

"You are a medical doctor, correct?"

"Yes."

"Dr. Wu, perhaps you could explain for the jury just what a PET scan is."

"Certainly," Dr. Wu replied. He explained that PET stood for positron emission tomography, which referred to a nuclear medicine imaging technique that produced a three-dimensional image. The PET camera detected radiation from the emission of positrons. Point was, the resulting image not only showed the physiological makeup of the brain, but also revealed the *level of activity* in each portion of the brain.

"How are PET scans taken?"

As was true of other internal examination methods, a preparatory radioactive "tracer" was introduced into the body, usually via direct inoculation into the bloodstream.

The PET scan system indirectly emitted gamma rays in pairs that could be captured in an image. The tracer was allowed to remain in the body for a waiting period before the scan was taken. Flat images were captured at minutely varying depths within the target organ, and a computer subsequently assembled those slides into a 3-D image. The scan created a picture that didn't just illustrate the size and density of a human organ, but also made sort of a map of its functional processes. You could tell which parts of the brain were functional and/or had structural differences from the norm.

"How long has this technology been around, Dr. Wu?"

"Approximately thirty years."

"You could, for example, use a PET scan to find a brain tumor?"

"Yes."

"Can a PET scan see even the smallest brain injury?"

"Often times, yes. It is quite precise."

The technology could also be used to monitor persistent neurological symptoms. It could be used in conjunction with the treatment of post-concussive syndrome, as well as certain types of chronic headaches.

Any neurologist would tell you that severe head trauma could have an effect on behavior. This was well known even before scientists developed a way to photograph the inner brain. Brain damage could result in psychosis. Dementia. It could be completely debilitating. Some don't recover, and the brain injury ends up affecting the rest of their lives. It was "fairly common" for brain injuries to result in patients who could no longer work for a living.

"Dr. Wu, when you first get your cases, is there already a belief that there is some abnormality? How do you get your cases?" Schlemmer asked.

"When cases are referred to me for imaging, it is usually the last step in a multistep process. PET scans are expensive, and are usually only done after patients have other types of clinical histories."

"Are there instances where you do your PET scan and find the brain to be normal, so you do not testify?"

"That happens on occasion—although a vast majority of patients who are referred to me do have a positive PET scan." That was, he explained, because patients he examined had a history of neurological abnormality. They did not represent a cross section of society.

Dr. Wu emphasized that PET scans would never be used as the sole criterion for diagnosis and treatment, unless the person was completely catatonic. Otherwise, the diagnosis would be based on a combination of a PET scan, personal interviews, and observations of social interaction.

"Where is the portion of the brain that controls behavior? Where is a man's conscience, his ability to appreciate right from wrong?"

"Here, in the front," Dr. Wu said, pointing at the center of his forehead.

"You took a PET scan of Michael King's brain?"

"Yes." The scan was made during August of 2008 at the National PET Scan Center. Conditions for making the scan were good, and there were no difficulties.

Dr. Wu was allowed to move from the witness stand so he could speak directly to the jury and operate a slide show from a laptop computer.

Schlemmer asked the difference between a PET scan and the more familiar MRI. Dr. Wu explained that the magnetic resonance imaging showed only structure. PET showed function. An MRI of a just-dead cadaver's brain might be normal, while the PET scan would be able to determine that all brain function had ceased.

Asked to explain how PET scans were made, Dr. Wu likened the process to "*Star Trek*'s *USS Enterprise* starship engine." He acknowledged that the show was fiction but said that the matter/antimatter science that the engine functioned on was a recognized principle of physics. Sugar was fuel for the brain. The PET scan determined function by measuring how much sugar was being burned in the brain.

A series of slides was shown: an Alzheimer's patient versus a normal brain; a patient with a tumor versus normal; an epileptic's brain versus normal; a traumatically injured brain versus normal.

A PET scan was shown that Dr. Wu identified as an image of the inside of Michael King's brain. Dr. Wu testified that the PET scan clearly showed that the defendant had abnormalities in his brain—not so much in the back of the brain, but in the front. There was an abnormal lack of frontal-lobe activity. To put it in automotive terms, the front of King's brain was not firing on all cylinders.

In a normal brain, the front burned as hot or hotter than the back. In King's brain, the front was cooler than the back. This was consistent both with brain injury and schizophrenia.

There was a hole in the frontal lobe, a "divot." The ratio of the back of the brain to the front was too high.

After a study of his medical history, it seemed a near certainty that this abnormality was damage caused by a snowmobile accident the defendant had when he was six. After the accident, Michael demonstrated a change in behavior. The description of the accident, which he'd gotten from King's two brothers, matched the injury he was seeing on the PET scan. Put everything together and you had a clear picture of what happened to Michael and what the results were.

Such an injury, Dr. Wu said, might cause an inability to express emotions or demonstrate rational, logical behavior—as well as psychotic-like behaviors.

"Such as?"

"Paranoia, catatonia, the inability to think, impaired cognition, delusion, a blunted effect. . . ."

"What do you mean by a 'blunted effect'?"

"We know that some people with this type of brain injury—patients will have little or no expression on their faces, as their brains have lost the ability to properly process emotion. These patients will demonstrate difficulty regulating their moods and will have a greater vulnerability to depression. These are all things likely to occur after someone has sustained a brain injury."

Dr. Wu also said this type of brain injury could cause schizophrenia, which impaired ability to separate fantasy from reality.

Not every brain-injured patient was going to become schizophrenic, or psychotic, or anything else. But the *likelihood* of developing those mental problems increased with people who had injured frontal lobes.

Dr. Wu used the analogy of smokers. People who smoked cigarettes were far more likely to develop lung cancer than people who didn't smoke—but that didn't mean that all smokers developed cancer, or that all nonsmokers didn't.

Studies had shown that Vietnam veterans were more likely to demonstrate aggressive behavior after their return to civilian life, but did that mean that all Vietnam vets were aggressive? Hardly.

People with frontal-lobe injuries were at a greater risk of behavioral difficulties, such as impulse control. A person who merely enjoyed gambling before an injury might find himself a compulsive gambler after the injury. What had really changed was his ability to tell himself no.

"Are symptoms that follow brain injuries constant and steady?"

"No, as a rule they are more episodic. They may be triggered by stress or some other factor."

Another analogy: the brakes on a car. A patient with frontal-lobe damage might have trouble hitting the behavioral brakes, and might just go ahead and do something because he had the urge at that moment—he'd do it without properly considering the morality or the consequences of his actions.

Dr. Wu discussed specific witness statements he'd read and how they reenforced his testimony. It was a statement from Michael King's ex-girlfriend, he felt, that best demonstrated the depth of the defendant's paranoia. The ex said King "always thought someone was following him." He'd nailed his windows shut, kept a handgun under his pillow. He was convinced there was a cop living across the street from him who was out to get him. On January 15, 2008, two days before the murder, the girlfriend reported that his paranoia was worse than usual, and she'd noticed that stress tended to make it worse.

According to one of the brothers' statements, King had had difficulty distinguishing reality from fantasy starting at a very early age. When he was in the third grade, he reportedly chopped down several trees because he was fearful that there were witches in them. His brothers thought, even back then, that it was very odd that Michael would have gone to such lengths, to the grueling effort of chopping down trees at eight years old, because of a fantasy.

"Dr. Wu, do you recall the so-called chain saw incident?"

"Yes, when Mike was seventeen, he acted out a scene from a horror movie called *The Texas Chain Saw Massacre*. He took a real chain saw, started it, and chased family members around the house with it. It was almost as if he placed himself in the movie and had difficulty separating fantasy from reality."

Throughout King's life, there were repeated episodes in

which King had difficulty regulating his impulses. At these times, witnesses said, his face was expressionless. When King was thirteen, he reportedly acted out a scene from a Bugs Bunny cartoon, shooting a bow and arrow at his brother. He even went so far as to say, "Say your prayers, rabbit," as the character in the cartoon had, just before releasing the arrow in real life. There was always a connection between King's aggressive behavior and the dull, blank expression on his face. The two went together. Once, when the defendant stole a car, he had the dull expression. Another time, he rode a motorcycle recklessly with no helmet—blank expression.

According to Dr. Wu's sources, in December 2007, a couple of months before the murder, the blunted effect on King's emotions regularly took on "catatonic-like proportions." By that time, his symptoms, when at their worst, resembled those you might see in an invalid, a psychotic.

All of this eyewitness data was important to Dr. Wu because it helped him interpret what he was seeing when he looked at King's PET scans.

"Did you receive information that there came a time when Mike King appeared to have blunted emotions all the time?"

"No, not all the time. Maybe with increased frequency. This is typical of episodes of catatonia. There were times when he could be loving."

"Were there other examples of bizarre behavior in the reports you read?"

"Yes. His brother Rodney reported that one time, Mike came to a stoplight next to girls in a car and he began to act peculiarly. Later he had no sense of himself behaving strangely, but he did wonder why the girls in the car were staring at him."

"When did you learn about Mike having severe head-aches?"

"His brothers reported that ever since his childhood accident, he had suffered from loud buzzing in his head, and he felt frustration because he couldn't turn it off."

Dr. Wu said that King's symptoms worsened in January 2008. Things went wrong in his life. He lost his girlfriend, declared bankruptcy, gave up custody of his son.

It was impossible to say if things went wrong because his symptoms were worse, or if his symptoms grew worse because things were going wrong. Most likely, both were true, and the two fed off one another.

Certainly, brain injury patients when stressed lost the ability to inhibit inappropriate acting out.

King's medical records, Wu said, indicated permanent brain damage in other ways. They showed two IQ tests—one before and one after his childhood accident, and a fourteen-point drop in his score. That disparity, in combination with the previously mentioned deteriorating cognition, was a solid and reliable indicator that King's childhood brain injury was permanent.

Today he measured seventy-one in the verbal portion of an IQ test, which was only barely "normal." A score of seventy or below would have qualified King as "mentally retarded."

Would King have been able to "deal with the law"?

The doctor replied that the defendant would be challenged to conform his conduct to the requirements of the law. Dr. Wu's diagnosis: Michael King suffered from post-concussive syndrome, an impaired ability to distinguish reality, with an increased chance of depression, dementia, and psychosis.

"No further questions," Carolyn Schlemmer said.

* * *

After a fifteen-minute break, court resumed. Dr. Joseph Wu returned to the stand, was reminded that he was still under oath, and faced the cross-examination of Lon Arend.

Dr. Wu listed all of the elements he'd used to come to his conclusion: the PET scan, interviews with brothers Rodney and Gary, interviews with King's friend Tennille Ann Camp, and his former girlfriend Jennifer Robb. He also used school and medical records, and the results of a legal evaluation done following King's arrest. He'd shown the jury two PET scans, one King's and the other a "normal" scan. Arend asked if Dr. Wu was allowed to identify the person whose brain represented "normal." The witness replied that he didn't think he was supposed to, but it made no difference, as he'd forgotten the name of the "normal" patient, anyway.

"Outside of those elements, you used nothing else to come to your conclusion, Doctor?"

"Not that I recall."

"Okay. You talked about conforming his conduct to the requirements of the law. That sounds like legalspeak. Could you explain what you mean to the jury in simpler terms?"

"That difficulty to conform to the law would be caused by an individual's neurological capacity to regulate his behavior to the degree that the law demands." The answer to the question obviously was no; he couldn't describe it in simpler terms.

Could he quantify King's inability to conform? Was it slight, mild, medium, or substantial?

"Substantial," the witness said.

Didn't he look at all of that time—Michael King's whole

life, for example—when Denise Lee's murderer *did* follow the law?

"I was aware that he was capable of following the law," Dr. Wu said.

"The fact that he was, for many years, a law-abiding citizen—that came through in the interviews you read?"

"Yes."

Arend asked where the witness got copies of those interviews. Dr. Wu received them from Carolyn Schlemmer.

"In order for those interviews to be helpful in formulating your opinion, Dr. Wu, you have to assume that they are factual and truthful. Isn't that right?"

"Yes."

Dr. Wu admitted that he had not received any medical records from the past that supported his diagnosis of a head injury. He had not received any medical records from King's distant past.

"Did you see any documentation that King had even gone to a hospital after his childhood accident?"

"No."

"Did Michael King's ex-wife provide you with medical records from shortly after his accident?"

"No."

"If you had received those records, would they have been helpful to you?"

"Yes. More information is always helpful."

Arend forced Dr. Wu to gauge the credibility of the information he did use. King's brother Gary, for example, was somewhere in the vicinity of twelve years old at the time of the snowmobile accident. Had Dr. Wu taken that into consideration when he used Gary's statement to formulate his opinion? The witness said he "was aware" that the brother was a child when the accident occurred.

Dr. Wu told Arend that he'd come to Florida in August

of 2008 for the specific purpose of making a PET scan of King's brain. He met King at that time and the two had an opportunity to "chat."

"When you formulated your opinion, Dr. Wu, did you take into account that the defendant had been a successful plumber?"

"I knew he was a plumber."

"And raised a son?"

"I knew he was a good father."

"And a good worker?"

"My information was not specific regarding his work success."

"And all you know about his accident is what you read of Rodney's and Gary's statements?"

"That, and his PET scan, which shows a lesion at the top of his head, where he would have struck his head."

Arend induced the witness to admit that he had testified in thirty murder cases—always for the defense—and in the great majority about diminished activity in the frontal lobe of the defendant's brain.

The frontal lobe provided humans with the capability to plan. That was where we formed our understanding and appreciation of "civilizing and socializing" behavior. It was that part of the brain that made us people, that allowed us to rise above the animals. Dr. Wu agreed that a PET scan in itself couldn't be used to diagnose anything. The image needed correlation, to be used in conjunction with other data, and was predominantly used to confirm other data. And yes, despite the fact that King had spent the great majority of his life abiding the law and staying within the social parameters of civilized behavior, it was Dr. Wu's testimony that, due to brain damage, Michael King was barely capable of following rules. And yes, because his opinion was based on cross-modality, it was to a large degree dependent on the credibility of the historical statements.

Arend tried to get the witness to simplify his explanation of the technology of PET scans, this time offering his own language. The red dots on the PET scan were sparks of heat caused by the brain breaking down sugar, right? Dr. Wu said that was basically correct. The colors on the image were not real; they were assigned by a computer to make the image easier to read and interpret.

"Can PET scans, by themselves, predict violent behavior?"

"No, only that there is an increased likelihood of violence."

"Isn't it true that experts disagree regarding the limitations of PET scan technology?"

"There are different perspectives, yes, of course."

"Some experts, for example, believe that we simply do not know enough about the brain to gauge impulse control from reading a PET scan, true?"

"Some hold those views, yes."

"And the PET scan in no way excuses Michael King's behavior?"

"I am not trying to excuse his behavior," Dr. Wu replied firmly. He was merely saying that this was a man who had suffered a significant head injury as a child, and thereafter had episodes of fantasy/reality confusion, and an episodic inability to regulate impulse. He wasn't basing this solely on the fact that Michael King had raped and killed a woman, but also on the chain saw and bow-and-arrow incidents as well.

Arend asked if it wasn't true that there were a considerable number of people in the world whose PET scans would resemble those of King, with its diminished frontal-lobe activity, with a similar history of brain injury, who did *not* have trouble regulating their impulses and were never violent.

Dr. Wu agreed that was true. The witness added that there were other variables that would increase the likelihood of violence, such as drug use and sexual abuse. No, he had no reason to believe King was a drug user, or that he'd been abused.

On redirect, Dr. Wu noted that he had received money from the government for PET scan research. The reason he usually testified for the defense, rather than the state, was because they were the ones who hired him, Dr. Wu stated. The reason he always testified that PET scans supported brain injury was because in cases where the PET scan came back normal, he simply did not testify, he reasserted.

The witness was excused, and court broke for lunch.

In retrospect, Lon Arend was pleased with the way things went with Dr. Wu: "I felt like after I was through cross-examining him, anyone who believed anything he said would be naïve." In the days and weeks that followed, Arend would receive many letters and e-mails from people who had seen the cross-examination on TV and thought the same thing. "Holy cow, you destroyed Dr. Wu" was a common sentiment.

"That made me feel good," Arend later said, "that we were able to do what we were supposed to do. I don't know if PET scans show anything or not. I do know that his interpretations of them were subject to debate."

* * *

When court resumed, a television with speakers was set up. Judge Economou explained that the next witness, Tennille Ann Camp, would testify via teleconference. Under Carolyn Schlemmer's questioning, Tennille said she was thirty-three years old, formerly of Ellenton, Florida, and currently living in Michigan. She was unable to testify in person because her grandfather was ill, and she'd spent the last several weeks caring for him.

Tennille said she met Michael King sometime during the summer of 2006 through his mom, and had an off-and-on relationship with him for the next year and a half.

She never knew him to use drugs, became close with the defendant's son Matt, and helped him move his stuff back to where he was staying, in November 2007. He had just broken up with his girlfriend, which didn't seem to upset him. He was determined to go back to Michigan and start a new life with his family.

Since she only knew him for a year and a half before 2008, she had no firsthand knowledge of his childhood accident, or the chain saw incident—but she did know that he suffered from headaches and regularly complained about buzzing in his head.

"Did you notice that he had more headaches after he broke up with Jennifer?"

"Yes."

"Did he take medicine for his headaches?"

"No."

"Why?"

"He didn't like to take pills."

Yes, King returned to Florida on January 13, 2008, and she saw him in person. No, he didn't seem spaced-out or anything. He seemed normal to her. There were instances when he seemed a little out of it, preoccupied. She remembered once she had to snap her fingers to get his attention after he was unresponsive.

"On January 15, 2008, did the defendant seem paranoid?"

"Yes, he talked about people looking in the windows to his house on Sardinia."

"Any other reason to think he was paranoid?"

"He had a brown gun, and he kept it under his pillow at night."

"No further questions."

Cross-examination began: "Did the defendant seem normal when you talked on the phone on January seventeenth?"

She'd even talked to him around six o'clock on the day of the murder. Very normal. Yes, he was intelligent, good with money, outgoing at times, and she still couldn't imagine him doing what he was accused of doing.

He did, however, have severe headaches and a persistent ringing in his ears. She recalled the day that January, after King's arrest, when police came to her home. She told them all about the headaches and tinnitus.

"Did you tell the North Port Police [Department] at that time that Michael King suffered from headaches?" Lon Arend asked.

"Yes."

"Did you also say that he had a persistent ringing in his ears?"

"I did."

There was a delay at this point. Arend wanted the witness to refer to a written transcript of an earlier statement that she had made, but she didn't have a copy. The jury was allowed to leave the courtroom as the long transcript was faxed to Michigan.

When court reconvened, Arend instructed Tennille Camp to look at the transcript from that long-ago interview. He asked her to tell him where, on which page, she said King was suffering from headaches and ringing in the ears.

"Okay," she said, and she began to read. And read. Arend took a seat and waited. Minutes passed. Turning the pages faster and faster, Tennille let out a loud and long sigh. Finally she finished.

"Well?" Arend said. Upon reconsideration, the witness admitted that, at that time nineteen months earlier, she had said nothing to police about Michael King suffering from headaches or experiencing a buzzing in his head.

On redirect, Carolyn Schlemmer asked, "When you testified about Michael King complaining of headaches, buzzing in his head, and demonstrating signs of paranoia, [were] you telling the truth?"

"Yes," Tennille Camp said firmly, and the TV was turned off.

Dr. Kenneth A. Visser testified that he'd been a psychologist since 1979, in Florida since 1973, and had worked at community mental-health centers until 1985, at which time he started a private practice. He was a trial veteran and had testified in court somewhere between two and three hundred times.

Dr. Visser explained to the jury that there were different IQ tests, but one of the most respected tests was the Wechsler test, which had been around since the 1940s. It was the gold standard of IQ tests, and was comprised of verbal and mathematical questions. Affecting the score was not just whether or not the subject got the questions correct, but also how long it took for the subject to come up with the answers. To test the subject's visual perception, he was shown illustrations in which elements were missing, and was asked to fill in the blanks.

Also gauged was the subject's ability to determine how things went together. Dr. Visser personally administered the Wechsler IQ test to Michael King, and his observations led him to believe that King was giving maximum effort.

Visser repeated a statistic the jury had heard earlier from Dr. Wu, that King scored a seventy-one on the verbal portion of his IQ test, which ranked him as borderline retarded.

Under normal circumstances, one would expect a subject's IQ to remain more or less the same throughout his life, and a dwindling IQ would be an indication of disease or injury to the brain.

King had scored an eighty-five in the verbal portion of an IQ test that he'd taken as a child, leading Dr. Visser to conclude that something happened between the two tests to slow down King's brain.

"Some sort of trauma would need to have happened for the score to drop like that?"

"Yes."

During Arend's cross-examination, Dr. Visser admitted that the IQ test in which Michael King scored a verbal eighty-five had been administered in 1984, when King was thirteen years old, well after his known head injury.

"In order to determine if the defendant was doing as well as he could on the June 2009 IQ test, you interviewed him, had conversations with him?"

"Yes."

"You asked him if he'd had any medical problems during childhood?"

"I don't recall that."

"You don't recall King telling you about a snowmobile accident?"

"No."

Dr. Visser said he'd asked King about head trauma in his past, and King said he didn't remember any. King said that he played football as a kid—that was about it. The witness asked the defendant about his recent past. King told him he worked as a plumber. He enjoyed working on cars. He had communicated his personal history in a "logical manner" and appeared fully alert.

"How could you be so sure that, during the 2009 IQ test, the defendant was giving full effort?"

"The test has some tricks in it that expose malingerers."

Despite his testimony here that King was not a malingerer, Dr. Visser admitted that, during a previous written statement, he'd opined that King's working memory was better than his IQ score indicated. That was because he did both well and poorly during the exam on questions of similar difficulty. He had the ability to look at a photo and predict the consequences of what it depicted, indicating that he distinguished right from wrong and understood why laws were necessary.

On redirect, Dr. Visser testified that he was familiar with Michael King's school records, which reflected a student who did not learn easily. He'd repeated the first grade, and teachers later commented that he fell further behind his classmates with each passing year. When King was eight years old, he still could not correctly write all of the letters of the alphabet. Because he was not learning at what was considered a normal rate, he was given an IQ test in 1984. The written report that accompanied those test results noted: *King has language impairment which has impeded his achievement.* He had speech and language difficulties, qualified as a "learning disabled" student, and spent time in special education.

Danielle Rossi, SCSO custodian of records, testified that she had reviewed Michael King's jail records and found them devoid of disciplinary reports. King had been a good boy behind bars.

During cross-examination, Rossi admitted that for King's entire jail time he'd been in solitary confinement, locked away from other prisoners, so opportunities to have discipline problems were limited.

On redirect, Rossi said that although he didn't have contact with other prisoners, King did have contact with guards, so opportunities to misbehave did exist.

Rossi was replaced on the stand by Deputy John Lima, who worked for the SCSO as a correctional deputy, providing supervision for prisoners.

He testified that Michael King had had opportunities to interact with other prisoners during his time in jail, and that there were no problems. Deputy Lima had firsthand knowledge of King's behavior and would characterize it as "good." There was no cross-examination.

The defense had gotten in a solid day of witnesses, and Judge Deno Economou sent everyone home for the day, ordering them to return at nine-thirty on Wednesday morning.

Outside the courtroom, Rick Goff was asked what he thought of the defense's expert witnesses. He responded that he was going to be nice, so he called it "crap," although he claimed that wasn't the first word that popped into his head.

Asked specifically about Dr. Joseph Wu, Goff commented, "He looked like a paid witness."

CHAPTER 21

SEPTEMBER 2, 2009

Wednesday's first witness was Jim King, the defendant's oldest brother. He was forty-five years old, married to Carrie, worked as a mechanic and as a maintenance manager, had two kids, one grandchild, and had served in the U.S. Navy for three years. His three younger brothers were, in order: Gary, also a military veteran who was forty-three, Mike, thirty-eight, and Rodney, thirty-six. Their parents were Patsy and James King. His parents remained home in Michigan, as their dad had recently had open-heart surgery and was unable to travel. Jim admitted that he had no first-hand knowledge of Mike's childhood accident, but he'd certainly heard all about it. His other brothers would be more helpful with that because they were there when it happened. Sure, he had heard about the chain saw and bow-and-arrow incidents as well.

Carolyn Schlemmer asked, "Do you remember Michael having nosebleeds?"

"All the time," Jim said. He remembered his mother

tried to take Mike to the doctor for his nosebleeds, but Mike ran out of the doctor's office, terrified of doctors. He couldn't swallow pills—in fact, none of the King brothers could. He had never seen Mike use alcohol or drugs.

"I show you now defense exhibit E. Do you recognize it?"

"Yes, it's a photo of us at our parents' place taken sometime in the 1980s. It's all of us kids on the steps." Jim ID'd another photo, which showed Michael as a baby.

Did Jim recall Mike's marriage breaking up? He did. Mike had gotten custody of his son, Matt. Jim recalled that in late 2007, Mike left Florida and came to Michigan. It was Christmastime, late 2007 or early 2008, just before Matt's birthday. He wanted to get some stuff straightened out, but the economy in Michigan was horrible. Mike spent all of his time looking for work, but there was nothing. He was facing foreclosure on his Florida home. During this period, Jim remembered Mike being quiet and sad. Eventually, in January, Mike left Matt behind with Jim and his wife and returned to Florida alone to look for a job and try to get back on his feet. Mike said he'd come back and get Matt when he could.

The witness testified that Matt was now thirteen, that he and his wife had official custody of him, were raising him, and that the boy was doing fine. The boy stayed with him in Michigan because he didn't want to go to a new school.

Back in 2008, on Matt's birthday, that January, Mike called his son and also talked to Jim, thanking him for looking after the boy.

Jim explained that there was quite an age difference between him and his siblings. When they were growing up, the age difference was more dramatic. He was usually doing his own thing rather than hanging out with his baby brothers. He worked after school and didn't even see his brothers that much. After school, he went directly into the navy. When he got out of the military, he immediately went to trade school, worked full-time, got married, and had kids. He'd been busy. There were things about Mike's childhood that his brother Rodney would know far better than he.

Lon Arend cross-examined: "Let me clarify a few things. When you say your brother Rodney will remember the accident better than you, you are referring to someone who was five years old when it happened?"

"Yes."

"When you were all boys, you used to talk about Mike's accident?"

"Yes."

"Joke about it?"

"Yes."

"In what way was it funny?"

"You know, like saying, you were okay till someone dropped you on your head. It was just a funny thing to say."

"You don't recall Mike having troubles in school?"

"No."

"And you said you've heard about the chain saw and bow-and-arrow incidents as well."

"Yes."

"When was the first time you heard about the chain saw and bow-and-arrow incidents?"

"A couple of weeks ago."

Arend paused a beat, and let that sink in. He then said, "When he returned to Michigan for Christmas, 2007, did you notice any change in his behavior?"

"Just that he seemed depressed."

"Was there a change in his appearance?"

"I don't know. I hadn't seen him in so long."

Jim said Mike was appropriately grateful for Jim and his wife taking care of Matt, and that Mike understood the importance for the boy to have a stable home.

And Matt *was* doing well. He was happy, and got straight A's in school.

To Jim's knowledge, Mike was never treated in a hospital, had no anger issues, and had no history of mental illness. This last answer spawned a sustained objection from the defense on the grounds that it called for a conclusion in a field in which the witness was not an expert.

"Let me put it this way," Arend said. "Did you ever see anything in your brother's behavior that led you to believe he might do something like this?"

"No."

"Is it hard for you to believe that Mike would do something like this?"

"Yes."

On redirect, Carolyn Schlemmer asked if there was any doubt in Jim King's mind that the accident was real. Jim said no doubt whatsoever.

On recross, Arend made Jim admit that he'd never noticed any scars on Mike's face or head consistent with the accident, as it had been described to him. He had no way of knowing what was causing Mike's nosebleeds. He had no reason to connect the nosebleeds with the accident, and he didn't know if Mike's nosebleeds were unusually severe. Jim admitted that when he said he'd heard about the chain saw and bow-and-arrow incidents, he didn't mean he'd heard about them when they occurred. Rather, he'd heard about them in the recent past, during what he thought

were unnecessarily intense interrogations by a detective on
this case.

Looking back on it, Karen Fraivillig felt sorry for
Michael King's parents and brothers. They were a somewhat desultory clan and their minds were boggled. How
could their child and their brother do something this horrible? They were just trying to explain the inexplicable—
and they came up with this accident. Of course, it couldn't
have happened the way they said. It was preposterous.
Mass times velocity squared—that was the formula. If
what they said was true, little Michael King's head would
have been applesauce.

Next on the witness stand was Kerry King, Jim's wife—
the defendant's sister-in-law. She testified that she'd started
dating Jim when she was fifteen years old, so she'd known
Mike King for a long time—twenty-seven years. She knew
that in early 2008 he was on the verge of losing his home
and declaring bankruptcy for the second time. He'd been
living with a woman named Jennifer Robb, but they had
had a fight. A depressed Mike came to Michigan. Kerry
went into some detail regarding Mike's job search while in
Michigan. He wasn't only looking for plumbing jobs, but
for anything that would pay his bills. He joined an employ-
ment agency called Michigan Works, but they couldn't do
anything to help him. He tried retail jobs, Walmart, and all
that sort of thing—but there was nothing. She remembered
that Christmas. They'd gotten Guitar Hero that year and
everyone, but Mike, was having fun with that. He wouldn't
play. He only wanted to watch. Kerry thought that Jennifer
splitting up with Mike was only part of the problem. She

believed Mike was still hurting from the breakup with his
wife, and he was upset that Matt's mother had not called the
boy to wish him a merry Christmas. Mike's ex-wife, Kerry
recalled, left him for a man she'd met on the Internet. Kerry
recalled the severe nosebleeds Mike had. He would bleed
profusely and afterward he would have to lie down for a
couple of days to recover. She'd never seen anyone else
have nosebleeds like that.

"Did Mike remember to call Matt on his birthday in
January?"

"Yes."

Like her husband before her, Kerry King was cross-
examined by Lon Arend. She repeated that she'd known
Mike for a long time. She knew him to be a good plumber,
who kept an updated résumé during his job search. He
was concerned about his son, concerned about Matt being
troubled about his mother. He had helped his son get
counseling when the boy blamed himself for his mom not
being around. Arend's questions portrayed Mike King as
a guy who, in contrast to the defense's portrayal, had his
act together.

On redirect, Carolyn Schlemmer wanted to know if Matt
knew about his dad's current legal difficulties. He did, and
was quite upset about it. He grieved for his father.

Schlemmer's point was that although Michael King
might have taken steps to help his son in the past, he'd done
the boy no favors when he raped and murdered Denise Lee.

Jennifer Robb took the witness stand and told the jury
that she was thirty-three years old, had two kids—a girl,

six, and a boy, thirteen—and was currently unemployed. She had known Michael King for two and a half years, and it was a fair characterization to refer to him as her ex-boyfriend.

"We've seen photos of Mike's home on Sardinia. There is no furniture—"

"I have it."

Carolyn Schlemmer directed the witness's attention to Thanksgiving, 2007, when she broke up with Mike. She recalled feeling that something was wrong with Mike right from the moment he woke up that day.

"He acted differently from normal?"

"Yes, he was distant. Cold and dazed. He didn't talk. He was very quiet. He was flat."

"Did he have a blank stare?"

"Yes."

Usually, she explained, he would get up and get ready. But on this day, he woke up but just sat on the bed. She spoke to him, but it was as if he didn't hear. "He acted like he was someplace else," Jennifer said.

"Prior to that Thanksgiving, had you ever heard Mike complain about headaches?"

"Yes. Bad ones. His head would really, really hurt. He said that he felt a freight train inside his head. He would have to lie down. He didn't like to take pills, so he never took anything for it."

"Did he have any other complaints regarding his head?"

"He said he heard a buzzing. He would wake up with a ringing in his ears." She added that it seemed to her as if his symptoms got worse leading up to the Thanksgiving when they broke up. He began to wake up in the middle of the night with the severe ringing.

"Was it constant?"

"No, it came and went—but it was happening more in the middle of the night."

"Describe the progression."

"It was getting worse."

"Did you see Mike after you broke up?"

"Yes, twice."

"Was he depressed?"

"Yes, really sad—and cold. He wasn't the same." He'd been a mischievous risk taker when he was normal, popping wheelies on a motorcycle and jumping out of trees—but all of that personality was dulling out. He was beaten down by life. Even before they broke up, she saw a steady increase in his paranoia as well: He thought he was being followed, that people were breaking and entering the house. He screwed the windows shut and put new bolts on the doors.

On cross-examination, Lon Arend asked Jennifer Robb to describe in detail the day she broke up with Michael King, the trip to Michigan for Thanksgiving, her mother being ill, and her being worried. King, meanwhile, was in no way cooperative, obsessing over a pair of pants, refusing to get in the truck, refusing to help with the preparation of Thanksgiving dinner, to eat or to help clean up afterward. That evening, he yelled at her for the first time in front of her parents. She told him to get the bleep out of her life.

She felt his personality change was significant, clear evidence that something was wrong with him. She didn't fear him, but she did feel he'd gone off kilter.

"The Michael King you knew wouldn't have done those things, correct?"

"Yes."

"He was the best man you ever had?"

"Yes."

"He was never violent or threatening with you in any way?"

"No."

"He was great with your kids?"

"Yes."

"How did he act when he had his severe headaches?"

"He heard buzzing in his head—asked me sometimes if I could hear it."

"So, at the time you left him, you felt there was something seriously wrong with him—his headaches, paranoia, depression, bizarre behavior?"

"Yes."

Arend paused, letting that sink in; then he moved forward in the chronology of the witness's testimony: "After the abduction of Denise Lee, two detectives drove to your house. Is that right?"

"Yes."

"Did you tell the detectives that King was showing signs of mental instability?"

"No, they were still looking for her at the time, and the focus was on that. The questions were more along the line of how I met him."

"Now, at some point in your relationship, isn't it true that you were the aggressor?"

"Yes, sir."

"There were times when you would be physical with Michael King?"

"Yes, sir."

"You struck him?"

"Yes."

"And at those times, he never struck you back. He walked away?"

"Yes."

"He was never violent with you, was he, Ms. Robb?"

"No."

"What would he usually say to you after you hit him?"

"He'd ask me, 'Why'd you do that?'"

On the surface, Arend's cross-examination might have seemed supportive of the defense's case, but the jury picked up on the subtleties. Sure, Michael King was showing signs of stress, but it wasn't so much that he was sick. It was more that he was a jerk, a guy whose pressure cooker had no release valve—a guy ready to blow. "Thank you, ma'am," Arend said.

There were no questions on redirect, and Judge Economou declared a long lunch break. He suggested the jurors go outside and take a walk, get some fresh air. There was some business the court needed to attend to before they could proceed.

Judge Economou didn't like the look in the defendant's eyes, hadn't for a while. It wasn't that he saw evil in those eyes; rather, he saw nothing at all. Michael King was inanimate, dulled, devoid of emotion—to the point where the judge wondered if he was still cognizant of his trial's significance, that his life was on the line. So the judge ordered that two court-appointed doctors examine King to determine if he was still competent to stand trial. As it turned out, the doctors were available that afternoon.

The defendant, of course, had been examined before the trial began and had been judged competent, but that might have changed. Although it was rare, cases existed in which a defendant was competent before a trial began but—because of stress or whatever—became incompetent. More common were malingering defendants who faked incompetence to stop their own trial.

This turn of events made Denise Lee's loved ones anxious. They wondered what would happen if King proved incompetent. Would they lose their chance to hear him condemned to death? Their stress only grew as the examination process took longer than expected. Court did not resume until Friday morning.

CHAPTER 22

SEPTEMBER 4, 2009

With the jury out, Dr. Ed Regnier testified regarding the defendant's competence. The court officially recognized him as an expert. Dr. Regnier said he'd seen Michael King in jail the previous day for more than two hours, and had performed on him a clinical review. King answered all questions and was cooperative. Dr. Regnier reviewed reports submitted by Dr. Kenneth Visser and Dr. Michael P. Gamache. Taking all of that into consideration, Regnier declared the defendant competent to proceed. King understood what was going on around him and appreciated the gravity of his predicament. He even understood the rules of court, and distinguished the guilt and the penalty phase of the trial.

None of that should be taken as an indication that Michael King was a mentally well person. During the previous day's exam, he also demonstrated paranoia and confusion. He experienced difficulty, for example, recalling the events of his life in chronological order. Twice during the exam, Dr. Regnier recalled, King was overcome with emotions. He required a pause in the questioning in order for him to regain his composure. He said he was overcome with grief, although it was possible that he only grieved over his own dilemma.

There were times when Dr. Regnier found the defendant to be malingering, using the opportunity of the exam to better his own condition. King realized a poor diagnosis might take the death penalty off the table.

As an example of King's malingering, Dr. Regnier found it unlikely that the defendant remembered being a plumber but could not recall the number of inches in a foot or a yard. It took King a very long time to solve even the easiest of math problems.

"The confusion was manipulative and served his purposes," the witness said.

When it came to his trial, and the charges against him, King proved to be an expert. He could quote the charges against him in detail. King told his examiners that he not only understood the charges, but he was innocent of them. He said that the prosecution was merely out to get him, that he was being railroaded—and the tape recordings that he'd listened to in court were fabrications of the state, created out of thin air in order to incriminate him.

Dr. Regnier saw no evidence of delusions, and found that many of the defendant's concerns betrayed a three-dimensional appreciation of his infamy, the spotlight of notoriety that relentlessly illuminated him. He heard people say horrible things about him, and he didn't like that. He said that he didn't like the idea of the media "covering" his ex-wife, that she didn't deserve that kind of publicity.

The subject's voice was clear and soft when he answered questions. He was familiar with what was and wasn't appropriate behavior in court. He knew when he could speak aloud and when he had to keep his mouth shut.

King told his examiners that he felt a personal disconnect between the things he knew to be true about himself and the horrible things people were saying about him in the newspapers and on television.

This represented a normal defensive posture, and it was possible that the defendant believed the things he said, as those beliefs made it easier for him to cope with the fact that his own impulsiveness had destroyed his life.

King denied that he had mental-health issues, and his examiners tended to agree. He wasn't even borderline, but "quite competent" to continue. The defendant was asked about the snowmobile accident, and he verified that it had occurred. He understood that the state attorneys were not in court to help him, that there was an adversarial aspect to a trial. He "couldn't believe" that the jury had convicted him.

King said he heard a voice sometimes, that he was distracted about half the time, that sometimes the voice in his head was so loud that it made it difficult for him to hear or pay attention to what was being said in the courtroom. He heard the voice every day, but not all day. When asked if he thought the voice in his head was a symptom of mental illness, he said no. It was not his imagination. The voice was real. He did not believe the voice was human. It didn't have a body. It wasn't "the Devil" or any other sort of religious being. He never heard the voice until he was arrested and jailed. The voice, he maintained, had the power to alter his perceptions. It could—and he used an odd phrase—"flip him pain."

Dr. Regnier told the jury that his examination of the defendant took place during the early-morning hours, beginning at five-thirty, and that lawyers from both sides were present.

Dr. Greg DeClue took the stand and identified himself for the court as a forensic psychiatrist who had earned his Ph.D. in psychology at the University of Missouri in 1983, and was fully approved by the American Psychological Association (APA). His specialties included forensic psychology, psychology of interrogation and confession, and the assessment and treatment of sex offenders. He had been in a private independent psychological practice in Sarasota since 1987. Dr. DeClue said that he, too, had examined Michael King the previous day and determined that, without exception, the defendant understood and appreciated the charges against him, the range of penalties he faced, and showed "some ability" to discuss legal strategy with his defense team. If he chose to testify during the penalty phase of his trial, there was no indication that he lacked the capacity to do so properly.

After listening to the doctors' testimony, Judge Economou declared Michael King competent to continue, and the jury was brought in. The defense called their first witness of the day, the defendant's brother, a heavily tattooed Gary King, who was questioned by Carolyn Schlemmer. His voice shook as he said he was forty-three years old and drove a long-haul semi for a living.

"Are you nervous?"

"Yes, ma'am. It's been a long time since anyone asked my age."

Gary's nervousness gradually dissolved, and he grew animated and loud when he spoke. He explained that he lived in Memphis, Tennessee, but wasn't home much as he drove trucks across the nation. Michael King was his younger brother, about five years younger. Rodney was the only brother younger than Mike.

"Let me direct your attention now to the accident Mike had back in the 1970s. Do you remember that?"

"Yes, ma'am." Gary recalled driving a snowmobile and pulling Mike on a sled. Mike was wearing a ski mask, and the rope connecting the snowmobile to the sled was twenty to twenty-five feet long. When the snowmobile turned from side to side, Mike moved back and forth. As the turns became sharper, Mike was sort of whipping from side to side, holding on for dear life. Gary took the snowmobile down the side of a large hill, the hill by the red barn, where the boys used to play king of the hill. He took it easy at first, but then he looked back and saw the sled was traveling faster than the snowmobile. The rope had an increasing amount of slack. So, to pull the rope taut once again, Gary gunned it down the hill. By the time they passed a shed, he figured the thing was going forty, forty-five miles per hour. Gary went to make a right turn.

"We were going *supersonic speed,* and I yelled, 'Mike, let go!'" But Mike didn't let go. The kid had his head down, so he couldn't see where he was going, couldn't see what was about to happen. "I was watching him go and go, and there was slack, and he went *boom!* Into a wall with his head down."

"What was your reaction when that happened?"

"I said, 'Oh, my God!'" Gary ran over to his brother, but Mike wasn't moving. He shook him, but his brother remained motionless in the snow. Gary pounded on Mike's chest. He screamed that he was sorry and begged his unconscious brother to forgive him.

Mike was bleeding from his nose and mouth. Gary

picked him up, and Mike's eyes popped open. "Praise the Lord," Gary said. But blood continued to pour out of his nose. His face was covered with blood. Gary carried Mike to the house and told his mom that Mike had been in an accident. They got ice from the freezer and put that on his head. They grabbed the frozen meat from the freezer and used that, too. They tried to get the swelling down, but Mike's face and head were visibly growing. Their mom put everybody in the car and drove to the emergency room at the hospital. Gary remembered that he was in the backseat holding a frozen steak to his injured brother's head. As they were heading into the hospital, Gary got his first look at Mike's teeth and could see that they were "all mangled up."

Inside, Mike was treated by a really old doctor, who said they couldn't do anything for head injuries, and that Mike's teeth might fall out. They were ordered to take Mike home, continue administering the ice, and to make sure he didn't fall asleep for the next forty-eight hours. If he did, he might slip into a coma. The incident badly upset Gary. Schlemmer asked why.

"I felt bad. It was an accident, but I felt responsible. He was a young person. I think it contributed to things he later told me about his life. I felt responsible, but it was an accident."

"Did anyone else see the accident?"

"My brother Rodney was also outside when it happened." Gary explained that Rodney was not on the snowmobile or on the sled. He might have been the best witness.

"Back in the 1970s, all doctors could do with head injuries was say 'put ice on it' and 'don't let him sleep'?"

"Yes."

"And there was severe bleeding?"

"Yes, from the nose and mouth. When he hit that pole,

he was embedded in the pole. If only he had missed that pole . . ." Jurors had now heard that the defendant had hit a shed and a pole, and some may have wondered which it was, if either.

"Mike still had his baby teeth?"

"Some. His teeth were mangled for the rest of his life."

"You are six years older than Mike?"

"I think five."

"And this happened in January or February of 1978?"

"Yes."

"This was a traumatic event for you?"

"Yes, ma'am. I thought he might not live. I didn't think someone could take that kind of impact and survive. I think God helped Mike that day."

"You and your brother Mike did a lot of things together when you were kids?"

"Not a lot. We played Frisbee and stuff together. Mike was closer to Rodney's age. Jim was older, higher in school."

"Speaking of school, of the brothers, was Mike slow to learn things in class?"

"Yes, he was a slower developer."

"Was there a change in Mike's personality after the accident?"

"Yes, he was happy-go-lucky before, but after, he was— well, just different. Later, through the years, I knew he was having problems."

"Did he tell you about his headaches and the buzzing in his head?"

"Yes, he would complain, and I would bring up the sledding accident. He would say yeah, he still had a buzzing in his brain. I never knew what to say or how to help him. The doctor said there was no treatment for brain damage."

Gary figured the accident had to be what caused the buzzing. Mike simply didn't have vices. He didn't smoke or drink. He didn't own guns and he had no tattoos. "He was normal, like society wants a person to be," Gary said.

After the accident, Mike sometimes seemed as if he had a tenuous grip on reality, hallucinating and exaggerating.

"Could you give us an example of Michael's being out of touch with reality?"

"One time, he told me he saw ghosts and that he had been shooting at ghosts."

"And what did you and your other brother do when he said things such as this?"

"We teased him about it."

Gary then told the jury about the chain saw incident. It occurred in 1988, when Michael was seventeen. He'd brought the chain saw into the house.

"Mike, my girlfriend—who was pregnant at the time—and I were watching a movie on TV. *Texas Chain Saw Massacre.* You can tell exactly how long ago this happened because my son is twenty now and in college. During the movie, Mike got up and walked outside. I remember being traumatized by the movie. I couldn't believe that they could make a movie like that. Seemed evil. Next thing I heard *reeeeeeeeeee,*" Gary said, imitating the sound of a chain saw. "Mike had the chain saw going and he was cutting branches off of our father's blue spruce trees."

"What happened next?"

"I told him, 'What are you doing?' I told him he was going to get in trouble."

"What did he do?"

"He looked up and then he went inside the house. Mike came into the kitchen with the chain saw still going. He filled the kitchen with smoke, and he was twirling circles with the chain saw. I told him to turn it off, *turn it off.*"

"Then what, if anything, did Mike do?"

"The next thing I know, he started walking toward me

with the chain saw. There was a scary look in his eyes. He had a ghostlike look in his eyes. It was like he couldn't hear what I was saying. It was very loud. *Reeeee, reeeeee.* I told him I was going to hit him if he didn't turn that thing off."

Mike did turn it off, and left the house via the garage. He still had that vacant "nobody home" look on his face, and Gary asked him why he did that. "Did what?" was his reply. Mike had no idea what he'd just done. At the time, Gary admitted, he couldn't believe it. He was shocked. He never told his parents or his big brother, Jim, who weren't home at the time, about the chain saw incident. Gary and Rodney cleaned up the mess, picking up all of the blue spruce limbs off the lawn and throwing them out into a field.

Afterward, Mike never said anything about it. He didn't say he was just kidding. He didn't say it was a joke. He never even acknowledged that it had occurred.

"And when did the chain saw incident happen?"

"During the summer of 1988," Gary replied. That meant that the witness was twenty-two and the defendant was seventeen. Gary said he saw to it that his parents never found out what happened.

"Let's move forward in time now, Mr. King, to late 2007. Did there come a time when Mike came back to Michigan to visit?"

"Yes, in January of 2008."

"At that time, was Mike acting paranoid?"

"Yes, there was something about wolves in the woods. He thought they were chasing him. Around that time, he also complained that he'd been harassed by an automobile that was trying to run him off the road."

"Mike was no longer a boy, right?"

"Oh, no. He was a man in his thirties."

"And this was at your parents' home, correct?"

"Yes, in a farming community in Michigan."

"Were there times when Mike was nonresponsive?"

"Yes, Mike sat there for eight hours in a trance and didn't move. We would say, 'What's wrong?' And he would say, 'Leave me alone.' I tried to communicate with him, but he sat there like a vegetable. He was in a trance. My girl-friend tried to joke with him, but he didn't laugh or show emotion. His face was white, like a ghost. He was upstairs in bed, in a trance. Eventually he did come downstairs, but he just stood there. I asked him what he was doing, and he said he didn't know."

Gary remembered thinking that Mike was getting worse, that the same head problems he'd had as a kid were still there—only now, they were worse. The same buzzing in his head was there, but now was worse. Gary felt helpless. He didn't know what to do. He couldn't think of a way to help his brother.

"Was he like that all the time, or were these episodes you saw?" Schlemmer inquired.

"Sometimes he was just talking, but he couldn't really hold a conversation because he didn't understand what you were trying to say. He didn't get it."

"Was there a time when [your] brother Mike and your nephew Matt came to live with you?"

"Yes. For a short time, I went to work with Mike to kind of help him out. Everyone loved Mike. He tried to do the best he could."

Carolyn Schlemmer had no further questions.

On cross-examination, Lon Arend asked the witness if there was anything else he thought the jury should know. Gary said there was: another example of how reckless Mike was. He recalled a time when Mike was riding a motorcycle with a throttle wide open—no clue that the smallest bump in the road could have killed him. "He had no concept of danger," Gary said, adding that he believed all of the mental problems and strange behavior was caused by the snowmobile accident. Gary felt bad because the injuries Mike suffered when he was six and a half impacted so negatively upon the rest of his life.

"You said Mike was normal, like society wants you to be. . . ."

"Because he doesn't drink or do drugs. I guess Mike was square in some people's eyes."

"You said earlier that everyone loved Mike. . . ."

"Yes, as a worker, everyone loved him. He didn't make waves. He did the best he could."

"He was a hard worker?"

"We were raised to do our very best."

"You clearly love him."

"Yes."

"And you wouldn't want anything bad to happen to him, right?"

"No, sir."

Arend wanted to know if Mike was a good plumber. Gary said he was, although sometimes Mike would try to go too fast and would make mistakes. He never tried to take advantage of anyone. Others sometimes tried to take advantage of him.

"But you knew him to work and have jobs?"

"Yes, but not very many. He dealt with things from day to day." Gary explained how Mike got himself into financial difficulties. He bought a house and then remortgaged it in order to pay for his wife's education. His wife then left him and he couldn't pay his bills. Regarding Mike's ex-wife, Gary said, "Mike loved her and wanted to be with her, but she was in her own world, with men on the computer."

Arend wondered how Mike managed to get so much credit when he didn't make that much money. Gary explained that creditors adored Mike because he had cars and four-wheelers, and he figured the wife was helping him with all that, the paperwork and the like.

"You're saying she took care of that?"

"Yes."

"You have said that you looked up to your brother Mike. Is that correct?"

"Yes. He was doing what a person was supposed to be doing in society."

"In January 2008, were there any other examples of Mike having hallucinations?"

"Well, I remember he told me how much he loved California and visiting the redwood forest. I had to tell him that he'd never been to California in his life. He said, in this life maybe he hadn't. It might have been a previous life."

"You knew him never to be violent with women?"

"Yes, he would get upset with his ex over playing on the computer and not paying her bills, but never violent. She took the money she was supposed to use to pay the bills and used it to buy new clothes. But Mike remained in love, even after she left. He said he would take her back in a minute—but it didn't work out that way for him."

"Would he get upset because she refused to do any housecleaning?"

"Yeah, but Mike dealt with it. He loved her."

Arend then shifted the subject back to the sledding accident, an incident he clearly believed had been—at the very least—exaggerated. There weren't even medical records to corroborate that it had occurred. Yes, Michael hit at forty to forty-five miles per hour; yes, the doctor said there was nothing they could do but ice it and keep him from sleeping.

"Did they tell you what to do if Mike did slip into a coma?"

"The doctor said in that case bring him back to emergency."

Gary reiterated that Mike's symptoms grew worse, until they peaked in January 2008 "when it was like [a] rubber band in his head snapped."

Regarding the chain saw incident, Arend found it curious that no one called the police; no one tried to get Mike psychiatric help; no one even told the teenager's parents. Again, as was the case with the accident, there was no official paperwork to back up the witness's credibility. The jury just had the brothers' word for it.

"It wasn't that big of a deal. I wasn't worried about him hurting me. I didn't take him to a hospital because I didn't want to get him in trouble," Gary said.

"You say that he was in a trancelike state in January 2008?"

"Right."

"Did you see Mike on January 17, 2008?" Arend asked, referring to the day of the murder.

"No."

"Do you know if he was in a trancelike state on January 17, 2008?"

"No."

"No further questions, Your Honor."

Because of logistical problems, Rodney King, the defendant's youngest brother, testified from Michigan via video.

Rodney, questioned by Carolyn Schlemmer, said he was thirty-six years old, unemployed, and living on disability.

There were a couple of reasons why he was teleconferencing his testimony—he had a few serious health problems, including lung and kidney disease. He couldn't be there because he was on breathing medications, a nebulizer.

He was testifying from his father's house, where he was trying to help out as much as he could, do a little yard work now and again. Dad recently had a triple bypass; and once he recovered from that, he was scheduled for more surgery because he had another blockage.

Today, Rodney was glad to say, was a pretty good day for him. He had three kids—sixteen, fourteen, and eight— and had been married for sixteen years.

He remembered that Mike was held back a grade in school, but wasn't sure if he repeated second or third grade. Rodney's parents held Rodney back at that time as well, because they didn't want the two of them in the same class. They didn't want people making fun of Mike because his little brother caught up with him in school. Mike was held back because he "wasn't getting anywhere" and "didn't understand." Rodney admitted that in junior high, both he and Mike were in special education.

Schlemmer asked if Rodney recalled Mike's sledding accident. Rodney did, because around that same time he had hurt his chin. He and Mike went to the same doctor. Mike's accident was traumatic for Rodney. He remembered how bad it felt wondering if Mike was ever going to wake up.

Rodney explained that he always remembered those events in the order they happened. He got stitches in his chin; then after, Mike got knocked cold. He saw it happen, and it really affected him badly. The three brothers were having fun: Gary driving the snowmobile; he and Mike taking turns on the sled being dragged around in the snow. Mike could hold on better than Rodney, so Gary drove faster with Mike on the sled. When the accident happened, Rodney was standing in the snow, waiting his turn. Then Mike's head hit the shed and "that stopped him in his tracks." How fast was the snowmobile going? "Eighty-nine miles per hour," Rodney guessed. Nobody really knew. The snowmobile had no speedometer. There was so much blood coming from Mike's mouth, where his teeth were mangled, that they didn't even know at first that he had a serious nose-bleed as well. Rodney approached tentatively, in shock. Gary took charge and tried to wake Mike up. Rodney was too scared to think. Gary picked up Mike and carried him into the house, where they told their mom what had happened. Rodney didn't recall his dad being there. Dad came in a few minutes later, and it was then that they began to put ice on Mike's swelling head. Frozen hamburger and chops were used to slow the swelling. Dad said it was time to go to the hospital, so they all piled into their "Brady Bunch station wagon," the one with the wood-grain panels on the sides. Rodney recalled that at first the roads were bumpy. Then they were on a main road and went to a doctor, the same one who put stitches in his chin. After that, Rodney wasn't sure what had happened. He got stuck in the waiting room. The next thing he remembered, they were on their way home. His mom was saying that they had to keep Mike up and continue icing his head. Mom said they had to check on Mike every twenty minutes, half hour, to make sure he was awake. After that, Mike had regular nosebleeds. Real gushers, too. He'd be fine, and then, in a snap, blood would pour out for no reason. Mike would have to lie on his back with a bloody washcloth on his face.

"Did Mike like to go to doctors?"

"No, he hated it. He was always too scared."

Once they took Mike to the family doctor, where they wanted to take a blood sample to perhaps help determine why Mike was getting the nosebleeds. Mike saw the needle and ran right out of the office, got in the backseat of the family station wagon, and refused to come out—so the tests were never done.

But Mike did go to dentists. Rodney was the scaredy-cat when it came to dentists. Mike had to have his wisdom teeth out, and he took it bravely.

"When Mike was growing up, did he ever exhibit any bizarre behavior?"

Rodney recalled the days when Mike and he rode their bikes through a stretch of woods, as a shortcut, on their way to and from school. One day, Mike refused to go that way. He was too scared—claimed there was a witch after them. He would act weird sometimes.

Once, Mike showed him a pair of trees next to each other. Mike would point up there and say that was the spot where the witches hung up their victims, and that was what was going to happen to them if they kept taking the short-cut. One time, he took his rifle, and made Rodney bring a BB gun, and they went in the woods to shoot the witches. Mike, Rodney testified, told him never to tell their parents about the witches or they would be in trouble. Eventually, it seemed to Rodney, they just forgot about the witches and continued to ride their bikes through the shortcut.

Sure, Mike complained of buzzing in his head. He always related it back to the accident. But his brothers never thought it was an issue. His head was constantly buzzing for no reason. They didn't know it was bothering him that bad.

Rodney gave his version of the chain saw incident. He re-membered the cover-up as clearly as the event. They made desperate attempts to air out the house so it wouldn't stink of chain saw smoke when their parents got home. He'd lopped off a bunch of tree branches out by the garage, and those had to be hidden as well. Gary and Rodney did the cleaning up. They kept waiting for Mike to say he was just joking, but that never happened. In fact, Mike never even knew what was going on. Rodney had thought about the chain saw incident a lot in the years since it occurred, but it still made no sense to him. Mike suffered from memory loss. You couldn't automatically assume that he was going to remember something he should remember.

Rodney gave the jury his version of the bow-and-arrow incident. That happened sometime in the 1980s. They had a big bow, and the arrows had rubber tips. Mike would shoot the arrows at Rodney. Sometimes he would "get brave" and take the rubber tips off before shooting the arrows at his little brother.

"Did he hit you?"

"Yes."

"How did that feel?"

"It stung!"

Then came the day Mike went into Gary's room, and came out with a real arrow, like the kind you could kill a deer with. Mike shot the arrow at him. Rodney managed to duck behind a door. Mike had fired the arrow so hard, it went through the door. Later, when their dad came home, Rodney told him Mike caused the hole by firing a real arrow and it "accidentally went through the door."

At times, Carolyn Schlemmer had to steer Rodney through his testimony.

"Did Mike do other things that were strange?"

"He used to act out cartoons—'Say your prayers, rabbit.' Uh, I got sidetracked."

"Did Mike do strange things throughout his life?"

"Yeah."

"Any other things you could tell us about?" the defense attorney asked patiently.

"I'm trying to think more."

"I can direct you. Let me direct you to late 2007. Was Mike up in Michigan?"

"Yeah, Mike was in Michigan, at my mom and dad's house, and I went over there one time to visit." That was when Mike was in some kind of trance, lying in a reclining chair, just staring, not understanding. Rodney couldn't even tell if Mike knew who he was, or even knew anybody was there.

"My wife went right up to him and snapped her fingers in his face."

Rodney had been told that Mike had been like that all day. It started with a fit of paranoia: Mike claimed that there were wolves in the woods, and they'd been chasing him. Next Rodney brought up the sledding accident, noting that Mike had never been right after that. Now, all those many years later, he was "in outer space."

"Do you know anything about Mike's breakup with his ex-wife?"

"I know she was always on the Internet talking to other guys."

"Did his wife leaving him have an effect on Mike?"

"Yeah, of course. I have been married sixteen years. When you have kids, you want to stay together and live as a family. That's the way I look at it."

Rodney told the jury that there had come a time when Mike wanted to put together a résumé that he hoped would lead to him getting better jobs as a plumber. But he had struggled. He was not very good at reading and writing, so his brother decided to help him. They tried to list past jobs and the dates of those jobs, but it wasn't easy. Mike didn't remember nearly as much as you'd think he would. The brothers couldn't help, because he'd lived in Florida and they had no idea what he'd done while down there. Their dad helped him a lot with the résumé, helping him put the dates together.

The witness suddenly hit upon a new strain of testimony. He recalled that there was always a problem with Mike and directions. That was a good indication that there was something wrong with his brain. You couldn't just give him directions to a place. You had to give him directions on how to get back as well, or he'd get antsy. Heaven forbid you should give him two roads to choose from. Sometimes you could take two routes from one place to another, because it was six of this and a half-dozen of the other. Mike, however, would get scared and think something bad was going to happen to him if he chose the wrong road. You could explain to him again and again that there was no wrong road, but he wouldn't listen. Sometimes he wouldn't go to a place at all because he was confused about the directions, so he'd end up staying where he was. This was the biggest handicap for Mike in terms of trying to find work, Rodney thought. His suspicion was that Mike sometimes didn't show up for job interviews because he was petrified of getting lost.

Carolyn Schlemmer knew this registered with the jurors. Earlier they had heard Robert Salvador say that giving King directions to the firing range hadn't worked, and King was only willing to follow Salvador there. That tended to corroborate Rodney's testimony.

When Mike showed up in Michigan after years in Florida, Rodney was under the impression that he'd already lost his house down there. Later, he found out that Mike still had the house but had lost the furniture. Rodney admitted that he wasn't sure when that was, when Mike had returned to Michigan.

On the witness stand, Rodney King was beginning to lose momentum. "I'm having trouble with my short-term memory," he said, an out-of-the-blue admission that could not have pleased Schlemmer. He did recall that Mike had to return to Florida. Mike had to declare bankruptcy, and their dad took Mike to a lawyer for advice.

When was the last time Rodney talked to Mike before Mike's arrest? That was around New Year's Day, 2008. The brothers got together. Rodney brought a six-pack of beer, but no one drank. He talked to him once after Mike returned to Florida. He was trying to get his electricity turned back on down there, and he was living by flashlight.

"No further questions," Schlemmer said.

On cross, Lon Arend took the witness back to the time when he and Mike were little and each had an accident that required a visit to the same doctor. How had Rodney injured his chin? Fell out of a bunk bed.

"When Mike said there were witches in the woods, did you believe that he was saying those things because of the aftereffect of his sledding accident?"

"To me, it didn't make sense. I didn't know the reason behind it."

"Do you believe it was a result of brain damage, or was it just children pretending?"

"I believe the accident was why Mike acted differently."

"According to the testimony you just gave, the witches were a result of his accident?"

"Yes."

"And you believe the *Texas Chain Saw Massacre* incident was a result of his injuries?"

"Yeah, I do believe that. I believe it goes back to that."

"When Mike was in a trance in December of 2007 or January of 2008, and your wife snapped her fingers in

Mike's face, you believe that behavior was a result of his sledding accident?"

"Yes, his eyes were bugging out. It seemed like a lingering head injury."

"When Mike was worried about getting lost on the roads of Michigan, you attribute that anxiety to his sledding accident?"

"Well, he could never take directions. He never stopped asking directions. All those years later, why was he still acting that way? Had to be the accident."

"You agree that you yourself do not have a good memory—"

"I have a short-term memory problem. I have trouble remembering dates. I have lung disease, and that affects it, too." His long-term memory was fine. Things that happened long ago he recalled pretty well.

"You don't have trouble remembering the chain saw incident?"

"Right."

"Do you recall on February 5, 2008, a detective came to visit you in Michigan?"

Rodney did remember. Yes, he answered questions about the sledding accident. Yes, he told them he thought the snowmobile was going ninety miles per hour. Maybe it seemed faster then than it would today. Today he would revise his estimate of the speed: eighty miles per hour. The pole Mike hit was "like a telephone pole." Rodney had previously called the object Mike hit a "shed." The defense smoothed out the seeming discrepancy by suggesting the pole was at the corner of the shed.

"Do you remember telling the detective on February fifth that you didn't remember whether or not Mike was bleeding?"

"I don't. That would be short-term memory."

"Do you, in fact, remember Mike bleeding after the accident?"

"I remember it had something to do with his teeth."

"You don't remember telling the detective you don't remember?"

"No. I was on medicine at the time."

"This was three weeks after Mike's arrest. You knew it was a serious situation?"

"I thought maybe they had the wrong person. My brother wouldn't do that. I remember that the police from Florida were not nice."

Arend produced a transcript of the February 5 interview. In it, Rodney didn't recall the bleeding. He remembered Gary carrying Mike inside and putting a frozen pork chop on his head. During that same interview, he said he didn't recall if Mike was taken to see a doctor after the accident.

The jury had the idea. Arend moved on.

"When you boys were growing up, your mom and dad were good parents?"

"Yes."

"No abuse?"

"No."

No, Rodney had never seen Mike get violent. Never saw him yell or scream or hit anybody. No fights when they were kids. Oh, sure, they would wrestle around, goofing around, like brothers do, but no real fights. Maybe during a previous interview, he had referred to his brother "going off," but he didn't know what he meant by that. His answer to the question here today was that Mike was never violent, not that he knew of.

During that February 2008 interview with police, Rodney was asked if he'd seen any changes in Mike after the sledding accident. He'd said Mike was prone to exaggeration, couldn't tell the truth about the size of the fish he'd caught, always making things seem more dramatic. There was a time when they were little when Mike and their dad went into the woods. Mike carried a cork gun. Came back saying he got a rabbit with the cork gun. "Today, he still believes that. Ever since his accident, he believes all that stuff. Your imagination believes anything's possible."

In 2008, Rodney mentioned nothing about the buzzing in Mike's head. Now he said there was buzzing just weeks before Mike was arrested. How did the witness explain the discrepancy?

"I was in a hurry with their questions," Rodney said. "I couldn't think at the time."

The witness was showing signs of mental fatigue as he tried to field Arend's increasingly rapid-fire questioning. He hadn't told the cops about the witches Mike claimed were in the woods; now he did tell that story. How come now, but not then?

"I'm getting sidetracked," Rodney said again.

"I'm looking at the overall picture of Mike's history from birth to now," Arend said.

"I think I'm lost. It could be my short-term memory," Rodney said. Arend knew he scored a point with the jury each time the increasingly confused witness talked about his poor memory and faulty answers due to "taking medicine." The jury was getting the point. This guy wasn't sure what happened yesterday, much less the year before, or thirty years before.

"Did you tell the police in 2008 about the chain saw incident?"

"I believe not. It was hard to sum up Mike's entire life in one hour. This was a shock to me, and nothing made sense."

"Did you tell police in 2008 about Mike being in a trance and your wife snapping her fingers in his face?"

Rodney didn't remember, but suspected he hadn't—or Arend wouldn't have asked that question. No, he hadn't told them about the wolves, either. But that didn't mean Mike wasn't in another world. His brain was like a computer that crashed. No, he didn't mention to the police that Mike always got lost when driving.

That concluded Arend's cross-examination.

On redirect, Carolyn Schlemmer did her best to rehabilitate the witness, a tough task considering Rodney's inclusion of his own mental problems.

"Mr. King, back in 2008, did detectives sit down with you for hours and discuss every detail of Mike's life?"

"No, they didn't give me a chance to talk. I tried to explain, but they told me to keep my answers short and sweet."

The 2008 interview was further complicated when, in the middle, the batteries in the detectives' tape recorder went dead. Rodney's son was running back and forth looking for fresh batteries to put in the machine. Rodney repeated that he was sick at the time, on meds, and they told him that it didn't matter if he left things out. There would be a chance to tell the story in greater detail later. So stuff was left out. Plus, just because he recalled things now, that didn't mean he recalled them then. "They caught me on the spot," Rodney said. His mom called, complaining that the police had been there, too, harassing her, being mean, asking if Mike was gay. The cops had been mean when he talked to them as well, and some of the questions were rough. Rodney had been embarrassed because the cops asked these things in front of his kids. "If they wanted me to tell them everything I knew about my brother, then they should have given me more time!"

"Thank you, Mr. King," Schlemmer said.

Judge Economou called for the lunch break.

When court reconvened that afternoon, Rodney was gone. On the TV screen was seventy-year-old James King, the defendant's dad. He told the jury his wife was named Patsy and that he had four sons, James Jr. (Jim), Gary, Michael, and Rodney.

"Are you sure that you are okay to testify?" Carolyn Schlemmer asked.

"Yes, I'm fine," James said. Then he explained that he couldn't be in court in person because he'd recently undergone open-heart surgery—triple bypass.

"Was Mike at all sick when he was a young child?"

Yes, the father said. When Mike was eighteen months old, he came down with double pneumonia and needed to be hospitalized for "quite some time." He recalled Mike's sledding accident very well. He'd heard a commotion on the farm and saw Mike being carried up to the house. The lower half of his face was covered with blood, and there was a huge knot on his head. He remembered very well trying to clean the boy's face off, but there was blood all over the place. Then he put ice cubes on Mike's head. They took him to the doctor, who said Mike's teeth should eventually be okay, because he still had his baby teeth, but the head injury might be serious. Mike had to be watched closely, and his mom sat up all night with him. After that, in school, Mike was slow. He was in special ed because of a learning disability. Yes, he had nosebleeds—so bad, they took him to the doctor once, but Mike ran out of the office.

James recalled asking the doctor what to do, and the doctor said to bring him back another time.

Switching to Mike's adulthood, his father remembered him getting a divorce, after which Mike and son Matt moved to Florida, where James had a house and a trailer. They could live with them down there, Matt could go to school, and they could get Mike a local plumbing job. James remembered Mike having his problems in Florida, breaking up with his girlfriend and moving back to Michigan, where he couldn't find work. He tried everywhere. Even Burger King wouldn't hire him. Matt stayed with his uncle Jim and aunt Carrie, and Mike returned to Florida.

During Lon Arend's concise cross-examination, James admitted to being biased. After all, Mike was his third son, and he loved him very much.

"Would it be fair to say that you can't believe he did what he's been convicted of doing?"

"No, I can't."

The witness was dismissed, the TV turned off, and the defense rested.

The jury was ordered out of the courtroom so Judge Economou could talk to the defendant outside their earshot. The judge explained that there were certain decisions in a trial that the defendant had to make for himself. He'd not wanted to testify during the guilt phase, but now had to decide again if he was going to testify during the penalty phase. The defendant said he'd discussed the matter with his counsel and would not be testifying this time, either. The jury was brought back in, and the state announced it had about an hour's worth of rebuttal testimony.

* * *

The state called Dr. Michael P. Gamache. He was a forensic psychologist who had a doctorate in clinical psychology from the University of Missouri, and was a professor at the University of South Florida. His job, he said, was to interface between mental-health issues and the law. He'd been the recipient of federally funded grants to do research involving serial murders, lust murders, and the treatment of sex offenders within a community. He'd been a licensed psychologist in Florida for a quarter of a century. Although he had a private practice, he was routinely hired to evaluate accused criminals and was a courtroom veteran. He'd worked for both the state and for defense attorneys. In this case, he'd twice examined Michael King, first on April 2, 2009, and then again on August 31, 2009.

"Did you also receive documents to review [for] this case?" Lon Arend asked.

"Yes, I got five volumes of documents," Dr. Gamache replied. These included handwritten correspondence between the defendant and his family and friends. There were also school, work, criminal, driving, and police reports. Dr. Gamache had been a spectator in the courtroom during the entire penalty phase of the trial and had witnessed the testimony of Dr. Joseph Wu. He'd also had a private conversation with Dr. Wu.

Dr. Gamache wasn't a big believer in PET scans as indicators of behavioral problems, and preferred his own method: two tests that could better determine the existence and extent of neuropsychological problems. Yes, he'd administered both tests to the defendant. One was completely nonverbal. The subject was shown a picture in which something was missing, then two other pictures—one of which logically completed the first picture. The subject had to choose which one it was. The test divided subjects into three categories: healthy people, those with brain damage, and those who were faking brain damage. The second test, which also screened malingerers, was verbal. During one portion of that test, the defendant was given a list of words and had to determine which two were similar. The tests put King in the last category—the results of the tests were invalid because he was not trying as hard as he could.

Dr. Gamache said, "Mr. King's test results were not an accurate reflection of his abilities. I believe his true abilities are superior to his performance when I tested him." Why would someone take these tests but not give full effort? There were three possible reasons: 1) He was deliberately attempting to do poorly. 2) He was not motivated to do well. 3) He was distracted.

The witness had also given King an IQ test. He scored a seventy-six. King had received two other IQ tests in his life, scoring eighty-five in 1979 and eighty-two in 1984. All three tests were given after the defendant's sledding accident and were similar. It was Dr. Gamache's opinion that King's IQ was, and had been for most of his life, in the low-average range. Average was one hundred. About 95 percent of subjects would score somewhere between seventy and 130. Those who scored below that range were considered mentally retarded; those who scored higher were considered intellectually superior. With King, there was no evidence of mental retardation, and his IQ put him in a potentially functional range. Many subjects with similar IQ scores were "street-smart," held down jobs, married, and raised children.

In addition to his belief that the PET scans as interpreted by Dr. Wu were a misapplication of technology, the witness had another bone to pick with Dr. Wu.

"Paranoia is not a symptom of frontal-lobe damage," he said.

Difficulty in controlling impulses, yes; difficulty in mood regulation, yes; paranoia, no. Bottom line, it was Dr. Gamache's opinion that Michael King's ability to conform to the law was not impaired. From a psychological point of view, the defendant was fully responsible for his own actions.

Carolyn Schlemmer began her cross-examination by chipping away at the doctor's credibility. No, he wasn't a psychiatrist. No, he wasn't a medical doctor. Board certified as a psychologist? No. He didn't create or interpret PET scans. Lon Arend had hired him.

And why was Michael King distracted during Dr. Gamache's tests? Could it be because they were administered on the same day that the defendant was found guilty of capital murder? A little thing like being found guilty of murder could distract a person, couldn't it?

Dr. Gamache reiterated that the test he'd administered on the day of King's conviction had been the one he'd found to be invalid, and distraction was one of the possible reasons why.

The witness had testified that he'd looked at volumes of documentation before passing judgment on King. Now he admitted that every single sheet of those documents had been supplied to him by the prosecution.

"Would you agree that inappropriate aggression and sexual behavior can be signs of brain damage?"

"Yes."

"My last question," Schlemmer said. "How much are you getting paid?"

"Two hundred fifty dollars an hour."

"You're charging Mr. Arend two hundred fifty dollars an hour for this entire week?"

"Yes."

Dr. Michael Gamache was allowed to leave the witness stand, and Detective Christopher Morales, who had already testified during the guilt phase of the trial, now returned.

"Detective Morales," Lon Arend said, "how much time did you spend with the defendant on January 17, 2008?"

"Nine hours."

"During those nine hours, was the defendant lucid?"

"Yes."

"No further questions."

On cross, Carolyn Schlemmer asked if Detective Morales had ever had any dealings with Michael King before this case. The witness said there had been a civil dispute in 2003 that resulted in no charges being filed. Was it true that the witness monitored King's phone calls while he was in jail following his arrest in this case? The detective said it was.

"Were there indications of paranoia on any of those tapes?"

The witness said that wasn't his call. He was a cop, not a shrink. But he could describe what he had heard. The defendant was kept on the fourth floor of the jail, in Cell A, which was suicide watch. He'd called one of his brothers and had told him about a conspiracy theory he had: "They were out to get him, and that he feared he was to be raped and murdered by his jailers. He asked his brother to call 911 from Michigan and to get him out of jail."

Schlemmer allowed the jury members, who weren't

shrinks any more than the detective, to make up their own minds as to whether King was paranoid. That concluded Detective Morales's testimony, and the presentation of evidence. As it was past three in the afternoon, Judge Economou dismissed the jury for the evening. He ordered everyone back the next morning for closing arguments and deliberation.

With the jury gone, Carolyn Schlemmer objected to four of the state's aggravating factors. Firstly she claimed that because the defendant had already been convicted, the second trial represented double jeopardy. The prosecution had also argued that the motive in this case was cold-blooded, a simple case of witness elimination, but Schlemmer said there was no evidence backing that up. They had no idea what the motive was. There was no tape of the defendant saying anything to the effect of "Well, I guess I'll have to kill you now." The prosecution's theory was merely surmise, and the cold-bloodedness of the murder should not be an aggravating factor.

When asking for the death penalty, unless the victim was a cop, the state had to prove motive, Schlemmer argued. She said there was not even evidence that the murder was premeditated. A plan to murder, on King's part, could not be inferred from his plans to commit another felony.

Lastly she objected to the aggravating factor that the murder of Denise Lee was "atrocious and cruel." Again—no evidence. There was no testimony substantiating pain endured. They didn't even know if the victim was conscious when she was killed. As a matter of law, gunshot wounds were not considered cruel. That aggravating factor was usually reserved for cases in which there was evidence of torture, and there was no such evidence here. Even if the victim was conscious, there was no evidence of cruelty. There was evidence that there was duct tape over the victim's eyes—in which case, she might not even have known the gunshot was coming.

Schlemmer could see and hear that spectators were horribly revolted by her argument, and she apologized for upsetting people, adding that she was speaking merely of aspects of the law.

Judge Deno Economou quickly overruled all of Schlemmer's exceptions, stating that the prosecution had presented evidence demonstrating that, before her murder, Denise was kidnapped and confined—*which in itself was cruel.* He also stated that the borrowing of the shovel while the victim was alive, and the fact that the victim was found buried, was evidence of premeditation.

CHAPTER 23

SEPTEMBER 4, 2009

A cogent Lon Arend told the jury that the defense had tried to *distract* them from the facts of this case. They'd seen pictures of Michael King's childhood, met members of his family who loved him. It was all a diversion. The only thing the jury should focus on when making their decision—life or death—was what the defendant did to Denise Lee.

"Think about the *way* he ended her life," Arend said.

The jury's job was to weigh the mitigators against the aggravators; so each time the defense talked about a mitigating factor, they should weigh that against the evidence they had heard about just what a horrible, premeditated, and cruel crime this was.

Michael King had had the opportunity to let Denise go, right up until the moment he pulled the trigger. There was only one reason why he made the decision he did. He did not want her testifying against him for the kidnapping and rape he had already committed. Nothing could be colder than that.

Arend understood how brave the jury would need to be—condemning a man to death was a very heavy thing. But they were there to answer the question of punishment, and there was only one punishment that fit the crime: death. Even if one assumed that *all* of the defense's mitigating factors were true, hardly a given, they didn't come close to outweighing the aggravators.

And were the mitigating factors true? The defense would argue that the defendant had a brain injury and lost his ability to resist impulses. Okay, how did that fit in with what they knew? Truth was, the murder wasn't impulsive at all. It was cold-blooded. They shouldn't forget that shovel he borrowed. With Denise Lee in his car, alive and surreptitiously on the phone, the defendant already knew how this would end.

They said he had a low IQ, that he was a good worker, boyfriend, and father. How much weight should the jurors give that? It was up to them.

The defense would argue that the death penalty was not necessary because the defendant was a model prisoner and had presented no disciplinary problems. Well, sure, he was in solitary confinement. How much opportunity did he actually have to break jail rules? How much weight to give that? Up to them.

He asked them to think about the testimony of Jane Kowalski, who'd heard the victim scream. It was not a light scream, but rather a scream like she had never heard before.

The defense would argue that evidence suggested Denise was blindfolded with duct tape when she was shot, that she didn't see the gun; therefore, the crime was not cruel. But that ignored the fact that her eye was missing, exploded from her head, an impossibility if there was duct tape over her eyes.

Everything they knew about Michael King on the day of the murder indicated that stress had nothing to do with it. He'd been calm and acted normally at the gun range. His girlfriend at the time spoke to him on the phone *during the abduction:* calm and normal. They heard him on that horrible, horrible 911 tape. Calm and normal. Just mean.

The defense would have them believe that the defendant was incapable of following laws; yet, he had successfully followed the law his entire life. He didn't even have a reputation for losing his temper. His ex-girlfriend testified that she hit him during arguments, but he wouldn't hit her back.

There were contradictions in the defense's argument that he wanted the jury to consider. On one hand, they said, he couldn't follow rules. On the other, he was a perfect prisoner. Which was it?

The prosecutor suggested the defendant's so-called history of violent behavior was largely a construct of the defense. Jim King, the defendant's older brother, testified that he'd heard about the sledding accident but never had a reason to give it much thought. He hadn't even heard about the chain saw and bow-and-arrow incidents until a couple of weeks ago.

Dr. Joseph Wu's fancy photos of the defendant's brain supposedly indicated brain damage—but there was no corroborating medical evidence. None of the doctors who examined the defendant diagnosed brain damage. The only corroboration came from the statements of the defendant's family regarding what they claimed was bizarre behavior.

The family didn't want to believe that Mike really did what he did—so they desperately scanned past incidents searching for something, *anything,* that might explain the unexplainable. And they settled on this sledding accident. The snowmobile was going ninety—no, eighty miles per hour! If a six-year-old's head hit something as solid as a pole or a shed at even forty miles per hour, he might have been decapitated. Arend wasn't suggesting that the family was lying, just that they were justifying, using hyperbole to soothe themselves, to lend sense to the nonsensical.

How tenuous was the connection between the sledding accident and the murder of Denise Lee? There were thirty-seven years separating the two events, years during which the defendant had a job, a family, and a home. Since the murder, he'd been a model prisoner. The *only time* he demonstrated poor impulse control was on January 17, 2008.

The defendant's IQ didn't set him apart. His PET scans didn't distinguish him from the masses. The only thing that distinguished Michael King on that day was that he kidnapped, raped, and murdered Denise Lee.

Arend recommended that the jury listen to the victim's 911 tape one more time during their deliberation. He suggested that was all they were going to need to know when deciding what punishment King deserved.

Carolyn Schlemmer told the jury that they were *never* required to recommend a death sentence. Even if they found that the aggravating factors outweighed the mitigators, they still didn't *have* to recommend death. Even if *all* of the factors were aggravating and *none* mitigating, they could *still refuse* to send the man to his death.

She understood the emotions the jurors were feeling: anger and sadness. It was perfectly natural after learning of the loss of Denise Lee. But the law said they could *not* recommend death based on anger; they could *not* recommend death based on sympathy for the victim. Emotions, the law said, could have *nothing to do with it.*

She asked the jurors to take a deep breath and base their decision on the evidence. A punishment of life in prison without parole did not diminish Michael King's responsibility for the crime. It did not diminish the value of the life that was lost on that tragic day.

Schlemmer argued that the first aggravating factor—that King murdered the victim in the course of committing a felony—was inherent in their guilty verdict. To consider it again represented double jeopardy.

She argued that the aggravating factor—that the murder was especially heinous or cruel—had *not* been proven beyond a reasonable doubt. She firmly disagreed with Lon Arend on this point. From the time King pulled his Camaro onto Toledo Blade to get away from Jane Kowalski until the time he was arrested hours later, *no one knew for sure what had happened.*

It was the medical examiner who had suggested that the victim's eyes might have been covered with duct tape, that the killer might have been standing either on the side or behind the victim when she was shot. These were things they should consider when weighing the heinousness and cruelty of the murder.

Schlemmer reminded the jurors that *nothing* the defendant did after the murder weighed on the question before them. She suggested that King's IQ was so low that premeditating a murder and eliminating a witness were concepts that were beyond him.

She shifted from hammering away at the aggravators to promoting the mitigators, and she referred to the defendant by his given name. Mitigating factors, unlike aggravating factors, *did not* need to be proven beyond a reasonable doubt.

They had seen and heard Mike's family describe his head injury. They could decide for themselves if Mike's dad and brothers were lying. Dr. Joseph Wu's PET scans scientifically corroborated that eyewitness evidence. Dr. Wu said symptoms could wax and wane, and witnesses agreed that the buzzing in Mike's head came and went. Everyone who described Mike's inappropriate behavior said it came and went.

She had one comment about the prosecution's rebuttal witness, Detective Christopher Morales. He was more cooperative with the prosecution than with the defense, so the jury shouldn't think they were getting fair and balanced testimony. When the prosecution asked the detective if Mike was lucid, he enthusiastically said yes. When the defense asked if Mike was paranoid, he said he couldn't answer because he wasn't an expert. He was an expert in lucidity and not paranoia, it seemed.

Dr. Gamache, who administered an IQ test to Mike the day after his conviction, said he found the results invalid, but he used those results to attack the PET scan evidence, anyway.

All of those professional experts testifying on behalf of the prosecution were being paid very, very well for their testimony—another thing that had to be weighed when determining their credibility.

Mike had been depressed during the weeks leading up to the murder, acting very strangely—and there were a lot of real factors in his life that explained that depression. Here was a man whose life should be spared—this good father, good boyfriend, this good prisoner.

Lon Arend would have them believe that there was something sinister afoot with the family's description of Mike's head injury. That was bull. The sledding accident *happened*. Everyone agreed it happened in more or less the same way. That wasn't any less true if the brothers, who were children at the time, overestimated the speed of the snowmobile when Mike's head impacted the pole. They all agreed that he received medical treatment and there was nothing doctors could do—which would have been exactly what doctors would have said if the diagnosis was a severe concussion.

It was *so important* that the jury look at the totality of Mike's life: a good person, but with academic difficulties, such a good father that he got custody in the divorce, law-abiding, no trouble, no drugs or alcohol. His life was spiraling down, down, down. He was suffering losses—his wife left him twice for a chat room Romeo. Depression, peculiarity. The prosecutor wanted them to think Mike's lack of violent behavior before January 17, 2008, was a contradiction when it was merely *context.*

The jurors did not have to limit their deliberations to the examples she was giving them. If they remembered something from the trial, any little point, that made them think executing this man was wrong, they should listen to that voice.

It was easy to concentrate solely on the terrible pulling of that trigger and the ending of a wonderful life, and it was easy to say that this was a case that was "crying out" for the death penalty. But that was only true when taking the horrible event out of the context of Mike King's entire life.

"I submit to you it is hard to do," Schlemmer said. "You must set aside the enormity, the sympathy, the anger—and look at the totality." To do anything else would be to make a terrible, terrible mistake. No one was asking them to excuse Mike King for the thing he did. They should not underestimate the severity of the punishment that was life in prison without chance of parole. Mike King would lose everything, his family, his son, his freedom—and he would lose those things forever, for he would *die in prison.*

Carolyn Schlemmer said that she had confidence in this jury, that it was comprised of levelheaded men and women who would not do anything rash. They would take a breath and weigh everything. This was nowhere near to being the most egregious case. She begged them to choose life in prison.

"He will die in prison," she repeated.

She thanked them for their time and attention; then she sat down.

After a twenty-minute break, Judge Deno Economou gave the jury its instructions. He explained that, technically, he was the one who decided the defendant's punishment. What they were working on was their recommendation, an "advisory sentence." They shouldn't take the matter lightly, however, as he promised to give their recommendation "great weight."

The jury was to decide, in essence, if the defendant's crimes were especially heinous, shocking, or cruel. Were the crimes cold and calculated?

On the other side, they were to consider whether Mike King could appreciate the gravity and quality of his actions when he was committing his crimes.

Was his ability to distinguish right from wrong impaired? Was his life worth sparing?

How much weight they gave to each piece of evidence was completely up to them. *They were the judges* when it came to the honesty and straightforwardness of each witness. Were some witnesses testifying because they had a personal interest in the outcome of this case?

They were to infer nothing from the defendant not

testifying on his own behalf. If they felt aggravators out-weighed mitigators, they could, if they chose, recommend death. They were not required to decide on death, no matter how they felt about the weight of the evidence. The vote did not need to be unanimous.

Any questions before deliberation began? Yes, the foreperson responded. Could the whiteboard be moved into the jury room? No problem, Judge Economou said, and deliberation began.

A half hour later, the jury had another question. Could a juror vote for death even if he or she didn't agree with all four of the aggravators? Judge Economou wasn't allowed to answer that one and responded merely that the answer was in the instructions he'd already given them. They were the jury; they decided what to do.

After three hours of deliberation on Friday, September 4, the jury sent a message to Judge Economou that it had reached a decision. At 2:41 P.M., Michael King was brought into the courtroom. A minute later, the jury filed in.

North Port police chief Terry Lewis, a spectator in the courtroom, quickly crossed himself and then held his head in his hands in silent prayer. Nate Lee was also praying. He sat between his parents, who locked their arms behind his chair. Rick Goff wore a cross and held his wife's hand.

Absent from the courtroom were any King supporters, including members of his family.

The jury unanimously recommended the death penalty.

The judge thanked the jury for doing its civic duty: "For three weeks, you have given a part of yourselves to this process."

Judge Economou said that sometime in the next two

months, he would announce his verdict. Economou said he "rarely" went against a jury's wishes, but he would give everything the once-over before confirming the recommendation for death.

The judge reminded the jury that no one could force a juror to talk. If any of them wanted to, they could slip out of the courtroom and remain forever silent and anonymous. On the other hand, if they wanted to speak with the media, they had that right as well. No one could force them to be quiet. It was their decision, and their decision alone. The judge repeated that at some point in the future, not then and there, he would announce the date for sentencing. He offered the jury his profound thanks, adding that the system wouldn't work without citizens who were willing to make the sacrifice.

The panel of twelve peers was discharged.

Hearing the verdict, the members of the Lee and Goff families cried and smiled, sometimes at the same time. Chief Lewis hugged Nate Lee, Rick Goff, and other family members. Nate was struggling. He still looked to be in shock.

"Mr. King, you are remanded to the Sarasota County Jail," the judge said. The defendant looked less catatonic than he had during the bulk of the proceedings. In fact, he appeared angry.

Six bailiffs surrounded Michael King, who was handcuffed, wrists behind his back, and escorted him out.

Right up until the very end of the trial, Amanda Goff, Denise's twenty-year-old sister, continued to take notes for the college paper she had promised to write, in exchange for permission to attend the trial and miss school. The deal with her teachers had changed since the trial began, however. The original agreement had been that she would write a paper about every detail of the trial and case. However, when members of the North Port Police Department, as well as representatives of victims' advocate groups, heard about the arrangement, they contacted Amanda's teachers. They stated that, because of the nature of the case, they didn't think it would be good for Amanda's well-being to write such a paper. So a compromise was made, and the young woman's teachers agreed that she should write her paper about just the trial procedures, leaving out the obviously upsetting details of the case. Her new focus was on the testimony of doctors and mental-health experts on either side.

King's defense team—Carolyn Schlemmer, John Scotese, and Jerry Meisner—announced that there would be an appeal, hardly a surprise since an appeal was mandatory in Florida for capital murder cases. They then quickly left the courtroom, leaving the winning side alone. Lon Arend, Suzanne O'Donnell, and Karen Fraivillig hugged Denise Lee's family, friends, and members of the law enforcement community. Fraivillig gave Nate Lee a big squeeze and looked into his eyes.

Outside the courtroom, Chief Lewis expressed surprise that the jury had recommended the death penalty following a unanimous vote. "I expected ten to two, or eleven to one, but twelve to zero speaks volumes about the quality of the prosecution. It was a group effort on behalf of many community agencies in our area."

Because Denise was the daughter of a cop, law enforcement was well represented in the spectator section of the courtroom throughout the trial. Chief Lewis, as well as four members of the North Port Police Department, had been in the courtroom for every day of the trial.

Rick Goff told a reporter, "Denise took another piece of trash off the street. She put him where he belongs. I'm sorry for King's son's loss, but we are without Denise, and her boys are without their mother."

Nate Lee added that justice had been served. "I'm sick of going to court and hearing all of the horrific evidence. I want to move on and spend time with the boys." During the penalty phase of the trial, he had sensed his wife holding his hand and giving him strength. "And she was with me today, I know she was," he said.

Nate Lee's mother, Marguerite, better known as Peggy, said she understood why the jury had voted unanimously for the death penalty. It wasn't just "because of who King was, but because Denise was so wonderful."

The jurors, of course, were under no obligation to speak to the press, but neither were they forbidden to do so, and one juror, Marcia K. Burns, said that Denise Lee was an amazing woman to have the presence of mind, in the face of knowing what was going to happen to her, to leave enough evidence to allow them to convict her murderer. She didn't think the average person would have been able to do that, and she hoped that Denise's family felt pride in addition to their heartache.

Another juror explained that the vote for death had not been unanimous at first. It was eleven to one. One person had a problem with the wording of something. Once that was cleared up, it was twelve to zero. Despite the horror of it, they relistened to the victim's 911 tape. The killer could be heard saying something to the effect of "I was going to let you go, but . . ." The statement seemed to define "heinous" and "cruel."

It was going to feel good rejoining society after three weeks of living in a bubble and watching only the NFL channel on TV, a channel where they could be certain they wouldn't inadvertently hear any real news.

The hardest part was to delay deliberation until the trial was over. The jurors were stuck together for hours at a time, and the only thing they had in common was the case—the very thing they were not allowed to discuss. It seemed like they spent most of their time sitting together in silence, doing their best to ignore the four-hundred-pound gorilla in the room.

When the time to deliberate did come, they gave great weight to the borrowed shovel. King knew then and there what he was going to do—which made the crimes as cold and calculated as they could get. He might have been overheard on the 911 tape saying he'd planned on letting her go, but he never did.

They gave much, much less weight to the scientific evidence. The panel didn't particularly care how doctors interpreted a PET scan of Michael King's brain.

A reporter asked if the jury had been bothered by the fact that the defendant's mother had not testified, despite the fact that she was alive and well and had, according to the story, been the one to sit up at night with her son during the days and nights following his head injury.

Yes, the subject of the silent mother had come up, and it was agreed that the only explanation was that she had information that would come out that would not be helpful to the defense.

Some of the jurors were experiencing anxiety because of the nature of the trial—some of the things they'd had to hear, some of the exhibits they were obliged to view. Jurors were experiencing insomnia. They wondered how long it would take for them to decompress, now that it was over. Hopefully, everyone would eventually be able to move on.

The jurors who spoke publically agreed that they would

return to the courtroom in three weeks for the sentencing hearing. They had invested so much time and emotion into the case that they did not want to miss Judge Economou confirming their decision.

Following the trial, Lon Arend took a moment to reflect on what had occurred. He was asked about the testimony of Michael King's family.

Early in the investigation, he had asked law enforcement to get in touch with King's family as quickly as possible and to interview them separately before they had a chance to get together and come up with a story that would put their Mike in a good light. The plan had worked. Both King's mom and his ex-wife had told police the day after the murder that he had never suffered a significant head injury.

Years and years in law enforcement had taught Arend a few things about human nature. One thing you could count on was that when someone does something this horrible, his or her family members would sit, think, and wonder, *how?* How could it have happened? And they would remember back to things that had happened, and they would start projecting importance on those occurrences. By the time they came to testify, they believed what they were saying—even though it was, often, a construct of their inability to process what had occurred. They weren't technically making stuff up. They were trying to come up in their own minds with an explanation for what had happened. When they did that as a group, they'd tend to formulate one story and stick to it. So, coming into the trial, Arend knew that the relatives, the ones he hadn't gotten statements from, were going to come into court united with a wild story, but he couldn't have anticipated that it would be as wild as it was. His head hit a pole—or a shed, whatever it was—at ninety miles per hour? If the story had been more feasible, Arend could've used the statements of the defendant's own mother to send him to the executioner, and he was glad that wasn't necessary. The obvious conclusion, Arend said, was that the whole story of Michael King's head injury was "fabricated, embellished, or exaggerated."

The prosecutor's impression of Jim King and his wife was that they were very nice people and did not want to lie—and that the things Mike had done horrified them. "I felt really bad for them," Arend said.

Rodney, on the other hand, seemed hell-bent on saving his brother. "Either he was better focused on the task than the others, or he was coached really well," Arend said. The prosecutor remembered that once Rodney got started talking, he had a hard time stopping. He would inevitably give an answer that journeyed beyond the scope of the question. In some cases, a prosecutor would want to stop this, would want the witness to stick to answering just the questions as they were being asked, but not in this case. Rodney rambled; and when he did, he often said things that told the jury just who he was and what he was up to. Arend just sat back and let him go. A couple of times, Rodney's monologues journeyed into the realm of the ridiculous. When he said Mike hit the pole at eighty to ninety miles per hour, Arend thought to himself, *Goodness, I gotcha now.*

"After the trial, one juror told me that when Dr. Wu explained that there was a divot in Michael King's head, he looked at the heads of King's brothers, and it looked to him like one sibling had the same divot—that it was a genetic trait, not a result of a head injury," Arend recalled. "The juror said, 'Holy crap, they've all got it.'" Arend added that he personally did not remember seeing a similarity in the shape of the brothers' heads.

Was there ever a moment when he knew he was going to win? "Oh, no!" Arend said. He claimed he worried to the point of panic throughout the trial. You never knew what a jury was going to do. Not so much in the guilt phase, but in the penalty phase. The biggest concern was that the jurors, despite his successful cross-examination, would buy Dr. Wu's presentation and rule against the death penalty. "The key to Dr. Wu wasn't what he said, but what he was basing it on. He hadn't interviewed anybody," Arend commented.

In his years as a prosecutor, how many murderers had he sent to death row? "One," Arend said. Michael King. Arend had prosecuted about twenty non–capital murder cases, and maybe twenty capital cases, but in each of those, the defendant had pleaded guilty and received a life sentence. A couple of times, he started the case as capital but, for one reason or another, took the death penalty off the table.

The penalty phase of King's trial was a first for him—and regardless of the circumstances, it was hard for a person to put another person to death. Luckily, you didn't need a unanimous vote by the jury in Florida to put a prisoner on death row. All that was needed was a simple majority. When it came down to it, though, they did get a unanimous vote, and that was an indication that the entire prosecution team had done a good job during death qualifying of the jury pool and voir dire.

"In our circuit, we only have six people on death row," the prosecutor said. "So it is very uncommon for the death penalty to stay on the table all the way through a trial."

The slow pace of the process would frustrate those in a hurry to see Michael King executed. One of the men on his circuit's death row had been there for more than twenty years. Even if all went smoothly, the earliest one might expect to see King executed would be 2017.

Jane Kowalski was asked for a comment from her home in Tampa. "If there was any case for the death penalty, this was one," she said. "It shouldn't be anything else."

In a poignant moment, North Port police chief Terry Lewis gave Denise's ring and necklace—which for two years had been kept in a bag marked "evidence"—back to Nate Lee.

Rick Goff said he couldn't wait for Michael King to die. "I will rent the bus for us to go up there and watch that man die." He was aware that the day might not come soon because of appeals. "I may have to go in a wheelchair, but me and my family will be there."

Goff again spoke of the pride he felt for his daughter. "We wouldn't have found Denise or him (King) if it weren't for Denise leaving behind clues. I could not have done what she did. She was a great detective."

Lon Arend agreed with Goff's assessment: "Denise was the best witness we had," he said.

EPILOGUE

On October 14, 2009, Nate Lee filed a seventeen-page lawsuit against the CCSO. The lawsuit stated that Denise Lee would still be alive if not for their bungling. The suit claimed that the botched handling of the 911 calls in the CCSO dispatch center "helped lead" to Denise's death, that the search for Denise Lee was *unfortunately plagued by poor law enforcement communication in a way that proximately caused* her death. The suit demanded a trial by jury for damages for wrongful death, damages for negligence, costs, and attorney's fees, and *such other and further relief as the Court deems just and proper.* The suit claimed the dispatcher proved "severe incompetence" in the handling of the 911 calls—in particular the nine-minute Kowalski call—and "breached their duties" by repeatedly making incorrect choices. There were five 911 calls in all, but the mishandling of the Kowalski call was most damaging because that caller had been able to pinpoint the victim's precise location in real time. Those errors included the failure to issue a timely BOLO regarding the location of King's Camaro from the North Port Police Department to deputies, failure to relay the information being provided by Jane Kowalski to those in the field in a position to prevent

Denise's death, and failure to log the Kowalski call into the system until twelve minutes after the call was made. The suit claimed that Jane Kowalski might have taken further action to help Denise but did not, because she had reported what was going on to the sheriff and had a reasonable expectation that the sheriff would respond in a timely fashion to her call. So, when the sheriff's office did not respond in a timely fashion, it, by taking Jane Kowalski's further assistance out of the equation, *increased the risk of harm faced by Mrs. Lee.*

The suit used information gleaned from Captain Donna H. Roguska's internal investigation, as well as the letter written by Susan Kirby Kallestad regarding what she perceived to be negligence on the part of Kowalski's call taker, Mildred Stepp. The suit was an action for damages that exceeded $15,000, exclusive of taxable attorneys' fees and costs.

No one expected the CCSO to roll over and play dead in the face of the lawsuit, but its defense against the charges was somewhat startling. They claimed in a thirteen-page motion that the suit was without merit because the CCSO had given *no specific promise to protect [Denise] Amber Lee,* and therefore were under no obligation to do so. They, after all, were not responsible for her death. The mishandled 911 calls had not killed her. Michael King killed her.

In November of 2009, Lee, after learning of the police response to his lawsuit, told a reporter, "I just think people who live in Charlotte County should be concerned that CCSO are saying they had no duty to protect Denise. It's so unbelievable to say."

The suit did not specify a dollar amount. Florida state law allowed only $200,000 to be awarded as a settlement in a suit for wrongful death, but if the case went to trial, a larger award could be granted by a jury.

In April 2010, the judge originally scheduled to hear the civil suit recused himself because he knew and had worked with Rick Goff.

In 2010, a Denise Amber Lee Foundation was set up dedicated to improving the 911 systems all around the country so that tragedies such as the failure to prevent Denise's murder were never allowed to happen again.

Nate tried to go back to work not long after his wife was murdered, but it didn't go very well. He was a meter reader with Florida Power and Light, but he soon left his job and requested a new assignment. He said his old job was making him crazy. All he did was walk and think. He was in a place in his life where he didn't want to think.

Prosecutor Suzanne O'Donnell wanted to thank the victim for making the solving of this case simple, easy. Denise Lee's abilities as a detective, planting clues, was at its sharpest in the car, where, in the course of a few minutes, she was able to make a 911 call from the murderer's phone, establishing an identifying link right there. She was able to talk to the operator and her abductor simultaneously without letting the man know what was up, and she took off her ring and planted it in the backseat. During that same stretch, she was making the loudest fuss she could, and managed to attract the attention of two motorists, who themselves called 911. *Wow.*

"She was amazing," O'Donnell said.

After all of those weeks together, O'Donnell's heart still

went out to Denise's family. "What a wonderful group of people—and what a heartbreak for them," she said. She recalled Denise's dad as a rock, an anchor, the point man for the family, taking so much onto his shoulders and being strong enough to bear it all. And Denise's mom was "so regal," in so much pain, and yet maintaining such a presence about herself: in control. The Goffs were cooperative with the state every step of the way, understanding and approving of the decisions—such as the playing of Denise's 911 call in court—that the prosecutors had to make.

O'Donnell also wanted to give a shout-out to Rob Salvador, who—through no fault of his own—had to endure accusation after accusation from Michael King's desperate defense team. He wasn't the type to let things go, either, and had been "genuinely disturbed" by the horrible thing that had happened and his bizarre connection to it. As he was her witness, O'Donnell had done her best to ready Robert for the difficult cross-examination she knew was coming—but even she underestimated how scathing it would be. She warned him that they might insinuate that since he had been target shooting with the killer on the day of the murder, he might have had something to do with it. Instead, he was asked if it wasn't true that he, himself, had been the one to pull the trigger and kill Denise Lee. Luckily, there were no surprises in Robert Salvador's testimony for the prosecution, no *aha* moments. That was because, except for that first night when he'd played his cards close to his chest for the police who were pounding on his door, he had been completely forthcoming with law enforcement.

"His life had been an open book," O'Donnell recalled, which helped in the long run—but he was still shocked by his ordeal on the witness stand.

* * *

Trooper Eddie Pope, used to being in the right place at the right time, hadn't run out of luck—and his cool head during emergencies still set him apart.

He remarried. He and his son from his first marriage both enrolled in college; the elder finishing up his bachelor's degree at Florida Gulf Coast University, and the younger on a full football scholarship at Heidelberg University in Tiffin, Ohio. (He also had two teenaged daughters.)

He had the honor of traveling to Washington, D.C., to be part of the security for the incoming commander in chief at President Obama's inauguration.

His ambition to one day become a federal peace officer was derailed once more, and for good, when he learned he had grown too old to apply.

"After I finish my bachelor's and my master's, I'm going to run for sheriff in Charlotte County," he said good-naturedly.

In March 2010, Pope was once again named the Trooper of the Month. On March 12, he was dispatched to a medical call, a baby choking. He hurried to the scene and talked to the mother, who explained that her son was turning blue and she couldn't dislodge the obstruction. Pope gave the child "back thrusts," the obstruction propelled out, and the child resumed breathing.

On April 14, 2010, Patrick Dewayne Murphy pleaded guilty to raping and murdering six-year-old Coralrose Fullwood, thus closing North Port's other notorious violent crime. Murphy was caught when DNA he left at the crime scene matched that taken from him while he was in jail on burglary charges. Just because the case was closed didn't mean investigation was halted, however. According to an informant, Coralrose's rape and murder were videotaped. A close relative of the little girl was in prison after pleading no contest to felony possession of child pornography, and police would not rest easy until they determined for certain whether there was a connection between the relative and the murderer.

Assistant State Attorney Lon Arend briefly ran for county judge in 2010, but withdrew from the campaign before the election. The Denise Amber Lee Foundation backed his campaign, but Arend eventually came to the conclusion that he could better serve the public as the chief homicide prosecutor for Sarasota County. Family considerations contributed to Arend's decision. He had two small children and the rigors of campaigning were not conducive to being the best dad he could be.

"I wanted to believe that you could do both," he said. "But it turns out if you do both, you will do both at less than one hundred percent."

In response to cries for reform led by Nate Lee and Rick Goff, the Florida Legislature passed the Denise Lee Law, setting voluntary standards for 911 systems throughout the state. The governor signed the new law in 2010.

On August 8, 2010, a plaque with Denise Lee's likeness was unveiled at the Englewood Sports Complex, where she often took her children. The plaque read: *It was at this play-*

ground that Denise would bring her two sons to play. Her family meant more to her than anything. On January 17, 2008, Denise gave her own life to ensure the safety of her children. It is because of her heroism that not only her sons can continue to come here to play, but also their children and all generations to come. The dedication ceremony was held the day after what would have been Denise's twenty-fourth birthday.

Denise's parents are very different types of people. Her dad, the career cop, had only taken two sick days during his twenty-eight years on the force. (He'd accrued enough sick time to take almost two years off with pay.) He was stalwart and hesitant to show his emotions under even the most extreme circumstances. Denise's mother, on the other hand, was more visibly affected. She had clearly been dealt a blow by Denise's death, from which she would never recover. It has helped that Nate and Denise's two little boys spend a lot of time with Denise's mom and dad, so they can put all of their love and caring toward the boys. Denise had left them a beautiful and precious legacy.

Denise's kid sister was getting on with her life, working hard to get her college degree. She was in her senior year in 2011. Although she never did get a grade on the paper she wrote during the trial, she passed that course. Getting back into the rhythms of being a student after the trial was difficult for Amanda, but she never complained. "I am very proud of how well she has handled this," her mom said.

Denise's brother, Tyler, was a remarkably talented baseball player. In 2011, he was a junior in high school. He'd been a starting pitcher and shortstop on his high-school baseball team since he was a freshman, and played year-round on a travel team out of Fort Myers. He was considered one of the top prospects in the country for his age.

Looking back on her experience with the case, 911 caller Jane Kowalski said that she had come to grips with the fact that there were seemingly many chances to save Denise Lee, and yet Denise wasn't saved. She understood that the 911 system simply wasn't prepared for an ongoing emergency that was moving from place to place, and was being seen from different angles. She applauded Nate Lee's reformation efforts, and felt hope that one day 911 systems everywhere would be up to snuff, and nothing like this would ever happen again.

The thing that still stuck in her craw, however, were the ugly things about human nature that this case had revealed. How many motorists on that horrible evening saw and heard Denise Lee in distress—and only two had called 911. That old wheeze of a line—"We thought it was a domestic dispute, we didn't want to get involved"—drove Jane crazy. How could people turn away, stick their heads in the sand, when a person was in trouble? It was the most pathetic thing. Even if Denise Lee had been "just" a battered wife, her screams made it clear that she was in a car with a guy who wasn't kidding around—a guy who had been, and planned to continue, doing a number on her.

How could anyone ignore that?

Prosecutor Karen Fraivillig said she hoped never to get another case as disturbing as this one. The case was so fraught with human error. The 911 people—what were they thinking about? 911! That's what everyone relied on. It was the first thing parents taught their kids when they were little. If there was an emergency, call 911.

Harold Muxlow. If only he'd done something more quickly. Denise Lee had had so many chances to be saved, but no one stepped up.

And, of course, there was the heinous nature of the crimes themselves that Michael King had perpetrated against this little girl—and Fraivillig did think of her as a little girl because she was so young and tiny.

Did the prosecutor believe in evil?

"Yes, I do. I think there are people out there who are truly evil. Michael King is one of those people. This crime went on for hours. This was not an isolated crime of passion. First he had to think about it a long time, because he took steps, like getting duct tape, preparing the rape room in his house, took her from her babies, raped her for hours. He still could let her walk away. Then he went to Harold's house, already knowing that she was going to die. He borrowed the gas can and the shovel. She was a smart girl. She saw those items and she knew what was ahead for her. He didn't have the decency, the human compassion, to hide those items from her. That is evil to me—truly evil. Then he took her out, and I think he tried to rape her again, because she was naked when she was shot. After killing her, he showed no remorse and told some half-assed story about him being a victim, too. You look at what he did, step by step by step, and the feeling you come away with is that there is something missing in him. I know that people call him [4a] sociopath or psychopath—but to me, there is just a void in there that is evil. I don't think he deserves to walk among his fellow human beings. I don't even think that he's a human being. He doesn't deserve to be called that."